More

FOR THE LOVE OF A DOG

"Gives fascinating insight into the emotions we always knew our furry companions possessed."
—*Dog Fancy*

"A fascinating, highly educational read. McConnell alternates between expressing empathy with our canine friends and taking a step back to explain the scientific limits of any attempt to get into their heads."
—FRANS DE WAAL, author of *Our Inner Ape*

"For anyone who's ever wondered how to pick out a well-adjusted puppy, McConnell's explanation of the neurology of emotion is a must-read."
—*Newsday*

"Patricia McConnell skillfully blends cutting-edge scientific data with examples from her personal experiences with dogs to produce a clear picture of the emotional life of dogs. In the process, we learn more about how the mind of a dog works, and how to better understand and interact with them. This is a must-read for all dog owners."
—STANLEY COREN, author of
The Intelligence of Dogs and *How Dogs Think*

"A compelling combination of stories, science and practical advice to show how understanding emotions in both people and dogs can improve owners' relationships with their pets."
—*Publishers Weekly*

"Brilliant! *For the Love of a Dog* is a perfect balance of science and soul. These stories will keep you up reading long into the night knowing that with your dogs, you love and are loved, need and are needed."
—DR. MARTY BECKER, resident veterinarian on
Good Morning America and co-author of *Fitness Unleashed!*

"In *For the Love of a Dog*, Patricia McConnell provides a fascinating window into the workings of the canine mind. It will bring people who live with and train dogs to a new level in understanding and communicating with their canine friends. This is another excellent book from a renowned author, and everyone who loves dogs will want to read it." —WAYNE HUNTHAUSEN, DVM, animal behavior consultant

"Yet another utterly delightful book from Dr. Patricia McConnell—such a fine storyteller and such a good scientist—the Jane Goodall of the dog world. *For the Love of a Dog* is an authoritative review of emotions in dogs and people. Thoroughly interesting, intriguing, entertaining, and such a pleasure to read. You'll love this book."
—IAN DUNBAR, PH.D., BVetMed, MRCVS,
founder of the Association of Pet Dog Trainers

"This exciting book is a welcome addition to our understanding of companion dogs and our relationship with them. At turns engaging, funny, joyous, passionate, sad, and poignant, it is a wonderful blend of science, social commentary, and great story telling."
—DANIEL Q. ESTEP, PH.D., CAAB,
Animal Behavior Associates, Inc.

FOR THE LOVE
OF A DOG

FOR THE LOVE OF A DOG

Understanding Emotion
in You and Your Best Friend

PATRICIA B. McCONNELL, Ph.D.

BALLANTINE BOOKS · NEW YORK

2007 Ballantine Books Trade Paperback Edition

Published in the United States by Ballantine Books, an imprint of The Random House
Publishing Group, a division of Random House, Inc., New York.

BALLANTINE and colophon are registered trademarks of Random House, Inc.

Originally published in hardcover in the United States by Ballantine Books, an imprint of
The Random House Publishing Group, a division of Random House, Inc., in 2006.

A portion of Chapter 7 initially appeared in the
November 2005 issue of *The Bark* magazine.

ISBN 978-0-345-47715-6

Library of Congress Cataloging-in-Publication Data
McConnell, Patricia B.
For the love of a dog : understanding emotion in you and your best friend /
by Patricia B. McConnell.
p. cm.
ISBN 978-0-345-47715-6 (alk. paper)
1. Dogs—Behavior. 2. Dogs—Psychology. 3. Dog owners—Psychology.
4. Emotions in animals. 5. Human-animal relationships. I. Title.
SF433.M34 2006
636.7—dc22   2006045200

Printed in the United States of America

www.ballantinebooks.com

2 4 6 8 9 7 5 3 1

Book design by Susan Turner

To my guys
Jim and Luke

Daily, in the morning, this faithful dog,
silent, sits near me,
till I recognize him
with a touch.
At my little notice
his body erupts in waves, streams of joy.

—RABINDRANATH TAGORE, "Recovery 14"

CONTENTS

NOTE FROM THE AUTHOR

The stories in this book are all true, although I have changed the names of all of my clients and most of their dogs in order to protect their privacy. I doubt that the dogs would care if they knew you were reading about them, but I can't ask them, so I've covered my bases and changed their names. I kept the names of my own dogs—that's what they get for living with a writer.

Although I've changed the names of individual dogs in the book, I have chosen to identify them by breed, even when the story included a dog causing serious injury. I realize that might result in some criticism: no one wants to hear about an individual of a breed they love causing serious harm. Two of the breeds I mention are Rottweilers and Pit Bulls. Because of the negative publicity those breeds tend to attract, I thought long and hard about changing their breed designation in the case stories recounted within the book. But then, changing to another breed would anger lovers of whatever breed I chose. I considered changing all the dogs to mixed breeds, or never mentioning breed at all, but that seemed dishonest and contrived. I finally decided that the best thing to do was to simply recount what happened, the way it happened. However, I don't want the stories in this book to add to stereotypes of those breeds—any more than I want people to believe that Labradors and Border Collies are "dangerous dogs" just because there are stories in the book about ones who have caused serious injuries. As readers will see, I adore Border Collies, but a problematic one can be a nightmare. The truth of the matter is that dogs who can open their mouths can bite, and big, strong dogs are more dangerous than little ones, and, most important, a tragically large number of dogs are being bred and raised by people in this country for all the wrong reasons.

On another note, some progressive readers will notice that I have not used the term "guardian" for those of us who live with and love domestic dogs. I have chosen to use the more traditional term, "owner," although I understand that the choice can be interpreted in different ways. I'm the first to admit that "owner" is not a perfect description of who we are to our dogs, but being perhaps too old and set in my ways, I find the term "guardian" a bit awkward. I'm working on it, but I just can't make it feel right yet—it feels formal and lawyerly, and somehow less intimate than my relationship is with my dogs. Lacking a better alternative, I have used the term "owner" throughout the book. Of course, the term "owner" itself can also be off-putting; one would never talk about being a child's owner, after all. But all words can have different meanings, different connotations, and when I say "owner," I mean simply that they are my dogs and I'm responsible for them. I'm reminded of a woman who introduced her significant other thus: "This is John. *My* John." My dogs are just that, *my* dogs. They are also my friends and my co-workers, and I have the deepest respect for them.

Readers should also be aware that the term "behaviorist," used frequently in this book, has many different meanings. "Applied animal behaviorists" are people like me, who use their academic background in behavior to solve problems and issues related to nonhuman animals. These issues can vary from working with aggressive dogs, to enhancing the habitat of animals in zoological parks, to saving endangered species. Our academic background, however, can vary. My Ph.D. major was in zoology, in which I was trained as an ethologist, or someone most interested in how an animal's behavior interacts with its genetic heritage and its environment. My minor was in psychology, where historically the focus was on how an animal's behavior is influenced by learning, and on discovering how the process of learning works in both animals and people. This is the source of the other use of the term "behaviorist," which refers to a perspective that endorses, à la B. F. Skinner, giving scientific attention only to an animal's *external* behavior. Animals' *internal* processes (such as thoughts and emotions) were believed to be inaccessible to scientific inquiry. To the benefit of all, both fields are now integrated to a large degree. The term "behaviorist" is used in both senses in the text of this book, I hope in a way that keeps its meaning clear to the reader.

I have also chosen to put references to most of the research described in the book in the "References" section, rather than in the body of the text. I hope the authors of the papers I mention do not take offense. Books like this could never be written without the hours and hours of hard work put in every week by scientists of all descriptions. My goal, in writing this and other books, is to provide a bridge between the knowledge derived from their work and the general dog-loving public. Moving the citations to the back allows for a freer flow of narrative and, I hope, results in a book that keeps the interest of all dog lovers, even if they didn't love science class in high school.

And finally, if your or your dog's emotions are causing behavioral problems, don't hestitate to seek professional advice. Even the best tennis player in the world has a coach, and dog training is a sport as much as anything else.

ACKNOWLEDGMENTS

My first thanks are to all the dogs I've known who have given me joy, insight, and purpose. I thank my clients' dogs for all they have taught me, I thank dogs I've only read about for their inspiration, and, with no apologies for the lump in my throat, I thank my dogs Lassie, Pip, and Tulip—my friends and family for over a decade. I thank Cool Hand Luke for being Cool Hand Luke, and for taking my heart and running with it. This book is for you.

Jennifer Gates continues to be the agent of every writer's dream, and I am grateful every day for her support, knowledge, and wisdom. I thank my editors Dana Isaacson and Caroline Sutton for their help and advice, and for skillfully escorting the book through the labyrinth of publishing. I am grateful to all at Ballantine/Random House for the hard work involved in bringing any book into the light of day, with particular thanks to my walk-on-water copyeditor Jolanta Benal. Earlier drafts of the book profited greatly from readings by Jim Anderson, Rick Axsom, Jeffrey Baylis, Jim Billings, Jennifer Gates, Andrea Jennings, Karen London, Aimee Moore, Nancy Rafetto, Charles Snowdon, Tony Stretton, Denise Swedlund, and Chelse Wieland. I also owe a debt of thanks to Paul Ekman for his insightful comments about the chapter on visual signals. Julie Hecht did a yeoman's job in her research for the book, and I thank her not only for that, but also for her support and enthusiasm while the book was being written.

This book could never have been written without the dedication of the staff of Dog's Best Friend, Ltd., who continued to help people and dogs while I spent the mornings writing. I am deeply grateful to Andrea Jennings, Aimee Moore, Denise Swedlund, Chelse Wieland, and all the trainers at DBF for their commitment and hard work to members of both species. I thank veterinarians John Dally, Chris Bessent, and Kim Utech for their caring and extensive efforts during Luke's illness and death—I count myself lucky to have them on the team.

Many people helped me round up photographs for the book. I am very grateful to Marc Bekoff, Peter Burghardt, Jim Billings, Julia Dayoub, Corey Dingman, Khris Erikson, Carl Fritscher, Aimee Graham, Suzanne Hetts, Dana Isaacson, Karen B. London, and Sarah and Tim McClure. Sue Sternberg provided several of the most dramatic photos, and deserves special thanks. You can learn more about her work by going to www.roundoutkennels.com. The North Shore Animal League America, which sponsors and provides care for needy dogs, also graciously allowed me to use one of their photos, and you can go to www.nsalamerica.org to learn more about the organization. Dog Days of Wisconsin summer camp (www.dogcamp.com) for dogs provided the photo of the smiling Rottie, and I thank them and the photographer both.

Several professional photographers also stepped up to the plate, and I am grateful to Dan Becker in Gurnee, Illinois (www.pyrphoto.com); Chip Peterson in Decorah, Iowa (chip@petersonphotography.com); Monty Sloan at Wolf Park in Battle Ground, Indiana (www.wolfphotography.com); and Holly Montgomery in Calgary, Alberta (www.mutshotsphotography.com) for their generous assistance. Chelse Wieland gets lots of credit for posing for some of the expressions—here's a happy face right back at you, and I thank Paul Ekman for the use of some of his examples of human facial expressions. The photo of the recumbent black dog with the huge fear grimace was given to me many years ago by a client, who was happy that her dog might help others understand their dog's emotions. It's a great photograph, and I'm very grateful for the opportunity to use it.

I thank Wendy Barker, Saranindranath Tagore, and publisher George Braziller for the use of an excerpt from the poem "Recovery 14," published in *Rabindranath Tagore: Final Poems,* selected and translated by Wendy Barker and Saranindranath Tagore. It's worth obtaining a copy of the entire volume—just the one poem itself is so exquisite that it is worth the price of the book. I am also grateful to *The Bark* magazine for permission to reprint a column on how to pet your dog included in the chapter on happiness. *The Bark* magazine and its editors are committed to improving the lives of both people and dogs through literature and art, and the world is a better place for it.

I'd also like to thank two groups of people, who feed and nurture me in very different ways: the members of the Interdisciplinary Forum on Applied Animal Behavior, for the intellectual nourishment and support they provide, and the women of the Vermont Valley Vixens, whose friendship anchors me in place like oak trees on a savannah. Special thanks goes to Sandi Stanfield, who put up with me writing about her dogs Samson and Delilah in *The Other End of the Leash,* and to her dogs (who are now model citizens of the neighborhood). Thanks also to the people at Vermont Valley Community Farm for spoiling me and my staff with fresh, organic produce. Special thanks go to Carol Klapste, who introduced me to Father Murray and his dog, Blaze, and who was instrumental in turning a potentially tragic situation into one with a happy ending. I can't imagine completing this book without the support of my dear friends David and Julie Egger, whose friendship and support over the years means more than I can say.

And finally, I save my warmest and most oxytocin-enriched thanks to my other guy, Jim Billings, who stays steady and true within the roller coaster of my own emotions, and who, most remarkably, has never once complained about a house covered in dog hair.

INTRODUCTION

Tulip broke away from me as we approached the body of an ewe named Harriet, and sniffed her from head to hoof. Harriet's death was a significant event on my little farm. Until the very end, even at the ancient age of fourteen, Harriet was a remarkable individual. In her youth, her delicate bone structure and toffee-colored wool qualified her for supermodel status. In old age she was little more than a scraggly skeleton, but even when fed a liquid diet through a turkey baster, she managed a sense of dignity that elicited respect from sheep, humans, and dogs alike. I was fonder of Harriet than of any sheep I've ever had, and I'd already cried like a baby by the time Tulip and I walked down to visit her body, lying cold and stiff in the grass.

Tulip, my Great Pyrenees sheep-guarding dog, hadn't been in the barn when the veterinarian put Harriet down. I'd put Tulip in the house so that the vet could end Harriet's life with no distractions. It's Tulip's job to protect the sheep from the coyotes and stray dogs that flow throughout the Wisconsin countryside. Tulip's commitment to nonviolence is impressive, but she can be counted on to protect her sheep when they need her. Normally docile, Tulip can switch from gentle nanny into Xena, Warrior Dog, in a microsecond. Although she's never hurt a person, dog, or sheep in ten years of guarding my farm, she's roared in like a freight train when a three-hundred-pound ram attacked me, when a visiting dog tore into one of my own, and when a foolish Border Collie switched from herding sheep to hunting them in the excitement of youth. She's also playful and curious, so it seemed wise to let the vet do his work without her. Because of that, Tulip hadn't seen Harriet pass from life to death, and when she found Harriet's body lying in the grass, she seemed profoundly affected by it.

She sniffed Harriet's body, circling, sniffing, and repeatedly nudging her. After a few minutes, she lay down beside the body. She placed her big, white muzzle on her paws, sighed once—a long, slow exhalation of what we'd call resignation in a human—and then refused to move. She growled at the approach of my Border Collies; they withdrew and came over to sit beside me, about twenty-five feet away. I don't remember how long Tulip lay beside Harriet, but she wouldn't leave her voluntarily. Finally, as darkness softened the sky, I gently took her by the collar and walked her back to the house.

Tulip looked for all the world as if she knew that Harriet had died, and she looked as sad about it as I felt. There's only one catch. She behaves in similar ways to pigeons she's killed herself, and last week, to an ear of corn I'd given her to chew. While my three Border Collies munched away on their own corncobs, milky yellow juice running down their chins, Tulip carried hers with great gravity over to her favorite spot, gently and carefully placed it between her paws, and proceeded to guard it from all comers. She didn't chew it. She didn't lick it. She lay beside it, her face quiet and grave, just as she lay beside Harriet's body that sad morning at Redstart Farm.

I want it to be true that Tulip's behavior around Harriet was an expression of something more meaningful than her demeanor around an ear of corn. A respectful awareness of Harriet's life fits into my belief about who Tulip is, and, more importantly, who I want her to be. Perhaps it is meaningful that Tulip's behavior toward Harriet was not exactly the same as her behavior toward dead pigeons or corncobs. She never put her head down on her paws with food as she did beside Harriet, and she never sighed a great gulping sigh when looming over a dead pigeon. I find it hard to believe that my big-eyed, soulful dog had the same response to Harriet's dead body as she did to a vegetable.

But the truth of the matter is, I don't know what was in Tulip's head as she lay beside Harriet's body. Did she know that Harriet was dead, and understand what that meant for the future? I want to know what was going on in her mind that quiet summer evening after Harriet died, but how can I find the way into her head? For that matter, what can any of us know about the emotional life of any of our dogs? It's hard enough to know what's going on in the mind of another person, much less an individual of another species.

But we want to know. Understanding what someone else is experiencing is the key to feeling connected, and feeling connected is an integral part of any good relationship. "Penny for your thoughts" is more than an old-fashioned phrase—it's an expression of our desire to understand the thoughts and emotions of those we love. We humans are social animals, and our desire for connection is deep and relentless.

Those of us who love our dogs deeply, who consider our dogs friends and family, want to know what's going on in their minds as much as we do in our relationships with other people. We don't need to think of our dogs as furry little people to want to understand how their emotional life compares with ours. I, and many others, don't want to live with fuzzy, nonverbal humans who walk on four legs but roll in cow pies. We like it that our dogs are dogs. The differences between us enrich our relationships and increase our sense of connection to the world around us. But the genetic gap between us means it's even harder to know what our dogs are thinking and feeling than it is with our human friends. No wonder animal communicators, who claim access to the minds of our companion animals, have become so popular.

Sometimes, even without the benefit of language, we make deep connections to the dogs in our lives. Other times, just as in any relationship, things may not go so well. I'll never forget a dog—one of those special ones with penetrating eyes—who simply stopped looking at her owner. I watched the two of them for several hours at a herding clinic, a petite gray-haired woman with a tidy black-and-white Border Collie on a bright red leash. The dog looked everywhere but toward the woman who loved her, at one point sitting silently at the woman's side for almost an hour, with her head turned a hundred and eighty degrees away.

The woman who owned and loved the dog was well intentioned, but her words and movements were all so confusing that even I had no idea what she was trying to communicate. I didn't have the slightest idea of what she was trying to get her dog to do, much less what she was thinking. I suspect the smart, willing little dog found her owner so frustrating that she could no longer bear to make the attempt to communicate, and so she spent her time avoiding making any connection at all. I was reminded of the times I've turned off my car radio because, even though I could still make out some of the words, the static was so aversive I couldn't stand listening.

I found the mismatch so heartbreaking that at the end of the day I asked the woman whether I could buy her dog. I wasn't surprised when she said no, because she seemed to love the dog dearly, and you can't exactly walk up to a stranger and tell them that they're inadvertently torturing their dog and expect them to thank you and then hand over the leash. But I still can see the dog's sweet, honest face, and I wonder if she's still alive, looking off into space, turning off the static as best she can.

Most of us do a better job of bridging the gap between our minds and the minds of our dogs than the woman described above, but that doesn't mean it's not a struggle. We may think we know how our dog is feeling, but that doesn't mean we're right. We may be sure we know what's going on inside the heart and mind of our mother or son or partner, but the truth is we're often mistaken. Psychologists tell us that erroneous assumptions about what others are thinking and feeling cause no end of problems in human interactions. We don't even know what's going on in our *own* minds half the time. As we'll see later, much of our behavior is influenced by processes outside our conscious awareness. No wonder figuring out what's going on in the mind of your dog is a challenge.

Even though getting into our dogs' heads isn't easy, we're not utterly clueless. For a start, we are making tremendous strides in understanding how human brains work. We may like to talk about the heart as the seat of emotions, but it's the brain that lies at the center of our feelings. If we want to understand our feelings, we have to start by understanding our brain. Our emotional life begins and ends in our brains, and the more we understand how this amazing mix of neurons, hormones, and electricity works, the better we'll understand emotions. Right now there are legions of researchers working on the brain, riding a rising tide of scientific and popular interest in the mind and how it functions. Much of that interest and attention has been driven by the amazing new technologies that allow us to watch the brain as it works. One of the most useful of the new technologies, the fMRI, allows us to see which areas of the brain are active while the brain is working.[1] You can show people pictures, ask them questions, or inject hormones into their bodies, and learn which parts of the brain are engaged while they are sorting things out. Studies like this have taught us, for example, that most people have a particularly sophisticated area of the brain designated to recognize faces, while a less powerful area is programmed to recognize objects. Autistic people, on the other hand, use the object-recognition part of their brains when looking at faces; no wonder they have so much trouble reading emotional expressions on the faces around them.

Neuroscience may be exciting, but it's not for the faint of heart (or, for that matter, the weak of mind). Brains are absurdly complicated things, and understanding the role that they play in our emotional life is no small challenge. Just the language used to describe the structure and function of the brain is, well, uh . . . elaborate. In his wonderful book *A User's Guide to the Brain,* John J. Ratey says that after the brain itself, "the second most complex object in the universe is the body of language we use to talk about the brain." How true that is. I howled when I read it, having started the daunting process of wading through articles on, for example, the role of the anterior cingulate gyrus in ideomotor apraxia.

As luck would have it, more and more books are being written by neuroscientists for those of us who aren't in their field but who are interested in how our brains affect our behavior. Whether you're interested in why you left the house intending to buy a Beagle puppy but instead brought home a Jack Russell Terrier, or why you still cry over your Golden Retriever who died ten years ago, these books can help you bridge the gap between the dual, but related, mysteries of brain and behavior. Books like *Descartes' Error: Emotion, Reason, and the Human Brain,* by Antonio Damasio, and *Biology of the Mind,* by Deric Bownds, allow us non-neuroscientists to share in the fun.

Our focus on mental processes may have been encouraged by new technologies, but interest in the workings of our own brains isn't new.

1. The abbreviation fMRI stands for "functional magnetic resonance imaging." This procedure allows you to follow the flow of blood in the brain, and thus determine which areas of it are active at any given time.

However, our interest in the minds of nonhuman animals has waxed and waned over the centuries. Thirty years ago, at least in this country, scientific interest in the minds of animals was barely perceptible; at the moment, it's increasing by leaps and bounds. One of the most interesting results of that research is the realization that thoughts and emotions can't be separated from each other as neatly as we once believed. Justifiably proud of our own intellectual abilities, we've paid most of our attention to the thinking, problem-solving part of our mind, comparing it (favorably, of course) with the brains of other animals. However, new ways of studying the brain have resulted in an expanding focus on emotions—what they are, how they are generated, and what their purpose might be. Not only are we starting to understand what emotions actually are, we're starting to understand their importance in humans and animals alike.

This increased interest in the inner lives of animals is a wonderful thing for dog lovers, because the burgeoning interest in the mental experiences of animals has resulted in a parallel interest in the minds of our dogs. Dogs are finally getting some of the attention they deserve, having been proof for decades of the saying "Familiarity breeds contempt." Scientists could study right whales or Serengeti lions or scissortailed flycatchers, but heaven forbid you tried to make your name as a researcher studying dogs. However, that has changed in just the last few years, and lately there have been articles in prestigious scientific journals, from the *Journal of Comparative Psychology* to *Science,* that add to our knowledge about the cognitive abilities of dogs. That interest has been reflected in a group of thoughtful books written specifically about the intellectual abilities of the dog. For example, *How Dogs Think,* by Stanley Coren; *If Dogs Could Talk,* by Vilmos Csányi; and *The Truth About Dogs,* by Stephen Budiansky, act as welcome bridges between what people want to know about the minds of their dogs, and what science has actually discovered.

Our dogs may not be lying around pondering the evolution of emotion and whether their humans experience emotions the same way they do, but it's the most natural thing in the world for us to wonder about the emotions of our dogs. How could we not? We've called dogs our best friends for centuries, and what is more basic to friendship than an emotional connection? A friendship with no emotional component is no friendship at all, it's a business arrangement (and even those usually have their share of emotional loading attached). Our dogs evoke a veritable sea of emotions in us, and we ride the waves back and forth between love and joy and sadness and anger almost on a daily basis. For centuries, dog lovers have believed that we're not paddling by ourselves—surely our dogs are out there with us, experiencing emotions similar to our own. Who could watch puppies play, or observe dogs lying motionless for days after losing a good friend, and not believe that our dogs have emotions as we do?

In contrast to the beliefs of most dog lovers, current beliefs among scientists and philosophers about the emotional life of dogs are all over the map. Some argue that only humans can experience emotions, while others argue that nonhuman animals experience primitive emotions like fear and anger, but not more complicated ones like love and pride. At the other end of the continuum, some say it's good science to believe that many mammals come with the whole package, being capable of experiencing emotions in ways comparable to the way we experience them.

The fact is, we don't know enough yet to be sure exactly what's going on inside the minds of our dogs. But we know enough to consider the topic thoughtfully, and we know enough to stop and look around at what we do know, what we don't know, and what we still want to learn. That's what this book is about. It's an inquiry into the emotions of dogs and of the people who love them. It is written in the belief that the issue is both gloriously simple and painstakingly complex. On the one hand, *of course* dogs have emotions. It seems so patently obvious to most of us that we feel foolish at having to say it. As much as any animal on earth, dogs express emotions as purely and clearly as a five-year-old child, and surely that's part of why we love them so much.

And yet, once that's acknowledged, things quickly get more complicated. Emotions are amazingly complex and, as is often the case, the more we know, the more complicated things get. As our knowledge of the brain deepens, we're starting to understand that emotions are vital parts of our conscious and unconscious lives, integrally involved in our ability to make good (or bad) decisions. While we've historically considered rational thought to be superior to our emotions, it turns out that "rational" thought uninformed by emotion can cause us no end of trouble.

Trouble, the kind between people and dogs, is one of the reasons I'm interested in this topic. I'm a Certified Applied Animal Behaviorist who has worked with dogs with serious behavioral problems for seventeen years. Part of my job is to try to get into the heads of dogs whose behavior is problematic. Most of what motivates people to come to my office involves canine aggression—dogs who snarl when you take them by the collar, who bite the neighbor, or who start fights at the dog park. Other people come because their dogs panic when they leave the house, or leap through the plate-glass window when it thunders.

All these problems, I will argue, are influenced by emotions—by fear, by happiness, or by anger born of frustration. It's important for me to know what emotions are involved, not just to help the dog and his owner, but to keep myself safe in a small room with a dog who bites people. Contrary to the belief of some, behaviorists, trainers, and veterinarians don't come with a shield that protects us from being bitten. I don't know how many times I've heard "Oh, my, usually he would have bitten you by now!" from an owner whose prediction that their dog was going to bite didn't result in any preventative steps on their part. But those of us who work with aggressive dogs usually don't get bitten, because we've learned to read dogs and can make guesses about their emotions and motivations. Those guesses help us predict what a dog is about to do next, and how to respond, like a good dance partner, in a way that helps us both.

Of course, observing that a dog looks fearful doesn't mean we understand how much of her experience of fear is like our own. But professionally, it matters that the outside of a dog can tell me something about the inside of a dog. That allows me to design a treatment plan that takes the personality of the dog into account, rather than provide a cookie-cutter approach straight out of a textbook. And even if it weren't useful, the fact of the matter is, I simply want to know what it's like to be a dog. As Jeffrey Moussaieff Masson said in *Dogs Never Lie About Love*, "I know them as well as I know my closest friend, and yet I have no idea who they are." What an exquisite paradox. It sends shivers up my spine.

I want to know more about what dogs are feeling, and how those feelings compare with mine. I want to know because I was trained as a scientist and am driven by the druglike excitement of discovery. I want to know because I think it's important for our species to understand where we fit in with the rest of life. In addition, so much suffering—in both species—could be prevented if we had a better understanding of the emotional lives of our dogs. But most of all, I want to know because of my own dogs. My dogs are as important to me as my human friends. They are my buddies, my family, my co-workers, my therapists, and, like all good friends, occasionally thorns in my side. I want to know more about who they are, and what they are feeling—partly from a desire to give them the best life I can, and partly from a desire to deepen our friendship.

I have three dogs now. Three dogs and a gravestone in the pasture for my soul-mate dog, Cool Hand Luke, who died recently and still seems as much a part of the farm as I am. His daughter, twelve-year-old Lassie, is always at my side—a hardworking Border Collie who works the sheep, helps with dog-dog aggression cases, and joins me in public appearances. Lassie is buttery soft, as responsive as a race car, and, I think, worried much of the time.

Fifteen-year-old Pip is also a Border Collie, but she's the one who didn't read the book about how Border Collies are supposed to behave. Quiet and docile even as a puppy, Pip wags her tail to stubborn sheep and runs in terror if an ewe so much as turns and looks at her. Pip was always the quiet one, the nanny dog, the dog you could count on to stay at home and take care of the kids while the rest of you went out to a play. A spirit guide to fearfully aggressive dogs, Pippy loved other dogs and men with equal devotion, and I've always wondered whether, if she had the choice of families, she would've chosen a home with a quiet, single man. Pip looks like a Border Collie crossed with a Labrador, complete with the sweet, goofy expression typical of retrievers on the outside, and a mind like a steel trap on the inside. Pip can learn a new trick in a session or two, while it takes Lassie days or weeks to figure it out. At fifteen, Pip is old now; she can't hear very well and she follows me everywhere, breaking my heart when she stands watching out the window as I drive away on business trips.

And then there's Tulip, my eleven-year-old Great Pyrenees, the poster child for dogs as emotional beings. She radiates joy like the sun shining on a winter's day. Tulip is a huge, fluffy, leap-spinning playground unto herself and I love her so much I can feel it in my chest just writing about it.

And that is what it's all about, isn't it? Our connection with dogs is based on emotion—on the joy they give us, the love we feel for them and from them. If we're honest, it also includes the anger and hurt we experience when we feel betrayed by them, and the fear they engender when they flash their teeth or bite our faces. Dogs evoke emotions in us as if wringing water out of a sponge, and so discussions about whether they have emotions themselves seem like arguments about whether there's a sun in the sky. But for all the love that we have for dogs, for all the joy and the tears, we have a lot to learn about our own emotions around them, and their emotional responses to us.

Love, as any partner or parent can tell you, isn't the same as understanding. Like the woman who loved her Border Collie as much as she confused her, we all can profit from learning more about emotions in both species. Some people who love their dogs are oblivious to blatant expressions of emotion on the dogs' faces (just ask any dog trainer). Others, not very good at controlling their own emotions around dogs, cause, at best, confusion; at worst, terrible suffering. Many dog owners don't know that dogs, like kids, need to learn to control their own emotions. I've seen countless dogs who bit someone out of what I think was frustration, lashing out in an emotional outburst that could have been prevented if they'd learned what all individuals who live with others need to learn: that patience is a virtue.

Many emotions support or undermine our relationships with dogs, but fear stands alone as the single most common cause of serious behavior problems in dogs. Dogs destroy the house because they're afraid of being alone, or tremble in the closet because they're thunder phobic, or cower when the neighbor kids come over to play—and end up lashing out when the children trap them in the corner. Many people don't realize how often dog bites are motivated by fear, or how yelling at them only increases their fear, making them more likely to bite again.

My hope is that this book, besides being intellectually interesting, will prevent some of those bites, and decrease some of the suffering that occurs when individuals love each other without the understanding necessary to keep the relationship healthy. *For the Love of a Dog* is a combination of stories, science, and practical advice about how under-standing emotions in both people and dogs can improve your relation-ship with your dog. It's not a dog training book, but it's full of information that can help your dog be better behaved, and help you to be a better handler. It doesn't begin to discuss everything we know about the biology of emotions—that book would be too heavy to pick up. I've focused on the emotions I think are most relevant in dog-human relationships: fear, anger, joy, and joy's cousin, love. My goal is to be both interesting and helpful to those of us who are, quite simply, crazy in love with our dogs. I wrote this book as much for dogs as I did for us, in the hopes it will, albeit indirectly, help dogs to better under-stand us—surely the world's most confusing species.

FOR THE LOVE
OF A DOG

1

EMOTIONS

An explanation of emotions,
and why they are so controversial in animals

At first, all I saw was a white blur out of the corner of my eye. It was a long way away, maybe five hundred yards, and initially I wasn't sure what it was. Most of my focus was on my Border Collie Luke, who was running his fastest about two hundred yards away. I'd sent him on a long out-run toward a flock of sheep during a "fun day," when herding enthusiasts get together and revel in dogs and sheep and the sloppy kisses of young puppies.

Many people there that day were serious competitors in herding dog trials, and were grateful for the opportunity to hone their skills away from home. Luke and I, however, were there just for the pure joy of it. We loved working together, Luke and I, finessing sheep gently and quietly across the countryside. A classic workaholic, Luke loved working sheep so much he had no interest in food, tennis balls, or even bitches in heat when there was a job to do. For me, watching my trustworthy black-and-white dog doing a perfect outrun on an emerald-green hill made my heart get bigger and my soul feel full. That's how I was feeling that morning as I watched my good old dog run perfectly and reliably toward the woolies on the far hill.

But all my feelings changed as I realized that the white blur running toward Luke was a hundred-and-twenty-pound working Great Pyrenees who had escaped temporary confinement and was barreling down on Luke to protect his flock. We were on a large, isolated farm with several dispersed flocks of sheep—a smorgasbord to the coyotes and stray dogs that commonly roam the countryside. Many of us in southern Wisconsin need working guard dogs to keep our flocks safe, and this farm had two of them. Unlike my guard dog, Tulip, who now protects the farm from the living room couch, these dogs lived exclusively with the flock, and were serious to the bone about killing anything that threatened their sheep.[1]

As I watched the guard dog run toward Luke, my feelings of joyful fulfillment were transformed into abject terror. The thought that I was about to watch my dog being attacked and possibly killed overwhelmed me. I love Luke so much it almost hurts.[2] In Dog Is My Co-pilot, in an essay about why we love dogs so much, I said about Luke: "And I still love him so deeply and completely that I imagine his death to be as if all the oxygen in the air disappeared, and I was left to try to survive without it."

Horrified at what I thought was about to happen, I screamed, "The guard dog is out, the guard dog is out!" Stating the obvious wasn't going to solve the problem, but it seemed to be all I could do. For the longest second imaginable, my mind was a black hole, as if my emotions had sucked away the rational part of my brain and left a cavernous skull full of nothing but fear. I can remember that terror now, and can visualize the scene as if in a photograph: emerald-green pasture, black-and-white Luke in full stride just where he ought to be, and a white bullet of doom streaking across the grass toward him.

But what of Luke? What went through his mind as he dashed through the grass with a canine hitman running toward him? Was he as scared as I was? And if he was, how much did his version of being scared resemble mine?

Luke and I were best friends, just as many dogs and humans are best friends all over the world. As friends do, we shared long cool walks in shady forests, tasty dinners of roast chicken or lamb, and long sleepy cuddles on the couch in the depth of winter. We shared hard times loading wild-eyed market lambs on to the truck, getting lost on back highways late at night while traveling, and making mistakes while working sheep that cost us valuable time, energy, and on occasion, a blue ribbon at a herding dog trial. We played together, worked to-

1. I envision Tulip on the couch, looking out the living room window beside a bank of video screens, talking into her head set: "Coyote at the west gate, coyote at the west gate."

2. Luke is gone now, having died of kidney failure, but I still love him as much as I did when he was alive, and I can't yet bring myself to say "loved" in the past tense.

gether, comforted each other, and had an occasional spat. In many ways, our lives were bound together as tightly as the lives of two human best friends.

But all those experiences don't say much about how we experienced the world inside our heads. We may have shared external experiences like walks in the woods and napping on the couch, but what of our internal experience? How much of that did we share? I've said that sometimes Luke lost his temper with me—but how could I know that? Without language as a bridge, how can any of us really know what goes on inside the heads of our dogs?

In one sense, we can't. We can't ever know what it is like to be a dog; some argue we shouldn't even try. But many of us try to understand the mental lives of our dogs every day, and we're not going to give up just because the task is difficult. One of my earliest childhood memories is of lying on the living room floor wondering what was going on in the mind of my dog, Fudge. I wanted to know what she was thinking, what she was feeling. Even at the age of five or six I wondered, What is life like inside her soft, furry little head? Is she happy? Is she sad?

These are reasonable questions for any dog lover to ask. Our emotional connection to our dogs is the fundamental glue that binds us to them, and it's natural to want to know more about their emotional connections to us. We can't have long intellectual discussions with our dogs as we do with our human friends; perhaps that's part of the attraction. Our intelligence and ability to use language can make our human relationships pretty complicated, as any marriage and family therapist can tell you. Our relationships with dogs are simpler in many ways than our relationships with people, but simplicity doesn't necessarily make something less important. $E = mc^2$ is simple, but it's an equation of great value. Perhaps our emotional connection to dogs is similar: pure, primal, and as basic as oxygen and water.

I don't remember whether I ran forward or stood frozen in fear during that endless second when Luke was in danger, but it was only a moment or two before a woman behind me calmly said, "Down your dog." I will forever be grateful to her, because this was perfect advice. A working guard dog is unlikely to be aggressive to a dog who lies down and stays still when approached, rather than running at the sheep like a hungry wolf. "Lie down!" *I bellowed, and two hundred yards away, Luke hit the dirt like a Marine on maneuvers.*

If Luke had been a much younger dog, he might have kept running. Asking a dog to stop on his outrun goes against his nature, and although an experienced trial-ready dog should be able to do it, it's an advanced skill that takes some serious teamwork to achieve.

Luke's age and training might have saved his life, because he dropped to the ground at my first request. Just in time: the guard dog got to him within seconds. "Stay there," I said in a low, steady voice, finally coming to my senses enough to be able to function. Luke stayed motionless, glued to the hillside, while the Pyrenees sniffed him from head to toe. (Well, really it was from rear end to muzzle, but you know what I mean.)

Although I was still terrified about what might happen to Luke, my brain was working again, and I was able to remember that my own guard dog insisted on inspecting any visiting dog from tail to collar. Tulip has been aggressive toward a visiting dog only once—when it ran away from her instead of standing still for scrutiny. I'm reminded of airport security guards, who are benevolent if we accept their inspections, but who react instantly to anyone who resists. Tulip behaves in a similar way, and once she's cleared canine travelers of harboring some doggy equivalent of sharp objects, she ignores them or invites them to play. That's exactly what happened that morning at the fun day. After a round of intense sniffing, the dog trotted off to check in with his flock. Soon his owner came and put him away, and Luke was able to complete his outrun and ease the sheep down the hill to me.

We had a great time working the flock after the interlude with the guard dog, and drove home tired from our day outside in the fresh air. Later I told a client about what had happened, and she suggested that Luke had probably been traumatized by it. "Look at poor old Brandy here [the dog lying at her feet, in my office for a serious case of dog-dog aggression]. He's never gotten over being attacked by that Black Lab at the dog park. You can see it right now in his eyes."

It was hard to see Brandy's eyes, covered as they were by champagne-colored bangs, but what I could see looked pretty much like the eyes of a dog happily chewing on the bone I'd provided. I'm not saying Brandy couldn't have been traumatized at the dog park. (We'll talk later about how traumatic events can affect the behavior of a dog years after their occurrence, just as they can in humans.) But if I had to make my own guess about what internal state Brandy's eyes were expressing in my office, it would have been contentment, not trauma.

WHAT ARE EMOTIONS, ANYWAY?

It's not surprising that people don't always agree with others about what emotion their dog is feeling. Emotions are complicated things, and it's worth taking a fresh look at them before we try to expand our understanding of our dogs' emotional lives.

Emotions may be primitive and primal, but that doesn't mean they are easy to understand. Now that we're finally getting around to studying them, emotions are turning out to be amazingly interesting and complicated biological processes. Most scientists agree that mammals such as dogs are capable of basic emotions like fear, anger, and happiness, but they don't agree on how they actually experience them. Surely, on the one hand it's a simple issue—if Luke saw an aggressive dog running toward him, why wouldn't he be fearful in much the same way that I was?

Ah, but on the other hand being scared is an emotional experience driven by the brain, and the only simple thing about the brain is the fact that we still haven't begun to comprehend it. No wonder: there are about a hundred billion neurons in the human brain, all linked together by ten trillion connections. Because of this level of complexity, our understanding of the biology of emotions is primitive at best. This makes it especially challenging to compare emotions in people and dogs, but the last few decades of research have taught us so much about the biology of emotions that it's more than reasonable to try. A good place to start is an examination of what we know about our own emotions.

Surely we all know what we're talking about when we're discussing emotions, but what would you say if someone asked you to define them? Beyond the labels we give them—fear, anger, joy—what exactly are emotions, and how are they created inside you? If you struggle with a precise definition, don't feel bad: you're not alone.[3] According to Antonio Damasio, an internationally acclaimed expert on emotion and

---

3. The inclusion of "don't feel bad" in a sentence about feelings wasn't planned, but it serves as a reminder of how central the emotions are to our existence.

the brain, our feelings are the least understood of all mental phenomena. They are also the most ubiquitous and probably the most ancient, so it's surprising that we've only recently attempted to sort them out. It took scientists like Damasio to dismiss the arguments of early behaviorists that we shouldn't attempt to understand emotions because, as subjective internal processes, they were "beyond the bounds of science." It turns out that's not even close to true; Damasio and others have proven that the biology of emotion is as accessible as the biology of hearing, vision, or memory.

This doesn't mean that research on emotions is easy. Emotions are slippery things, in some ways as hard to separate from our bodies and minds as it is to separate egg yolks from egg whites once you've mixed them together. As the neurologist John Ratey says: "Emotion is messy, complicated, primitive, and undefined because it's all over the place." You can't sit back and examine your own emotions as if in a petri dish, because they come along with you. We do know that emotions— like joy, fear, and anger affect the mind and body in predictable ways. An emotion like fear includes physiological changes in your body (your heart starts pounding when you see your dog running toward the road), visible changes in expression (you freeze in place, your pupils dilate, your eyes widen), conscious thoughts ("Oh no! There's a car coming!"), and feelings (your conscious experience of fear and panic). Thus, every emotion includes (1) changes in the body; (2) changes in expression; and (3) the feelings and thoughts that go along with them.

What we're not sure about is what comes first. Are you conscious of fear because your heart is racing and your eyes widen, or does your heart pound after your mind tells you your dog may be killed by a car? It seems reasonable to most of us that our bodies must be reacting to our thoughts—we see a car bearing down on our dog, we know enough about physics to know this is not a fair fight, so our bodies react with the feeling of fear. But research has shown that much of what we experience actually flows in the other direction. Often, it's the changes in your body that create the thoughts in your mind.

We've long known that you can stimulate different areas of the brain with a mild electrical current to evoke feelings of fear, sadness, or amusement. What's most remarkable about those cases is that the research subject, wide awake and in no pain, always comes up with an intellectual explanation for his or her feelings *after* the emotion is elicited. In my favorite case, a woman reliably burst into peals of laughter every time one area of her brain was stimulated. When the attending neurologists asked her what was so funny, she said: "You guys are just so funny . . . standing around!" Apparently needing to explain her amusement, her brain turned a circle of serious researchers into a knee-slapping vaudeville act.

You can even create emotions by moving parts of your body into different positions. You've no doubt read about experiments in which people were asked to raise or lower the corners of their mouths, and later asked how they were feeling. Just as our moms told us to put a smile on our face to cheer up, the people whose mouths moved into a smile felt better, while the frowners felt worse than when they came in. You can try it right now: hold a pencil in your back teeth for a few seconds and notice how you feel (besides silly). Most people report a mild boost in mood, because your mouth has to move as if it was smiling to hold the pencil. Now take the pencil out, drop your shoulders, droop your head, and slump down as if the air had come out of you. Feeling chipper? Probably not.

There's a long list of surprising ways you can influence your emotions by changing what you're doing with your body. One researcher noted that people in love tend to gaze into each other's eyes for prolonged periods of time. Wondering whether the process could work in reverse, she asked strangers to do the same for two minutes. After that amount of mutually agreed-upon eye contact, the people in the study reported feelings of attachment and attraction to the other person. (Of course, this long period of eye contact was by mutual consent, and had nothing to do with a stranger walking up unannounced and staring straight into your eyes. That would probably elicit the opposite of attraction. If the stranger was a dog, it might even get you bitten, so please don't go experimenting with a nonconsenting partner of any species.)

You never know where and when these postural changes might affect your mood. The famous jazz singer Ella Fitzgerald reported that one year she had become so tired she couldn't get out of bed in the morning. She went to several doctors until finally one asked her what she did during the day. As she thought through her day, she realized she was singing her hit song "I'm So Tired" over and over again, changing her posture each time to match the emotion she was expressing. The doctor prescribed eliminating the song from her repertoire, and Ella recovered in days.

As we all know now, our emotions can also be affected by our internal physiology. This was not Nobel Prize–winning news to women with premenstrual syndrome, but an understanding of the impact of physiology on emotion is relatively new. Decades ago—before PMS was acknowledged—my best girl friend and I wondered why we could be blissfully happy one day, but, with no discernible changes in circumstance, be depressed and irritable the next. Eventually we noticed a pattern and figured out on our own that the mood changes correlated with our menstrual cycle. Right around that time, a physician in England began arguing that hormonal changes could radically affect mood and, in extreme cases, could lead to suicide or institutionalization.

Now that we have a much better understanding of neurochemistry, it's universally accepted that the body's chemistry affects our emotions. As I write, millions of people are taking SSRIs (selective serotonin reuptake inhibitors) to improve their mood by changing the ratio of neurohormones in their brains. An acknowledged side effect of being on a heart-lung machine is the onset of depression in patients who have never experienced it before. No one knows why, but it probably has something to do with a change in internal physiology created by the heart-lung machine itself. Three decades after my conversations with a friend, women with PMS are now taken seriously by the same doctors who used to do little more than pat them on the head.

Of course, in addition to the powerful effect of the chemistry within our bodies, we all know that external events drive our emotions on a daily basis. A perfectly good mood can be soured by stop-and-go traffic. The impending death of a beloved dog is heartbreaking, because we intellectually understand what that death will mean to us. Once those thoughts arise (and in some cases, even before we're conscious of them), our bodies respond with the cascade of changes that define our different emotions. It seems reasonable to believe that something similar occurs in our dogs as well. Pick up the leash, and your dog radiates with excitement; tell him that he can't come with you this time, and watch his body slump and his face droop, just as yours does when you've been disappointed.

EMOTIONS AS PRIMITIVE LINKS
BETWEEN BRAIN AND BODY

In spite of the "Which came first, the chicken or the egg?" controversy about emotions, neurobiologists agree that the primary function of emotions is to keep the brain in touch with the rest of the body. Emotions are a kind of bridge between the "thinking" part of the brain and the rest of the body, acting to keep the organism moving toward its ideal state. Emotions allow each of us, from an award-winning neurobiologist to a hungry bloodhound, to respond to the world in ways that allow us to keep growing.

Before the invention of things like caramel corn and Krispy Kremes, what made us feel good was good for us. That's still true of animals who live in an environment with limited resources, in which they don't have the opportunities that we do to pig out on too much of a good thing. This general rule works just as well in reverse: in the wild, what feels bad probably isn't good for you, so you should avoid it. One of the first things you learn when you study animal behavior is that animals move toward pleasure and comfort, and away from pain and discomfort. Emotions are the mechanisms that allow animals to do that; they are the Geiger counter of the body that informs the brain what to do next. Did your eyes spot a predator behind the bush? Then it's good when your heart starts to race and more blood pumps to your muscles and your brain tells you to get ready to run. Feel warm and cozy and content? Then you're probably in an environment that is safe and healthy for you.

Emotions are profoundly basic things, seen in a myriad of species in their physiological reactions, their expressions, their brains, and their neurochemistry. That's one of the many reasons why it's illogical to claim that animals like dogs don't have emotions, even though some people still make that argument. If something happened right now to terrify you and your dog, his posture and expression would be a close replica of your own. This isn't new knowledge—in 1872, Charles Darwin published *The Expression of the Emotions in Man and Animals,* in which he doesn't hesitate to illustrate the posture of a "terrified" cat or a "humble" and affectionate dog. In the book, Darwin emphasizes that basic emotions like fear and disgust have the same outward physical expression in many species. Well over a hundred years old, the book is used in every class worth its salt on evolution or behavior.

Now that we're able to look beyond changes in behavior and go deep inside a functioning brain, we've found that we share a lot more than just outward expressions with other animals. In his book *Affective Neuroscience,* Jaak Panksepp argues that mammals have the same basic emotion-related structures and the same emotion-related physiology as we do. The area of the brain that mediates emotion is called the limbic system, and it's so basic to the brains of both you and your dog that it's often called the mammalian brain.

The limbic system nestles deep in the middle of your brain, tucked between the truly primitive areas that keep your head up and your lungs working, and the wrinkly, newer areas of the cerebral cortex, which integrates information and makes decisions. In both you and your dog, it includes three vital little structures called the amygdala, the hypothalamus, and the hippocampus. The amygdala attaches emotional significance to the information coming into the brain, and has been called the command center of the emotions of surprise, rage, and fear. As we learn more about the complexity of the brain, we've learned that this is a vast oversimplification, but then, just about everything we've learned about the brain fits into that category. (The brain is so complicated that it's almost impossible to talk about it without over-simplifying something, so bear with me.) Suffice it to say that your amygdala is a crucial player in your emotional experience and your dog's amygdala a crucial player in his. The amygdala is not only important in generating your own emotions, it's a key player in reading the emotions of others. People with damaged amygdalas can't discriminate between others' facial expressions of joy and anger.[4] As we'll see in later chapters, the amygdala is a very busy place if something happens to scare or enrage either you or your dog.

The amygdala passes on its emotional judgments to other structures that collate memories, pass information on to the cortex, and release hormones appropriate to whatever emotion has been generated. This system as a whole, relying on both innate responses and stored

---

4. They can recognize familiar faces because facial recognition is mediated by another part of the brain, but they can't tell if the person is happy, sad, or angry without a fully functioning amygdala.

memories, was a major player in my feelings of terror when I realized that Luke was in danger. We can't know how much Luke's internal experience was like mine, but he and I both had the same structures in our brain that mediate the fear, and it's this structural similarity that underlies the argument of many of us that the emotions of nonhuman mammals must be similar to those of humans.

Surely, fear is the most fundamental of emotions. It's hard to imagine living in a world full of predators and poisonous plants without a brain that motivates you to be careful when you're in danger. Even skeptics of emotions in animals agree that fear is the most basic of emotions, an adaptive response for any animal able to make choices to protect itself in the wild. Most biologists agree that the other "basic" emotions are anger, disgust, and joy. These primal emotions are seen clearly in all individuals of our own species, and are expressed in similar ways, no matter where the person is or what the culture.[5]

Three of these basic emotions—fear, anger, and happiness—are so important to us (and I will argue, also to our dogs) that we'll discuss each of them in its own chapter. Love, as a cousin of happiness, deserves its own chapter, as only seems appropriate in a book about emotions and our relationships with dogs. Besides these four basic emotions, there are others, such as guilt and pride, that appear to be more complicated. Perhaps they are combinations of basic emotions, as green is a combination of the primary colors yellow and blue. Some people argue that while all mammals experience fear, anger, disgust, and joy, emotions like guilt and pride require higher cognitive abilities and can be felt only by humans. We'll talk about these more complex emotions later in the book, but for now, what's important is that our basic emotions don't separate us from the rest of nature; they link us to it. As Diane Ackerman put it in *An Alchemy of Mind,* we may have sophisticated brains, but the emotions that blossom within them are crude and primitive. At their most basic level, surely we share the experience of them with our dogs.

5. Some people argue that while animals have these emotions, the perception of them—the actual feelings associated with anger, fear, disgust, and joy—can't exist without consciousness. If you want to delve into an intellectual morass as sticky and opaque as molasses, jump into the debate about consciousness in nonhuman animals. We'll do that later on in the book (remember, molasses is sweet—it's not all bad in there), but for now, there's value in staying with what we do know about emotions.

THROUGH YOUR EYES ONLY

In November 2003, Tammy Ogle's head was run over by the car she was driving. She was cruising down a county road, her three Labradors lolling in the back, when her SUV flipped in circles like a spinning ball, and threw her out the window and under the wheels of her own vehicle. When the dust settled, she lay unconscious with ten broken ribs and a smashed, scalped head. Tammy's three Labs, Double, Lily, and Golly, escaped serious injury and scrambled out of the vehicle. (Tammy told me that she always crated her dogs in the car, and has no idea why on this particular morning she let them ride loose.) Double, a handsome black three-year-old, stayed with Tammy, while Lily and Golly ran half a mile to the nearest house, where they proceeded to bark and scratch at the door until someone came out. Golly grabbed the homeowner's sleeve to pull him toward the road, where he was able to see Tammy's overturned vehicle.

If you'd like to get into an argument, ask several people whether they think Tammy's dogs were consciously saving her life. Some will say: "Of course they were. It's perfectly reasonable to believe that (1) the dogs recognized that Tammy was seriously injured and desperately needed help; (2) they loved Tammy and wanted to help her; (3) knowing they couldn't help her themselves, they consciously decided to run down the road and find someone who could help her; (4) when they arrived at a house, they barked and scratched at the door to get the attention of whoever was inside; (5) Golly became aware that the homeowner hadn't yet noticed the accident, so she tugged on his sleeve to try to direct his attention.

Other people will see the story above as a prime example of dog lovers being foolishly anthropomorphic, imagining mental processes in dogs that are actually exclusive to humans. People with this perspective might argue that the dogs ran down the road because they were mindlessly frightened and wanted to get away from the site of the accident. Their barking in the farmyard had no strategic purpose, but occurred because the dogs had unconsciously learned to bark around humans to get attention, or because the dogs were emotionally aroused without knowing why. Perhaps Golly often greets people by grabbing at their sleeves—heaven knows Labradors love to put things in their mouths, and there are lots of Labradors who can't resist a friendly "handshake" with their mouths.

You can see it's easy to come up with stories about why an animal is doing something. Both of the stories above are just that—stories. None of us can prove that our own version is the accurate one, but no one can disprove the alternative either. In the absence of any more information, it's pretty seductive to believe your own version and dismiss others. That's one of the reasons why scientists have historically argued that being anthropomorphic is to be avoided at all costs. It's easy to make up a story about what's going on in an animal's mind that's based on putting yourself in the animal's place. It's also easy to be really, really wrong.

There are endless illustrations of the trouble we get into by imagining animals as furry people, and not just in the world of dogs. I darn near killed my first flock of sheep by closing them into the barn in winter in a misguided attempt to keep them warm. I couldn't imagine them outdoors without my assistance when it was 20 below—simply because I couldn't imagine staying warm if *I'd* been left outside all night. But sheep aren't wooly people, and as long as they have enough fuel in the form of good food, they are much healthier if left in the fresh air than closed into a barn. Shut into a confined area they are likely to get pneumonia from air dampened by moisture from their own breath (which is exactly what happened to mine). Now I'm smart enough to give them the choice, and most nights they choose to lie outside, perhaps covered in a blanket of snow, contentedly dozing in weather that would chill me to the bone.

That same year I obsessively stuffed soft fresh straw into the outdoor doghouses, worried sick that the dogs who slept in the kennels at night would suffer from the cold.[6] In the morning I would find that Bess, a brilliant and strong-minded Border Collie, had dug out every strand of straw. After just a week or two, during which I relentlessly ignored my dog's behavior and continued to try to make the doghouses softer and warmer, Bess began digging out the straw before I had finished putting it in. Finally I figured it out, probably on the morning when the temperature was 5 below and I found Bess sleeping content-

6. At that time I was married and had agreed to a "no more than two dogs in the house" rule. Now even the sheep-guarding dog sleeps inside. The dogs and I like it better that way, although the living room couch will never be the same.

edly outside her doghouse, curled up on a patch of snow and ice, apparently as comfy as warm toast.

Misplaced anthropomorphic concerns about animals go far beyond the boundaries of dog lovers. In a classic case, a British committee charged with improving the welfare of commercial chickens was about to mandate that the chickens be housed on wire thicker than what was commonly used. The traditional wire was so thin it looked as though standing on it with bare feet would be painful. Rather than dispensing tennis shoes to the chickens, the committee thought that producers should provide thicker wire. But before the producers were forced to spend millions of dollars on new caging, good science prevailed in the form of objective tests to see what the chickens preferred. Contrary to all expectations, the chickens chose the wire that to humans seemed intuitively the least comfortable. Subsequent tests showed that the thin wire actually dispersed pressure more effectively, and was far kinder to the feet of the chickens than one would have thought.

Forgetting that other mammals are not furry people with paws is a mistake that dog lovers frequently make. In an earlier book, *The Other End of the Leash,* I talk about how humans hug as a sign of affection, while a dog's version of hugging is a display of social status. Dogs may love to be stroked and massaged, but hugging around the shoulders and chest is something most dogs only tolerate in exchange for cozy couches and a guaranteed dinner. I've learned to be careful when I talk about hugging dogs, because some people get angry with me when I suggest that their dog doesn't adore being squeezed around the shoulders. Hugging is such an important part of expressing affection in our species, it's impossible for some people to imagine that their dogs don't necessarily like it. This is compounded by the fact that we can't see the expression on our dog's face when we're hugging her. If you change perspectives, and watch a dog's face when someone else is doing the hugging, you'll get an entirely different picture. I have about fifty photographs of people hugging dogs, in which the human is beaming and the dog is looking miserable.

Usually this difference in interpretation doesn't lead to serious problems, but sadly, many dogs don't tolerate our bizarre need to squeeze them around the shoulders. They take our hugs as serious violations of canine social rules, and lash out in protest. This has resulted in countless numbers of dog lovers being bitten, and countless numbers of dogs being put down for biting a child on the face. Of course, we all should be working toward breeding and raising dogs that tolerate typical human behavior, but we're also always going to have to acknowledge that if we're the "smart" ones, then we have to meet dogs more than halfway. The fact of the matter is, dogs don't always want what we want, and forgetting that can cause a lot of pain and suffering.

Most examples of this aren't so dramatic, but can still cause great harm. I'm amazed at the number of people who still believe that their dog potties or chews in the house to "get back at them" for being left alone during the day. People imagine that their dog is angry because she's been left behind, and assume that the pile of poop in the living room was left as a statement of disgust. But there are a lot of problems with this scenario, not the least of which is the fact that dogs aren't disgusted by poop. They love the stuff. Eating feces, whether that of another dog or a pile deposited by sheep or horses, seems to be a highlight in the life of many a dog. When people visit my farm they often envision their dog, finally off-leash in acres of safely fenced countryside, running like Lassie in a television show, leaping over fallen tree trunks, shiny-eyed with joy at the chance to run free in the country. While they're imagining that heartwarming scene, their dog is most likely gobbling up sheep poop as fast as he can. Dogs aren't people, and if they have their own image of heaven, it most likely involves poop.

Why on earth, then, would a dog defecate in the house to get back at you? If he was trying to communicate with his owners by defecating (which I doubt), the message would more likely have been "Look what I've left you! A really great pile of poop!" Neither does it make sense that a dog would chew on the couch (or the remote control—one of the all-time favorite chew toys for dogs, by the way) as a way of punishing you. It's far more likely that the dog is either frustrated, anxious, or bored. Short of going on the Internet or watching soaps, what is your dog going to do besides chew on something?

So often people think their dog "knows" she shouldn't potty in the house because she greets them at the door looking "guilty," with her head and tail down, her eyes all squinty and submissive. But this is a posture of appeasement, not guilt. The poor dog has learned that her owners are going to yell at her if there's a puddle on the carpet when they come home. All that crouching and groveling is a white flag to avoid her owner's wrath, not a sign she's aware she's broken some moral code of dog/human relationships. A dog cowering at the door when the owners come home is trying to keep them from yelling at her, poor thing, and it's the last thing she'll think of later on in the week when they're gone and she needs to pee. But people still yell at their dogs, hit them, and shove their noses into puddles in the belief that the dog looked guilty when they returned home, and therefore has proved that she "knew" better all along.

"ANTHROPOMORPHIC" ISN'T ALWAYS A DIRTY WORD

The examples above illustrate why many people consider anthropomorphism dangerous. Being anthropomorphic originally meant ascribing human characteristics to the gods; the word is now used any time humans try to understand the world by putting themselves in the place of another animal. The attempt is considered such a sin in some circles that "anthropomorphism" might as well be a dirty word. Luckily, it's a bit too long to be a satisfying expletive. "You anthropomorphic idiot" has a certain ring to it, but it's not going to replace any four-letter words.

I, along with legions of others, was taught in zoology and psychology classes to avoid anthropomorphism like the plague. However, as often happens in our species, many took a reasonable perspective to extremes, and began to speak as though comparisons between animals and people were always incorrect. To them, any property that seemed part and parcel of who we are, like thinking, planning, and even feeling, became off-limits for nonhuman animals. However, although rationality and reason are the traits most often considered unique to our species, there's a surprising lack of reason when you look at the "human" traits the skeptics *have* been willing to attribute to other animals.

Many people who warn about the dangers of anthropomorphism don't hesitate to talk about animals as being "selfish" or "competitive." It seems that the attribution of negative human traits to animals rarely receives criticism. Animals can be "manipulative" or "selfish," but heaven help you if you talk about animals as "affectionate" or "conciliatory." The primatologist Frans de Waal was roundly criticized when he first described "reconciliation behavior" in common chimpanzees, even though the evidence for it was overwhelming. Even seemingly neutral terms can make some scientists uncomfortable. Two excellent scientists, Donald Owings and Eugene Morton, whose work I greatly respect, recently argued that it is wrong to look at animal communication, like the song of a whale or the whine of a puppy, as "information transfer." That is an anthropomorphic concept, they argue. Rather, we should discuss animal communication as examples of "assessment, manipulation or management." I'm very much in agreement with the idea that communication is often about trying to get others to do what you want. But I don't see why the terms "manipulation" or "management" aren't anthropomorphic, when "information transfer" is.

Another example of our hesitancy to attribute positive motivations to animals occurred in 1996, when a three-year-old boy fell into a gorilla enclosure at Chicago's Brookfield Zoo. Binti Jua, an eight-year-old female gorilla, picked up the child, cradled him in her arms, and then gently handed him over to one of the keepers. The story hit the national media, and within hours, experts were interviewed about this "amazing" event. Some argued that it was foolishly anthropomorphic to attribute kindness or compassion to Binti, and that she was simply doing what she'd been taught to do by her keepers.[7] In his book *The Ape and the Sushi Master,* Frans de Waal points out that we'd never dismiss the similar actions of a human child, even if she, too, had been taught to be gentle and nurturing by her parents. What Binti did is typical for gorillas, not in any way unusual. Gorillas are generally quiet, gentle vegetarians, who spend most of the day munching on wild celery, benevolently tolerating the antics of the youngsters. It would be a different story altogether if the boy had fallen into a pride of lions and a young female picked him up in her jaws, walked through the pride, and handed him over to a keeper. Little boys look like dinner to lions, but to gorillas they look like, well . . . little boys. What's most amazing to many of us was not Binti's behavior, but the outcry from some that attributing something akin to human compassion to a gorilla was hopelessly romantic and unscientific.

It's not just scientists who appear to be more comfortable using negative rather than positive terms to describe animals. Dog owners,

7. Binti's keepers had been helping her learn parental skills with a stuffed animal, much as young children are taught with dolls by their parents.

even those who love their dogs, do it too. Millions of hapless dogs have been yelled at or even beaten because we so readily attribute our species' worst traits to them. How quick we are to project our worst attributes onto dogs. Think how rich you'd be if you had a dollar for every time someone said "He's doing it just to spite me!" or "He *knows* better than that!" Well, maybe your dog does "know" not to jump up onto visitors, but haven't *you* ever forgotten your manners when you got excited, or forgotten what you wanted to say when you were nervous? What did "knowing" have to do with it when you dropped your fork at your in-laws' house during Thanksgiving dinner? Did you do it on purpose, to spite your new spouse? I doubt it. Why are we so willing to attribute willful disobedience to dogs, but unwilling to attribute to them things like anxiety or confusion that compromise our own performances?

Perhaps the answer lies in what psychologists call the fundamental attribution error. It seems we humans tend to assume that the behavior of individuals we don't know is based more on their underlying dispositions than on external influences. This is best illustrated by one enlightening study, in which students spoke to a woman who was told to be either warm and friendly, or cold and aloof. Half of the students were told that the woman was behaving one way or another because she had been instructed to act that way by the experimenters. The other half was told nothing that would explain her behavior. Amazingly, both groups of students rated the aloof woman as being *inherently* unfriendly, even if they'd been told she was just acting. It turns out that we all do this; it's almost impossible to avoid. You may know your best friend well enough to know that her rude remarks to a salesclerk are a result of the terrible day she's had, but if you see a stranger doing the same thing you're likely to assume it's because she's a nasty person. Sadly, dogs can't tell us that they've had a bad day, or that their hips hurt, and too often we assume the worst about them.

Of course, some dog owners go to the opposite extreme. Just yesterday I talked with a good friend who expressed her belief that dogs are the epitome of absolute love. I share her view that dogs can give us a pure and uncomplicated kind of love, but I don't believe that dogs channel love, and nothing but love, every moment of every day. To imagine that everything a dog does is motivated by love and compassion is as inaccurate as adopting the other extreme. I had a client who explained that the scars on her arms were "love bites" from her eighty-pound Lab. After watching the dog show no regard for her personal space, slam into her as she walked across the room, throw himself into her face, and repeatedly bite her arm for attention, I had a slightly different interpretation.

Either way, surely what's best for our dogs is to find a balance between rejecting all "human" traits in our dogs and projecting our fondest dreams or worst fears onto them. It seems to me that the question of what parts of our mental life we share with dogs is a "glass half full, glass half empty" issue. Of course, our subjective experience of the world is profoundly different from that of our dogs, but we share so very much with them—surely it's bad science to ignore that. The glass may be half empty, but it's a big glass, and that means there's a lot of liquid in it that shouldn't be ignored.

An increasing number of scientists *are* looking at the glass as half full, taking the stand that being anthropomorphic isn't always all bad. How else are we to begin, they argue, except with our own experience? Surely it is reasonable, when animals have similarly organized brains, similar physiologies, and similar behaviors, to speculate that, to some extent, they might be having similar experiences. What's needed is a balanced perspective, in which we avoid imagining animals as mute, hairy versions of people, but continue to do all we can to understand how our experience compares with that of other animals. Not too long ago a scientist named Jacques Vauclair disagreed, saying, "Fortunately the principal aim of scientific study of the minds of other animals is not to find out what it is like to be a certain type of animal, but rather to clarify how mental states cause observable behavior." But when asked why they began studying animal behavior, the participants at an annual meeting of the Animal Behavior Society replied that their primary motivation was to see the world through the eyes of other animals. This motivation has inspired thousands of scientists to work exceptionally hard, for relatively little money, usually in mud, rain, or tropical heat, all because they want to expand their understanding of the universe. Accordingly, we dog lovers shouldn't apologize for wanting to know what it is like to be a dog. Trying to imagine what life is like from the perspective of another animal is one of the abilities that might actually be unique to humans—why should we be ashamed of it? Of course, we'll never completely know what it is like to be a dog, or a warthog or a grasshopper. We'll never *really* know what it is like to be another human either, but surely that shouldn't stop us from trying.

There's no question in anyone's mind that Tammy Ogle was rescued from near death by the actions of her dogs. The story was so compelling that the Wisconsin Veterinary Medical Association inducted the dogs into their Hero Hall of Fame in 2004. For what it's worth, my own interpretation of what happened is that Double, Lily, and Golly were well aware that she was badly injured, and were also aware, in some way, that she needed help. Rather than being overly romantic, this seems like the simplest explanation. Science may get complicated, but all budding scientists are taught that in the absence of certainty, the best explanation is the simplest one. It seems far more complicated, even unwieldy, to imagine a world in which Ogle's dogs were reflexively responding to external events and had no awareness of her injuries. As highly social animals, dogs are one of the few species in which individuals will sacrifice their lives to save a member of the pack.[8] They are predators who hunt cooperatively, so it is part of their biological makeup to collaborate. They evolved to be problem solvers, team players, and concerned, nurturing elders who take care of needy pack members. It is not foolish romanticism that suggests that Tammy's dogs were trying to help her. It's good biology.

It is foolish, however, to imagine that Tammy's dogs engaged in a sophisticated analysis of the problem, with their minds working exactly as ours might have in the same situation. My own belief is that both of the explanations we examined at the beginning of the chapter have merit, although I suspect the truth is closer to the former rather than the latter. It's true that the more altruistic explanation makes me feel better, but that doesn't make it wrong. The fact that the story of Tammy and her dogs makes some of us feel all soft and melty inside doesn't mean that our interpretation of it automatically violates the tenets of good science. Just because an explanation makes us feel good doesn't mean it can't be true. It's a foolish fallacy that emotion is the enemy of reason, as we'll see later on in the book. I will continue to believe that Tammy's dogs knew she needed help because it's a

---

8. Wolves will always feed their puppies, even if they themselves are starving. Lions eat first, letting their young starve if there's not enough food. I love my cat more than I can say, but I wouldn't want to count on her to risk her own life to save mine.

reasonable explanation for their behavior, and because I watched my own Luke, the dog who started this book, save my life by risking his own.

I'll never know exactly what he was thinking when he scrambled, unasked, over a tall wooden fence to save me from a horned sheep who was out for blood, but he'd worked sheep long enough to know he could've been badly injured himself. I know that he leaped over the fence on his own initiative, without me saying a word. He never did that before, and he never did it again. He went after the horned sheep just long enough for me to get to the gate, and then he bolted out behind me. And I know that as we lay panting and bleeding on the barn floor, both exhausted and exhilarated, we were two friends gulping oxygen and relief after our shared adventure. We may be members of different species, but what we share—what Tammy and her dogs share, and what so many of us share with all of our dogs—is surely greater than what we don't.

THE CONTROVERSY OVER EMOTIONS IN ANIMALS

We may share a lot with dogs, including parallels in brain structures, the similarity of changes in brain chemistry and activation, and the similarities in facial expressions, but that isn't enough to silence the naysayers who argue that animals like dogs can't experience emotions. As recently as 1989, a philosopher named Peter Carruthers wrote that unless animals have the kind of consciousness that we do (and are thus able to "think about thinking"), they may have what look like emotions, but they can't feel them. This is not a new perspective. In the 1600s, the philosopher René Descartes argued that animals were not only incapable of thinking or having emotions, but that they couldn't even feel pain. He illustrated this principle by nailing live dogs to barn walls and eviscerating them. While the dogs writhed and screamed, he told the crowd of onlookers that their struggles were merely automatic movements of the body—no more felt by the dog than a clock feels the movement of its hands.

As horrific as this practice was, at least Descartes had the excuse of ignorance about the biology of emotion and sensation. That excuse is no longer available, but in spite of the current state of knowledge of the shared anatomy and physiology of emotions, a small number of educated people still resist the idea that animals experience the world around them in ways similar to ours. Carruthers, the philosopher mentioned above, went on to argue that any concern about the "pains of brutes" (*brutes*?) is unethical. He says that nonhuman animals can't actually feel anything, no matter how they behave, and so concern about them is unethical, because it takes time and money away from helping humans. This is a not a man I'll be inviting to the farm to meet my dogs.

Others argue that although animals such as dogs may think and feel, their mental lives are inaccessible to us, and so there is no point in trying to understand what goes on inside their heads. If, these people argue, we can never *really* know what's going on in our own minds, much less how a dog is feeling, then attempts to guess at it can never be more than speculation. Since good scientists aren't supposed to settle for guesses, the argument goes, we should avoid that inquiry altogether and get on with collecting hard, solid facts.

Much of the adherence to this perspective was driven throughout the twentieth century by America's influential behaviorists John B. Watson and B. F. Skinner. Both Skinner and Watson were committed to avoiding speculation about those messy and unapproachable aspects of behavior, like emotions, thoughts, and consciousness. Skinner argued that it can't ever be known what goes on inside an individual's head (whether human or animal), and so we must focus exclusively on observable behavior. Skinner did *not* say, as some do, that there is no such thing as consciousness in humans or animals. He argued that because we can't possibly know what an individual is really thinking and feeling, we should avoid trying to find out. Just days before his death in 1990, Skinner argued against any scientific consideration of "thoughts, perceptions and expectations." To his credit, he wasn't just talking about your dog or your cat; he held the same views about studying human emotions. But as this perspective became pervasive in science and society, others began to argue not that we couldn't understand the mental life of animals, but that animals simply didn't have one.

Especially in the United States, the distinction between "human" and "animal" grew in the mid-1900s, such that any experience beyond simple learning was judged to be exclusively human.[9] This view was pervasive in some fields of science and in society in general. The early

---

9. People (at least, in the West) in the 1800s had a much more accepting viewpoint of animals as thinking, feeling creatures, and romanticized descriptions of them were common.

work of the primatologist Jane Goodall was roundly criticized because she used the term "personality" in relation to chimpanzees: ascribing a "human characteristic" (the subtext being *exclusively* human") to a nonhuman animal was considered sloppy science. David Bodian, one of the researchers responsible for discovering the polio vaccine, was criticized at a 1952 scientific conference for referring to one of his research chimpanzees as a "he" rather than an "it." His critic argued that the use of "he" made the animal the "equal of men." I sent my first research paper to the journal *Animal Behaviour* in fear and trepidation, because I purposefully gave the subjects (puppies) names instead of numbers. At the time, that was a relatively radical thing to do; the belief was that naming an animal in an experiment might lead to an unscientific assumption that the animal experienced a life of hopes and fears, as would any human with his or her own name.[10]

Based on the principles of learning theory, parents were advised to employ the basic laws of learning by reinforcing good behavior, ignoring or punishing bad behavior, and inhibiting their foolish tendencies to show affection randomly. Dog owners were demeaned for attributing "exclusively human capacities" like emotions, expectations, and, worst of all, "thinking" to their dogs. The cautions of many of these scientists are with us today. Most scientists, biologists, and health care workers have been carefully trained to avoid ascribing human emotions or thoughts to nonhuman animals. In a recent article in the popular Sunday magazine *Parade*, a pediatric neurosurgeon said: "Animals are victims of circumstance. They can only react to their environment. But humans, thanks to our frontal lobes, can plan, strategize and exercise control over our environments. We don't have to be *victims who simply react*" (my italics).

Even veterinarians can argue either side of the coin—dogs as thinking, feeling individuals or as fuzzy, mindless machines. While I was working on this very section, a veterinarian on a television show was asked: "Can we tell our animals' emotions by looking at their body postures?" "Well," said the vet, "emotion is a human term," and went on to say he hesitated to use it in relation to dogs. Given the primitive nature of fear and rage, I was more than a little surprised by his state-

10. The paper was accepted, although at least one reviewer objected to my "unscientific" terminology and advised I change the names to numbers. The editor, bless his heart, stood by me.

ment. I was reminded of Darwin's *Expression of the Emotions in Man and Animals,* in which he draws parallels between the expressions of people and animals, and of how, although the topic may be controversial, scientists still consider the book a classic.

Darwin's work is a good reminder that the controversy about emotions in nonhuman animals doesn't have animal lovers on one side and all of science aligned on the other. Nothing could be further from the truth. There's as much disagreement among scientists about the mental states of animals as there is in the general public. If you pick up some of the many books written by scientists in the last twenty years about animal minds and animal thinking, you can see just how heated the debate has become. (See the references for Chapters 1 and 9 for a list of some truly great books on those topics.) In 1984, a scientist named Donald Griffin, well known for his rigorous research on the navigation abilities of bats, published a book on the mental lives of animals titled *Animal Thinking.* It generated such heated controversy in the world of science that it's since been called the "*Satanic Verses* of animal behavior."

Donald Griffin was castigated by some for allying himself "with the layman, the affectionate pet owner and curious huntsman," simply because he argued that animal thinking was an important subject for scientific inquiry. Comparing a scientist with an "affectionate pet owner," is, in some circles, a scathing rebuke. Luckily, scientists like Griffin seem to take it in stride. He volleyed back by calling his critics "mechanomorphs," whose narrow views demean animals into little more than automatons. A more recent discussion of the controversy is found in *Affective Neuroscience,* in which Jaak Panksepp argues that the basis of human emotions lies in our evolutionary heritage, and counters the arguments of critics that animals may "have" emotions but are unable to "feel" them.[11]

And so, the debate rages on, with some believing not only that animals like dogs can think and feel, but that it's possible for us to inquire into what they're thinking about and how they're feeling.[12] But to oth-

11. If you'd like an interesting and entertaining survey of how scientists vary in how they talk about emotions in animals, get a copy of Marc Bekoff's *The Smile of a Dolphin: Remarkable Accounts of Animal Emotions.*

12. I use the word "rages" purposefully. The process of science may be objective, but individual scientists aren't, and disagreements between them can get heated, personal, and, on rare occasion, even physical. In one infamous incident in the seventies, someone at an academic conference threw a bucket of water in E. O. Wilson's face for his comments linking human and animal behavior.

ers, attributing a "mind" full of thoughts and feelings of any kind to a dog is unscientific and objectionable. It's not just scientists and veterinarians who argue about what goes on between the ears of your best friend. A student in my "Human/Animal Relationships" class at the University of Wisconsin–Madison told me that a philosophy professor informed his class that not only are animals unable to think and feel, they can't learn anything either. To him, the behavior of all animals, from bumblebees to Black Labs, is simply a series of mindless, mechanical responses to the world around them. Given that virtually all of the early studies on learning were done on animals, that's an amazingly ignorant statement.

Ignorance about what goes on in the minds of animals appears to be an equal opportunity employer. Just about everyone seems to have a strong belief about the mental lives of animals, unrelated to their level of knowledge about the topic. Not too long ago I sympathized with a dog having what looked like a painful medical procedure done without anesthetic. "Oh, it can't feel anything," the owner said. "It's just a dog." The other end of the spectrum is equally easy to find, and equally astounding. I had a client who told me flat out that the reason her dog pawed obsessively around his dinner bowl was that he knew her mother was coming to visit. It seems Mom was a fastidious housekeeper, and my client thought the dog was trying to help clean up before she arrived. I don't remember any more details of her explanation; I was too busy trying to keep a straight face. Stanley Coren tells a laugh-out-loud story in *How Dogs Think* about an attorney who called and asked him to interview the Akita involved in the O. J. Simpson murder case, quoting him as saying, "Couldn't you just come down here and interview the dog?"

You can easily find the same dizzying variety of opinions in your own life. Just start paying focused attention to what you hear and read. You'll find that there are few, if any, fields of science and popular belief in which there is so much disagreement. It's as though some people, from scientists to pet owners, believe that the earth is flat and all of existence ends at its edge, while others are working on how and why the universe is expanding into infinity. I wonder whether this level of controversy suggests that we are talking about something that is deeply important to us, but that we know little about. I'm reminded of the bitter debates in the 1800s when Darwin proposed that animals evolved through the process of natural selection, and that humans share common ancestors with apes. The idea of any kind of continuity between humans and animals so threatened people's beliefs about the unique status of humans that debates about the topic were frequent and heated (as they can be today). One of my favorite remarks from Darwin's time was made by the wife of the Bishop of Worcester: "Descended from monkeys! My dear, let us hope that it isn't true. But if it is true, let us hope that it doesn't become widely known."

Perhaps her fears are relevant today. Perhaps it's fear that drives some of the critics, because the more we uncover about the mental processes of animals like our dogs, the more we will have to examine our relationship with them. Arien Mack writes, in *Humans and Other Animals*, that "the delineation of human/animal relationships occurs in all cultures, and in all cultures this boundary is a matter of great significance." Redefining who we are in relation to the dog at our feet or the horse in our barn can be a scary prospect. No wonder it generates so much controversy.

HOW TO BE THE JANE GOODALL OF YOUR LIVING ROOM

There is one thing that's not controversial among dog lovers: we want to know what's going on inside the minds of our dogs, pure and simple. We don't need them to think and feel about the world exactly like we do. Rather, we want to know how much of our experiences we share with our Lukes, our Gingers, and our Goldies. And so, all of us make guesses about the thoughts and feelings of our dogs. It's unavoidable.

Our guesses are usually based on a variety of factors. Some are good objective ones, like a careful description of our dog's expressions, postures, and behaviors. Other factors, colored by our own experience and projections, can lead to mistakes about what's going on inside the minds of our dogs. Those mistakes help drive criticisms of our inquiries into animal thinking: beliefs that horses can do math and that dogs take it upon themselves to clean up before your mom comes to visit haven't helped convince skeptics that we can look at this issue objectively.[13]

---

13. In the 1880s, a horse named Clever Hans had most of Europe fooled into thinking he could do addition, multiplication, and long division until a scientist named Oskar Pfungst figured out he was using visual cues inadvertently supplied by people who knew the answer. See the references for a book about Clever Hans.

It's true that all of us, to some extent, project our own feelings onto our dogs. This is the dark side of our remarkable ability to be empathetic, and it can lead to no end of problems, as we'll see throughout the book. However, the opposite problem—obliviousness to the expressions of dogs—is all too common as well, even among people who really, really love their dogs. No matter how many years you've taught dog-training classes, it's always amazing to watch people who are clearly smitten with their dogs miss what seem like blindingly obvious signals on their dogs' faces. In every class you can watch someone enthusiastically "praising" their dog, while the dog shrinks back in fear or disgust. To some extent, this happens because of ignorance about the meaning of a dog's expressions. However, sometimes it happens because we pay too little attention to what our dog is trying to tell us, just as sometimes we pay too little attention to the faces of our human friends when we're busy inside our own heads, thinking of other things. Accurate, objective observation is a skill that requires practice, but it starts with asking your mind to focus on what you see, not on what you think it means. A very small amount of time and energy spent in reminding your brain to make accurate, objective descriptions of your dog can radically improve the relationship between you and your dog. The section below encourages you to become your own field biologist, and practice making thoughtful, detailed descriptions of your dog's behavior. The better you get at it, the better you'll be at avoiding the problems associated with attributing emotions to dogs, and the closer you'll get to connecting with your dog in the way that so many of us desire.

You'll be in good company. All students of animal behavior, whether they focus on learning (behaviorists) or on genetic and environmental influences on behavior (ethologists), are rigorously trained in the accurate observation of behavior. This might sound simple, but it's not. It takes concentration and practice to accurately observe an animal's actions, but it's even harder to develop the discipline to objectively describe the behavior, rather than skipping to a belief about what an animal is thinking or feeling when performing it. For example, here's an all-too-common scenario: "So, what is your dog Murphy doing that's causing problems for you?" I might ask a client. "Well," says the owner, "he goes crazy when visitors come over." "What does he do that makes you say he goes crazy?" I inquire, trying to get a picture of what the dog is actually doing. "Oh well, he goes out of his mind, I mean he's just completely out of control." "Could you tell me *exactly* how Murphy behaves when visitors come that makes him look 'out of control'?" I ask. "Well, I told you, he just goes crazy. . . ."

This conversation could continue into infinity, with me having virtually no idea what the dog is actually doing. "Going crazy" tells me nothing at all about the dog's actions—"going crazy" could range from catatonically huddling in a corner, to leaping onto everyone's shoulders, or to barking bug-eyed while trying to bite the nearest thigh. I have learned to say: *"Imagine you're watching a videotape and describe to me exactly what you see when your dog greets visitors."* That helps quite a bit, although the best way to get information about the dog's behavior around visitors is to be a visitor myself. That's why people in my profession stress that house calls are always the most effective way to help dogs who are problematic around visitors. However, we're always reliant on the descriptions of owners to some extent, and the more accurate the description, the better.

The tendency to make assumptions about what a dog is thinking and feeling, rather than to simply describe his behavior, is overwhelming. It also seems to be universal, so don't start feeling guilty when you catch yourself doing it. It's actually an interesting ability, and it often serves us well. Being able to empathize, or to put yourself in another individual's place and imagine what's going on in his or her mind, is a handy skill. If you have it, then you can use that information to predict an individual's behavior in the future, and decide on your own course of action. Say, for example, that your dog is behaving in the same way that you'd behave if you were nervous around visitors. Using your ability to imagine his internal feelings, you might put him away in his crate instead of making him defend himself in a forced interaction. Later, you can use your belief about his emotional state at the front door to help him be more comfortable with visitors. Although we take empathy for granted, and use it all the time, it's actually an advanced mental ability, so advanced that we don't even know to what extent other animals can do it.

As useful as empathy is, it can also be the road to trouble. Inaccurate guesses about what's going on in the mind of another individual have ruined many a marriage, and have confused the relationship between no small number of dogs and their owners. I've had clients tell me that their dog was "angry" when they left the house, even though the dog's visual signals were all about anxiety and fear. Some dogs who "go crazy" when visitors arrive act as though they are terrified, while other dogs similarly described are beside themselves with glee. Because it can lead to so much trouble, one can sympathize with radical behaviorists who argue that we must avoid making any "attributions" about an animal's mental state. But ignoring an animal's mind and emotional state in order to avoid mistakes about them is like throwing the baby out with the bath water. Surely there's a way to toss out the dirty water but keep the baby in the tub. One way to do that is to learn to distinguish between an objective description of your dog's behavior, and a guess about what's going on in his mind.

The first step is easy—simply start paying attention to your own descriptions of your dog's behavior. Are they clear descriptions about exactly what your dog is doing, or are you jumping to conclusions about why your dog is behaving in a certain way? Keep a mental log of how often you describe your dog's behavior in an objective, descriptive way ("When the doorbell rings he begins running in circles and leaping up at the door. He barks with high, rapidly repeated notes, his tail is wagging so hard his torso is wagging along with it, his eyes are sort of squinted half-shut and his mouth is open.") versus describing what you think he's thinking or feeling ("Oh he just loves visitors! He goes crazy when they come over"). Don't misunderstand me: I'm not suggesting that we're necessarily wrong when we describe what we believe about a dog's mental state. I have every reason to believe that the dog in the description above does indeed love having visitors over. Nor am I suggesting that you sound like you're reading from a scientific journal in your daily speech. But it's important to be aware of the difference between a description of a behavior and your interpretation of what it means.

While you're at it, you might do the same in your interactions with members of your own species, asking yourself how often you objectively describe someone's behavior in your mind ("Her voice was flat; her lips smiled, but her eyes didn't") versus jumping right to an attribution ("She hates me") or a judgment ("She is *such* a witch"). I suggest this not in the vein of a dog trainer/ethologist morphing into a self-help author, but because paying attention to all your social interactions might teach you something about your interactions with dogs. One of my clients consistently interpreted her new dog's behavior as "testing" her. With every misdeed, the dog was purportedly attempting to gain "dominance" over her and push the limits in his new home. However, every time I met the dog, he bent himself into a pretzel to keep his tail down, his head lower than his shoulders, and his mouth in a submissive grin. He behaved the same way to my client, and so I suggested that the dog bolted through the door, leaped up onto the beds, and chased the cat only because he didn't know he shouldn't. As I got to know his owner better, I realized that she interpreted the behavior of all her human friends in the same way. Just like her, we all have filters through which we interpret the world; be careful that yours aren't filtering out who your dog really is.

YOUR DOG IS WATCHING YOU

And what about our dogs? Are they observing us and making their own interpretations? Your dog may not be conducting complicated intellectual analyses of your every move, but I suspect the well-known trainer and writer Brian Kilcommons is right when he says that dogs are brilliant at reading the emotional states of their humans. What else do they have to do all day, he asks, but watch us like hawks, taking our pulses moment by moment? "Is she happy?" your dogs might wonder. "Angry? Should I leave the room?" It makes sense that it is relevant and important to dogs to have some idea of what we, their social partners, are thinking or feeling. This does not mean that dogs lie at our feet wondering if we're wondering what they're wondering about. But surely it is to their advantage to understand enough about our emotions to know how they might affect the immediate future ("Uh-oh, she's sitting at the computer and she just made that low, hissy sound she makes right before she yells that loud, yucky one. Better get up quietly and go lie down in the living room.").

A great question to ask yourself is how your dog would describe your behavior, and what interpretation he or she might make of it. One of the most common mistakes dog owners make is assuming that their dogs "know" what they are thinking or feeling. Often that's based on little more than a wish and a prayer, since even another human can't figure it out. For example, go to any dog training class in the country, and sooner or later you'll see some gruff guy thumping his shy little Sheltie for coming when called. In a deep booming voice, he'll say "GOOD DOG!," slapping the Sheltie like a good ol' boy at a bar, while the Sheltie shakes and cowers at what she interprets as a punishment.

Try putting yourself in your dog's place for a day or two, and ask yourself how your dog would describe your behavior, if he or she could write it down. (Heaven help us if they could.) Your dog is probably a far better observer than you are—we humans pay so much attention to language that it often interferes with our ability to see what's happening around us. A tremendously useful (and sometimes painful) way of seeing yourself through your dog's eyes is to have someone videotape you while you interact with your dog. If you're like most of us, you probably do things you didn't know you did. Your dog knows what they are, but short of asking her, your best bet is to watch yourself, just the way your dog does. Every one of us performs habitual movements and has habitual expressions that our friends are more aware of than we are. And why not—who walks around with a mirror attached to his face all day long? We see ourselves from the inside out, but our friends and our dogs get an entirely different view. You can also benefit (as will your dog) by carefully watching other people around their dogs, trying to interpret the person's actions through the eyes of a dog. Trying to watch ourselves through our dogs' eyes will do a lot more than shed light on the behavior of our own species. It can teach us a lot about our dogs' behavior as well, because so much of what our dogs do is in response to us.

2

EMOTIONAL EXPRESSIONS

People and dogs share expressive faces,
and use surprisingly similar expressions

"He's just fine with visitors, aren't you, Buddy? He's fine, really he is."
Buddy's owners had asked me to their house to help them with their beloved
Labrador Retriever, who had bitten their neighbor the week before. Barbara and Peter couldn't understand it: Buddy was a loving family dog who
doted on their children, was easily housetrained as a puppy, and was a star
at obedience school. They couldn't have loved him more, and the feeling
seemed to be reciprocated. Members of the family could take away his food,
pull toys out of his mouth, and trim his nails without eliciting the slightest
protest. In their eyes, it seemed that the bite had come out of the blue, and
although they had responded responsibly by calling in a behaviorist, deep
down inside they didn't think it would ever happen again.

I did. Buddy may have been "fine" to them, but as I entered the house,
he and I were having another, unspoken conversation. To judge by his expression, Buddy's side went something like this: "I don't know who you are,
and I'm nervous about that. For all I know, you might be dangerous. If you
stay there and don't move forward, I'll stay here, but if you move fast or
reach your hand toward me, I'll be forced to protect myself. I am uncomfortable, on guard, and perfectly willing to bite you."

Of course, all that is just a bunch of words I strung together to describe
my interpretation of Buddy's emotional state and his probable behavior if
I tried to pet him. I can't possibly say exactly what was going on inside his
brain, but I can make predictions about his future behavior on the basis
of his expression. Rather than showing the relaxed, open mouth of a dog

who loves visitors, Buddy kept his jaw closed tight, except when his tongue flicked out in an expression of anxiety. His entire body was stiff and unmoving—in sharp contrast to the loose and flexible body of a relaxed dog. Buddy's eyes were big and round, rather than the squinty eyes of a dog who loves company. As if that weren't enough, Buddy was staring dead straight into my eyes, and his own eyes were as cold as ice.

"I AM GOING TO BITE YOU. HONEST."

Peter and Barbara thought Buddy was "fine," because he wasn't barking or growling at me, but to me, Buddy had a neon sign over his head that said I AM GOING TO BITE YOU IF YOU GET ANY CLOSER. Good dog trainers and behaviorists learn to read these signals in their most subtle form, because if we don't, we get bitten. We hate it when that happens, so we learn fast. There may be controversy about how dogs experience emotions, but there's universal agreement that a dog's expressions have a lot to tell us about what he's likely to do next. As Darwin noted so long ago, many of a dog's expressions are blindingly obvious; few people misinterpret the combination of deep growls, a snarling face, and flashing teeth. But other expressions, like the ones from Buddy, are more subtle. That doesn't make them any less important in predicting what a dog is about to do, and the better you learn them, the more you can be proactive rather than reactive.

Some people are really good at reading their dogs' visual signals; I have observant clients who keep dangerous dogs out of trouble because they can see their dogs tense up long before they strike out. Others—I don't know how else to say it—are virtually illiterate in the language of dogs. The ability to read a dog's face and posture seems to have no correlation with how much you love your dog. I've seen clients who were devoted to their dog, and yet while they were chatting about how their dog Lucky is cheerful 24/7, Lucky was pacing around my office with a tense, anxious face.

Differences in sensitivity to the expressions of others aren't confined to dog owners. Not surprisingly, some of us are better than others at reading the facial expressions of members of our own species. Introverts are better at reading the expressions of others (while extroverts are more expressive themselves). According to Paul Ekman, who has been studying facial expressions around the world for over forty years, women and men are equally adept at reading facial expressions, but there is tremendous variation between individuals of either sex. Dog trainers see the gamut, from people who read dogs like a book, to those who seem almost oblivious. This shouldn't be surprising; even other animals vary in their ability to read faces. The primatologist Barbara Smuts described a male olive baboon who received favors from females by being especially adept at reading subtle indicators of their emotional states.

TRAINING MATTERS

No matter where you fall on the continuum, the good news is that there's a significant practice effect on the ability to read facial expressions, whether on a dog or a human. I am reminded of this every time I show a particular video sequence of an adolescent dog hovering over a stolen toy. The dog trainers go on alert when the dog's face becomes still and his eyes go round, because they know what's coming next. In contrast, the general public watches the video in innocent silence, gasping in shock when the dog lashes out, snarling and lunging toward the owner. The professionals know that freezing in place with rounded eyes is a threatening posture, but because the dog was neither growling nor showing his teeth, the general public is stunned by his attack.

You can see milder versions of this all the time in training classes. Most often, we'll see an expression of distaste on a dog's face while an oblivious owner does something he thinks the dog loves. Whether they're slapping a touch-sensitive dog on the head ("Gosh, she just loves this," the owner says while the dog grimaces and turns her head away) or shouting "Good dog!" to a cringing, sound-sensitive Cocker Spaniel, otherwise loving owners commonly miss expressions as obvious as fireworks to people with experience.

Although I know of no research on our ability to interpret the facial expressions of dogs, there's a lot of research on our ability to read the faces of other people, and much of what we've learned can help us better understand our dogs. For example, study after study shows that the more training you receive about the meaning of facial expressions, the subtler the signals you'll be able to read. A good example is our ability to detect deceit in others, surely a behavior with which we've all had a lot of experience. The easiest form of dishonesty to learn to detect is an insincere smile. Natural smiles go far beyond the mouth and affect the muscles around the eyes, but insincere ones usually only include movements of the mouth. Most of us aren't aware of the difference on our own faces, but extreme examples are easy to spot on others, and with training you can get really good at seeing subtle examples.

LESS CAN BE BETTER

The reason most of us aren't as good as we'd like to be at identifying dishonest expressions is that we haven't been taught to look for the subtle changes in facial expressions that are usually generated by even accomplished liars. The best human lie detectors are U.S. Secret Service agents, CIA agents, and clinical psychologists who study lying. These are the only groups of people who can reliably detect dishonesty, and it's their training and experience that give them this advantage. The rest of us aren't as good at it as we think we are. Parents take note.

The more training and experience you have at reading expressions in dogs or people, the more your brain is able to focus on the important signals and ignore the extraneous ones. At any given moment, your brain is flooded with information, only some of which is relevant to any particular issue. In many situations, it turns out all you really need is a tiny piece of information, as long as it's the right piece. Called thin-slicing by the researchers who discovered it, it's the equivalent of finding your lost wedding ring in the woods, because your brain is focused on "sparkly" and is ignoring everything else. The dog trainers who watched the video of the dog about to lunge were thin-slicing, because they knew that, in that context, "freezing with a closed mouth" was the only thing they needed to see to predict the attack.

Thin-slicing is best illustrated by the work of psychologist John Gottman, who has been studying interactions between married couples for decades.[1] After eavesdropping on more than three thousand couples, Gottman can listen to a couple chatting about nothing in par-

---

1. See a full discussion of this, and thin-slicing in general, in the brilliant book *Blink,* by Malcolm Gladwell. *Blink* is so good I want to tell you to put this one down right now and run out to buy it, but on second thought, I'd rather you finished this one first.

ticular for an hour, and then predict, with 95 percent accuracy, whether they'll still be married in fifteen years. Other people, even marriage counselors, aren't able to do any better than guessing, because they haven't learned which visual or verbal expressions signify a healthy relationship. After years of analyzing tiny changes in expression and tone of voice, Gottman and his colleagues have found that signs of defensiveness, stonewalling, criticism, and contempt are red flags that trouble is brewing. But all they really need to see is the expression of contempt by one of the partners (picture someone ever-so-slightly rolling his eyes) to know that the marriage is doomed. No matter how many times the members of a couple smile at each other, laugh, or cuddle, if one suggests contempt for the other with the subtlest of expressions, they might as well call the lawyer and get it over with.

These results represent far more than just some trendy pop psychology that makes interesting reading. There's overwhelming evidence from a variety of studies that experienced observers are able to make accurate judgments about the feelings of others, based on amazingly small samples of their behavior. The psychologist Elisha Babad and his colleagues found that viewers needed only ten seconds of a video clip to accurately judge whether a teacher liked the child to whom he or she was talking. The teachers themselves were quite sure that they were concealing their feelings, but their faces gave them away. That's because, more than any other muscles, the muscles of the face are hard to control consciously—our eyebrows can change the tiniest bit when we're concerned, angry, or frightened, but we don't consciously decide to make those movements in the same way that we decide to move our arm.

THERE'S AN ESSAY ON YOUR FACE

It's hard to consciously control your facial muscles because they are intimately connected with the emotional centers of your brain. Much of this wiring bypasses the rational, thinking part of your brain altogether, so the process of conscious decision making is out of the loop. That's why face-to-face contact is always the best way to communicate, and why behaviorists and trainers always want to meet your dog face-to-face. Our species' ability to use language may allow us to say anything we want (whether it's true or not), but our faces remain more honest indicators of our internal emotional state.

Somebody came to my office once, on an ostensibly friendly visit, and I'll never forget seeing his eyes go cold and hard while at the same time he was complimenting me. I knew instantly that the words were meaningless, because the message on his face expressed his real feelings. Those feelings weren't pretty—they made the hair stand up on the back of my neck—but at least I had gotten an accurate view of how he really felt.

The eyes of my not-so-friendly visitor were icy cold, but I don't think I would have been so aware of them if I hadn't seen that same expression in the eyes of dogs who are about to bite. Seventeen years of reading the faces of dogs who may be about to bite me has made me much better at reading the faces of people. Other trainers have the same experience—it's so common that we swap stories at conferences about how our improved ability to read faces has helped us through tricky negotiations with an increased awareness of a person's true feelings, regardless of the words he or she uses. That wouldn't be true if we humans didn't share many basic expressions of emotions with our dogs. The faces of dogs are almost as plastic as our own, able to morph from disappointment to joy in the blink of an eye. We read our dogs' faces as we read the faces of people, looking for information about how they're feeling and what they might be about to do. Experience may improve our ability to read between the lines, but, as Darwin reminded us a long time ago, the basic emotions of fear, anger, joy, and disgust look the same on the faces of our dogs as on the faces of our human family.

It's no coincidence that highly social animals like people and dogs have exceptionally expressive faces. Solitary animals, pandas, for example, have relatively impassive faces that make it difficult to figure out how they're feeling. That makes sense, because if you're a solitary animal, it doesn't matter whether others are able to evaluate your emotions: there are no "others" to begin with. But if you live in a tight-knit group, it matters greatly whether you're scared or frustrated, because your emotions are excellent predictors of what you'll do next—handy information when you are affected by the behavior of those around you. Emotional expressions act like lubricants in social interactions, and the more important your behavior is to those around you, the more important it is that they are able to read your emotions from your expressions.

Thus, the expression of emotion, and the ability to read it, aren't random—they're crucial components of a social relationship in which the partners can choose how to behave. The participants in a complex social relationship must be able to take the emotional temperatures of their partners, and that's hard to do if the emotions are hidden inside. The important role of emotional expressions in social relationships is highly relevant to our interactions with dogs. Dogs behave as though they expect us to be able to read their expressions accurately. When we don't, either because we aren't able to or because we aren't paying attention, both dogs and people can get in a lot of trouble.

THE MOTION OF EMOTION

It makes sense to assume that our dogs' expressions are honest indicators of their internal emotional states, just as in our own species. After all, the word "emotion" is mostly made of (and derived from) the word "motion," and that turns out to be a telling relationship. An emotion, as described by the neurobiologist John Ratey, is a "movement outward, a way of communicating our most important internal states and needs." As we discussed in Chapter 1, the expressive movements on our faces are part and parcel of our emotions—you simply can't talk about them as if they were separate things. If you want to understand your dog's emotions, you need to be able to read the expression on his face.

The rest of this chapter is designed to polish your ability to understand your dog's emotional expressions. Although everyone gets better with practice, the good news is that we all have a solid foundation on which to build. In general, people are pretty darn good at reading intense emotions from the facial expressions of other people, no matter where they're from or what language they speak. Paul Ekman, who has spent decades studying cross-cultural expressions of emotion, has found that anger, happiness, fear, surprise, sadness, and disgust look the same the world over. When he asked members of an isolated tribe in New Guinea to "pretend your child has died," their faces moved into the same expression you'd see on the face of a Japanese computer programmer or an American shoe salesman if you had asked them the same question. In spite of the vast cultural differences between people, we all express our basic emotions the same way.

Not only do our faces change in predictable ways when we're happy or sad, our expressions are interpreted the same way on every continent. Dozens of studies show that people in many countries and cultures, including people in isolated hunter/gatherer tribes, make the same interpretations of photographs expressing basic emotions. Even children who have been blind from birth, who can't possibly have learned by imitating others, express emotions that can be read correctly around the world. There are cultural differences in how likely individuals are to express basic emotions—the Japanese, for example, are less likely to express negative emotions than are Americans—but both cultures agree on what the emotions look like once they are expressed.

As we've discussed, many of these expressions are shared by dogs and people; but reading them through floppy ears and long, fuzzy muzzles can be a bit tricky.

Even people who've lived with dogs all their lives can benefit by training their brains to look for those important signals—to thinslice—so that they can better understand what's going on inside their dog's head. It's particularly valuable to learn to perceive and interpret what Paul Ekman calls "micro-expressions," or fleeting and subtle indicators of emotion that require training to notice. The more skillful you get at this, the easier it will be to know when Buster isn't comfortable being petted, so you can move on before his discomfort turns into a growl, snap, or bite. You'll be able to see when your dog is starting to become stressed during a training exercise, and know it's time to lighten things up or clarify his confusion. You'll also be better at knowing when your dog is really, truly happy, and so you'll get better at making him so.

A NOTE OF CAUTION

One caveat before we move on to highlighting important expressions in dogs: there are a few things, unrelated to your dog's actual emotions, that can influence your interpretation of her expressions, and it's useful to keep them in mind. One is your own experience, which research has shown affects how you read another's face. For example, in one study, children who had been physically abused in the past were asked to label photographs of faces as fearful or angry. The facial expressions in the photos had been computer modified to combine equal amounts of both emotions. Abused children were much more likely than other children to label the faces as angry.

Additionally, it's tempting to project your own emotions onto your dog. My dear mom, who loved both her dogs and the visits from her daughters, consistently pointed out that her dogs looked depressed during the last days of a daughter's visit. "Look at poor Jenny," she'd say. "She knows you're leaving tomorrow and she's just miserable about it." A glance at Jenny found her sound asleep on the couch, looking exactly as she had the day before, and the day before that. Mom did this so much we began to tease her about it. She put up with our teasing, but I don't think she ever stopped believing that, long before we got out the suitcases, her dogs knew our departure date and shared her feelings of sadness about it. Be careful, then, that you're not projecting your own feelings on to your dog. Remember the advice in the first chapter, and use your skills of objective observation to read what your dog is trying to tell you with her facial expressions.

SHAPE MATTERS

One last thing to remember is that the shape of your dog's head also has an influence on your perceptions. Because of our extensive efforts to create designer dogs, your dog may have anything from the baby face of an American Cocker Spaniel to the grown-up, wolfy look of a Malamute. We know that people respond differently to a baby-faced person than to one who looks more grown-up. The key features that make faces look infantile or grown-up are the size of the forehead in relation to the rest of the face, and the size of the eyes. Babies have proportionately larger eyes and foreheads than adults, and if you change just the size of the forehead, keeping all else the same, you can change how people respond in a variety of circumstances. For example, all else being equal, we are more protective of people who have babylike faces, and we are less likely to judge them guilty of a crime. There is even evidence suggesting that a baby face inhibits aggression and elicits nurturance: the facial proportions of children who have been physically abused are more likely to resemble those of older people than are the facial proportions of nonabused youngsters.

The importance of facial proportions appears to be replicated in our interactions with dogs. I am often amazed at the lengths people will go to to defend an aggressive dog with a puppylike face, even strangers who have been bitten by the dog. Being bitten by a German Shepherd, a dog with a more "adultlike" face, is another matter. Of course, the overall size of the dog is always a factor, bigger dogs being more frightening than smaller ones. However, I've seen some truly dangerous baby-faced dogs of all sizes, dogs who have ripped and torn enough human flesh to count as weapons of mass destruction, but these dogs are rarely judged as dangerous as adult-looking dogs who have caused far less injury. Even sheep seem to respond to infantile versus grown-up features on the face of a dog. I once saw a flock of sheep chased around a pen all day long by out-of-control Corgis, Border Collies, Pulis, and spaniels at a herding dog clinic, but when a docile German Shepherd walked into the ring, the sheep panicked as if he'd walked in with an automatic rifle. They literally crawled over one another in a desperate attempt to jump out of the pen when the well-behaved, prick-eared, wolfy-looking dog entered the ring and quietly sat down. Like it or not, our own reactions share something with those of the sheep, but at least we can be consciously aware that we are being influenced by anatomy as much as by honest expressions of emotion.

What follows are the expressions and behavioral changes that professionals count on to tell them what's going on inside the head of a dog. It is not an exhaustive encyclopedia of all the expressions and postures made by dogs. I have highlighted some books that do that in the Reference section, but I want to focus here on some of the more subtle signals that allow professionals to thin-slice a dog's expressions and evaluate his internal state in an instant. It will help to go back and forth between the text and the photographs to get the best sense of what to look for, and to compare the expressions of dogs with those of our own species.

OPEN MOUTH/CLOSED MOUTH

One of the most important things to notice about a dog's face is whether her mouth is open or closed. Relaxed, happy dogs tend to have relaxed and often slightly open mouths. In its extreme form, biologists call the look the "open-mouth play face." Aspects of this expression are not unlike a human smile—if you smile right now, you might notice that your teeth are not touching and your lower jaw is relaxed, rather than tense. When dogs come to my office I am always aware of whether their mouths are open or shut. Most dogs who come for appointments start out with their mouths closed up tight. I don't even think about petting them at that point, not until their mouths relax and open up an inch or two. (Keep in mind that most of the dogs I see in my office have serious behavioral problems, most often aggression related, so I see a disproportionate number of dogs with their mouths locked shut.) Whether a dog's mouth is open or closed is so important to me that I write in my records how long it takes a client's dog to relax enough to open her mouth—ten minutes? Thirty? Some dogs never relax enough to open their mouths in the presence of a stranger, and that tells me a lot about the seriousness of the problem.

Your dog isn't going to have her mouth open all the time, no matter how joyful she is, but if you learn to watch for *open mouth/closed mouth,* you'll be amazed at how much you learn about her internal emotions. You might see her close her mouth as she sees a squirrel across the road, or another dog walking down the street. Dogs will close their mouths when they're on alert, and watching a mouth go from open to closed is a good way to know your dog has begun to concentrate on a change in the environment. Dogs will also close their mouths when they're serious about something. Mine often close their mouths when I put them on a down/stay for photographs. A closed jaw by itself can't tell you whether the dog is alerting to the chirp of a chipmunk or signaling to you that he's about to bite, but going from open to closed is a key indicator that your dog is no longer in a happy-go-lucky frame of mind. Look at the photographs in the middle of the book for some examples of dogs with open and closed mouths, and compare the open-mouthed dog faces to the faces of happy humans. The similarities are truly striking. We all recognize the relaxed face of a happy-go-lucky dog, but fewer people are aware of the opposite, the dog whose mouth is closed and tense. Start watching for when your dog's jaw opens and shuts, and in just a few days you'll understand your dog better than you did before.

There are times, however, when an open mouth on a dog can confuse us. People often interpret a high-energy dog with a wide-open mouth as "extra friendly," but sometimes these dogs are physically overheated or emotionally aroused. "Oh, he just loves everyone," I've heard owners say, as their dogs repeatedly leaped up toward my face, their mouths open to give off the heat generated by their highly charged bodies. Unable to cool their bodies by sweating, as we do, dogs open their mouths to cool down, so don't assume that every open mouth is an invitation to cuddle. However, there's a lot more to a face than a mouth, and, just as we do in our own species, we can learn the most about how a dog is feeling by looking at all his facial features together.

WHEN BODIES FREEZE LIKE POPSICLES

If a dog's mouth is closed *and* his entire body is frozen in place, you'd better pay attention. This is the thin-slice that professionals learn to look for early on, because if you ignore it, there's a possibility you're going to get bitten. If I meet a dog who reacts to me by closing his mouth and stiffening his body, I stay well away from him. I might talk to him in a singsong voice, keeping my own body loose and fluid, but I'm not going to reach out to pet him. A stiff body and a closed mouth are signs of a dog on high alert, whose next move may be to lunge forward. Buddy, the dog in the earlier story, stood like a statue for several seconds when I met him at the door. Because he was so stiff and was staring straight into my eyes, I read him as a dog who was uncomfortable about my presence, and willing to go after me if I made the wrong move.

There's a downside to this knowledge, because now you're going to join the hapless group of people whose hearts stop beating on a regular basis when they see a little boy across the street petting a new dog in the neighborhood, and the dog's mouth has closed and his body has gone still and silent and the adults continue to chat on in oblivion while you wait for doom to fall, teeth to flash, and little Johnny to start screaming. Sorry. Ignorance can be bliss. But knowledge can avoid problems, so if you're witness to a scene like the one above, you can call Johnny over to you or try to ease the tension by calling "Who wants to go on a walk?" You'll also know to tell a visitor to stop petting your own dog if your dog's mouth shuts and her body goes still. If the general public learned to look for this important warning signal, tens of thousands of bites could be avoided every year.

Dogs frequently use "freeze" as a signal to other dogs. If you see two dogs greeting each other who are both stiff and still for more than a second or two, you'd better do something to break the tension. Things might get dramatic if you don't. Clap your hands and suggest "Walkies!" throw a ball, sing out "Who wants *dinner*!"—but whatever you do, don't go all stiff and immobile yourself, or you'll make things worse.

You can also see a less problematic version of freezing when dogs are romping together. First they'll be frolicking with loose, relaxed bodies, and then you'll see one dog stop and freeze for just a moment.[2] Often the freeze is accompanied by a turn of the head directly toward the other dog—a good descriptive title for that is "turn to face." Tulip does this when a dog she's playing with attempts to mount her. Queen Tulip loves to play, but nobody gets to mount the queen. Mounting in play isn't about sex, it's about social status, and Tulip isn't interested in sharing her title. If you know what to look for—it happens oh so fast—you can see Tulip whip her head around and freeze for less than a half a second as a dog tries to mount. The other dog will stop what he was about to do, perhaps play-bow to return the mood to frolicsome, and off they'll go, bodies back to being fluid and relaxed.

You may have seen such a "micro-freeze" in some dogs when you trim their nails or pull burrs out of their tails. Groomers and trainers know to go on alert when a dog abruptly whips her head around toward their hand and freezes her body for a microsecond. I take it as a threat, a clear warning not to repeat what I just did. If a dog does this with a closed jaw, she is most likely communicating to you that she is objecting to what you are doing. It's a great signal to be able to spot, and if you can do it, you'll be ahead of 99 percent of the dog lovers in the world.

Whether another's body is relaxed or stiff is important information

---

2. I used "moment" on purpose—a second is much too long a time period for this signal. This type of freeze may last no longer than a quarter to a half of a second, so watch closely. Better yet, watch a videotape you can play in slow motion.

in dog-to-dog communication, and there's no question in my mind that dogs interpret similar postures in humans in the same way. When I met Buddy I was careful to stay relaxed and fluid, because going still yourself is a signal to the dog that you, too, are on guard. That one change in your own body might be enough to get you in trouble, or, if used in reverse, prevent a bite from happening. A good example of that occurred at a seminar during which I saw a cute little Lhasa apso snuffling her way across the floor. As she turned toward me, I began wagging my body back and forth like some crazed two-legged Labrador, along with turning sideways, adopting an open-mouth play face, and crinkling my eyes in the universal sign of friendliness. As I approached her, she turned and cuddled against my leg, raised her head, and leaned into my hand as I stroked her neck. "Oh my," said her owner. "That's not what she usually does. She's here as a case study because she snaps at people when they try to pet her."

Just as predicted, when the dog came up on the stage and was approached by strangers, she stiffened with concern. If I hadn't stopped people several feet away from her, I have no doubt she would've snapped or bitten. The difference was in the approach: I was focusing on behaving like a friendly dog, while most people were acting the way people naturally do. The usual approach of all people, when greeting human or dog, is basically the opposite of a polite approach in dog society. Dogs approach one another from the side, curving their line of approach and avoiding eye contact, while keeping their bodies loose and fluid. We do the opposite: we keep our bodies upright and relatively still, and make direct eye contact while reaching out with our paws before we've even so much as exchanged scents.

This is so important in canine interactions that professionals learn to breathe deeply and keep our bodies fluid and relaxed even if we're feeling afraid of the dog in front of us. (Make that, "*Especially* if we're feeling afraid.") If you go still, close your mouth, and stop breathing, the dog you're with may decide that he had good reason to be on guard, and he will be more likely to do something aggressive. If you want to greet dogs like a pro, be sure to keep your mouth open slightly and relaxed, slowly wag your shoulders and your hips back and forth just the tiniest bit, and move your head to the side as if you were cocking it. (Dogs cock their heads to get more visual and acoustic information when they're curious about something, but they don't do it when they're nervous.) Don't go so far overboard that you end up scaring the dog ("I have *never* seen a human behave like this before . . ."), but consciously stay loose so you don't lock up yourself and inadvertently send out signals of potential aggression.

I'll never forget a session long ago with a client in which her dog was freely interacting with my dog Pip. Before she retired at thirteen, Pip seemed to love working dog-dog aggression cases with me. Pip adored other dogs, and was a master at calming those who had been aggressive to others because they were nervous. As usual, I asked her if she wanted to work with this particular dog, and she answered by running to the gate with enthusiasm. (Sometimes she'd take one look at a dog and walk away, and I always respected that, assuming she was better than me at reading another dog's emotional temperature.) Pip seemed enthusiastic about working with this particular dog, so I let them greet each other off leash in a half-acre fenced pen behind the house.

But the dogs weren't the only ones in the pen. I hadn't paid enough attention to the owner, who was extremely nervous about the arrangement. While the dogs greeted each other, she stood to the side, frozen in place and barely breathing while I tried to assuage her fears. My mistake, because while the owner stood stock-still beside me, her dog looked up into her eyes, just for an instant. The owner's face was as stiff as a Halloween mask, her eyes were huge with fear, and her mouth was rounded as if she was saying "Oh!" This is the face of a dog about to attack, and after one glance at it, that's exactly what the dog did. Before I could react, he attacked Pip, growling and snarling while she rolled over on her back in fear. I had the dog off in an instant, and Pip wasn't hurt, but both of us were shaken up. Pip got more than her share of treats that week, and I got less sleep than usual, worrying about what might have been. Pip is fifteen now, and the incident was long ago and far away, but I've never forgotten the hard-won lesson of how important our own expressions can be to a dog's behavior.

WAGGING THE DOG

Stiff, frozen postures are so important that they trump the signal that people often associate with friendliness—a wagging tail. Tail wagging is most commonly interpreted as a signal of friendliness, but that can be a big mistake. What *is* friendly is a loose, relaxed tail that wags the hindquarters along with it. "Wagging from the shoulders back," I call it, and it's a great indicator that the dog is happy to see you. However, if the body of the dog is stiff, the mouth is closed, and the tail is raised and only wagging from its midsection, watch out. A stiff body and a stiff tail base constitute the thin-slice that tells you this dog isn't necessarily feeling friendly, no matter how hard the tail tip is wagging. Those of us with cats know that swishing tails and stiff bodies don't always mean good things, and in this case, it's accurate to generalize that to dogs.

FORWARD AND BACKWARD, STRAIGHT ON OR SIDEWAYS

It's worth making one more comment about a dog's overall posture before we go back to facial signals. That's because, just as in our species, all of a dog's expressions have to be taken in context with the signals being given by the rest of her body. One of the most important of those is the direction of a dog's energy. When you meet a dog, or watch your dog meeting others, ask yourself: which way is the energy directed in the dog's body? You'll notice many dogs whose bodies are shifted forward, whether they're greeting you at the door or saying hello to another dog. Dogs can have their bodies leaning slightly forward as a sign of friendliness, or as a sign of being on the offensive. Either way, the dog is letting you know that he's in a relatively confident state. If a dog comes toward me willingly, wagging his tail from the shoulders back in a "full-body wag," head lowered, mouth open, and eyes squinty, I'm going to squat down and have a love fest with him. If a dog's body is shifted forward and he's stiff and immobile, with his mouth closed shut and his tail wagging only from the tip, I'm going to stay where I am, and ease the tension by turning away, or pulling out a treat or a ball. However, if the dog is close and begins to advance on me, mouth still shut, body still stiff, I'll turn my head quickly toward him (there's that "turn to face" I was talking about) and speak in a low, sharp voice. This is a dog who is on the offensive, and who needs to be stopped without adding to the tension; as soon as I can, I'll face him off, but then break the tension by saying "Wanna go on a walk?" or "Dinner!"

On the other hand, dogs whose energy is directed backward are dogs on the defensive, even if they're growling and flashing their teeth. These are dogs who have a lot of fear in them, and you need to be sure not to put any pressure on them by cornering them or reaching to pet them. Remember that a dog on a leash or a tie-out is essentially trapped, which is undoubtedly why so many bites occur in that circumstance. In *The Other End of the Leash,* I talk at length about how you can use a dog's awareness of whether another's body is directed forward or backward, so I won't go into it here. However, just keeping in mind whether a dog is directed forward or backward can go a long way to helping you predict his future behavior.

You can also learn a lot about a dog's motivation by watching him approach other dogs. Polite dogs greet one another by approaching from the side, as if following a curved line toward the other dog's flanks, rather than taking a straight, head-on approach. Direct straight-on approaches are part of polite greetings in our species, but not in dogs, so pay attention to this aspect of the dog's body as well. You might have noticed that I approached the nervous Lhasa at the seminar by turning my body sideways. You can do the same thing when you meet a new dog—just turn slightly sideways, and approach as if walking forward along a curved line. You'll be amazed at how many dogs will be thrilled to meet you.

FUZZY GRINS/OFFENSIVE PUCKERS

We talked earlier about how our mouths are relaxed and open when we're smiling; the other key component of a smile is the movement of the corners of the mouth. Retracting the corners of the mouth and raising them is what makes a smile a smile. Even insincere smiles widen the mouth toward the ears. Try it yourself; go to a mirror and smile with just your mouth, and then let your smile move all the way to your eyes. The difference is striking, both in your expression and how you feel when you do it. A sincere smile, which engages the muscles of the mouth, cheeks, and eyes, is the easiest of all expressions to read. A smiling face is evaluated as happy by virtually everyone around the world.

Interestingly enough, unlike expressions of fear or anger, smiles don't happen as often when we're alone as they do when we're with others. Human smiles appear to be important signals in social contexts, because they are almost always given while facing another person. Bowlers who get a strike usually don't smile until they turn around to face their friends; Olympic athletes receiving their medals smile when they turn to face the crowd. Of course, we all smile on occasion when we're alone (I can't seem to stop doing it right now, as I write this—are smiles catching like yawns?), but not with the frequency with which we do it in public. Wherever we smile, and whether we smile sincerely or not, our smiles are always defined by the mouth being partially opened and the corners of the mouth pulling upward and back toward our ears.

Paying attention to the corners of another's mouth isn't unique to our species. Many species of mammals pull the corners of their mouths back when they're nervous, which is why ethologists call that movement a fear grimace. In some species, in social contexts, it's called a submissive grin, because it's always given by an individual in a subordinate position. Like many other animals, humans pull back the corners of their mouths when they're scared. Universally, our species expresses fear by retracting the corners of the mouth, along with rounding the eyes and raising the eyebrows. (See the photo section for examples.) Even human smiles aren't always expressions of pure joy—many a smile relates to nervousness rather than happiness. Ethologists suggest that our smiles derived from submissive grins, in which the person smiling is signaling that he has no offensive intentions.

As you can see in the photographs, dogs move the corners of their mouth too, and just as in humans, the direction of the movement tells you a lot about how the dog is feeling inside. The corner of the mouth is called the commissure, and dogs, wolves, and coyotes all pull it back when they're being submissive, defensive, or fearful. Even when dogs are playing, you'll notice it's usually the one on the bottom whose commissure is pulled back. That's not random, it's an expression of the dog's internal state. The "defender" has the commissure pulled back, while the pup in the role of offensive tackle has the commissure forward.

Humans also move the corners of our mouths forward when we're on offense, in our own version of what's called an "offensive pucker" in dogs and wolves. The commissure of an angry human moves in the opposite direction of a smile, moving forward toward the center of the face rather than back toward the ears. Make the "mad," pouty face of an angry five-year-old right now, and notice how your mouth closes and your lips pucker forward. Dogs do something very similar, although I wouldn't say that they are always angry when they're doing it. I'll bet the farm, though, that they're not scared or submissive. An offensive pucker is one of the best indicators I know that a dog is ready to go on offense, and it doesn't seem surprising that it correlates with our version of an angry face.

Look at the photographs and consider the difference, in both humans and dogs, between a commissure pulled back and a commissure pushed forward. Like a lot of things, the movements of the corners of the mouth are blindingly obvious once you learn to look for them, but they get little notice until they're pointed out to you. Start to pay attention to your own dog, and ask yourself which way your dog's mouth is most likely to move, and in what circumstances. If your dog lunges at another dog with his commissure forward, he's in a very different state than if he retracts it in a fear grimace. He could be barking and lunging in both cases, but the position of his mouth will help you understand how he's feeling inside when he does. If your dog puckers her mouth forward when your child tries to take a toy out of her mouth, she's telling you that she's standing up for what she believes is her property, and that she's willing to use her mouth to defend it if necessary. If she growls at a visitor with her commissures retracted, she may be afraid of strangers, and so needs help overcoming her fears when the doorbell rings.

You can see how these facial signals can be useful when you're working on a treatment plan for a dog who snaps at visitors or won't let you take the rawhide chew toy away. We'll talk in later chapters about how to match treatment plans with dogs in different emotional states, but for now, concentrate on being a field researcher in your own living room, and learn to watch which way your dog's mouth is moving. Think of it as "lip reading," one species to another.

SMILE FOR THE CAMERA

Dogs do something that looks to some like a human smile, and to others like an aggressive baring of their teeth. "Smiling" dogs raise their upper lips, usually so much that the skin over the top of their muzzle becomes wrinkled. Because the lips are raised vertically, the dog's teeth are exposed. There's nothing like a full set of flashing white teeth in the mouth of a predator to get an emotional reaction out of a primate like us, but these dogs don't seem to have an aggressive thought in their heads. Surrounding those shiny, sharp teeth are a loose, relaxed body, a lowered head, and the friendly, squinty eyes of a dog who is glad to see you. You see the smile most often when dogs are greeting you after an absence, or welcoming strangers into the house. Smiling dogs usually have a goofy look about them, with their whole body wagging from the shoulders back and their head held parallel to the ground.

I remember one house call at the home of a Golden Retriever. The owners said the dog was becoming aggressive to them and to visitors, although he had yet to snap or bite. I was greeted by a tail-thumping, body-wagging mush-bucket whose lips seemed to have a mind of their own and kept rising upward to expose his teeth. This dog's posture was the exact opposite of Buddy's, who never showed me any teeth, but who stood rigid and cold-eyed as I entered. The Golden all but melted into a puddle as I entered the house, but there were those teeth—huge and white and gleaming, and right by my face. It is understandable that visitors weren't quite sure what to make of them. What a pleasure to be able to tell the owners that their Golden was as dangerous as a stuffed dog, and that those teeth had more to do with a human smile than a warning of potential aggression. We don't know exactly what emotion a "smiling" dog is expressing, but it doesn't seem to be associated with anger or fear-related aggression. One good guess, my favorite at the moment, is that it's an expression of a dog in an ambivalent state, with the primary emotion being one of submission or docility. I think of it as the kind of goofy, nervous grin you'd see on the face of a shy adolescent guy when he picks up his date for the first time.

TONGUE FLICKS

Another important expression of your dog's internal emotions is the "tongue flick," in which your dog's tongue extends straight out of the mouth and retracts again immediately. Don't confuse it with the side-swiping tongue of a drooling, hungry dog who anticipates dinner. In a tongue flick, the tongue is moved in a straight line, forward out of the mouth, and then immediately pulled back in. These little tongue flicks are either expressions of low-level anxiety, or are appeasement gestures from subordinate dogs to higher-ranking ones. How far out the tongue goes is probably dependent upon the extremity of the emotion.[3]

Once you start looking for tongue flicks, you'll see them everywhere. Your dog might tongue-flick when you pick up her paw to trim her nails, or perhaps when that big bruiser of a Chesapeake Bay Retriever comes over to play. You can see an example of it on a video clip that's all over the Internet in which the handler of a newly acquired police dog is being interviewed by the local hometown reporter. Squatting down just inches from the dog's face, the reporter places his hands on either side of the dog's head as he begins to stand back up. The dog's mouth is closed up tight, and although he isn't growling or showing his teeth, experienced dog handlers can tell that he's uncomfortable with the situation. The reporter didn't pick up on the signals, but he probably figured things out after the dog bit him full on the face—right after the dog's tongue flicked out in a clear expression of anxiety.

I often see dogs tongue-flick at the vet's office, at training classes, while greeting other dogs, and when owners hug them or do anything else that makes them uncomfortable. I also see tongue flicks from submissive dogs who are continually signaling to those around them that they don't want to be in charge. Of anything. Ever.[4]

How often a dog tongue-flicks can tell you a lot about her personality. My sweet, submissive Pip tongue-flicks to just about everything, including me when I quietly walk over to pet her. She loves me dearly—at least, I think she does—but she is so submissive she responds to almost any social encounter with a tongue flick. I stopped working her on sheep when a ewe turned to face her, and Pippy responded by wagging her tail and tongue-flicking. Border Collies the world over would have been appalled. On the other hand, Cool Hand Luke almost never tongue-flicked. Luke loved taking charge of recalcitrant sheep and lived his life brimming with confidence. The only time I remember him tongue-flicking in his prime was at the vet's when he

---

3. Or the length of the tongue? Pip has the longest tongue of any dog I've ever known, and on occasion her tongue comes out so far, I have wondered if it had become disconnected.

4. Many other species exhibit tongue flicks when they're feeling submissive or slightly anxious, including humans and many other species of primates.

was being treated for cancer. Years later, when his kidneys were failing, I had to give him subcutaneous fluids twice a day through a huge needle that caused him to whimper plaintively every time I inserted it. After four days of that, he tongue-flicked one morning as I approached him. It was so out of character that I stopped dead in my tracks. I was sure he'd done it because he had learned to associate me with pain. I called the vet's office in distress (that's code for "sobbing uncontrollably"), and told them I simply couldn't be the one to hydrate Luke any longer. In hopes that extra fluid would keep his kidneys from crashing, we kept it up for a few more days, but I drove him to the vet's twice a day so that our last times together were characterized by love rather than fear. I'm so thankful I knew what that tongue flick meant, because, as sick as Luke was, he never tongue-flicked again, and we were able to spend our last days together in a bittersweet haze of love and grief.

You can tell by the stories above that every dog is different. Start watching your own dog to see when her tongue flicks forward out of her mouth. You might never see it, or you might see it all the time. Picking up the back paw elicits it in some dogs, because most dogs don't like having their back paws handled. Submissive or slightly nervous dogs will tongue-flick in response, but status-seeking ones will go stiff and clench their jaws.[5] (And the in-between dogs will squirm and squiggle, lick your hand, or roll over on their backs.) If you get a good idea of your dog's "baseline" frequency of tongue flicking, it will help you know when she's nervous, or feeling submissive. You can also use it around other people's dogs. A dog who wags his whole body and comes toward you with head down, tongue flicking in and out, is submissively soliciting attention. If, however, a dog stands still, tongue-flicks out of a closed jaw, and then stiffly turns his head away from you, mind your manners. You are being told loud and clear that Fido is uncomfortable, and isn't interested in a date right now. Ignore this message at your peril.

"I'M NOT YAWNING BECAUSE I'M BORED"

Yawning can be another sign that your dog is uncomfortable. Yawns are often given by slightly anxious dogs, and all trainers and behavior-

5. I wouldn't be a good idea to try this out on unfamiliar dogs, any more than it'd be a good idea to saunter up to some stranger and, unannounced, begin staring deeply into his eyes.

ists pay a lot of attention to them. Of course, sometimes dogs yawn when they're waking up and are just sleepy, so don't worry that every time your dog yawns it's cause for alarm. However, paying attention to your dog's yawns can help you understand her a lot better. Yawns themselves are an excellent introduction to what have been called calming signals by a Norwegian trainer named Turid Rugaas, who's written a fascinating book, *On Talking Terms with Dogs*. In it, she argues that many of the signals discussed in this chapter are used by dogs to calm other dogs, and she cites yawning as one of those. She even suggests that people try yawning themselves to calm their dogs in stressful situations. However, she agrees that yawns are produced by anxious dogs and are usually seen when dogs are being hugged, in veterinary clinics, or during stressful encounters with others.

This raises two interesting issues related to the function of many of the signals we've been discussing. One is that the same movement can have many meanings, just as a smile in humans can signal nervousness or joy. If a yawn is due to sleepiness or relaxation, then it makes sense that it would have a calming effect on others. If a yawn is the result of anxiety, then its effect on others is less clear. A second interesting question relates to the function of the yawn itself. Is the yawner, the "sender of the signal," purposefully attempting to calm (or excite) another individual, or is the expression an involuntary result of the sender's internal emotions? I suspect that the latter is most often the case, at least with signals like tongue-flicking and yawning. An anxious dog who is tongue-flicking or yawning is probably not intentionally trying to calm another individual—remember, we talked about yawns being involuntary, and tongue flicks might be as well. However, it makes sense that such behaviors can indeed be called calming signals, in that they are the opposite of the signals of a dog about to attack. Dogs who tongue-flick and yawn are not radiating the kind of "I'm not afraid and I'm about to bite you" message sent by a frozen body and hard, cold eyes. It makes sense that signals like yawns could influence the emotions of the dog who sees them, and so it makes sense to call them calming signals.

Yawns are an especially interesting signal, not only because they are usually involuntary but also because they are almost impossible to watch without yawning yourself. We're still not even sure about the function of yawning, but we know that watching others yawn elicits a yawn in return in most people. Even just talking about yawns (or writing about them for that matter) can cause people to yawn. In a perfect example of our emotional interchange with dogs, a yawning dog can set you off just as easily as a yawning person.

WRINKLES ARE GOOD

I hope no one ever uses Botox on dogs, because a dog with wrinkles around her eyes is a dog who's glad to see you. The eyes of dogs are wonderful sources of information about what's going on inside their minds. It takes experience to learn to interpret some of the expressions within a dog's eyes, but wrinkles around the eyes are easy to see. Just like smiling humans whose eyes crinkle with delight, dogs who are happy to see you often have squinty eyes with lots of furry crow's-feet around them. Look for the muscles around their eyes to constrict, just as ours do when we're feeling happy or amused. Compare the eyes of the "happy face" dogs and humans in the photographs, and you'll see that in both species, the muscles around our eyes are important parts of our expressions. My impression is that the more submissive the dog, the more his eyes will crinkle up, so I'm not sure that squinty eyes correlate as directly with happiness as they do in our species. It seems that the most docile dogs squint during greetings, an observation similar to the reports of wolf researchers, who include crinkled eyes as one of the many expressions of submission or appeasement.

On the other hand, dogs who are on alert, who are surprised or frightened, often have rounded eyes. In this they are not unlike humans, who round their eyes in fear or surprise. You can see clear examples of these emotions in the photo section, on the faces of both species. Pip used to be afraid of thunder, and when she leaped up into the bed after an especially loud boom, her eyes would be as big and round as pancakes. Rounded eyes are a sure sign that a dog is either frightened or highly aroused. Dilated pupils also correlate with fear or arousal, but they can be hard to see—sometimes the last thing you want to do is get closer to a dog to see whether her pupils are dilated—but you can always tell when a dog has rounded his eyes from their normal shape. Keep in mind that different breeds naturally come with differently shaped eyes—Malamutes have almond-shaped eyes, while Chihuahuas and Cavalier King Charles Spaniels come with big, round ones. What's important is how the eye changes from its neutral state. If you become acquainted with the appearance of your dog's eyes when you're hanging around the house together, you'll be more able to see subtle changes in eye shape when you're at the vet's or meeting a new dog in the neighborhood.

WARM EYES, WARM HEART

There's another quality about the eye that is important, but it's harder to describe. Any one who has ever worked with aggressive dogs knows what I mean when I talk about a dog's eyes turning "hard." Clients often will describe a "cold" look in the eyes of their dog, right before he snaps or bites. This change is not about pupil dilation, and it's not a change in color, but something about the eyes changes so that they harden like cooling steel. The look resembles what we call a glare from a human.[6] Friendly, relaxed dogs have the soft, dewy eyes that we associate with babies and lovers, while dogs who are about to hurt you have the hard eyes we associate with cold-blooded killers. You may never have seen this look, from either species. If you're lucky, you never will. When I first got serious about dog training, I spent a few years looking for it, and was frustrated because I thought I just wasn't skilled enough to see it. Then a visiting dog turned to face me when I picked up something she wanted, and in an instant, everything changed. Her eyes, as hard and cold as a Wisconsin winter morning, seemed to cut right through to my heart. Long before my conscious brain said, "Oh, that's the look!" my body had reacted by shooting adrenaline throughout, first stopping my heart for a moment and then sending it pounding like a hammer in my chest. In a perfect example of thin-slicing, my brain knew right away that out of all the signals coming from her face and her body, the only important one was the hardness in her eyes. I can remember exactly what they looked like to this day, although I have virtually no memory of anything else about the incident.

6. Psychologist Paul Ekman tells me that this same look in the eyes of a human is predictive of a premeditated assault.

I wish we knew exactly what it was about the eye that physically changes, but all we can do is guess. Jeff Baylis, my major professor in graduate school, came up with the best hypothesis I've heard so far. It's based on the fact that the eyes of mammals actually move back and forth all the time, so rapidly and so minutely that we don't notice it. This is one of our brain's ways of getting as much information as possible about the world around it. By moving back and forth, or triangulating, the eyes can continually send the brain information from two different perspectives. The shifts might be small, but they must be valuable, or else we wouldn't spend so much energy on them. When this movement increases enough to be visible—something that usually happens during a seizure or some other electrical dysfunction in the brain—we call it nystagmus.

Perhaps the usual microscopic movement ceases when the emotions of a dog, or a human, change to pure anger. This hypothesis is consistent with our knowledge that an alerted brain stops dead in its tracks, just for an instant, before responding with a storm of electricity and chemical messages. We can reasonably speculate that there is an equivalent micropause in the body's machinery, right before it acts on the emotion of anger.

Whatever causes this change in eye expression, don't worry about training yourself to see it. If a dog's eyes go cold and hard on you, believe me, your body will let you know. Just be sure to pay attention to what your body is trying to tell you, because it's sending you some very important information. I'll never forget calling the animal behaviorist John Wright after I'd seen one of my first clients. I was just starting out, and John had been working with aggressive dogs for several years, so I valued his opinion. I didn't call for advice about a treatment plan; I called for solace, because I had become deeply afraid of a Standard Poodle whose eyes raised the hair on the back of my neck. Like many novices, I had a fantasy that my commitment and knowledge should preclude feeling afraid while working with dogs. That fantasy fell apart as the dog began to leap toward my face, higher and higher each time, without a shred of friendliness in his eyes. In seconds my body and brain were in complete agreement. "Be afraid," they said. "Be very afraid."

I had been afraid, and felt like a failure. "How could I be so scared and call myself an animal behaviorist?" I asked John. "How could you call yourself one if you weren't?" he countered. "The dog was threatening you, and your body knew it right away. Listen to your body when you're working with dogs: it's giving you invaluable information." He was right. The dog's eyes were as cold as flint, and now that I have seventeen years' experience under my belt, I have no doubt that I was being threatened by a dog who was serious about hurting me. That case helped me learn to use my body's wisdom to my advantage, and to welcome those signals rather than trying to suppress them.

Expressions of the eye may be the hardest to describe in words, but experienced canine behaviorists and dog handlers of all descriptions agree that they are key to the way we evaluate dogs. Psychologists tell us that humans read fear and anger mostly from the eyes, and happiness from the mouth. Certainly an offensive pucker is an important cue to anyone observing a dog, but nothing compares to the look of pure rage that can be expressed by a dog with hard eyes. If you encounter a dog who turns his head to look directly into your eyes, and whose eyes go cold and hard as he looks into your own, you're much better off trying to ease the tension by speaking quietly and calmly, changing the focus onto "Walkies!" or "Dinner?" than you are confronting the dog directly. A direct stare with a hard eye usually means the dog is willing to fight, and unless you want to be involved in a barroom brawl with someone better armed than you, you're better off finessing the situation until he calms down. I don't want you to teach your dog that all he has to do is glare at you to maintain possession of the couch or the chewy toy, but those problems are better solved before a face-to-face confrontation occurs, not during it. If your blood runs cold when a dog looks you directly in the eye, listen to your body, stop doing what you're doing, look away yourself, and change the focus to walks or dinner. Then put your energy into finding a skilled and understanding behaviorist to help you out.[7]

7. Keep in mind that a "hard eye" is a bit more difficult to read in a dog with blue eyes, which tend to look a bit "colder" than brown eyes. It's also helpful to remember that herding dogs, like Border Collies, were bred to show what's called eye, which translates into an almost obsessive direct stare, originally used to intimidate sheep. It's not necessarily aggressive, although it can get downright tiresome when you're trying to relax on the couch and your dog stares at your face throughout an entire feature-length movie.

WHALE EYE

There's another expression related to the eye that the pros look for when evaluating the emotional state of a dog, but that's not intuitively obvious to the dog-loving public. Labeled "whale eye" by Sue Sternberg, an expert on canine aggression, it appears when your dog's head and eyes aren't pointing in the same direction, so you see the whites of your dog's eyes on one side or the other.[8] Look at the photo of the dog exhibiting this expression and you'll see what I mean. This nervous dog is so anxious about what he's looking at that he wants to turn his head away, but he's too afraid to take his eyes off the anxiety-provoking object of his focus. I see this expression most often in dogs who are fearful of strangers or of unfamiliar dogs. If you want to get a good look at this expression on a human, just go to a scary movie. When something terrifying occurs, you'll see people turn their heads away, but keep their eyes riveted on the monster on the screen. Our rational brains may understand that the danger is confined to the screen, but our emotional brain knows at any moment the alien in the movie is going to leap out and attack us, so we need to keep our eyes on him at every moment.

Dogs appear to evaluate the situation in a similar way, because fearful dogs turn their heads away as if they can't bear to face the monster, but keep their eyes riveted on whatever it is that has scared them. This expression is very different from the hard, direct stare of a confident dog. Either dog could cause all kinds of trouble, but the dog that shows you whale eye is telling you in no uncertain terms that he's really, really nervous. You'll do him no favors if you either ignore it or force him to confront his fears right then and there.

There is an exception to the caution about a dog showing the whites of his eyes. I've seen this same expression on the faces of completely relaxed dogs who appear, for want of a better description, to be purely and simply amused. Look at Luke's face on the last page of photographs. His head is partially turned toward me and partially toward the camera, while his eyes are looking directly toward the lens. You can see the same look on the faces of Elizabeth Marshall Thomas's dogs in

8. This term came from a client of Sue's who had been observing whales and noticed that the whale's eyes showed lots of white when she kept her eyes on the people around her, no matter which way her head was pointed.

her author photo for *The Hidden Life of Dogs*. It's not a look I've seen often, and I want to be crystal clear that I'm only guessing, but it looks for all the world to me like the dog is sharing a joke with the person he's looking at. In Luke's case, I suspect he was laughing at my hair.

LOOKING AWAY

While we're talking about the direction of a dog's head, it's important to be aware of the times your dog goes out of her way to avoid looking directly at a person or another dog. You'll see this when one dog turns her head away as she passes by another dog, perhaps if there's tension between them or the dogs haven't met each other yet. If you start paying attention to which way a dog's head is oriented, you'll discover that dogs spend a lot of energy avoiding direct eye contact with one another unless they are good buddies. The best place to see this is in a group photo of people and dogs: all the people will be looking at one another or the camera, while all the dogs are looking away from one another.

This isn't a problem, at least not if we respect our dogs' attempts to stay out of conflict with one another. Some dogs appear to use a "look away" to defuse tension, and it's often a sign of a well-socialized, friendly dog. Luke and Lassie both worked hundreds of dog-dog aggression cases with me, and they'd always turn their heads away when a defensively aggressive dog looked in their direction. If they had stared right back, the other dog would have erupted into low-pitched barks; by turning their heads, they were keeping things relaxed and avoiding the kind of staredown that sets dogs off.

Sometimes confident, high-status dogs turn their heads away from the submissive greeting of a lower status dog. In this case, it's as if the dog is playing a canine version of hard to get, or communicating that they will favor the other with attention only when they feel like it. However, dogs may also "look away" because they are nervous themselves. A dog who tongue-flicks and turns his head away from an approaching stranger is communicating anxiety, and is not a dog who's going to appreciate petting. Start noticing the orientation of a dog's head when he's meeting new people or unfamiliar dogs—you'll learn a lot about how he's feeling inside.

TALKING EYEBROWS

When humans frown, we move the centers of our eyebrows down and toward each other. Dogs frown, too, and it's another relatively easy signal to read once you learn to look for it. It's clear that these are important signals in social communication—in both species the muscles above the eyes are accented, by hair (in our case) and coloration changes (in the case of most dogs).[9] Look at the photos of Lassie, who has the most expressive face of any dog I've ever had. When we're on our way to the barn to herd sheep, elation flows like sunshine out of every pore of her body. Her mouth opens—heck, her entire face opens, in the kind of relaxed, joyful look that makes you happy yourself just to look at it. However, when she's lying on the floor watching me pack my suitcase for yet another business trip, her eyebrows wrinkle forward in a stunningly obvious analogue of a human frown. Lassie frowns so much that one of her nicknames is Frownie Face.

Her oft-wrinkled brow is one of the reasons I believe that she's not always a happy dog. Certainly she was a wreck when she came to me, after being raised by a mother (the canine one) who hated her puppies, and then spending her first year of life in a home with four small children and an overwhelmed single mother (the human one). Living at the farm did her a world of good, and after a year of working sheep, intensive training, and playing with her father, Luke (whom she worshipped), Lassie stopped compulsively spinning in place and licking anything within reach of her tongue. Eleven years later, at the mature age of twelve, Lassie still seems to take the world with great seriousness. If you took a photograph of her every five minutes, most of the images would show a dog with her eyebrows ever so slightly scrunched together. Psychologists tell us that people have a "setpoint" of happiness, based on both genetics and early experience, and I have no doubt that's as true of dogs like Lassie as it is with humans.[10]

Some dogs rarely frown, so you might not see this expression in

9. Have you ever thought about why there is hair above your eyes and not on your forehead? Hair has probably been retained in part to protect the eyes, but it makes sense that the hair also works to accentuate the movements of the muscles above your eyes, since they are such an important part of facial expressions.

10. We'll talk about the setpoint more in the chapter on happiness.

your own dog. I don't think I've ever seen Pip or Tulip frown. Luke frowned on rare occasions, when I irritated him with a foolish command while sheepherding or when I called him off sheep when he didn't want to stop working. He'd also tense up many of the muscles in his face when he was, I believe, anxious about something. In sharp contrast to the smooth, loose muscles of a relaxed dog, Luke's facial muscles would visibly tighten over his entire head; the tension was especially obvious under his eyes. Look at the three photos of the dog named Gus in the middle of the book for a great example of the transition from "relaxed and happy" to "tired and grumpy." Besides his mouth going from open to closed, the most obvious difference in the images is the tension of his facial muscles, especially under his eyes. The faces of worried or tense dogs look almost as if someone had drained the fluid out of them. They lose the full, smooth look of relaxed muscles, and give the face a worn-out appearance.

"ARE YOU ALL RIGHT?"

Ever had someone say to you, "Oh dear, you look so tired. Are you all right?" You may have wondered if that was an expression of concern or a comment about how bad you look (thanks *ever* so much), but the relevant question here is: What was it about your face that led someone to say that? In many cases, our faces get the same look when we're tired as I described above in dogs. We describe exhausted or stressed faces as being "drawn," as if someone has drained the rounded fullness of rested and relaxed tissue right out of them. Learn to see this same expression on your dog's face, because exhausted or grumpy dogs can be at the limit of their patience. I don't know how many times brokenhearted clients have told me that Barney had been doing *so well*; he'd handled the noise and chaos of the family picnic all day long, but just when everyone was about to leave, he fell apart and snapped, or nipped, or bit. As someone who loves social gatherings but finds them tiring, I have great sympathy for any dog who stays patient and polite all day long but finally has had enough after ten hours of commotion. I am grateful, as I suspect are my friends, that I have never bitten, but I know too well the feeling of being emptied of energy. If people could just see the signs of exhaustion or worry on their dogs' faces, there'd be a lot fewer bites in the world, a lot fewer tears, and a lot more dogs living to old age.

DISGUST

There's another facial expression you share with your dog, and that's the expression of disgust. When people are disgusted they raise the upper lips (which makes the corners of the mouth appear lower), squint their eyes and turn their heads away. In extreme cases, they'll wrinkle their noses. Dogs do the same thing, and you'd do well to recognize the look on your own dog's face. I can't tell you how often people in beginning dog training classes will reward their dogs by giving them a few happy slaps to the top of the head. It may make the owners feel good, but most dogs don't like it any more than young children do, so they turn their heads away and look disgusted. Rather than reinforcing the dog for coming when called (for example), the owners are inadvertently punishing them. If the owners knew to watch for their dog's expression, they'd understand right away that the dog didn't like what he got for coming when called, and might well ignore the signal the next time he hears it.

I suspect the primary problem is that we do what feels good *to us* when we're praising a dog, and often forget to pay attention to how the dog feels about it.[11] Professionals learn to pay attention to a dog's expression as they reinforce a dog for doing what was asked—if we don't, then we can't be sure we're really reinforcing the dog. "Positive reinforcement" means adding something that makes the dog want to perform an action again (like giving her a tiny, tasty treat for sitting when asked), so by definition it has to be something that the dog really, really loves and is willing to work for. Rewards, on the other hand, are things that are handed out by trainers (or bosses and parents) that may or may not be something the receiver wants or cares about. You may get a trip to Hawaii for selling more widgets than anyone else that year, but if you travel all the time for a living, maybe you'd rather have two weeks at home.

Dogs can't tell us what they want with words, but their faces speak volumes, so next time you praise and pet your dog for doing something you asked, pay careful attention to her face. The easiest situation to observe is when a dog is rewarded with pats on the head when she is in play mode. Just like us, dogs like to be touched and petted *some* of the time, but not all of the time and not in every context. We humans can

---

11. See *The Other End of the Leash* for a discussion about how much we, as primates, love to pat others on the top of the head (as well as a photograph of a dog turning her head away in disgust).

barely keep ourselves from reaching toward our dogs with our paws, because that's natural to us, but most dogs don't want pats on top of the head when they're in play mode, any more than young boys want their mommies to come give them a hug when they're on the playground. If you're not sure what disgust looks like on a face covered with fur, spray some perfume on your wrist and put it right under your dog's nose. We may love flowery and musky smells, but if dogs could make perfume it would contain the essence of horse poop and rotted squirrel. Let a dog smell some perfume and you'll know right away how he feels about it. If he doesn't like it, which most dogs don't, he'll pull down the corners of his mouth and turn his head away. You and your dog may be disgusted by different things, but you express the feeling in the same way. Keep that in mind when your goal is to reinforce your dog for doing something you requested.

SIGNAL STEW

I guarantee you that soon after you become adept at reading canine expressions, some dog is going to confuse the heck out of you. Innumerable trainers ask my opinion about perplexing expressions on a dog. One moment they'll think a particular dog is fearful, because his commissure is pulled back straight to his ears in a fear grimace, but the next moment they think he's not, because his eyes are cold and hard. Perhaps his ears are up while he's leaning forward and barking, but his tail is down. "I just can't figure him out," they say. "I'm so confused." If this happens to you, don't feel bad; you're not as confused as you think you are. If you think the signals are contradictory, they probably are. I'd estimate that over half of the dogs I've seen in my office exhibit some combination of emotions when they're about to get themselves into trouble.

This mixture of signals suggests that dogs can experience two different emotions simultaneously. However, some neurobiologists argue that even humans can't experience different emotions at the same time, although they can rapidly alternate between them. Temple Grandin, the brilliant, autistic expert on animal welfare, makes that claim in her book, *Animals in Translation*.[12] This is one of the most important books

---

12. This is another must-read book if you want to get a better idea of how nonhuman animals perceive the world.

about animals written in the last century, so Dr. Grandin's argument deserves careful consideration. However, it does seem reasonable to think that dogs can be ambivalent, just like people can. That's the best explanation I can muster for the hundreds of dogs I've observed whose expressions and behavior suggested that there was an emotional battle raging inside their brains and bodies. Although we don't yet have a definite answer to what's going on inside them, it should be mentioned that ethologists have argued for decades that many signals used by animals to communicate express conflicting emotions.

Most commonly, I see what looks like ambivalence in certain aggression cases, those involving what I call alpha wannabe dogs—dogs who want to be in control of everything and everyone around them, but who are also fearful and have little confidence. This personality type can take some real finesse to work with, because once you successfully treat the dog so that he's no longer fearful, you might be left with a dog who still wants to take over the house. Such dogs do best with a combination of classical conditioning to assuage their fears, a program that helps the owner teach the dog new behaviors, and an understanding that some dogs desperately need their owners to be benevolent leaders. (See the Chapter 6 references for problem-solving resources.)

READ ME IF YOU CAN

No matter how good you get at reading subtle changes of expression, some dogs are going to make it harder than others. I think of Black Labradors as the iconic American dogs, because both Labs and Americans tend to have such emotionally expressive faces. I met an expressive Lab last week with a face so plastic he reminded me of the actor Jim Carrey, whose face can morph from extremes of joy to concern to anger in a microsecond. Other dogs—often individuals of breeds with fighting in their genetic backgrounds—are much harder to read. Fighters aren't interested in letting you know how they're feeling at the moment; it's to their advantage to keep their emotions to themselves. Because of that, it takes a lot more skill to read changes in expression in these dogs, just as it's harder to read the faces of people from cultures that value hiding emotions, not expressing them.

I compare the ability to read canine facial expressions with the skill of reading radiographs. My vet can look at a bunch of fuzzy white blobs on an X-ray film and immediately focus on something relevant, while I'm stuck sorting out the dog's intestines from her stomach. Great dog trainers can do something similar with the expressions on a dog's face. The more experience you have, and the more relevant signals your brain has been taught to look for, the better you'll get. You may not have the time or opportunity to work yourself up to complete literacy, but every one of us, no matter how skilled, can continue to improve his or her ability to "read dog."[13]

LISTENING WHILE YOU'RE LOOKING

Your dog's vocalizations are also a good indicator of how she's feeling inside. This book focuses primarily on visual expressions, but the sounds your dog makes also contain a lot of information. The barks and whines of our dogs follow the rules laid out years ago by Eugene Morton, who suggested that the vocalizations of all mammals follow certain general principles. Sounds related to offense tend to be low in pitch and "noisy," like a low, growly bark, while sounds related to fear or appeasement tend to be higher pitched and more pure in tone, like the yelp of a frightened puppy. Excitement also tends to raise pitch, as anyone knows who has exclaimed "Wheeee!" as they sped down a hill on a sled.

Tulip barks deep and low when she hears coyotes, but as I run downstairs to put her outside, her barks rise in pitch. While I fumble with the front door, Tulip spins in circles and barks higher and faster, I suspect because she is excited and frustrated that she has to wait for me to perform my part of the job. As soon as I open the door and snap her collar to her tie-out line, her barks lengthen and lower.[14]

One of the most practical applications of this knowledge is the evaluation of playing dogs. It's often difficult for people to distinguish exuberant play from a serious scrap, but you can use the sounds you hear as a good indicator. If you start to hear the dogs' vocalizations become lower and more growl-like, don't wait for the fight to break out. As we'll discuss in a later chapter, dogs can become overly aroused during play, and end up fighting like out-of-control sports fans, so listen

---

13. See the references for some books and videotapes that can improve your skills.

14. If I just let her go, she'd run across a county highway and chase the coyotes. That's far too dangerous, so she does her night-time protection work on a thirty-foot line. So far it's worked; I haven't seen a coyote footprint on the farm since Tulip came, although my neighbors see them often.

for a change in pitch and redirect the players if things start to sound "offensive" or overexcited.

CAN YOUR DOG READ YOUR FACE?

All this brings up a question: what about your dog? While you're reading subtle changes on your dog's face, what is your dog doing? How literate are dogs at reading human faces and postures? I've been writing as if it was a fact that dogs respond to our expressions and postures the way they would to the expressions and postures of another dog. We desperately need more research on this topic, but the anecdotal evidence, and the biology of dogs, suggest that they are brilliant interpreters of our expressions. In *The Other End of the Leash,* I wrote about how minor changes in your posture can have major effects on your dog, and I've yet to hear a trainer or behaviorist disagree.[15] Our mutual experiences support the belief that dogs get a tremendous amount of information about our emotional state (and thus what we're about to do next) from our postures and our faces.

There are logical arguments as well: if dogs weren't good at reading emotional expressions on the faces of others, they wouldn't be so expressive themselves. If the point is to communicate, then signals have to be interpreted by a receiver; otherwise there's no point in sending them. You wouldn't spend a half hour typing out an e-mail to someone who doesn't have a computer. It isn't surprising that dogs can interpret expressions on the faces of another species—not when they share many of the same expressions and are hard-wired to understand them. Surely our shared expressiveness and our mutual ability to read the expressions of others is part of what makes our relationship with dogs so emotionally powerful. We're bonded to dogs not just because we are both emotional beings, but because we express our emotions so freely, and are so good at interpreting them on one another's faces. (Although I suspect our dogs are better at reading our faces than we are at reading theirs!)

15. This is a profoundly rare experience in the world of dog training, in which different methods of training can take on almost religious significance to some people. The standard joke among dog trainers is that the only thing two trainers will agree on is that the third trainer doesn't know what she's talking about. My own version is that the only two things *all* trainers agree upon are (1) dogs are highly responsive to our expressions and postures; and (2) humans are harder to train than dogs.

BE CAREFUL WHAT YOU "SAY"
(OR WHAT YOUR DOG *THINKS* YOUR FACE IS SAYING)

Sometimes what's on our faces turns out *not* to be an accurate expression of how we're feeling inside. A few years ago, I worked with an American Eskimo Dog who illustrated this point by reacting with friendly relaxation to the approach of one person, and nervous aggressive barking to another. The first person who approached was a relatively short woman who walked toward the dog with her body turned slightly sideways, avoiding direct eye contact and squatting down about three feet away from the dog. She kept her hands to herself, and in seconds the dog ran up to her, body loose and bendy, sniffed her hands, and leaped up to lick her face. Minutes later, a man with a hat and sunglasses approached the same dog, this time with a hand extended. Before he could get anywhere near the dog, she exploded in high-pitched barking. With rounded eyes, dilated pupils, and an offensive pucker, she made it perfectly clear that the man continued his approach at his own risk.

Any one of several different factors could have affected the dog's response. Shy dogs are usually more afraid of men than women. (Is it their large jaws? Big chests? Deep voices? We're not really sure, but the tendency is almost universal.) The man had walked directly toward the American Eskimo Dog—unlike a friendly dog, who would have approached laterally rather than head-on, and who would have avoided direct eye contact. The hat could also have been an issue. I think hats confuse dogs because they don't seem to get the "removable parts" aspect of human couture. But there's no question that sunglasses, looking like huge, rounded eyes with completely dilated pupils, are particularly scary to dogs. The dog turned out to be most affected by the sunglasses—she'd let the man approach without them, and then bark herself silly when he put them back on. Same man, same dog, same seminar room. Sunglasses on: dog barks and lunges forward. Sunglasses off: dog lets man approach and allows herself to be petted under the chin.[16]

16. Sunglasses also make it impossible to read a person's eye expression, which is one of the reasons that law enforcement officers don't like talking to people wearing them. You'd be wise to remember this next time you get stopped for speeding or are going through customs at an airport.

I don't know how many times I've taken one look at a dog and told my companion to quickly take his or her sunglasses off, but I'm convinced that by doing so I've avoided lots of sticky situations. I've also seen dogs react in my office to a beautiful painting of my first Great Pyrenees, Bo Peep, that hangs above the chairs in my office. Dogs can be in the office for an hour before they happen to look up and see two large, round, brown eyes staring right at them, at which they erupt in a volley of barks loud enough to wake the dead. Lest you feel smug that we humans are too advanced for such primitive reactions, keep in mind that even as infants, we respond to an image of two dots above a curved line by smiling in return. Our brains are so programmed to those basic units of expression that we respond to them even if they are completely out of context. Think of the popularity of the "smiley face" that is used universally to convey happiness. There's no reason to believe that dogs don't do the same thing, responding to what they perceive as signals on our faces that are relevant and important to their interactions with us.

I would guess that anyone who's ever owned a dog believes strongly that their dog gets a tremendous amount of information from looking at their face. Certainly our dogs look to our faces all the time when they are confused and want more information. Herding dogs who are unsure of what to do will turn their heads and look back at their humans, in apparent hope of additional direction. Just as children who are unsure of how to solve a puzzle will turn and look at an adult's face for more information, performance dogs will stop what they're doing and turn and look at their handler's face. We can get a tremendous amount of information by looking at an individual's face. What we see there may not always be an accurate reflection of what's going on inside his head, and it may only give us part of the picture, but the study of faces is one of the best means we have for gathering information about the world around us. That appears to be equally true for both people and dogs.

Surely one of the reasons we have such amazing relationships with dogs is our shared reliance on facial expressions in social interactions. These expressions are windows to what is perhaps the most astounding aspect of our shared biology—the mammalian brain. You can't have emotions without having a brain, so the next chapter takes a look at your brain and your dog's brain, and how they function to create emotions.

3

EMOTIONS AND THE BRAIN

The master of ceremonies of emotion,
in both you and your dog

I met Bo Peep when she was an eight-week-old fluffball who grinned and thumped her tail as I approached. She lay curled up in the barn, close to the sheep that Great Pyrenees dogs like her were bred to protect. There was no worry that she'd get into the trouble common to young pups, playing too hard with the lambs or eating the grain meant for their hungry mommas. Bo Peep was born with back legs so crippled that she couldn't stand up; she could move only by hauling her hips forward with her front legs. After two months of life, with little chance to develop muscle, that wasn't far.

Euthanasia was a reasonable consideration, and her breeders had discussed it at length. But they couldn't bring themselves to put her down, so they called a veterinarian to discuss their options. Bo Peep's back legs didn't work because her kneecaps were on the sides of her legs rather than the fronts. The problem could be fixed surgically, although this major operation was usually done on small dogs, not ones that grow up to weigh over a hundred pounds. Their vet said he'd give the surgery a try, as long as they understood the outcome was uncertain. He was sure about one thing: Bo Peep would need extensive rehabilitation during her long recovery. The breeders had full-time jobs, several young children, and about a dozen Great Pyrenees. That's where I came in.

One horrible day I lost twenty-nine ducks to a stray dog, not long after a neighbor lost a calf to coyotes. The rolling hills of southern Wisconsin may not look like a dangerous wilderness, but stray dogs and coyotes are common. After my own loss, and after neighbors regaled me with stories of at-

tacks on their horses, goats, and chickens, I started looking for a working guard dog. Only one problem: my flock of eight ewes was worth about $800, and I couldn't afford the $2,000 to $3,000 it cost to buy a mature, working Great Pyrenees. Bo Peep's breeders knew my story, and thought they'd found the perfect solution. "You could have her for free," they told me on the phone, "and the vet will do the surgery for only the cost of materials." Bo Peep would need a tremendous amount of care, they said, but with luck she'd grow up to be a happy, functional guard dog.

"Well, I'll come look at her," I said, as if meeting a helpless fluffy white puppy would help me make an objective decision. I don't need to tell you what happened next. If you care enough about dogs to be reading this book, then you know that my fate was already sealed. Granted, after I met her I said I'd go home and think about it, maintaining the pretense of making a carefully considered decision. I thought about it, all right—I couldn't think about anything else all night long. I brought her home the next day.

Weeks later, I watched in fascination as the vet cut open Bo Peep's leg, filed grooves in the bones for the appropriate tendons and then, straining and groaning, his foot on the table for leverage, pulled her knee cap into place. After a few weeks of recovery in a cozy pen in the barn, it was time for Bo Peep to begin walking on her first newly repaired back leg. (We had decided to do one surgery at a time.) But Bo Peep had never walked on her back legs, and things didn't turn out as expected.

No amount of coaxing or luring could motivate her to take even a single step. Bo Peep had spent her entire life, short as it may have been thus far, lying in one place within a flock of sheep, licking the faces of lambs who came to visit and thumping her tail when humans approached. For the life of me, I couldn't get her to try to use her new leg. Somehow I had to get her walking. During one frustrating attempt, I carried her a few feet away from the barn, perhaps just to get us into the warmth of the sun. For the first time in her life, Bo Peep was out of sight of sheep, and finally she was motivated to try to move. She began pulling with her front legs in an attempt to get back to her sheep, and I was able to curl my arms around her hips and lift her hindquarters so that her new hind leg could straighten and begin to carry her weight.

Thus began my personal weightlifting routine at Redstart Farm. Two sessions a day, ten to twenty times each, I picked up Bo Peep and carried her away from the sheep. First five feet, then ten, then twenty. Once she began to rock forward, I lifted up her hindquarters to get her started, and then cheered as she took first one step, then two, on her new leg. After a few shaky steps she'd collapse, and I'd pick her up again and lug her back to where she started. She accepted all this as she did everything in life, cheerfully and sweetly, licking my face as I carried her across the grass. As the months went on, the distance increased. Regrettably, so did her weight. I gave up somewhere around sixty-five pounds, having developed an impressive set of muscles and a tired back.

We did the surgery on her other leg four or five months later. This time, things didn't go so well. She seemed to be in more pain than after the first surgery, and it was harder to keep her immobile during recovery. A large metal pin didn't stay in place; I found her one morning with it thrust out of her skin like a dagger. Subsequent X-rays found that not only had her kneecap been out of place, but her thigh bone was curved like a bow, and couldn't support her leg even with a repaired knee. She would have needed a minimum of two more major surgeries to attempt a repair, with only a microscopic chance of success. As it was, her deformed leg was dragging underneath her "good" one, and impeding her progress. Appalled at the choices, I finally accepted the inevitable and had the problem leg amputated.

This was Bo Peep's third major surgery in nine months, and it took its toll. She looked pathetic for days after her surgery, her eyes filled with pain and a kind of weariness rarely seen in young animals. But I was buoyed by the knowledge that three-legged dogs usually thrive once they've healed. Someone showed me a video of a working cattle dog who'd had a similar surgery. It wasn't until he got a few feet from the camera that I realized he wasn't running on three legs, he was running on two—a foreleg on the left side, and a hind leg on the right. Amazing. I kept that image close to me while Bo Peep recovered. She was young and otherwise healthy, and once we had gotten her useless leg out of her way, she had every chance of being a happy and fully mobile teenager.

That's not what happened. She recovered from the amputation, but she never walked more than a few steps on her remaining, surgically repaired hind leg. The vets couldn't explain it, because the leg looked sound in the X-ray films. The University of Wisconsin Veterinary Medical Teaching Hospital even used the X-rays to illustrate the ideal surgical resolution to her problem. Everything was in the right place—bones, tendons, and car-

tilage all lined up perfectly for a fully functioning leg. But Bo Peep never used her leg for more than ten or twelve steps. She'd stand up and walk forward a few steps, then flop her hips sideways down to the ground and drag them like a seal. Finally, I figured out that it wasn't her leg that was the problem: it was her brain.

It seemed reasonable to focus on Bo Peep's leg as the source of the problem. After all, that was the part of her that didn't seem to be working. But as John Ratey has said in no uncertain terms, "Separating the body and the brain is rapidly coming to be seen as ridiculous." What the brain becomes, and how it functions to control your emotions, turns out to be influenced as much by the body and its early experience as the body is influenced by the brain. This is true for both people and dogs, and is one of the many things that make doggy brains much like ours. In spite of a perfect surgery, Bo Peep's leg could never function normally because the connections between her brain and that part of her body weren't made when they were needed—when her brain was developing into its final form. She managed well enough, having learned to drag her hindquarters with her strong shoulders and front legs, but she never fully recovered from growing up without the right connections between her back legs and her brain.

This interplay between body and brain is as important for emotions as it was for Bo Peep's legs. Our emotional life, and that of our dogs, is profoundly affected by how the brain develops early in life, and thus how it functions once we're mature. Our emotional experiences are not only centered in *both* the brain and the body, they are a vital link between the two. Because the brain's role is so important in the regulation and experience of emotion, it's impossible to understand how our emotions compare with those of our dogs unless we get to know the brain a little bit better.

USE IT OR LOSE IT

One of the most amazing aspects of the brain is its development. Far from being fully formed at birth, brains are like software programs designed to be customized once they've been taken home from the store.

What happens after birth literally creates who you and your dog become as adults, because the way a brain functions once it matures is dependent upon the information it receives as it develops. If parts of the body aren't used during early development, the brain discards the connections that control them, either eliminating them entirely or assigning them to other duties. "Use it or lose it" turns out to be a prophetic phrase. When we're young, our brains are busy creating travel routes for the signals that link them with our bodies. These connections aren't just direct routes from the brain to a limb or an organ; they also include complex pathways among interconnected nerve cells within the brain.

If nothing travels on them, these pathways become like unused trails in the woods, filling up with scrubby weeds and bushes, eventually unusable by even the most intrepid of travelers. That's what happened to Bo Peep. Not having received enough signals from her hind legs when it should have, her brain moved on, and instead created more internal wiring to direct her massive shoulders and front legs. At birth, the brains of both people and dogs are a little like tropical jungles, in which plants struggle against one another to fight for sunlight. In the brain, the limiting resource isn't sunlight, it's connections to other cells, and neurons that don't use connections early on are overwhelmed, and ultimately eliminated, by those that do.

The brains of human children provide innumerable examples. We know that the neurological circuits managing their muscles are completed at age two; if, for some tragic reason, a child isn't able to move her arms or legs by then, she'll never be able to. Babies born with cataracts will never be able to see if the corrective surgery is done after six months of age, because that's when the wiring system for vision is completed. It's as if the workmen for that project picked up their tools and went home, and once they're gone, it's too late to call them back.

The importance of this early wiring project goes far beyond the functioning of body parts. The tangle of trails between your brain cells is as essential to your emotional life as it is to the movement of your body, and is equally affected by what happens during development. For example, the psychiatrist Dan Stern has found evidence for critical periods in the development of emotion, just as there seem to be critical periods for the development of eyes and limbs. Stern found that babies whose parents responded to them with expressions of delight formed more connections within the circuits that generate positive emotions. On the other hand, a baby whose parents react to him or her with horror becomes hard-wired to experience negative emotions more easily than positive ones. It's not just that the baby learns a particular behavior early on; he or she actually ends up with a completely different brain, depending on that early experience. This interplay between emotions, brain circuitry, and experience occurs only in children between the ages of ten months and eighteen months, which suggests that there is a "critical period" for an individual's emotional software.

THE IMPORTANCE OF TOUCH

The implications of this knowledge are vital to the development of healthy people and dogs. We learned this lesson the hard way, from watching baby after baby die in orphanages in the 1930s and 1940s.[1] Concerns about germs were rampant, so caretakers were told to avoid touching the babies and to keep the rooms as empty and as clean as possible. Babies lay alone in their cribs, with nothing to look at but an unchanging ceiling, for months or years on end. They may have been protected from diseases, but many of them died anyway, because babies need physical affection and environmental stimulation to thrive. Those who died might have been the lucky ones; the survivors were so damaged they had no chance of a normal life, even if they eventually found their way into loving homes. We should have known better: as early as the thirteenth century, the Holy Roman Emperor Frederick II isolated babies to see whether they'd start talking without ever having heard the spoken word. Nurses could feed the babies but were forced to avoid all other contact with them. Frederick never was able to answer his question: the poor things all died before they would have been able to speak.

In recent decades, through experiments on the hardworking laboratory rat, we have begun to understand what happened to those children in orphanages and in Frederick's experiment. The brain simply

---

1. It had been found that 100 percent of the babies in orphanages were dead by the age of two, often from diseases like cholera or scarlet fever. See Deborah Blum's amazing book *Love at Goon Park* for a riveting account of the extreme and often tragic measures taken to prevent the spread of disease.

can't develop normally without a great range of stimulation—from different types of touch to a variety of noises and things to look at. Touch is just one sense that must be stimulated early on for normal development, but as we saw, it's a critical one. Brain scans of touch-deprived babies show that normally busy areas of their brains are alarmingly quiet. It took a few years for hospitals to realize that's why premature babies in incubators weren't thriving. Their brains were being starved of the input necessary for them to grow and function. Touch is so important that if massaged three times a day, babies born prematurely gain 47 percent more weight than if not. Touch does more than help the brain manage the body; it is critical to the development of a healthy emotional system later in life.

That early development has important effects on the emotional lives of adults appears to be true across the board in all mammals, from mice, to mastiffs, to the man next door. The more baby rats are gently handled by their keepers, the more serotonin they produce and the less aggressive they are as adults.[2] The same correlation is found in human societies: cultures in which people avoid cuddling their children are also cultures in which people are relatively aggressive as adults, while members of societies who receive a lot of gentle touch when young tend to be less violent when they grow up. As anyone who has considered throwing their computer out the window knows, aggressive behavior is highly correlated with strong emotion, so these are important findings for us all. The story that follows is a tragic example of the interplay between aggression, emotions, and the development of the brain.

Frisco, a five-week-old Pit Bull mix, was in the middle of a full-blown seizure when detectives found him during a drug bust in Madison, Wisconsin. His owners thought it would be fun to give him cocaine and see how he liked it. He didn't. His young, fragile brain went into overdrive, and the electrical storms within it almost killed him. He teetered on the edge of death for five days, pulled through, and was rescued by Karen, a

---

2. Serotonin is one of the neurohormones that affect mood and behavior. We'll talk about it in more depth later in this and other chapters.

kindhearted woman who fell in love with his sweet face and his sad history. I met him a year later, when she brought him in for possession-related aggression.

Eager for me to see what he did, Karen dumped an entire bag of toys on the floor and said, "Now watch." I couldn't do anything but, because Frisco's response was so dramatic. He became stiff as a board, shot his head up to look directly into my eyes, and began snarling and growling like a revved-up motorcycle. Although his behavior was extreme in its intensity, stiffening and growling are typical of dogs who are possessive about their toys. But while staring directly into my eyes, Frisco squatted and emptied his bladder, his hindquarters shaking like a frightened puppy's. Saliva drooled out of his mouth and pooled on the carpet at his feet. Frisco was a cauldron of conflicting emotions, from extreme rage to extreme fear. Even though I've seen thousands of dogs in my office, I'll never forget Frisco's face at that moment. His eyes were bulging almost out of his head, and they looked, well . . . crazy. I've always found eye expressions the hardest thing about dogs to describe objectively, and all I can say about Frisco's eyes is that they looked purely and simply insane. I remember thinking that this had to be one of the most dangerous dogs I'd ever met.

Every time either Karen or I moved, even to turn our heads, Frisco lunged forward and his growls got louder. Needless to say, for a while we stayed still, concentrating on breathing normally and keeping our own bodies as relaxed as we could. I finally found I could slowly edge my way to the door, as long as I moved in tiny increments. Feeling guilty about leaving Karen in the room with him, but knowing that movement was what set Frisco off, I elected to be the one to edge out the door. I made it out in one piece, and gathered more toys with which to lure him into another room. It worked. Once away from his own treasures, he calmed down in a matter of minutes and went back to being the cheerful, handsome boy he had been before.

After Frisco had settled down, Karen and I spoke at length about how much damage the early weeks of his life had done to his brain, and my concerns about his prognosis. It seemed likely that Frisco's extreme reaction was related to the abuse his brain had endured early in life. That meant it was impossible to know how much the usual treatment techniques would help, but she was willing to try and I was committed to doing all I could to help her. I sent her home with some techniques that help most resource-guarding dogs, and with the obvious instruction to put away anything that even vaguely resembled a toy. Even so, I was so worried about her and Frisco that I gave her my home phone number and told her to call me night or day if she needed help. She did, at eleven o'clock that Friday night. I picked up the phone to hear Karen, panicked, whispering like a kidnap victim who has sneaked away from her abductors to call 911. "Please come help me. Frisco's gone crazy and is stalking me. I've hidden upstairs, but he's trying to get through the door and I don't know how long it will hold up. I can't get out the windows and I'm terrified he's going to kill me."

I immediately called Esther Rasmussen, a friend and animal control officer who loves dogs, especially Pit Bulls. Smart, brave, and able to stay calm in a crisis, Esther leaped to the challenge. She knew as well as I that there are thousands of sweet, loving Pit Bulls in the world, but that an aggressive one, because of the breed's stamina and power, is not to be taken lightly. We met each other after midnight on the street in front of Karen's house, armed with a dart gun, a syringe full of tranquilizer, and a rabies pole.[3] We could talk to Karen by cell phone, and see her frightened face in the second-story window. We pounded on the front door to lure Frisco away from her, and sure enough, he charged down the stairs and attacked the front door. As he barked and lunged, I opened the door just enough for him to get his head out, and then instantly shut it to stop his shoulders from coming through. Esther snagged him with the loop on the rabies pole, and then handed it to me while she prepared the dart gun. Frisco stood still, sides heaving, drooling and snarling. I silently prayed my weak back would hold up long enough to keep him from pulling the pole out of my hands. Esther fiddled with the dart gun, to no avail; finally, she said, "Don't let him get me," moved directly to his hindquarters, and jammed the syringe into his hip. I held on for dear life, appalled at the thought that I might not be able to stop him from turning and biting her. Frisco tried his best to bite Esther, but to our mutual relief, she got away in time.

Esther's aim had been true, and in just minutes Frisco's eyes went soft. We removed the loop restraining him, and cradled his sagging body in our laps. We gently carried him into the van, and, at Karen's request, drove him to an emergency vet clinic to be euthanized. Overwhelmed with both

---

3. Rabies poles have a loop at the end that allows you to lasso a dangerous dog. The rigid pole keeps the dog a safe three or four feet away while you restrain him.

adrenaline and sadness, Karen, Esther, and I stroked Frisco while he slipped off to his final rest. Karen had done all she could to give him a good life, but I told her then, and I'll repeat it now: Frisco's first owners had killed him long ago, when they fried his poor young brain. It just took him a long time to die.

This true story, as tragic as it is dramatic, speaks to the terrible harm that can be done to the developing brain of a young dog. Once Frisco became emotionally aroused, the arousal increased until he became physiologically out of control. Arousal, like many other aspects of physiology in mammals, is regulated by mechanisms much like the thermostat on the furnace in your home. It's the thermostat that keeps your furnace from staying on all the time: once the temperature rises to a certain level, a feedback system kicks in, and the heat is turned off. As the air in the house cools, then becomes too cold, the furnace kicks in again. In a healthy dog, emotional arousal is regulated in a similar way, with what are called the sympathetic and parasympathetic systems acting like thermostats to keep the body and brain functioning at optimal levels. But the body and brain can spiral out of control, if the circuits that control this kind of feedback don't have a chance to develop normally.

Of course, most stories aren't as extreme as Frisco's, but I've seen too many dogs whose emotional health has been permanently damaged because their developing brains didn't have the right environment in which to grow. Illegal drugs are not the only means of compromising a dog's developing brain. Sterile, unstimulating environments can stunt a dog's emotional growth so that he is never able to cope with stress of any kind. Harsh, abusive situations in puppyhood can hardwire a dog to be emotionally overreactive as an adult. Of course, there are many reasons besides early development for the behavioral problems described above, but it's important to include development as one piece of the puzzle.

CLEANLINESS IS NOT ENOUGH

Many people know something about the importance of environmental stimulation for young children, but often we fail to apply that knowledge in picking or raising a puppy.[4] I've seen any number of clients who raved about the cleanliness of the kennel where they got their pup, but who had no idea of what the pup experienced after birth. "Cleanliness is next to Godliness" in America, and I've learned that clean and neat is what people look for when they're choosing a place to buy a pup. Clean is good, I'm all for it, but it's not enough to ensure that your pup has really had a good start in life. The extreme of "clean" is "sterile," and sterility, it turns out, is a good thing only if you're doing surgery. Sterility can equal environmental deprivation, and that can cause no end of trouble to a developing pup.

Environmental deprivation can happen anywhere. It can disable puppies born in filthy puppy mills as well as those raised in spotless kennels. Clean or dirty, if dogs grow up with little environmental stimulation they can turn into adults who are lacking in the ability to handle even minor stress. Stress is just change, after all, and if a pup has matured in an environment that never changes, she doesn't develop a brain that is wired to cope with it. Numerous studies on rats and nonhuman primates show that barren environments create individuals who are unable to cope with stress as adults, because the stress-related pathways in their brains aren't able to develop normally. Rats who were taken away from their mothers for fifteen minutes a day turn out to be *less* reactive to stressful events than those that weren't. (In an interesting link to our earlier discussion on the importance of touch, that result appears to be related to the amount of intensive licking that the mother rats do when the baby rats are returned.) Rats raised in the standard, sterile boxes used in most laboratories have fewer connections between their brains' cells, and thinner cerebral cortexes, than rats raised in "enriched" boxes.[5]

This is so important, and yet so often ignored, that I had to sneak toys into the kennels when I was doing research on dogs and their responses to different types of sound. I had four litters of puppies growing up in kennels in the middle of the University of Wisconsin campus, and was committed to raising healthy, normal dogs. That was important to me not just for their sake, which would have been important

---

4. Yet another example of our inability to be anthropomorphic when it makes sense to be!

5. It's regrettable that much of the medical research done on laboratory animals is done on animals raised in isolated, sterile conditions that can't possibly create a normal brain.

enough, but also for my research. Research on the behavior of abnormal dogs wouldn't be meaningful, so I wanted to ensure that the pups had plenty to feel, hear, and see as they grew. As it should, the university has strict regulations on the care of animals in research, but at that time the rules were all about cleanliness and physical safety. The kennels had to be spotless, but heaven forbid we should bring in a germ-laden toy or chew stick that would facilitate normal development. As a lowly graduate student, I knew that my chances of getting the regulations changed were negligible. I'd already pushed the envelope by creating a legal document that allowed my pups to be the first research dogs at the university to be adopted out into private homes instead of being euthanized at the end of the research project. There are just so many battles you can fight at one time, so I picked up the toys whenever I thought the lab might be inspected, and put them down when I thought the coast was clear.

That was a long time ago, and I'm happy to say that even at that time some people were acknowledging, and acting on, the importance of an enriched environment to captive animals. Although I'd argue that we have much to do to improve the lives of many research animals, some of the most impressive advances in creating enriched environments for developing animals have actually come from laboratories and zoological parks. Ironically, the general public, responsible for the lives of over sixty million dogs a year in just the United States alone, is often less aware of enrichment's importance. My associates and I often see dogs who were raised in conditions designed to handicap the development of their minds, not encourage it.

These poor dogs can't handle change of any kind, and depending on their genetics, they either slink into the office in terror or roar in like freight trains off the tracks. There's always a lot that can be done to help dogs like this—brains are amazing things and some rewiring is possible if you have the time and the patience—but just like a house built on a shaky foundation, the result is never as solid as it would be if you'd started out right from the beginning.

I don't want to discount the importance of genetics here; it plays a big role in who a dog is and how his or her brain reacts to the environment. You can usefully compare genetics with the ingredients in a recipe, and the effect of the environment with the method of putting them all together. The best eggs in the world aren't going to make a good omelet if you hard-boil them before you mix them with the other ingredients.

SESAME STREET FOR DOGS

Good breeders know about the importance of environmental enrichment and work hard to stimulate their puppies daily from birth. That includes ensuring that the puppies get lots of handling from the day they're born. Although pups are born deaf and blind, their sense of touch is fully developed at birth, and if their brains are to develop normally, their bodies must receive lots of physical contact. I've always suspected that's why single pups, with no littermates to poke into and push against, sometimes grow into adults who are more touch sensitive than pups with littermates. The impact of gentle handling can be seen even if it occurs before birth: puppies born to mothers who were petted during pregnancy tend to be more receptive to handling after birth.

The research on the effects of environmental stimulation and the ability to handle stress got a lot of attention a few years back from the U.S. military. In search of dogs who could perform difficult tasks under stressful conditions, the military developed a method of early sensory stimulation that they believe created adult dogs with superior problem-solving abilities and more tolerance of stress. The process takes only a few minutes a day, and involves five simple exercises, to be done on each pup in the litter, from birth to thirteen days old. The pup should be picked up in one hand and be tickled between the toes of one foot for just three to five seconds. Next, use both hands to hold the pup, again for three to five seconds, so that his head is directly above his tail. Carefully cupping the puppy in both hands, reverse his direction so that his head is pointing straight down, and hold again for three to five seconds. (Dropping the puppy is not advisable for optimum brain development, so do this carefully!) Next, hold the pup so that he is parallel to the floor, belly up, for the same amount of time as the other exercises. Last, put the pup on a cold, damp towel for three to five seconds; and then return him to the litter.

Carmen Battaglia, a Ph.D. scientist and American Kennel Club judge who has written extensively about this plan, cautions that breeders should follow it exactly: he suggests that repeating the exercises more than once a day, or doing them for more than five seconds each, can potentially cause harm. This does not mean that you should restrict the normal cuddling and handling that every puppy needs (and most of us can't resist giving). The exercises described involve stimulation that pups would normally never get, and possibly act to kick-start some aspects of neurological development. Because too much stress can backfire, if you're going to try this out, I'd suggest doing it exactly as described. I used the plan on one litter, and the pups did grow into calm, resilient dogs—but that doesn't tell us much, because who knows how the litter might have turned out otherwise. Maybe they would have been the same, or maybe they'd have been better if I *hadn't* done the exercises. However, the research suggests that the exercises do have value, and they are an important reminder to us of the effect of the environment on your pup's brain.

The exercises are designed to stimulate the senses that are fully functioning at birth: the sense of touch, another sense called proprioception, which involves the brain knowing where the body is in space, and the ability to sense warmth or cold. Once the eyes and ears of puppies are functioning, starting around fourteen days or so, they need stimulation in the areas that process sound and vision. That doesn't mean a pup should be bombarded with constant noise and handling. Pups, like babies, need lots of time to be left alone to sleep. But when they're awake, they need enough stimulation to encourage connections to form among neurons in different parts of their brains.

Keep in mind that environmental enrichment is different from "socialization," in which pups are introduced to animals with whom they are expected to form social relationships. We know from extensive research, first done by John Paul Scott and John L. Fuller in a groundbreaking twenty-year study, that pups are hardwired to learn, between the ages of about five weeks and thirteen weeks, what their social partners are supposed to look like and how they are supposed to behave. This time period is called a "critical" or "sensitive" period, because if you miss it you'll never quite get the same effect later on. That's one of the reasons good trainers and behaviorists encourage well-managed puppy socialization classes, so your dog's brain can record

what his playmates should look and act like. This is especially important for dogs, given that they come in a dazzling array of shapes and
sizes. You can hardly blame a Teacup Poodle for not knowing how to
react to a Newfoundland if she's never met any dogs besides other poodles.

Lots of people are aware of the importance of early socialization for
dogs, thanks to the efforts of people like Ian Dunbar, a veterinary behaviorist who spent the better part of twenty-five years encouraging
people to create and attend puppy socialization classes. But fewer know
about the important effects of environmental enrichment on behavior.
The good news is that you don't need to go too far out of your way to
provide an enriched environment for a growing pup. Puppies raised in
most homes hear a variety of noises, from the phone ringing, to the
kids coming home from school, to advertisements on television. They
are picked up and handled often and are more likely than kennel-raised
pups to be put on a variety of surfaces, amid a variety of smells. However, pups raised outside or in kennels can also get a tremendous
amount of stimulation. When I was breeding Border Collies, the pups
and their mom lived inside for three to four weeks, and then moved
into the old milk house in the barn. Lost in puppy rapture, I'd spend
hours outside with them; I brought each one into the house daily, took
them waddling through tall grasses, and allowed them to experience all
the sounds, sights, and smells of the Wisconsin countryside. What
matters, whether a pup is raised inside or out, is whether he spends
long days in the same place listening to the same sounds and seeing
the same things, or whether he experiences a bigger range of life's experiences.

WE ALL HAVE OUR LIMITS

Keep all this in mind if you're buying a puppy-mill puppy because you
fell in love with his sad, sweet eyes, or if you're rescuing an adult dog
raised in compromised conditions. Far be it from me to tell you to walk
away from some poor dog who's had a bad start—just ask Bo Peep how
well I did at making a cool, dispassionate decision after taking one look
at her crippled little body. But for the sake of both you and the dog, I
want you to be realistic about what to expect. Some dogs, probably be-

cause of superior genetics, can experience negligent, even abusive conditions, and still mature into emotional health. My Luke lived an isolated and unhealthy life between the ages of two months and eleven months, but because of his first weeks in a healthy, enriched environment and an amazing set of genes, he developed into one of dogdom's great ambassadors.

Luke adored people and dogs, and he tolerated just about anything from just about anybody. I hope you're as lucky as I was; I can't imagine ever again having a dog as noble as Luke. But for every dog like him, there are a hundred whose deprivation early in life results in their inability to tolerate change or stimulation of any kind. Perhaps the Australian Shepherd you rescued, the one who lived in a cage for three years pumping out puppies in a puppy mill, may never be able to compete in agility despite her phenomenal physical skills. The retired racing Greyhound you adopted might not be able to tolerate the cheerful pandemonium that goes along with four teenagers in the house. The show prospect who never left her spotless kennel until eight months of age may never be comfortable around unfamiliar men. I'm not trying to talk you out of adopting a dog who had a tough beginning in life. The world is full of dear, damaged dogs who desperately need homes. Lots of wonderful people rescue them, and those people deserve our heartfelt appreciation. If you want to join their ranks, my hat's off to you. In spite of the importance of early development, patience and hard work can go a long way to rehabilitate dogs damaged in their youth by unsuitable environments.

Just remember that this might not be the dog who wins you that obedience competition title you've always wanted. Victory with a dog who's been severely damaged by a neglectful upbringing is more likely to include finally enabling her to tolerate a house sitter when you go on vacation (rather than destroy the house or leap through the second-story window), or teaching him to walk politely down the street without leaping and snarling toward every dog he sees. Don't feel like a failure if you can't make a social butterfly out of the dog you rescued from a nightmarish beginning. Giving him a kind, loving home and helping him to relax enough to nap in your lap are achievements in their own right. If you can manage them, you deserve much more than a blue ribbon and a silver chalice. However, if what you absolutely have to have right now is a stable, easygoing dog who is adaptable to a changing environment, then you'd be wise to take this chapter to heart.[6]

Funny I'd use that phrase, "to heart," when writing a chapter about the brain. I doubt that the decision I made about bringing home Bo Peep was actually made in the chambers of my heart. That organ was too busy thumping away, pumping blood to the energy-hungry nerve cells inside my head. We may speak of the heart as the center of our emotions, but as we all know, emotions actually come from our brains. The brain is a kind of emotional master of ceremonies, and this is, yet again, something that we share with our dogs. Learning a bit more about how the brain works, once it is fully formed, can go a long way toward helping us understand the emotional connection between us and our dogs.

BRAIN BASICS

The complexity of a fully formed brain, whether it's yours or your dog's, is absolutely astounding. A piece of your brain no bigger than a grain of sand has 100,000 nerve cells in it. Each microscopically small nerve cell, called a neuron, is still big enough to connect with thousands of other neurons. (It is these vital connections that are lacking in animals raised in sterile environments.) In total, your brain contains over 100 billion neurons, with 10 trillion connections between them. Heaven only knows how many of those connections are being used as you read this, but if you tried counting them one by one, you couldn't finish in a lifetime.

Speaking of lifetimes, it would take forty-four thousand of them to count the sum total of *all* the connections between nerve cells in your brain. I don't know about you, but facts like this evoke the same feeling in me that I get when I look up at the stars at night. I don't care how many neurons we have, there aren't enough to handle the concept of 10 trillion, much less that of infinity.

All these connections allow the brain to act as a filter, a switch-

---

6. Keep in mind I've been talking about dogs from severely deprived environments. Many dogs from "rescue groups" are as stable and benevolent as the Dalai Lama.

board, a maintenance crew, and a board of directors. It weighs a total of three pounds in a 150-pound human, and about a fifth of a pound in the head of a Beagle. The brains of humans are huge compared to our body weight. The brain of a gorilla weighs only a third as much as ours, while a gorilla's body weight is two to three times that of a human. Even a whale's brain weighs only about four times as much as ours, when a whale's body weight can be more than four hundred times greater than ours. No doubt about it, our brains are phenomenally large. Even if your dog is a genius, his brain is proportionately tiny compared to yours. No matter how smart your dog is and how much you love him, the fact of the matter is that your brain, in some important ways, is different from his. These differences are important, and we'll talk more about them in a later chapter.

However, for all the differences between the size and function of our brains and the brains of our dogs, the similarities between them are amazing. Canine and human brains are made up of the same basic structures and they function the same way. The brains of all animals are made up of neurons, their tangle of connections, and a supportive scaffolding that provides structure and nourishment to the hardworking nerve cells. It turns out that it takes a lot of energy to keep all this activity running smoothly. It also turns out that the energy required to power your brain has an important effect on emotions.

THE HUNGRY BRAIN

Brains are energy guzzlers. In humans, they use 25 percent of the body's oxygen and many of the body's available calories. This hunger for energy means that blood flow is increased to areas of the brain that are actively working, as the blood brings fuel to the busy nerve cells. Thanks to new technologies like PET scans and fMRIs, we can track changes in blood flow, observe which neurons are active or passive, and thus know which parts of the brain are engaged when you're petting your dog, listening to music, or watching a monster in a scary movie.[7]

7. PET stands for "positron emission tomography," fMRI for "functional magnetic resonance imaging."

That ability has radically changed our understanding of how the brain works. Much of our new knowledge about brain function is based upon the brain's hunger for fuel and upon our ability to observe how energy is distributed while the brain is working (which, of course, is all the time).

The energy requirements of the brain are impressive. Our brains are indeed remarkable things, but they come at a high price. Think of them as the SUVs of organs, requiring disproportionately large amounts of energy compared with the rest of the body. No wonder we get so tired when we're learning something new. How many times have you said you weren't "physically tired," you were "mentally tired"? It turns out that both states are physical in nature, part and parcel of the same basic process, you just feel them in different ways. It all gets down to "Energy in, energy out"—if too much goes out because your brain is working harder than usual, you feel it in your mind rather than your muscles.[8]

This is vital information for those of us who need an arctic outfitter to walk our dogs in January, or who have high-energy dogs of herding breeds and yet no flock of sheep in the garage. You can spend a half an hour teaching your dog some new tricks and get almost the same effect as if you've walked her for an hour. Keep it lighthearted and fun, use lots of positive reinforcement, and try hard to motivate your dog to want to learn. Of course, your dog is still going to need some physical exercise, but the combination of the two will go a long way to keep Maggie from munching on your couch or bouncing off your walls.

The downside of all this is that your dog can get mentally overtired, just like you can. Remember those frowning dogs we talked about in the last chapter, the ones whose faces signaled that they were running out of patience? I've seen hundreds of them, I'm afraid, dogs who had been doing wonderfully at the family picnic or during the New Year's Eve party, but ruined the occasion by snapping at someone as the festivities were winding down. Many of these dogs were good dogs who, I believe, didn't want to hurt anyone. They were simply exhausted, not just from

---

8. If this is all true, and I am assured that it is, why can't we lose weight by just thinking a lot? Surely I should be no bigger than a size 3 by now. . . . Joking aside, this is a complex topic, but take my word for it that mental exercise is an important component of a well-exercised dog.

running or swimming all day long, but from the constant stimulation of being in a crowd of people. The dogs simply ran out of steam, and ultimately out of patience. Keep in mind that your dog needs you to protect him from mental as well as physical exhaustion. It's a wise and loving owner who gives his dog a break long before she's had enough.

TWO KINDS OF TRAFFIC

All mammals, including you and your dog, use a combination of electricity and chemistry to move signals around inside our heads. A neuron that's been "turned on" by something—from the touch of a nose to the sound of a bark—sends an electrical signal down its connections toward other neurons. In a human, the sum total of all this mental electricity is the equivalent of a ten-watt light bulb, a pretty impressive amount if you think about it.

Electricity isn't enough to move information through the brain, because the threadlike extensions of neurons that stretch toward other neurons don't physically connect. The gap between them is tiny, but electricity can't jump across it. Chemicals called neurotransmitters bridge the gap, moving through fluid from the end of one threadlike connection to another. As soon as the connecting fiber receives these chemicals, electricity takes over again. It moves the signal through the next neuron and down another connecting fiber, until it comes to another gap, where the neurotransmitters take over again. This alternation of electricity and chemistry is happening right now, billions of times, at blinding speeds, in both you and your dog. No wonder we can get tired just sitting at a desk all day.

The chemical messengers that travel between neurons do far more than move signals from one cell to another. They are vital to how you and your dog feel at any given time. In the last thirty years, we've learned that neurotransmitters, such as serotonin and dopamine, have a profound affect on our emotions. Serotonin acts to dampen feelings of fearful arousal, and is associated with the experience of pleasure and contentment. That's why so many depressed people benefit from mood-elevating drugs that increase the amount of serotonin available to the cells in their brains. Dopamine plays an equally important role in feelings of pleasure (and addictions). The roles these chemicals play are complex; many of them have complicated job descriptions that we haven't begun to sort out. Dopamine, for example, is vital to your brain's ability to focus your attention—its release causes all your brain cells to cease firing for a microsecond, and then prepares them to fire in anticipation of an important event—but it's also a key player in feelings of reward and satisfaction.

Neurotransmitters aren't the only chemicals in your brain that affect mood. Hormones move through the bloodstream rather than between the cells of our brains, and have a profound effect on emotion. For example, the release of the hormone oxytocin causes the uterine contractions that are vital during the birth of all mammals, but it also affects our emotional state. As we'll see in more detail in a later chapter, if you feel all warm and soft when you pick up a puppy, it's because your body is being flooded with a wave of oxytocin. Surges of oxytocin lead to strong feelings of love and attachment, and are so important that mothers who don't produce them can have problems bonding with their children.[9]

We'll talk more about neurotransmitters and hormones in the chapters about fear, anger, happiness, and love, but for now what's important is that these same chemicals play an equivalent role in the brain and the body of your dog. The evidence is overwhelming that other mammals, including our dogs, produce the same chemicals in their brains, and that these chemicals have much the same effect on them as they do on us. Indeed, our knowledge about the function of these substances comes largely from work done on other mammals. Healthy levels of serotonin have been found to inhibit aggression and encourage friendly social behavior in many species of animals, including humans, nonhuman primates, and rats. Sheep who have been given a drug that blocks the action of oxytocin reject their own lambs as soon as they are born. Dopamine plays an important role in addictive behavior in rats and monkeys, just as it does in humans.

Keep this in mind when someone argues to you that dogs don't have emotions. Not only do dogs show the same changes in facial ex-

---

9. Some people find this connection between a hormone and a feeling upsetting, as if the existence of a chemical basis of love demeans the emotion. To me it's yet another example of the wonder of biology, and how we have to stop thinking of our brains, our emotions, and our bodies as separate.

pression and posture that humans do, but their internal brain chemistry appears to parallel ours as well. The chemistry that controls our emotions is found in similar contexts and similar areas of the brain in dogs. Oxytocin appears to have the same effect on dogs as it does on us—not only stimulating uterine contractions but also facilitating bonding and nurturance. There is a growing body of research that correlates certain types of aggression in dogs with low levels of serotonin; this evidence replicates some of the findings in human neuropsychology. Hyperanxious dogs appear to suffer the same chemical imbalances that extremely anxious people have. Of course, I'm not arguing that dogs and humans have exactly the same emotions, or that they experience them in exactly the same way. But, as our ability to understand the biology of emotion increases, it is becoming increasingly clear that, in many ways, dogs may be more like us than they are different from us.

NAVIGATING THE BRAIN

The basic structure of your brain is also similar to the structure of your dog's. Both humans and dogs have brains that come in three main sections: (1) the hindbrain, comprising the brainstem and cerebellum, which keeps our lungs breathing and our bodies aligned in space; (2) the midbrain, which regulates our emotions and memory formation; and (3) the forebrain, made up of two cerebral hemispheres covered with a thin film of cells called the cortex. It's this area of the brain that we think of as the center of thought and decision making, and, not surprisingly, it's this area that is most different in people and dogs. Of course, things are much more complicated than that, but it's still helpful to start with the basics, and the basics are something we all share with our dogs.

No matter what you and your dog are doing right now, the brainstems sitting atop your spinal cords are efficiently sending out signals to the lungs and the heart. Breathe! Beat faster! Pretty important stuff, that. Imagine if you had to stay up at night to tell your lungs to breathe. "I'd forget my head if it wasn't attached" is true for many of us. Good thing our heads *are* attached, or we'd get too busy to remember to breathe. If we could misplace our brainstems as we do our keys, natural selection would have gotten rid of us a long time ago.

We tend to forget these basic functions, instead thinking of the brain only as the center of thought and problem solving. We don't call someone brainy because his heart and lungs work so well, but without these ancient areas of the brain, you and your dog wouldn't make it through the night. Ever wonder why dogs who like to hunt small animals grab them by the back of the neck and shake them? That's where the brainstem is, and serious damage to this part of the brain is fatal, pure and simple. It's the reason my blood ran cold when a couple told me that their dog had grabbed a child by the back of the neck and wouldn't let go. At the time, they were relieved that the dog hadn't harmed the child's face. I was sick with the knowledge that this could have been a killing bite, or could have paralyzed the child for life if the spinal cord had been severed. In seventeen years, I've had only two other cases where a dog bit a child at the back of the head and shook the neck. In one case, the child made it through with minor injuries. In the other, the child was killed.[10]

Besides regulating vital body processes, the ancient part of the brain also contains an area that coordinates movement: the cerebellum. When you reach down to pet your dog, your cerebellum is the stage manager that keeps things running smoothly. When you stop petting, and your dog nudges you for more, his cerebellum coordinates the movement. It's not surprising that this primitive part of the brain is integrally involved in movement, because it's movement that created the need for brains in the first place. Animals wouldn't need a brain if all they have to do is "just react" (as claimed by the neurosurgeon mentioned in Chapter 1). Plants "just react" all the time. For example, acacia trees release airborne chemicals that signal danger if a browsing antelope chomps on their leaves. The surrounding trees of the same species receive the message and quickly change their internal chemistry so that their leaves become less tasty.

It's movement from one place to another that requires a brain. If an animal is going to move, it has to make choices that immobile animals don't. What is it about to move into? Should it move this way, or that way? The proof is in an animal called a sea squirt, which has a brain and nerve cord while it's swimming around in the ocean. When it matures and permanently anchors itself to a rock, its brain is absorbed and

10. I'll talk more about this tragic case in a later chapter.

digested by the rest of its body. No movement; no brain necessary. Surely those of us who have spent just a little too long lying on the couch in front of some tawdry television show can relate to a lack of motion leading to brain absorption.

IT'S MIDNIGHT. DO YOU KNOW WHERE YOUR TOES ARE? (YOUR DOG DOES!)

It's a good thing that these ancient areas of the brain coordinate many of your movements, for it ensures that much of what your body is doing is controlled outside the realm of conscious thought. Your brain knows exactly where your toes and elbows are every instant of your life, but you're not consciously aware of this information unless you go out of your way to be. A circuit of signals runs between your muscles, your inner ear, and your cerebellum to keep you aligned in space, including being in the position you're in right now, without the need to think about it.[11]

Imagine being conscious of the location of every part of your body every moment of every day. Just thinking about it is tiring, and for good reason. Decision making and conscious thought take place primarily in the "newer" part of your brain, the cortex, which is famous for being an energy hog that requires a disproportionate amount of fuel to run. Better, then, to save the cortex for things that can't be relegated to the cerebellum, and not bother our pretty little heads unnecessarily. The cerebellum acts like the autopilot system in a plane, enabling us to "fly" without consciously monitoring every little movement, every single second.

It's this phenomenon that explains why teaching your dog new tricks can do almost as much to tire her out as taking her on a walk. When she's learning something new, she can't run on autopilot out of her energy-conserving cerebellum. She has to use her brain's energy-guzzling cortex, so a little bit of something new can tire her out as much as a long walk around the neighborhood. If that's the only thing you learn from this book, it still might be worthwhile, because so many of our dogs have excess energy that gets them into trouble. We all

11. One unlucky man who had nerve damage to this system is now able to function only if he can see his limbs and consciously direct their movement. If he's in complete darkness he crumples to the floor and can't get up.

know that dogs need exercise, but it's easy to forget that they need mental as well as "physical" exercise. (I put "physical" in quotes, because, as I mentioned earlier, mental processes are just as physical as those that take place in our muscles, even though we don't tend to think of them that way.)

Chris and Custer were a great pair, both young, healthy males who reveled in playing ball, running hard, and relaxing together on their old, musty couch. I met Custer first, all eighty pounds of him, lunging his way toward me, dragging his human behind him. "Isn't he great?" Chris beamed. And he was—Custer greeted me with a full-body wag, squinty eyes, and the open, relaxed mouth of a dog who loves people. After Custer and I had a love fest on the living room floor, I asked Chris why he'd requested an appointment.

"Well, he's a great dog, but he's not very good at listening to me. I've taken him to obedience class, but he still won't sit or stay when I ask him to, and he's too big to get too much older without some manners." I agreed, since Custer was only eight months old and already capable of flattening anyone smaller than a Green Bay Packer defensive end without even trying. "Why don't you ask him to sit and stay for me," I asked, "so I can get an idea of how things are going?" Chris asked Custer to sit, and sit he did—at least for about half a second, until Chris said "stay." As soon as he did, Custer leaped up, kissed Chris's face, and joyfully danced around his owner. They repeated this exercise three times, and each time, Custer sat for an instant, and then jumped to his feet as soon as Chris said "stay." However, when I tried it, Custer not only sat as directed, he stayed in place for a solid three to four seconds before I released him. A stay that short might not seem impressive, but given Custer's propensity to hurtle into the air as soon as he heard the word "stay," it seemed like a significant improvement.

Certainly, Chris thought so. "I've been trying for five months to get him to do that. How the heck did you get him to stay still?" It would've been great fun to answer that I've always had a special way with dogs (not true), and that even as a child my friends called me the "dog whisperer" (even less true), but the answer was far more mundane. The only difference between Chris and me was the movement of our bodies when we said "stay." Like most people, Chris hadn't learned to pay attention to the movements of his body when he was saying "stay." When he did, he unconsciously moved

backward a few inches and ever so slightly bowed forward with his torso.
That was exactly the same set of movements I'd seem him perform earlier
when he called Custer to come. Custer was doing what he was "told," but
was paying attention to Chris's body, not his voice. Once Chris learned to
match his movements to his voice, Custer was able to sort out "stay" from
"come" in a couple of days.

THE SPORT OF DOG TRAINING

The efficiency of the cerebellum, which allows many of our actions to be unconscious, has a price, and our dogs are often the ones who pay it. The fact that we can be oblivious to the position and movements of our body makes life difficult for our dogs. Living with aliens who speak another language, our dogs are desperately watching our bodies to get information about what we expect of them. Because we usually aren't paying conscious attention to how all our body parts are moving, we send confusing and inconsistent signals out on a daily basis, while our dogs have smoke coming out of their ears trying to figure us out. As I wrote in *The Other End of the Leash,* the biggest difference between dog lovers and professional dog trainers is that the pros know exactly what their bodies are doing when they're working with a dog, so they don't confuse their dogs with random and inconsistent movements. That's why I think of dog training as a science, a sport, and an art—and it's the *sport* part that everyone can learn if they are willing to practice a little bit.

If you want to be less confusing to your dog (and have a better-behaved dog as a result), put your cerebellum on hold for a while and use your cortex to monitor your movements. Focus your attention for a few weeks on how you move in space when you're working with your dog. You could even have someone videotape you, as suggested in the first chapter. The reason it's so shocking to see ourselves on video for the first time is that so much of how we move is out of the realm of conscious thought. Your friends might know that you put your hand over your mouth or play with your hair while you talk, but you probably don't.[12] Be assured, though, that your dog does, because she's been

12. If you do watch yourself for the first time on tape, I suggest that while watching you chant, "My friends see this all the time and they still love me. My friends see this all the time and they still love me."

watching you like a hawk for years. When you think about it, why *should* we know what we look like from the outside in? How could our brains record what we look like from ten feet away? That would be like asking a camera to take a picture of itself.

There's tremendous variation in people's awareness of their own body movements. If you don't believe me, just go to a beginning family dog training class. Some people can quickly switch their attention to how they are moving and, with little effort, start giving their dogs clear and consistent visual signals. Others have no awareness of how they're moving their body, no matter how hard they try to focus on it. Lesson after lesson you can coach them, and lesson after lesson they can't stop a hand or a leg from moving forward at the wrong time. It can be frustrating to coach someone like this, although surely not as frustrating as being the person whose body seems to have a mind of its own. But everyone can learn to increase their awareness of how their body moves. It just takes some people longer than others—a good example of the fact that all brains have the same general structure and function, but every one of them works a bit differently. Don't despair if you're slower than others to increase your body awareness. You may well be more adept at some other aspect of dog training.

IT'S GOOD FOR OLD DOGS TO LEARN NEW TRICKS

Whether you need a little coaching or a lot, don't feel too bad about your initial lack of awareness of your body's movements—your dog has the same problem. He, too, has an inner ear and cerebellum that work together to tell the primitive part of his brain where his body parts are in space. Just like you, he isn't always aware of where his body parts are. Perhaps that's why it's so much easier to teach a dog an action than a position. Say, "Sit," and most dogs will behave as though it means: "Go to your owner, face her, and move part of your body down toward the ground." Those are actions controlled by the cortex, not postures controlled by the unconscious cerebellum. Say, "Sit," to a sitting dog, and there's a good chance he'll lie down—which suggests that the signal relates to an action he makes consciously, rather than a posture he's in that he's not really thinking about.

There are other examples of both dogs and people being unaware of their bodies' positions in space. Many dogs behave as though they have no idea of the location of their back feet. Of course, they couldn't function if part of their brain didn't know, but put a novice dog on a narrow wooden beam in an agility course and he's likely to carefully place his front paws in the center of the beam, and then let his back paws go helter-skelter, sometimes straight off the beam and into thin air.[13] Most of the time, dogs don't have to think about where to put their back feet—following in the general direction of the front feet is usually all that's necessary, so that's a reasonable thing to delegate to the inner ear and cerebellum.

It might be good for your dog to become aware of her body in new ways. We know that one way to keep human brains healthy is to exercise them, by asking the brain and the body to learn new things. Although most of the connections between your brain cells are formed early in life, we've recently learned that you can form new links among neurons by engaging in activities that are new to you. We're advised, as we age, to do novel things like use our nondominant hand more often than usual, learn to dance, or learn to play the piano—all actions that engage both our thinking cortex and our cerebellum. There's no biological reason to believe that learning's not equally beneficial to your dog. If your dog is older, you probably won't want to introduce her to the athletic rigors of agility, but dogs of almost any age can learn new tricks. At fifteen, my oldest dog, Pip, loves learning new tricks. She may be hard of hearing and a bit wobbly on the stairs, but she just learned to lay her head down on the ground between her front paws when I say "Bummer," and I swear she gets as much of a kick out of it as I do.

EMOTION CENTRAL

As we've already seen, the brain is a complicated, integrated piece of work, and all parts of it seem to play some role in our experience of emotion. However, there's little question that the part of the brain called the midbrain is the command center of emotion in both you and

---

13. Agility is a great sport in which dogs run through a course of jumps, tunnels, and weave poles, competing against others for a clean run in the fastest time.

your dog. Nestled between the cerebellum and the wrinkled lobes of the cerebral hemispheres and cortex, this area of the brain has a profound effect on how you and your dog experience the world. The structures within the midbrain make up what's called the limbic system, which drives most of your emotions. Your eyes and ears send information to your brain about what's happening, but the small structure called the amygdala assigns emotional significance to that information. Did you just see an aggressive dog running toward your own? "Oh, no!" signals your amygdala as soon as it receives the information, and relays the emotions of fear and arousal to another structure in the limbic system, the hippocampus. This area integrates the information with stored memories of other events (perhaps a dog who looked much the same attacked your dog last year), and then passes the filtered and emotion-laden information to your decision-making brain, the cortex. In a fraction of a second, electricity sizzles and chemicals rush between millions of your brain cells, concluding with signals to your muscles to take action.

All this happens in the blink of an eye, but it still takes some time for the information to be moved from your body's sensory systems, through several different areas of your brain and back to the muscles of your body with instructions for action. But what if you have very little time, as little as half a second? That's when another important actor in the limbic system kicks in: the hypothalamus. It's called "the brain of the brain" because it regulates so many of your body's functions without involving your energy-hungry cortex. Once it receives information, the hypothalamus can directly signal your adrenal gland for "fight or flight," while skipping the circuitry that runs up to the rest of your brain. Years ago I was bitten by a dog who lunged directly at my chest. One moment I was walking past him, and the next I was watching him bite back and forth along my forearm, which had appeared as if by magic in front of my chest. What's relevant here is that I couldn't have had time to make a conscious decision to move my forearm to protect my body. It just happened, thanks to the quick work of my hypothalamus, my adrenal glands, and my cerebellum.

All the structures in the limbic system play a central role in the experience of emotion in both you and your dog. The limbic system is where neurotransmitters are most concentrated, acting in conjunction with structures like the amygdala to control your emotional life. Your dog has exactly the same set of structures, permeated with the same set of neurotransmitters. This part of the brain is commonly called the mammalian brain, because it is first seen in mammals and is absent in reptiles. It may not have been around for as many millions of years as the brainstem and the cerebellum, but it's been around for quite a while, and is considered a relatively primitive set of structures.[14] It is *not* the part of the brain that is unique to humans; we share it with other mammals, including the one who may be lying at your feet as you read this book.

This is yet another reason why biology suggests that dogs *do* experience emotions. Surely they don't experience them exactly as we do—the cognitive component of emotion, which we'll talk about later, makes our experience of emotion somewhat different from our dogs'—but to argue that they don't share the basics of fear, anger, and joy is to argue against biology as we understand it.

WE ALL PRODUCE OUR OWN REALITY SHOWS

So far we've been talking about the similarities between human and canine brains, but some parts of our brains are profoundly different, and they deserve our attention as well. The biggest difference between your brain and that of your dog is in the last major section of the mammalian brain: the big gray cerebral hemispheres. These hemispheres, in humans as wrinkled as a wizened old woman, are covered by a thin layer of cells called the cortex.[15] This is where we do most of our thinking and planning, and it's also the feature that makes our brains so disproportionately large. It's the cortex that ultimately receives information from the sensory system, and that informs the brain what it's seeing, hearing, smelling, and feeling. It's in the cortex that each of us constructs our perception of the world around us, and because each of us has a different cortex, each of us lives in a slightly different world.

That's partly because the brain of every mammal, including humans and dogs, is designed to perceive and react to only some of the in-

14. "A while" means since about 225 million years ago, when mammals first made an appearance.

15. The word "cortex" means "bark"—the kind that wraps around trees, not the kind your dog makes.

formation available to it. Just as reality shows on television are highly edited, so that they present only a portion of what really happened, our brains are always editing out information and keeping only a portion of it for processing. What your brain tells you about the world around you is not a complete picture. It has been edited to keep you from being so overloaded with information that you have a mental meltdown. Even 100 billion brain cells aren't enough to process every single piece of information available to you. Partly on the basis of genetics, partly on the basis of experience, your brain edits out things judged to be unimportant—perhaps the sound of the fan you've had in your home for three years, or the sight of the marks where your dog chewed on the table leg when he was a pup. Better to expend your limited brainpower to listen for the sound of your dog pacing because he has diarrhea, or to notice that his water bowl is empty.

Because of the editing function of the brain, every person, and every dog, sees the world a little differently. This is why law enforcement officials struggle to get accurate descriptions at crime scenes. It's not just that people aren't particularly observant of the kind of details that become important in crimes, it's that we actually record different things. Our brains are making continuous split-second decisions about what to attend to and what to ignore, and each brain makes a slightly different set of decisions. Some of those decisions are driven by emotional memories stored deep in the limbic system, and can vary greatly depending on what has happened to an individual during his or her lifetime. Some are based on genetics, and on how the individual is hardwired before and after birth. One dog will respond to the approach of a stranger as a life-threatening experience, while another interprets exactly the same event as a party about to happen. Both you and your dog, consciously and unconsciously, make decisions and judgments millions of times a day, about what should be filtered out, about what deserves your attention, and about how it should be evaluated. Because of that, no matter how close we are to our dogs, we'll never really live in quite the same world as they do.[16]

There's another reason that each of us lives in our own reality, and

16. This is, of course, also true of you and your parents, your partner, and your absolute best human friend in the entire world.

it's particularly important in comparisons between different species. Not only do our brains filter out different kinds of information, they receive different information in the first place. Though we share the same planet, the sensory systems of animals vary so much that we might as well be living in different worlds. Bees can see bull's-eye-shaped ultraviolet lines on flower petals that direct them to the pollen, when all we see is the pretty red color of the petal (and dogs can't distinguish the red flower from the green grass because they're red/green color-blind). In pitch darkness, bats navigate by bouncing sound waves off objects in the landscape: dogs would be using their noses to navigate, and people would be standing stock still, unable to locate much of anything at all. Some fish can sense electromagnetic currents, of which people (and, most probably, dogs) are completely unaware. These comparisons are more than just intellectually interesting in a golly-gee sort of way. They are relevant to our shared experience of emotion, because it turns out that many of our senses are closely connected to our emotions.

Like us, dogs use sight, sound, smell, taste, and touch to interpret the world around them, but, as we all know, they experience each of those senses differently from us. Vision is the most important source of information to primates, so, not surprisingly, we humans devote an inordinate amount of our sensory cortex to it. A casual look at our language illustrates the importance of sight to us. We say, "I *see* what you mean," and "*Look!* What I'm trying to tell you is . . ." Vision is such an integral part of how we see the world that I've inadvertently referred to it twice in the last few lines: "a casual *look* at our language" and "how we *see* the world." I didn't use those words on purpose to make my point. I didn't even notice that I'd written them until I reread the paragraph. I used them because that's the way we describe the world, through the principal sensory system of primates: vision.

THROUGH YOUR NOSE ONLY

Dogs rely on vision too, but if a dog were writing this book surely she'd be writing "how we smell the world" and "Sniff, I *told* you never to get into the garbage when your humans are home!" We all know that a dog's sense of smell puts ours to shame. It's been estimated that dogs can use their noses a thousand to ten thousand times better than we can. We may be structured to have impressive powers of abstraction and problem solving, but dogs are the ultimate smell machines. Not only do they have a nose designed to take in as many scent molecules as possible (can you move your nose from right to left?), they have a much larger surface area inside the nose to absorb scent molecules. Once the smells are received, they travel to the sensory cortex, which is proportionately huge in dogs. Their ability to experience the world through their noses means we'll never really know what the world is like to them, because so much of what they perceive is beyond us. Think of using scent to locate the one stick, among dozens of others, that you picked up and threw for your dog last week. Your dog can do it, even after the stick has been lying in the sun and the rain for six days. Dogs are so good at finding and identifying smells that we simply can't imagine how the world appears to them.

This difference in perception goes beyond dogs' ability to smell tiny quantities of something that would be imperceptible to us. Dogs can distinguish *between* scents to an extraordinary degree. When you pet a damp, dirty dog, you can easily recognize the smell of "wet dog," but you can't separate out the smell of the water from the smell of the mud on his paws and the dander in his coat and the scent glands behind his tail. And when you walk into someone's house for dinner and are overwhelmed with the good smell of homemade chicken soup, you smell chicken soup—but your dog smells chicken and carrots and onions, each as separate as they are when you look into the pot. If you see five objects on a blanket, your brain doesn't perceive them as a mixture of images, it sees them as six separate things: five objects and a blanket. That's what scientists think dogs can do with smells, separate them out, each from the others, rather than blending them together. We're so good at separating things visually that we take it for granted, but imagine being able to do that with smells. What a different world it would be.

Comparatively pathetic though our olfactory abilities are, scent still plays an important role in our lives. Much of the information about scent that we are able to perceive is relayed not to the conscious part of our brain, but to that ancient limbic system that drives emotions, mood, and memory. That's true for both dogs and us, and it means that the sense of smell has more effect on humans than you might think. Pheromones, a category of scent molecules that we take in but aren't conscious of, can change our sexual appetites, cause a man's beard to grow faster, help mothers recognize their babies' T-shirts merely by sniffing them, and cause men to rate women as more attractive.

In both people and dogs, the sense of smell is more closely linked with emotion than any other of the senses besides touch. Except for touch, smell is the most primitive sense, and its connections go directly to the more primitive, and emotional, parts of your brain. We've all had experiences in which we were flooded with emotion when we smelled the perfume worn by an old flame, or caught a whiff of Grandma's cinnamon buns. This is because, unlike the nerves that relay information about sight and sound, the olfactory nerves go straight to the emotional part of your brain, bypassing all the other departments usually visited by our sensory perceptions before they go to the limbic system. This is true of dogs, too, and given their amazing abilities to use their noses, I often wonder if we could be using scent more effectively to communicate with our dogs.

One way in which many of us are doing that already is by using food as reinforcement in training. Food is a great motivator to both people and dogs and is a great way to teach dogs both basic obedience, like "Sit" and "Stay," and advanced tricks, like rolling themselves up in a blanket when you say "Go to bed." This isn't just because food tastes good; in fact, dogs don't have taste buds as sophisticated as ours. It's also because food has strong odors associated with it, and the sense of smell is directly linked with the areas associated with pleasure (or disgust) in the limbic system. Indeed, the smell of food is so closely linked with primitive emotional centers that neurologists believe the limbic system first evolved as a way of evaluating whether food was good for you—or would make you sick. Good smells equaled good food, which made you feel good. Bad smells equaled bad food, which made you feel bad. Simple as that.

Now, of course, things aren't so simple, but both you and your dog are still strongly affected by what you smell. If your dog learns to associate the good smells of food with sitting when you ask, then you're teaching his brain to feel good when he listens to you. This is one of the reasons you can use food to get a behavior started, and then drop it out once the behavior has become a habit. You don't need to carry dog treats around in your pocket for the rest of your dog's life, because you've wired his brain to associate listening to you with feeling good. If, on the other hand, you train primarily using force (perhaps you use a leash correction to make your dog sit), you're missing out on a remarkable opportunity to condition a primal, positive association between obedience to you and his reaction to good food. Additionally, if you use force you're probably stimulating the fear centers in his limbic system, so that he learns to associate you with the potential of danger. It's a shame how common it is for people to use force and coercion on their dogs, when there's no question that positive techniques, besides being more humane, are simply more effective.

One of the important roles of the limbic system is not just to assign an emotional state to an event, it's to record those associations in an immediately accessible place. Even though we may not be as good at using our noses as dogs are, we can relate to the strong connection between smell and emotional memories. Perhaps the scent of pines brings back the happiness you felt every summer when your parents took you camping. You might notice a perfume you haven't smelled in years, and remember your first love as an adolescent. Of course, these associations are not always good ones. The smell of champagne brings back the day I combined my first hangover with my first sailboat ride on the open ocean. Forty years later, all I need is one sniff of champagne and my stomach begins pitching like a ship in a storm.

I've always wondered whether the relationship between smell, memory, and emotion explains a confusing kind of case related to dog-dog aggression. Behaviorists see a small but consistent percentage of aggression cases in which dogs appear to be acting like Dr. Jekyll and Mr. Hyde. At first, they send out all the signals of friendliness while greeting another dog—wagging from the shoulders back, mouth open, eyes relaxed. This continues until the dogs have greeted one another for a second or two, and then our previously slap-happy dog explodes, growling, lunging, and sometimes attacking and injuring the other dog. You can imagine how confusing and frightening this is to owners (not to mention the other dog), and I've been perplexed by it for years. I have an inkling that it's related to smell. The only pattern I can find in these cases is that the dog's friendly demeanor always changes right after he or she has gotten a good whiff of the other dog's anal-genital region. That suggests the dog's reaction is related to smell, although I'm not sure this hypothesis will help us to understand it better. We have so much to learn about the world of scent that our dogs live in—we don't even know what information they obtain when they sniff one another, or when they smell urine deposited by others as scent marks. Can they sense the emotional state of a dog from his urine? It's a reasonable possibility, given how the body's chemistry and physiology change as our emotions change, but we don't really know.

We do know that there is another relationship between smell and emotions that doesn't rely on memory or any kind of learning. Certain odors seem to have inherent effects on us, no matter what our early experience. The scents from the oils of some plants appear to improve our mood by changing our brain's chemistry so that it produces proteins that tend to make us feel good. Lavender, for example, is known for producing feelings of calm and well-being in those who smell it; even babies in nurseries sleep better and longer when the scent of lavender is in the air.

There's no reason that scent wouldn't have an equally important effect on your dog. One practical application of the relationship between smells and emotions is the use of DAP. "DAP" stands for "dog appeasing pheromone," and it seems to be useful in improving the mood in some dogs who are anxious about being left home alone or are afraid of thunderstorms. It is a replicate of the pheromone produced between the mammary glands of a lactating dam, and is presumably received by the pups when they're experiencing the happy feelings of getting a good meal. I've had clients who reported great success with it. Others couldn't detect any difference at all in their dog's behavior, so don't expect miracles if you try it. But it's clear that the relationship between smell, emotion, and canine behavior is an important one that we need to learn more about.

We could talk about the senses of a dog for a long time, but that's already been done beautifully in other books, such as Stanley Coren's *How Dogs Think*. That book is a great resource for how all of your senses compare with your dog's, and I highly recommend it. What I want to emphasize here is that there are many similarities between the brains of people and the brains of dogs. We share ancient systems found in thousands of species to keep the machine of the body running as efficiently as possible. We both have structures, shared by all mammals, that mediate fear, anger, and joy, as well as primal drives like hunger and sexual energy. Our brains are designed to filter sensory information coming from the environment, to process that information and compare it with memories stored in the midbrain before deciding how to respond. Certainly, our brains differ from those of our dogs in many ways—in the information that they take in, and in their abilities to form mental abstractions and to solve problems. These differences are important, but they don't override the fact that our brains and dogs' brains share much of their architecture and design. There is little question that the parts of our brains that mediate emotion are more similar in people and dogs than they are different. Your brain and the brain of the dog at your feet are amazing structures, fragile mazes of chemicals and electricity that are responsible for your fears, your occasional frustrations with each other, and the love that binds you together.

Bo Peep's leg never functioned very well, but her story ends happily nonetheless. She had used her forelegs and shoulders as a young pup, and the active pathways between them and her brain allowed her to develop tremendous strength in them. She'd flip her hips the way dogs do when they lie down, and pull herself forward with her massive front legs, dragging her hips behind her, her thick fur protecting her skin. She was amazingly fast and agile, and could scoot up the hill faster than I could. She lived happily with the sheep all her life, and I never lost an animal to dogs or coyotes again. Visitors would stop and stare dumbfounded when she flopped her way down the hill inside a flock of ewes, looking like some crazed white seal who had abandoned the ocean for green hills and the company of sheep.

She protected my flock for nine years and was as much a part of Redstart Farm as I was. She didn't know her hindquarters were supposed to work any differently than they did, and she remained sweet and cheerful her entire life. One afternoon, while working upstairs, I heard her alarm-barking and looked out the second-story window. Bo Peep had caught a large stray dog in the act of running off with my only male duck. While Uncle Bert the Stud Duck squawked and flapped his one free wing, Bo Peep streamed down the hill like frothy white water in a flood, picked up the intruding dog in her huge jaws, and shook him like a rat. She released him the moment he dropped Uncle Bert, and let him run away, yipping like a cartoon dog down the center line of the road. At first I had been frozen at the window in horror, but I finally ran down the stairs and flew out of the house to help. By the time I arrived, the dog had disappeared and Bo Peep was gently nudging Uncle Bert back toward the barn. She'd lick his injured wing, then nudge him toward the barn, let him walk a few shaky steps, then lick and nudge again. I stopped in my tracks, transfixed by their slow, dancelike procession.

Uncle Bert survived his injuries, but Bo Peep died a few years later of a hateful kind of cancer called hemangiosarcoma. I found her in a coma in the barn, carried her in a panic to the car and drove like a race car driver to the vet's office. She died, never having woken up, a few days later. Her death hit me so hard I attended a group counseling session for pet loss, where I passed around photographs and told her story to sympathetic listeners. I cried buckets for days on end, and finally planted a raft of white tulips in her honor. That's where the next big white dog on the farm got her name—Tulip, named after the flowers I watered with tears for Bo Peep.

It turned out to be the perfect name, because Tulip is the essence of springtime, year in and year out. She is playful and shiny-eyed and so athletic that in her youth she climbed my fences the way a fireman climbs a ladder. Just calling her name, "Twooooooooo-lip!" makes me smile. She and I visit Bo Peep's gravestone every day. For a while I didn't think there'd be room in my heart for another dog whose life was as big as Bo Peep's. Turns out I was wrong.

4

THE MANY FACES OF FEAR

By the time I met him, Blaze was in big trouble. He had a record of three serious bites, one for every year of his life. A strikingly handsome Border Collie, Blaze was owned by Father Murray, an eighty-year-old Irish priest straight out of central casting. They made quite a pair—Blaze with a generous ruff of black-and-white fur, Father Murray with dancing blue eyes, rosy cheeks, and an angelic sweetness that melted my heart the minute he walked into my office. But this wasn't going to be a fun consultation; I knew that before it started. A mutual friend had talked Father Murray into coming to see me, sick with worry about the future of both man and dog. The two adored each other, but Blaze had become so aggressive to visitors that no one could get out of their car in Father Murray's driveway without being bitten. Walking into the house was out of the question.

The problem was compounded by the fact that Father Murray was so hard of hearing I had to yell, even in my small office, so he could hear me. When visitors came to his isolated old house deep in the country, he couldn't hear the car drive up or the knocking on his door. His only clue that company had arrived was Blaze charging toward the window, barking so aggressively he became almost hysterical.

In short order, it became clear that Blaze was a danger to society. Even Father Murray was at risk, given the extremity of Blaze's behavior and the chance that he'd lash out at anyone in his frenzy. Father Murray would have done anything to rehabilitate Blaze, but the chance that he could manage a successful rehabilitation was almost nil. Blaze was a young, healthy dog, bred to work hard all day, with boundless energy that went in all the wrong directions. Father Murray may have been active for his age, but I'd be hard pressed to describe him as hearty or agile. His hearing problem and his isolation in the country complicated the situation. If he couldn't rehabilitate Blaze himself, the only alternatives were rehoming him or having him euthanized. I found myself forced to scream words difficult even to whisper—"I SAID, 'EUTHANIZE'"—desperately trying to communicate with this dear old man who loved his dog as much as life itself.

The thought of giving up Blaze devastated Father Murray. That's the only way I can describe it. He began to cry in that deep primal way we do when all our inhibitions have been overrun by emotion. I sat helpless at my desk while this dear old man sobbed in my office, until, in a classic case of emotion trumping logic, I offered to take Blaze and try to rehabilitate him myself. As soon as I said it, I knew it was crazy. Adding another dog into my already busy life was the last thing I needed. But I took Blaze home, wrapping my life and the life of my dogs around his rehabilitation for the next three months. I'm glad I did, although I've asked the office manager to carefully screen consultations with adorable, elderly priests for a while.

THE MANY FACES OF FEAR

Poor Blaze. There he was, terrifying visitors with his panicked barks and his flashing teeth, when all along he was terrified himself. Blaze was afraid of unfamiliar people, and rather than hide in the back of the house like some dogs, Blaze expressed his fear with that age-old "I'm going to get you before you get me" philosophy. Dogs like Blaze remind me of scraggly bearded hermits who threaten visitors with shotguns, in the belief that anyone unfamiliar must be dangerous.

Fear in dogs can be expressed in a multitude of ways, from cowering in the corner to lunging at visitors, but it's the emotion behind a multitude of behavioral problems. Like Blaze, lots of dogs behave problematically because they're afraid of people. Other dogs are afraid of members of their own species, and are defensively aggressive when encountering other dogs on neighborhood walks.[1] They may look scary

1. I'm using "aggressive" in the popular sense, when it labels any dog who growls, snaps, nips, or bites. Be aware, however, that the strict definition of "aggression" is an offensive [versus defensive] action coupled with "intent to cause harm," and thus does not include growling out of fear to try to defend yourself.

when they're barking and lunging, especially if their behavior is directed toward your own dog, but sometimes all that drama is just a desperate attempt to keep the other dog away.

While fear motivates some dogs to growl, snap, or bite, it causes others to melt into pathetic puddles, or to buzz up into panic-stricken whirling dervishes. Separation anxiety (the fear of being alone) and noise phobias can lead to some horrific behavioral problems in dogs. Missy the Weimaraner was so afraid to be left alone that she went through a plate-glass window and carved a road map of lacerations into her back. In ten short minutes, after a truck backfired on the adjacent highway, Frito the Golden Retriever did $10,000 worth of damage to his owner's apartment. The consequences of phobias in dogs are highly reminiscent of phobias in people, and are yet another reminder of how much of our emotional life we share with dogs.

Fear may cause a lot of problems in both species, but the good news is that there's a lot we can do to alleviate the problems caused by it. We can't cure every fear-related problem in dogs, any more than we can in people, but a little bit of knowledge can go a long way. That's why this chapter will begin (as will each of the chapters on three of our most primal emotions—fear, anger, and happiness) with information about the biology of the emotion. Next we'll talk about fear from three different perspectives: (1) *the genetics of fear*, and how some brains are hardwired to be overly reactive to the potential of danger; (2) *early development*, during which dogs can be programmed to be fearful of unfamiliar things or overreactive to stress; and (3) *learning and experience*, and how dogs can be traumatized just as people can.[2]

Each of these factors can influence how much fear an adult dog experiences, so it's useful to understand them if you want to understand fearful dogs. Fear is designed to be aversive, and it's an emotion most of us don't want our dogs to experience, except as part of learning to keep themselves safe. In this chapter we'll talk about the influence of each of the three factors, and in the next chapter we'll talk about practical and effective methods to treat behavior problems based on fear.

---

2. These three sources overlap to some degree, but our brains work best by dividing things into categories, so there's value in looking at them one at a time.

FEAR: DON'T LEAVE HOME WITHOUT IT

Surely fear must be the most universal of emotions, given its importance to survival. Without fear, even civilized urban dwellers wouldn't live to pass on any of their genes, because they'd stroll in front of buses and forget to lock their doors at night. People who experience little fear are at great risk: individuals born with no pain receptors in their skin have a hard time learning to be afraid of harmful things like fire and electricity, so they live far more dangerous lives than the rest of us.

Animals who don't feel fear aren't going to live long enough to reproduce: it's as simple as that. The value of this emotion is evident in studies in which mice have had their amygdalas, those almond-shaped centers of fear and anger in the brain, mechanically stimulated. The mice fearlessly attacked any animal brought into their cage, including fully clawed cats. This is not a good strategy for a defenseless animal that weighs less than two ounces. Fear, the brain's way of protecting the body, is one of the most ubiquitous and primitive of emotions. Puppies develop their first "fear period" right around the age they become fully mobile, which is the first time that a lack of caution could get them killed.

Given all we know about behavior and the brain, it's hard to argue that complicated animals like mammals aren't able to feel fear. While more complex emotions like pride, shame, and love may be controversial, almost all biologists are convinced that human and nonhuman mammals experience fear in ways at least somewhat comparable. Temple Grandin says, "Fear is so bad for animals, I think it's worse than pain." Although highly functional and with a Ph.D. in animal science, Temple Grandin is autistic. She argues, reasonably, that the biology of fear and pain is more similar in autistic people and animals than in typical people and animals, and that as an autistic person, she has centered her life around the management of her intense fears. She sees those fears reflected in the lives of other animals, especially herbivores like cattle and sheep, and she supports her argument with good solid biology.

One of the differences between autistic and typical people is a difference in the activity level of the prefrontal cortex, one of the areas of the brain involved in controlling fear. A high level of prefrontal cortical function—found in most humans—allows one to control fear, but is associated with higher levels of pain. Lower levels of the same function are found in nonhuman animals and autistic people; they correlate with reduced pain perception, but higher levels of fear.

FIGHT OR FLIGHT, BUT ONLY AFTER *FREEZE*!

As a universal emotion, fear has predictable consequences on an animal's behavior. These patterns can be useful to dog owners, in that they can help us decode our dog's emotions.

Imagine you're walking down the street with your dog, and suddenly there's a loud crashing noise right behind you. This information—"very, very loud noise, very, very close"—begins its usual path to the "thinking" part of your brain, but on its way, the signal runs through the amygdala, both in your brain and the brain of your dog, which takes over in a potential crisis before the cortex can evaluate the situation. The amygdala signals *"Emergency!"* in a split second, and initiates a flood of messages that prepare your body for action. No time for analysis here—every millisecond counts if you're in serious danger. "React first, and ask questions later" has kept many an animal alive, whether the danger was from a predator, a tree falling in the forest, or a car careening onto the sidewalk behind you.

We're all familiar with that visceral feeling of panic flooding through our bodies—our hearts beat faster and our blood pressure rises, accompanied by that hard-to-describe feeling of tightening and fluttering in our chests. Something similar must flow through your dog's body too, because she has all the same initial physiological responses that you have when she's startled. Remember, the thinking cortex—the part of you that is very different from your dog's—hasn't yet been engaged, so there's no reason to believe that at this point your dog's response would be any different from your own.

We call this universal response of the body to potential danger the fight-or-flight syndrome, but, to be accurate, we should include "freeze" in the equation. Freezing, ever so briefly, is the most common response to an emergency signal from the brain. In the absence of information, it can be hard to know what to do. Run? But what if you end up running *toward* the danger? Attack? But is that really your best choice? Most animals *freeze,* even if just for a millisecond, before they decide whether to stand their ground or run away. This is an involuntary response, in which the inhibitory part of the nervous system, the parasympathetic system, calls a screaming halt to everything for a microscopically brief moment of reflection.

Remember those extended freezes we talked about in Chapter 2? Now you know why they might be a signal of danger. A dog frozen in place over his chew toy could be feeling afraid or angry, but, either way, his body is ramped up for action. Don't be fooled by the stillness of a dog who isn't moving. His body may be still and silent on the outside, but inside it is a cauldron of activity. Stiff-postured dogs always remind me—bear with me here—of submarines in old war movies. If the camera is looking at the sub from the outside, all seems peaceful and calm as the sub glides soundlessly through the water. Inside, however, is a whirlwind of activity, with alarm whistles shrieking and sailors scrambling in response to an oncoming threat. Dogs who react by freezing in place may look passive on the outside, but they are usually highly aroused on the inside.[3] These freezes can vary in duration, from eternally long stand-offs between two stiff-legged male dogs, to the briefest of pauses to warn you away from a chew toy. Once you start looking for them you'll see them everywhere, and once you recognize the long, obvious ones your ability to notice the short ones will rapidly improve.

Dogs who freeze are both sending out signals and awaiting more information, so how you respond will make a big difference in their subsequent behavior. However, before we talk about the best way to respond to your dog's fears, it's useful to look at the factors that influence how they are experienced and expressed. Let's talk about genetics first, not only because it comes first chronologically, but also because it often seems to be the least understood. Let me start with a story about Tulip.

THE INHERITANCE OF SECURITY SYSTEMS

Frozen in place as if in terror, Tulip stood at the doorway to the living room. In the classic expression of a frightened dog, her mouth was clamped

---

3. The exception is a freeze in play, play being an activity in which all kinds of expressions and actions aren't taken as seriously as they would be outside of the playing field.

shut and her eyes were huge. For the longest time, I don't think she even took a breath. Tulip is a Great Pyrenees, a breed developed to guard sheep from wolves in the Pyrenees mountains, and I have no doubt she'd fight off a pack of them if they went after my sheep. Without any training in protection, Tulip watches over the sheep and the farmhouse, and, bless her, over me. Normally as quiet and sweet as a spring afternoon, Tulip has fearlessly leaped into the fray when something was in danger, whether that something was a sheep, another dog, or a person.

"Fearless" isn't the word that came to mind when my big, brave guard dog stood stock still in the living room doorway. Tulip was so frightened by what she saw that she wouldn't enter the living room for hours, and for days afterward would enter only through a different door. You might think there had been a wolf in the house, or at least a shifty-eyed stranger who appeared out of nowhere. But the problem wasn't that dramatic. The problem was an empty cardboard box, sitting in the middle of the floor.

Tulip stared at it, stiff and immobile, for two or three seconds, and then let out a series of barks that raised the house off its foundation. She barked as though we were all in peril of losing our lives. The cat dashed up the stairs, pursued by phantom demons. The Border Collies ran into the room, Luke and his daughter Lassie alarm-barking as they scrambled across the slippery kitchen floor. I ran to the window, expecting to see a truck the size of Connecticut in the driveway or a raging bull on the lawn. Nothing. Just a box. An empty cardboard box.

I'd bought a new VCR that afternoon, and had left the box it came in on the floor. That's what caused Tulip to first freeze, and then bark as if we were all about to die. After I finally realized the source of Tulip's concern, I tried to coax her over to it. She planted her feet and raised her head like a frightened horse. I threw food by the box. She wouldn't touch it. She wouldn't even take a piece of lamb that I offered in another room, out of sight of the killer cardboard box.

I carried the box to the garage and flattened it down into sheets of cardboard. When Tulip walked by it later that night, she paid it virtually no attention. But the living room was a different story altogether. For days afterward, she'd hesitate before entering it, leaning her body backward while she stretched her nose forward to investigate. She wouldn't enter it at all through the same door she'd used when she first discovered the box. That wasn't a crisis; she could use another door. But that door wasn't very handy, and it somehow seemed absurd that a Certified Applied Animal Behaviorist couldn't get her own dog through the room's most convenient doorway.

Tulip goes in and out of the living room now as if nothing had ever happened. It took a few days of classical counterconditioning and an old horse-trader trick I had learned years ago at a stable.[4] Because Tulip was comfortable going *out* of the room once she was inside it, I simply walked her one step out the doorway, turned her around in a circle three times in the middle of the doorway, and then walked back *in* without taking a pause. After you've spun around in a couple of circles, the difference between inside and outside gets pretty blurred, so this, along with the addition of some particularly tasty treats as she entered, helped Tulip put aside her fears and start acting like the living room was, well, a living room. But why did she react with such drama in the first place?

No doubt her reaction to the killer cardboard box was influenced by learning and early experience—as a sheep-guarding dog, Tulip lived in the barn for the first three years of her life, a place devoid of VCRs and cardboard boxes. She'd only been living in the house for six or eight months when the killer cardboard box arrived. Now that she's lived in the house for seven years, the arrival of a new box or piece of furniture might elicit a good sniff, but it won't produce signs of alarm.

However, it wasn't just a lack of experience that affected her response. Like most dogs bred for guarding, Tulip is extremely reactive to changes in routine. This makes a lot of sense when you think about it. It can be hard to know whether something new is dangerous or not, so for the one in charge of security, its very novelty makes it worthy of cautious attention. We all intuitively understand this to some extent, but security experts learn to be especially sensitive to change. We are often warned to "watch for anything out of the ordinary" in time of danger, so it makes sense that dogs bred to be four-footed security guards would have similar tendencies.

Some dogs take this to extremes—Bo Peep barked for two days when I moved the farm truck from the *right* side of the barn to the

---

4. More on the technique of counterconditioning in the next chapter.

left—but at normal levels caution is useful. It keeps wild animals safe more often than not, and so it tends to be a trait that hangs around in the gene pool. No wonder then, that the tendency to be fearful around unfamiliar animals and objects, often called "shyness" by biologists, has a high degree of heritability in dogs, as well as in people.

Lots of people are surprised that their dog's fears of strangers can, at least in part, be explained by inheritance. Behaviorists and trainers hear, almost on a daily basis, that a client's dog must have been abused, because she reacts so fearfully to strangers. However, many of these dogs are just shy, and they aren't any more comfortable around unfamiliar strangers than shy people are. Shyness exemplifies one of the many ways that genetics and brain function can influence how a dog experiences fear. This seems to be a concept to which we're resistant, although we have no problem associating other traits, like artistic talent or the gift of gab, with an individual's genetic inheritance. We all seem happy to accept that physical characteristics like eye color, coat color, and size are inherited, and that genetics influence certain types of canine behavior, such as retrieving and herding. It turns out that genes also influence how fearful or reactive dogs are, so part of how your dog behaves to visitors was already hardwired within her when you brought her home as a pup.

GENETICS AND FEAR

We're starting to understand a lot about how genes affect fearful behavior. One of the greatest influences of our genetic heritage is on which parts of our brains are most easily activated. We know that different versions of genes, the architects that draw the blueprints of our body, create different activity levels in the amygdala and other fear-related areas of the brain. For example, a study in 2002 found that one of the genes that help regulate levels of serotonin in the brain comes in two different versions. One version, interacting with certain experiences during early development, leads to too much serotonin, a neurotransmitter that in normal amounts helps to soothe and calm the activity of the amygdala. But more isn't always good, and too much serotonin sends the amygdala into overdrive. Overwhelmed with too much serotonin, the amygdala overreacts, creating a high incidence of anxiety disorders.

More evidence about the influence of genetics on fearful behavior comes from a surprising link between temperament and whether you are right-handed, left-handed, or ambidextrous. Researchers have found that people who express no preference for using one hand or the other have higher than expected levels of generalized anxiety disorders. A recent study on noise phobia in dogs found similar results—dogs who used either paw to stabilize a stuffed toy (so that they could lick out food) had a higher frequency of noise phobias than dogs who were right- or left-"pawed."[5] Handedness is inherited in humans, and we have every reason to believe it is in dogs too. If being ambidextrous is associated with an increased risk of generalized anxiety disorder, then the disorder itself is most likely passed on genetically as well.

More evidence relating brain function and fearfulness comes from studies of people with autism. Autistic people respond to faces as if to threats, not because they don't recognize them, but because autistic people's amygdalas are always overactive. We don't know exactly what causes autism, but there's no question that it has a lot to do with the function and chemistry of the brain, matters influenced both by genetics and, as we saw in the last chapter, early development. Individuals with a variety of anxiety disorders also have overactive amygdalas, and this relationship between genetics, the workings of the brain, and the experience of fear is just as pronounced in other animals, including our dogs.

A good example of the interplay between genetics and fear is the type of fear that biologists call shyness, one of the many aspects of life we share with dogs. Anyone who's ever had to walk into a crowded party, not knowing a soul in the room, can empathize with a dog cowering behind her owner's leg at doggy day care. Our level of discomfort around unfamiliar people varies—sales reps are known for their lack of it—but most of us have felt shy at some point in our lives. How often and how intensely you feel shy turns out to be influenced by your genetics, just as it is in your dog.

What's different about this type of fear in people and dogs is the

5. You may be interested to know that out of forty-eight dogs, twenty-one were "lefties," sixteen used their right paws most often, and eleven were "ambilateral," showing no preference. That is, of course, very different from humans, of whom about 10 percent are left-handed or ambidextrous and 90 percent are right-handed.

way it is expressed. We think of shy people as passive, retiring folks who stay in the background, speaking quietly if at all and avoiding the spotlight. However, to dog trainers and biologists, "shyness" refers to a specific type of emotion, the fear of the unfamiliar. What action a dog takes in response to this fear can vary widely, from hiding behind the couch to the canine equivalent of pulling out a shotgun when a car drives up.

"DO I KNOW YOU?"

Although the fear of meeting new people is common in our species, many dog owners seem surprised, even shocked, when their dog behaves one way to the family, and another way to strangers. "But he's so sweet!" they say, almost pleadingly, in a consultation, while their dog sits in the corner and avoids me. He may be hiding his head behind the chair, or he may be growling under his breath because he's trapped in a room with a stranger, but both responses are motivated by fear. I have no trouble believing that their dog is exuberantly friendly to the family, but that doesn't mean he will be to people he doesn't know. Shy people behave differently around their close friends than they do with strangers—why should dogs be any different?

Even so, it seems hard for some people to understand that the dog who is sweet and loving to them may not behave that way toward everyone. No one knows this better than delivery workers, whose amygdalas light up when they hear the words, "Oh, don't worry, he's just *fine!*" as a household dog tries to lunge through the screen door toward them. "Fine" often means the dog is wonderful with the family, but it doesn't say much about how he behaves toward anyone else. Dogs sort the world into "familiar" and "unfamiliar," and you can't understand dogs if you don't understand that. Of course, we humans don't see the world all that differently. If you woke up in the middle of the night and found someone standing in your bedroom, wouldn't it make a difference if he was a trusted friend instead of a complete stranger?

It's understandable that people have a hard time equating growls and bites with fear, especially the kind of fear that biologists and animal behaviorists call shyness. We're used to associating shyness with timidity, so it's hard to look at what appears to be an aggressive dog and think of her as shy. After all, shy people usually don't attack visitors; why would shy dogs?

There are probably many reasons that dogs and people express their discomfort around strangers differently. Surely one of them is that adult humans are often able to avoid social encounters that make them nervous, whereas our dogs are often not given the choice. There they are, tied up in the front yard, or trapped on a leash, unable to avoid contact with people they don't know. Even if they do have a choice, dogs have no idea who is an acceptable visitor and who isn't—how are they to know that the stranger at the door is delivering a package rather than threatening the den? With the rational, thinking parts of their brains radically smaller and less efficient than ours, dogs simply can't think through all the complexities of human social interactions and talk themselves down from feeling afraid. If they have what is called an active defense reflex, then they're going to go after what scares them, rather than run away from it.

It's also helpful to note that although most of us think of shy people as being timid, some shy people report that they become overly assertive, to mask their fears. Melvin Belli, the flashy American attorney, said he became flamboyant to "hide his own shyness." Here's a passage written by a boisterous woman who describes herself as very shy:

> I barge in, hog conversations, rattle on endlessly making an ass
> and nuisance of myself, appearing to be insensitive to others, all
> for the same reasons others attempt to fade into the woodwork.
> My underlying terror of being in public is no less, and my prob-
> lems are no less serious than those of wallflowers.

Statements like these make me think of dogs who barrel into my office and leap all over me, the desk, and anything else that gets in their way. These dogs are full of energy, but they are as quick to jump on the furniture as they are to jump on you. You get no sense of connection with these dogs—and if you look past the exuberant activity, they don't seem to have any interest in relating to you at all. I've come to think of them as frenetic rather than friendly, and increasingly I find myself wondering whether some of them are the Melvin Bellis of dogdom.

However it's expressed, there's little question that the fear of the unfamiliar is a common trait in the animal world. One early study on shyness in humans found that 80 percent of respondents described themselves as shy at some point in their life, and 40 percent of them said they were still shy as adults. Four percent said they were shy *all* the time, in *all* new situations. That study showed that shyness was relatively common, but at that time, we didn't know how it developed, or how much of it was learned and how much inherited.

People long ago came to suspect that this type of fear was heritable in humans, but the early studies were confounded by the influence a shy mother has on her baby. The evidence was overwhelming that shy mothers tended to have shy children, but until researchers looked at adopted babies, we couldn't separate out nature from nurture. It made sense that shy mothers would behave differently than bold ones, and that in itself might be enough to influence a child's behavior. In 1985, researchers answered the question by comparing babies raised by their biological mothers to babies raised by adoptive mothers. All the babies had been born to shy mothers, but the adopted infants were raised by mothers who were not shy. Such studies, called cross-fostering studies when performed on animals, help us sort out the influence of genetics from the influence of the mother during early development. Although the mothers' behaviors did indeed affect the children—shy mothers raised the shyest babies—there was also a strong genetic effect. Infants born to shy mothers were still somewhat shy, even when raised by moms who weren't. Advocates of the "nurture" side of the equation argued against the influence of "nature" (genetics) for decades, but countless studies have made clear that nature has a profound effect on whether an individual will tend to be shy or bold.

The same result has been found in many animals, including our primate relatives. Stephen Suomi, a primatologist at the National Institutes of Health, has spent decades studying shyness and has found that about 15 percent to 20 percent of several monkey species are "excessively fearful" of novel individuals or situations. Shyness has even been found to be heritable in one of the world's hardest-working animals, the laboratory rat. Perhaps you've heard about the work reported a few decades ago on "maze bright" and "maze dull" rats, in which researchers selectively bred rats depending on how quickly they could run a maze. In just a few generations, they'd bred a group of rats who were able to move through a complicated maze in no time, especially compared with the "dull" group, who were bred for their lackluster performance. Only there was one problem—it turned out that "bright" and "dull" rats (read "smart" and "stupid," although the researchers were too gracious to use those terms) weren't at all different in their ability to solve problems. The "dull" rats were simply afraid of new environments, and when placed in one were less likely to explore than the "bright" ones were. The "bright" ones may have won blue ribbons in the laboratory, but they'd be the first ones eaten by a hawk in the wild— a good reminder of why shyness tends to hang around in the gene pool.

A DOG'S FEAR OF THE UNFAMILIAR

Fear of the unfamiliar may not be blatantly obvious in laboratory rats, but it can be easy to spot in the dogs that live in our homes. We've all known dogs who were "a bit cautious" around visitors, or who were afraid of new places. This tendency to be cautious around unfamiliar things is as strongly influenced by genetics in dogs as it is in people. Studies done as early as 1944 supported the idea that the fear of strangers can be inherited in dogs. The researchers found that out of 178 dogs bred in one laboratory, 46 percent were extremely shy. This surprisingly large percentage turned out to be due to the disproportionate influence of one extremely shy Basset Hound bitch, who produced 59 of the puppies in the study, 43 of whom were "shy and unfriendly." Another study in 1958 reported significant breed differences in fearful responses to novel objects (for example, a mechanical snake or an inflated balloon), finding that individuals of breeds such as Collies, German Shepherds, and Corgis were most likely to be wary of unfamiliar things, while Boxers, Scotties, and Boston Terriers were the boldest. The famous twenty-year study done by Scott and Fuller on the genetics of dog behavior confirmed that shyness, although strongly influenced by experience during early development, was also affected by genetics.

More recently, some researchers have found that fearfulness was the one personality trait that could be predicted by puppy "temperament" tests, if the tests were given at twelve weeks (instead of the more common seven or eight weeks). The research also found that the tests were most predictive if given at six months of age, a good reminder that heritable traits don't necessarily appear in the first few months of life. After all, well-bred sheepherding dogs, whose stalking behavior around sheep is as hardwired as walking, often don't "turn on" to stock until adolescence, even late adolescence. I have always found it amazing that an inherited trait like the "Border Collie eye" was so variable in the timing of its first appearance. You can see it in some eight-week-old puppies, but others pay no attention to sheep until, one day, even as late as fourteen months of age, they happen to glance at the sheep and, in an instant, their heads drop and their eyes focus like a heat-seeking missile system. "Eye" doesn't develop step-by-step; rather, it's as though someone turned a light switch from "off" to "on." All this is to remind us that just because a behavior is influenced by genetics doesn't mean you're going to see it in an eight-week-old pup, although a tendency to be fearful appears to be relatively stable through time.

In the last few decades, scientists have capitalized on the genetic influence of behavior by studying a line of "genetically nervous" pointers. These dogs are so shy they can't tolerate any human interaction. They freeze and tremble when petted, and no amount of loving-kindness can calm their fears. The study has confirmed the genetic basis of their behavior: normal dogs raised by nervous moms did not become nervous themselves, while dogs from nervous mothers were fearful, no matter who raised them. Currently, Karen Overall and colleagues at the University of Pennsylvania are studying the neurophysiology of some of these dogs, and another researcher, Greg Acland at Cornell, is studying a line of more typically shy Siberian Huskies. The goal of these projects is to teach us more about the biology of fear and anxiety in both people and dogs, and they remind us yet again how much of our emotional life we share with dogs.[6]

DOGS, WOLVES, AND SHYNESS

Although the consequences of shyness can be a serious problem in both people and dogs, domestic dogs are actually much less shy than their closest relatives, wolves. Wolves are notoriously shy, so much so that researchers used to crawl into wolf dens and handle the puppies while the

6. Fear and anxiety are related, but aren't exactly the same thing. Anxiety is usually used to describe a low-level, chronic fear, often of something that might happen in the future, or a fear with an unspecified focus.

parents hid in fear.[7] These are the same animals who'll fight off grizzly bears to protect their pups, so bravery is not the issue—familiarity is. Remember, fear of the unfamiliar improves your chances of staying alive if you live in the wild. Domestic dogs, like many domestic animals, show a much higher tolerance for coping with unfamiliar things than do their wild counterparts. That's one of the defining characteristics of domestication. No one has illustrated this more clearly than the Russian biologist Dmitri Belyaev, who selectively bred only the tamest and friendliest of Russian fur foxes. Not only was he able to create foxes that acted for all the world like domestic dogs, he found that the friendliest foxes, whom he called the "domesticated elite," were physiologically different from the shyer, wilder foxes. The docile foxes had a delayed fear period during development, and their levels of cortisol, one of the products of an active amygdala, were lower.

Shyness, or the lack of it, is the basis for a popular, and very reasonable, hypothesis about the evolution of the domestic dog. In *Dogs: A Startling New Understanding of Canine Origin, Behavior and Evolution,* Ray and Lorna Coppinger argue that dogs are derived from a subset of wolves who were bold enough to forage on the outskirts of human settlements. The shyest wolves stayed away, and remained wolves as we know them today. The boldest ones hung around humans and, through both natural and artificial selection, became dogs. Perhaps that's one of the reasons it is so hard for us to equate human shyness with the behavior of our dogs—so many dogs seem oblivious to social stress, with the hearty boldness of a door-to-door salesman. But as we've already noted, a trait like shyness has a lot of value, so it's hard to eliminate from an entire species. It's no surprise then, that many of our dogs retain varying degrees of it.

GENETICS: BLUEPRINTS WRITTEN IN PENCIL

No matter how much research supports the influence of genetics on personality traits like shyness, there is still resistance in some quarters to the idea that there are genetically influenced personality traits that

7. That kind of disruption, done by researchers to check on the pups, is avoided at all costs now, since the parents may be so concerned about the safety of their pups that they'll risk moving the den, or may be so stressed that they'll abandon the pups altogether.

remain stable over an individual's lifetime. True, some studies show that experiences early in development can wipe out the effect of genetics; for instance, genetically shy rhesus monkeys can end up as functionally normal adults if they are cross-fostered with the right mothers. But other studies suggest that personality can be stable over time; children who were categorized as "timid" around unfamiliar people showed similar behavioral and neurological responses to the sight of unfamiliar faces when they became adults.

Perhaps some of the resistance to acknowledging the impact of genes on fearful behavior comes from the belief that "genetic" means "unchangeable." A book about shyness in people written by the psychologist Philip Zimbardo in the 1970s suggests that acknowledging a genetic effect on shyness is tantamount to assuming that all shy people are doomed to a life of fear and anxiety. He calls it the "born to be a loser" approach. The same assumptions appear today, in articles in popular magazines and newspapers. I read one recently that suggested if shyness is "genetic" then it is permanent and can't be influenced. I shouldn't be surprised then, when my clients ask, with drawn faces and held breaths: "Is it genetic?" as if "genetic" were a curse that no magic potion could cure. Yet that's not how genes influence a behavior as complicated as shyness or aggression. Think of genetics in these cases as creating a predisposition, or a tendency to behave a certain way. Like a driverless car rolling down a slight incline, these tendencies can be influenced by someone who hops in and puts on the brakes, or can cruise along on their own, picking up steam as they flow downhill, headed for who knows what.

How much you can affect a trait like shyness depends on the intensity of the individual genetic contribution to it. No one can cure the "genetically shy" pointers; the wiring in their brains is so extreme it can't respond to any type of treatment. That level of genetic influence, however, is rare. More often, one can do a lot to increase an animal's level of comfort; it's just hard to know how far you can take them until you try.

It's also good to remember that you can only work with what you've got—extremely fearful individuals may learn to be comfortable around strangers, but they're not going to love selling widgets door-to-door. The same is true for dogs. I worked with Kato, a Great Dane puppy who was so frightened of strangers that, at twelve weeks of age, he growled at me when I entered the house. Lucky for Kato, he was owned by Brenda Scidmore, now a professional dog trainer, who went into socialization superdrive when Kato was still a young pup. Kato lived the life of a social butterfly for his first year, never being overwhelmed, but given frequent opportunities to meet new people in a variety of environments. Kato learned to associate strangers with treats, and because of it, he grew into a dog who was gracious and polite. As an adult, Kato was quiet and reserved, and his owners were wise enough not to try to turn him into Larry the Labrador. However, his fear never evolved into something dangerous, which it well could have if the Scidmores hadn't taken that first growl seriously and taught him to associate strangers with yummy treats.

Most of us have a personal and intuitive sense of the interplay between an inborn personality trait like shyness and the influence of practice and experience. Shy individuals may make great strides in overcoming their timidity, even becoming great public speakers, but they're probably not going to become nightclub hosts. Keep that in mind if you're breeding dogs, or if you're picking out a puppy. You can only work with what you've got, and what you've got—a set of genes wrapped up in silky fur and floppy ears—was created a long time ago, in the heritage of your dog's ancestors.

BUYER BEWARE

I don't want to give the impression that shyness is always a behavioral disaster. A little bit of caution about new things can actually make a dog easier to manage, especially as an adolescent. It's the dogs with extreme shyness who seem to suffer so much, and who can cause untold suffering to their human family. Shyness doesn't combine well with some other genetically mediated traits. Dogs who are shy along with being territorial, overreactive, *and* quick to use their mouths are at risk of biting visitors who enter your house without knocking. The last thing most of us want is a dog who defines anything new as a crisis and feels he has to confront it with his mouth. Rather than run away from the killer cardboard box, Tulip could have charged at it, which would have been the response of a dog who goes on *offense* in response to her fears, rather than on *defense*. I'm eternally grateful that Tulip is on the lookout for anything new or different at the farm, *and* that in over ten years she's never taken it upon herself to charge into battle unless an animal was being physically attacked. Thus, the cardboard boxes at Redstart Farm remain safe—unless they take it upon themselves to attack me, another dog, or my sheep. I'm lucky that Tulip has the ideal combination of shyness, protectiveness, and docility to welcome visitors but protect the farm from danger.[8] That's not always the case, and we'd do well to remember it. Shyness in dogs can, and does, combine with other personality traits to turn into aggression. That important fact of biology requires more attention than it presently gets.

Far too many puppies are produced from shy parents, with little regard for the effects on the dog and on the family in the dog's new home. If you're looking to buy or adopt a puppy, ask yourself whether an adult version of a shy pup is going to respond to her fears on offense or on defense: that's the difference between a dog who hides behind your legs when the mailman hands you a package, and a dog who lunges out to bite him. You can get genetics on your side by using the information in Chapter 2 to read the emotional expressions of the puppies in a litter and by evaluating their relatives; most important, you can obtain a puppy from a reliable, responsible source.

Keep in mind that it's not just shy *parents* who can produce shy puppies; you can breed shy pups from parents who seem relatively bold, if one of *their* parents was a bit shy. Remember that shyness is a "conservative" trait, so it's going to hang around in the gene pool, even if only somewhere in the background. If you're the one doing the breeding, be sure, before you decide on a mating, that you've learned about the behavior of the entire line, not just the behavior of the parents. If you're the one doing the buying, do enough research to discover if your potential pup's parents, grandparents, and aunts and uncles ever had any problem with excessive shyness. This information is impossible to obtain if the parents have lived in kennels all their lives. In that

8. Luck has a lot to do with it, because you can never exactly predict the behavior of any one adult dog from their behavior as a puppy. I should mention, though, that I spent a great deal of time researching the genetics of Tulip's heritage and assuring myself that the behavior of her parents was the behavior I'd like to see at my house.

case, nothing ever changes, so how can you know how the dogs will cope with something new or different? This is one of the many reasons why we should all be actively fighting against the plague of puppy mills, from which millions of dogs are sold to unsuspecting people with no regard for the disposition of the parents.

BRINGING UP PUPPY

The story of Blaze, the dog who began this chapter, is a perfect example of the importance of *early development* on fearful behavior in dogs. Blaze was aggressive to people because he was afraid of them, but in this case the cause wasn't his genetics. Blaze warmed up so fast in my office, and seemed so happy to be around people once he relaxed, that it seemed impossible to believe he was hardwired to be fearful. I suspected that Blaze was afraid of visitors because he'd seen so few of them, especially during the phase of development called the *critical period of socialization.* Blaze had grown up in an isolated house in the middle of nowhere. Rather than being genetically shy, Blaze had had little exposure to people as he was growing up, and therefore he saw anyone who was unfamiliar as a threat. As he matured, he began to act on those fears, desperately trying to protect Father Murray and the house from invasion by aliens.

Blaze's story exemplifies how both nature (genes) and nurture (development and learning) play essential roles in behavior. If Blaze had been well socialized, I doubt very much that he would have become aggressive. If he hadn't inherited a certain amount of friendliness, I doubt he ever could have been rehabilitated. However, he was also hardwired to be exceptionally reactive, and he had a lot of trouble keeping himself from becoming overaroused. The combination of these factors created both the Blaze of the past, who would've bitten you, and the Blaze of today, who'll lick your face and welcome you to his new farm. We'll talk in the next chapter about how that turnaround happened, but for now, it's worthwhile to talk about how Blaze's aggression to visitors could have been prevented in the first place.

The period of early development has a profound effect on an individual's level of fearfulness about the world. We've learned that warm, supportive parents lead to bolder, more confident children. We know that genetically shy monkeys and human babies can be brought out of their shells by being cross-fostered with attentive mothers who provide what's called a "secure attachment base." We talked at length in Chapter 3 about the impact of an enriched environment with respect to a dog's ability to cope with change as an adult, and this effect is equally important on a dog's tendency to be fearful or bold. If you think about it, an enriched environment is not that different from a changing environment—even a complex environment stops being enriching if it never changes. You can't have something new without change. That's why any properly enriched environment includes chances to meet new people and dogs; that's why both puppies and children need to be introduced to enough new people and dogs that meeting individuals who are unfamiliar becomes familiar itself.

Both breeders and puppy buyers will have happier dogs if they are mindful of the importance of socialization. I mention breeders because we know that the primary "sensitive period" of socialization begins as early as three weeks of age, and is over as early as twelve weeks. Good breeders invite lots of friends (who have washed their hands and left their shoes outside, thank you) to interact with the pups. Good puppy raisers do the same, and take the pup out and about to meet people and polite, healthy dogs of all descriptions, making sure that the interactions are good ones. Effective socialization creates positive experiences that enable your pup to feel comfortable with a variety of people and dogs, and to learn that strangers, no matter how many paws they have, are a good thing.

Puppy socialization classes can be a great addition to a socialization program. The good ones get you started on lots of fun and practical training exercises, while introducing your pup to a variety of other sizes and shapes of dogs. Be cautious, though, about puppy classes in which all the pups are thrown together in a mosh pit of activity, with instructors blithely saying, "Oh, it's great for puppies to learn to work things out for themselves." Puppies work things out just like young children on playgrounds do—with little regard for emotional control or the social niceties of life. There's a reason that an adult is always assigned to monitor the playground at an elementary school; otherwise, we'd have *Lord of the Flies* acted out at schools all across the country. Unregulated puppy classes can create the same dynamic, by reinforcing bullies (yes, even young puppies can act like bullies) and traumatizing some of the more timid puppies. The problems associated with unregulated puppy classes are a good reminder that "socialization" doesn't mean throwing your pup into the deep end of social interaction and assuming he'll learn to swim. As we'll see in the next section, that can cause more problems than it solves. Be sure that your pup's socialization process is a series of positive experiences, not a series of negative ones.

A LITTLE BIT GOES A LONG WAY

Recently I saw a couple at a busy, noisy farmer's market with a terrified Boxer puppy in tow. "Oh, he's fine," they said. (There's that phrase again.) "We thought this would be a great place to get him socialized." It didn't seem like such a great place to me, and I don't think the puppy thought so, either. The tiny puppy was so scared he was trembling. Surrounded by hordes of noisy adults and screaming children reaching to pet him, the poor pup was overwhelmed. He was learning, all right— he was learning to be deathly afraid of people. Unfortunately, this scene is all too common and, ironically, is produced by people with the best of intentions. Too many puppies are inadvertently traumatized through a misunderstanding of what a healthy socialization process entails. Rather than being gradually exposed to different environments, pups end up traumatized by being thrown into scary situations that are over their heads.

A healthy period of development isn't about *any* kind of exposure, it's about exposure that allows puppies to learn about life at their own pace. Not long ago an eight-week-old puppy, let's call him Tigger, visited my office. His little jaw was swollen from a serious bite from another dog, although that didn't stop him from cheerily greeting all the people in the room. As bold as the pup seemed, I was concerned about his reaction to other dogs in the future—what effect would a bad bite (the poor thing's jaw was broken) have on the pup's relations to other dogs? As luck would have it, Lassie was in another office, and I knew I could count on her to be quiet and polite around a fragile young puppy. I wanted to start creating good experiences for Tigger, in case his earlier trauma had taught him that dogs were dangerous. As I feared, Tigger took one look at Lassie and flattened in fear, with the corners of his little mouth pulled back and his eyes rounded like Frisbees.

The worst thing we could have done was let Lassie run up to him when he was trapped in a small room, so as soon as I saw his expression, I asked Lassie to lie down on the other side of the room, and we let Tigger run back to "Mom." Secure beside his new, two-legged mama, Tigger stared at Lassie as if transfixed while the humans in the room chatted and paid little attention to either dog. Every few minutes, Tigger would lean forward and sniff Lassie's tail, then rock backward into the comfort of that "secure attachment base" I mentioned earlier. After a few minutes, without us forcing anything, Tigger got up and walked all the way over to Lassie's head, his confidence growing with each step. I kept Lassie on a down/stay, so that she didn't stand up and startle him, and Tigger sniffed her mouth, wagged his tiny little tail, and ran back to "Mom."

It was a perfect session. Rather than having his fears confirmed, Tigger had a secure place to run to when scared, and wasn't presented with anything that was over his head. A few days after this session, his owner introduced him to another friendly, docile dog, and soon the two were romping like old friends. That's exactly the kind of experience that can turn genetically shy monkeys into normal adults, and it bears no relation to the "Just throw them in the deep end" approach that many people take. That method can backfire on you more often than not; just ask my family, who still laugh about the time I got thrown in the deep end—literally. My mother took me to swimming class, which turned out to be taught by a big, ex-Marine kind of guy. Soon after we met, with little preparation, he swept me up and tossed me into the pool. I'm told I popped out of the water like a piece of toast out of a toaster, and ran screaming across the lawn. All I remember is running away from the pool, shrieking in fear, pursued by a huge, red-faced man, who was followed, cartoon-style, by my distraught mother. Needless to say, I didn't learn much about swimming that day, and for a couple of years afterward I avoided water whenever I could. That kind of experience, in which an individual learns to be frightened by something, is the third most common source of fearfulness, after genetics and a lack of early experience. There's plenty to be afraid of out there in the world, and dogs can be permanently changed by traumatic events, just as people can.

A good socialization plan should be designed to prevent traumatic experiences, not create them, so be thoughtful about where you take your puppy when you're out and about. Ideally, you're shooting for a balance between the right amount of exposure and stimulation and a sense of security and safety. As we've seen already, what balance is right for your pup is going to depend on his genetics and what kind of life you envision him living. Your best guide as to how to proceed is to use the signals described in Chapter 2 as a window into your dog's internal state, along with some thoughtful anthropomorphism and a dash of common sense.

Blaze, the Border Collie who hadn't been well socialized, is fine now, although I won't pretend it was easy getting there. It took a village of helpers and a tremendous amount of energy, but Blaze now greets visitors like long lost friends and lives in a home with an active young owner and lots of other dogs to play with. Father Murray is happy too—he rescued a sweet old dog who loves company as much as he loves Father Murray. We'll talk in the next chapter about how Blaze was rehabilitated, but next we'll look at the third common origin of fear in dogs and people—trauma.

LEARNING TO BE AFRAID

Lefty had been a friendly dog all his life—the dog everyone in the neighborhood knew and loved. An amiable Labrador, he loved nothing better than to play with the neighbors' kids on expansive suburban lawns. One summer his family took a vacation unsuitable for dogs, so Lefty went to a friend's house. A week later, the family returned and picked him up. They were recounting this story to me in my office, and they stressed that he seemed fine, just fine, when they brought him home. He was a bit quiet, but he'd played a lot with other dogs at the neighbors', and his family assumed he was just tired.

A week later, Lefty was outside in the backyard when one of his buddies, a twelve-year-old boy, came over to say hello. As the child reached out to pet him, Lefty exploded in his face. The frightened child rocked backward as Lefty barked BARR RARR RARR—deep growly barks that brought his owners running from the house. Lefty quieted as his family ran to him and the hapless boy withdrew, but everyone—the boy,

Lefty's owners, and possibly Lefty himself—was shocked. Lefty and the boy had been friends for years, playing fetch under summer sunsets and sharing hamburgers at neighborhood picnics. His behavior seemed inexplicable.

Lefty's barking and lunging toward the boy was so out of character, the family could barely believe it had happened. Perhaps, they thought, he'd been in pain for some reason, and would have lashed out at anyone. They decided to watch him closely, but couldn't imagine such a thing happening again.

It did. A few weeks later, Lefty lunged toward a seven-year-old boy, and a month after that he cornered the plumber against the bathroom wall. By the time Lefty's family came to me, his behavior had deteriorated to barking aggressively toward any unfamiliar male, young or old. He hadn't bitten anyone yet, but his barks were deep and threatening and the family was afraid of what he might do next.

As we talked, Lefty greeted me exuberantly, bringing me tennis balls to throw and chew toys to admire. His body stayed loose and his mouth was relaxed, and for most of the hour he appeared as happy-go-lucky as he'd been for most of his life. But when a man walked by the office window, Lefty dropped the tennis ball he'd been carrying and lunged toward the man with deep, threatening barks. The hair over Lefty's shoulders stood straight up, his body had become stiff and tight, his ears were pinned flat, and his eyes were round. Lefty may have been lunging forward, but if you looked at him closely, you could see that the corners of his mouth were pulled back in a fear grimace, and his pupils were fully dilated. Lefty's behavior may have been frightening, but Lefty was as scared himself as he was scary to others.

The family was scared, too, and confused about why, after six years as their sweet, loving, easygoing best friend, Lefty had changed into a dog who was not only untrustworthy around strangers but also jumpy and reactive to noises he'd previously ignored. We talked at length about what had happened in Lefty's life that could have precipitated his change in behavior, but couldn't come up with an explanation. Two veterinarians had carefully checked him for hidden health problems. Lefty had come up clean. The family hadn't changed his food or his routine, and nothing had happened at home that could explain his behavior. Finally, one of the children noted again how quiet he had been when he returned home from the neighbors' house. Looking for any insights into Lefty's behavior, I called them to find out whether anything could have happened while his family was away on vacation. The mystery began to resolve when they told me that a visiting relative had brought her twelve-year-old son with her, and on one afternoon they had seen the boy "teasing" the dogs in the house. At one point, the boy trapped Lefty in the laundry room and taunted him by screaming in his face. Lefty, by all descriptions, had been terrified.

Responsible dog lovers, the neighbors were appalled and put a stop to the abuse right away. To their relief, Lefty seemed none the worse for wear, happily greeting everyone who came to visit, playing politely as always with the other dogs at the house. But none of the family were twelve-year-old boys, and no one knew that the effects of trauma are not always visible on the surface, or that they can spread like ripples beneath the surface of a dog's future.

Besides a genetic predisposition and a lack of exposure during development, the third reason that dogs are fearful is because they have learned to be. Perhaps one dog has learned that a rolled-up newspaper means she's going to get hurt. Another dog may have had a painful procedure at the veterinarian's and begins to pant and drool the next time the car pulls into the clinic's driveway. I've met dogs who loved other dogs, except individuals of just one breed, or one color, who look like the dog who attacked them when they were younger. These dogs may send them shaking behind their owner's legs or barking hysterically in a desperate attempt to keep the other dog away.

Fear derived from traumatic experiences is actually less common than people imagine. Trainers and behaviorists see clients almost daily who say, "I'm sure she was terribly abused before I got her, because she cowers/growls/snaps/hides at every man/stranger/dog she sees." Most often these dogs are either genetically fearful, undersocialized, or, most commonly, a bit of both. Shy dogs are often more afraid of men than of women, so a dog doesn't have to have been abused by a man to be fearful of all men.[9] However, sometimes dogs do get hurt and scared

9. We don't know exactly why so many dogs are more afraid of men than of women, but it probably has to do with men's larger chests, larger jaws, lower voices, and tendency to approach assertively.

during their lifetimes, and these traumatic events can resonate through their lives just as they can through ours. We'll talk in the next chapter about what to do if that happens, but first it's worth looking at how it happens in the first place.

When people and dogs are frightened, parts of the limbic system, especially the hippocampus, record the details of the event like a detective at a crime scene. However, neither limbic systems nor detectives know which of the details might be predictive of a similar danger in the future, so they record whatever they can, in case it turns out to be important later. A dog attacked by a big, white dog may forever be afraid of white dogs, because "white" was one of the features his brain recorded at the time. Another dog, attacked by the same white dog as the first, may remember size, rather than color, and be afraid of big dogs in the future. We know from brain activation research that when a person is terrified, the brain recruits input from neurons all over the brain, sweeping up both significant and insignificant details at the same time. For example, an entomologist who was hit by a car still remembers the species of insects flattened on the license plate as it rushed toward his head. Unable to sort out which details were related to the danger, the brain reacts emotionally to all of the information that was included in the sweep. Our entomologist friend will probably always react differently to the types of insects he associates with his car accident, even though they had nothing to do with the danger. One of the challenges when trying to turn around fearful behavior is to figure out what features were recorded as being relevant to the problem. These features, or triggers, become an important aspect of soothing the fear, as we'll see in the next chapter.

How frightened a dog will be by any one event is driven in part by his genetics, in part by his experience during development, and also by the details of the event itself. Obviously, the intensity of the event makes a huge difference, just as it does with us. It's one thing to have a dog lunge at you and nip your hand before you knew what hit you; it's another to be the victim of a long-drawn-out, injurious attack. However, how you or your dog experiences the event isn't just a function of what happened, it's also dependent on your emotional state at the time. I just had a minor medical procedure that was about as risky and dramatic as eating warm oatmeal, yet I was trembling as if my life were in peril. The analytic part of my brain knew that was foolish, but my limbic system was on red alert. It had been primed by a terrifying incident in my car the night before, in which large sheets of particle-board flew out of a trailer toward my windshield, requiring me to drive like a stuntwoman in a James Bond movie to keep me and the dogs in my car alive. The physiological effects of an event like this can take a long time to dissipate, and I could tell that my body was still full of stress hormones the next morning. Additionally, I went to the hospital with the knowledge that my father had died tragically after a similar medical procedure, in which one small accident led to a series of others, and ultimately to his death.

The combination of factual knowledge about my father's death and the physiological arousal from the accident the night before turned me into a high-maintenance patient. The physician and CT scan technician get lots of points for bending over backward to soothe my irrational but deeply felt fears. Knowing that no amount of rational discussion was going to calm me, I stopped trying to talk myself out of being afraid. The only intellectual knowledge that helped was knowledge about the way the brain is wired. I remembered that there are fewer connections from the rational cortex of the brain to the limbic system than vice versa. Knowing that allowed me to stop trying to talk myself out of it, and instead spend my energy doing what I did the night before—comfort myself with support from friends, deep breathing, and a whole heck of a lot of petting of dogs.

Prior experience is an important factor in how a dog reacts to a frightening event. An attack by another dog is going to have much more impact if it happens to a pup who's never met another dog; that's why I was so worried about young Tigger. In contrast, Pip recovered from being jumped by a client's dog relatively quickly, because she had had years of good experiences with other dogs. It also matters to dogs, just as it does to people, what happened in the days preceding an incident. Just as I was primed by being frightened in the car the night before my medical procedure, so dogs can react differently depending on what has happened in their own recent past. A dog might react very differently to an attack if he'd been scared the night before by a thunderstorm, or just been to the vet's for vaccinations. The impact of the environment can be additive, which is one of the reasons that dogs *seem* to behave erratically. Perhaps your dog might welcome a guest one day, and bark like a banshee at the same person the day after. Don't let some inconsistencies in your dog's behavior throw you. Many factors influence how frightened a dog will be by any one event. What has happened in his past is just one of them. Usually the effects of any single incident fade away over a period of days, but on occasion, just as in people, one single incident is enough to change a dog forever.

PTSD: POST-TRAUMATIC STRESS DISORDER IN DOGS

Some dogs are so affected by what happens to them they behave as though they have been clinically traumatized. Someone rolled her eyes once when I used this term in relation to dogs. She asked, her tone dripping with sarcasm, if I wasn't being just a little bit anthropomorphic when I used such a "human" term in relation to a dog. No, I replied, I wasn't—at least, not in a problematic way. "Trauma" is defined as a serious shock or injury to the body or the emotions; an event that causes "great distress and disruption." There's virtually nothing about the way dogs are designed to preclude their being "distressed and disrupted" by a terrifying event. As we've seen, dogs share the brain design and neurochemistry that influence fear and anxiety in humans—if we didn't, people wouldn't be continuing a line of perpetually terrified pointers to better understand how to treat generalized anxiety disorders in humans. That dogs can be frightened by something, and that those fears can affect their behavior, is hardly surprising to any of us who know dogs. What did surprise me was my gradual realization over the years that dogs exhibit many of the same symptoms as people who have post-traumatic stress disorder.

Lefty, the dog whose story began this section, is a classic case of a dog who behaved much like a person with PTSD. As is often true in humans, his behavioral problems didn't begin immediately after he had been scared. Also, like a human PTSD victim, he began to generalize the triggers that he associated with his fear, first being afraid of just one twelve-year-old boy, then of other boys of similar ages, and eventually of males of any age. That's often how trauma affects humans—its effects aren't always obvious right away, and over time the victims begin to generalize their fears from one specific stimulus to wider and wider categories of events.

An infamous story about the progression of trauma comes from the work of John B. Watson, the behaviorist mentioned in Chapter 1. Watson wanted to show the power of associative learning, in which an innate reaction to one thing (like the fear of a loud, startling noise) can be transferred to another thing (a benign object, such as a small, furry animal). Watson brought Albert, an eleven-month-old child, into his laboratory and sat him down in front of a friendly little white rat. Albert was charmed by the furry creature in front of him, and cheerfully tried to pet it. However, every time Albert reached for the animal, Watson slammed a hammer onto a piece of metal just a few inches behind Albert's head. After one short session, poor little Albert burst into tears every time he saw a white rat. By the end of the week he had become afraid of anything furry, including a rabbit and a fur coat. This experiment was heartless enough given the knowledge of the time, but is made even more painful to contemplate by our current knowledge that Watson was permanently changing the function of Albert's brain, and predisposing him to be far more reactive to trauma than he would have been before his unknowing mother brought him into the laboratory.

Little Albert the boy and Lefty the dog have a lot in common: both suffered from an event that was frightening, and in both cases a specific fear became generalized to anything that their brains had associated with the trauma. Albert started with an attraction to white furry animals, and Lefty to little boys. However, when these things were paired with something frightening, they became frightening all by themselves. Over time, both boy and dog began to generalize their fears: Albert to anything furry, Lefty to anyone male. Lefty was friendly to me not because I'm a trained behaviorist, or because I love dogs, but simply because I'm not a guy.

The bad news is that trauma can stay with us forever; just ask the victims of war or other violence. We know this is true of many species besides ourselves—rats who have been traumatized by inescapable shocks have long-lasting changes in their physiology, and deficits in their ability to learn. Traumatic events can change the performance of an individual's amygdala, which, paired with its partner the hippocampus, can carry memories of past dangers for a lifetime.

One of the most common symptoms of PTSD in people is an increased level of reactivity to almost any stimulus that could possibly be associated with danger. I knew a Vietnam veteran who startled to any abrupt noise, literally throwing himself to the floor if a car backfired on the street below. His behavior and expressions were dead ringers for those of a client's traumatized Golden Retriever, who was the victim of a childhood prank. I don't know whether the kids who threw the firecracker meant it to land on the dog's back, but it did, a microsecond before it went off. Frito was terrified, and after that one incident he responded to any loud, abrupt noise with panic, just as my friend did after being in combat.

This hyperreactivity is the result of what researchers call "an overly efficient neural pathway" between the amygdala, the hippocampus and hypothalamus, and the production of stress hormones like cortisol and adrenaline. In these cases, the brain lives in a state of chronic over-arousal, which can inhibit the ability of the cortex to help the body decide what's dangerous and what isn't. This "priming effect" can result in some surprising findings, like that of one researcher who found that Beagles had higher levels of cortisol when taken back to an area where they'd been shocked *one month before* than they did immediately after they received the shocks. That means that one entire month after being shocked, the poor dogs were more stressed about being taken back to the location than they were after the actual event. That's a perfect example of the results of trauma, in which a single event can have pervasive effects on an animal's emotions, and after which the fear worsens over time rather than improves.

It's also a good example of how the brain does its best to record and remember things that are associated with fear or danger. The Beagles' brains told them that the place was dangerous, because they had been shocked there, even though the place itself actually had nothing to do with it. You might feel nervous when you hear a song that was playing on the radio when you had a car accident, although you won't even be conscious of the connection. Many of these associations are unconscious, but they probably drive our behavior as much as they do our dogs'.

There's good news, though, about trauma and its effect on people and dogs. For one thing, most frightening events don't result in clinical levels of trauma, and dogs can be as resilient as people can in recovering from a scare here and there. Being scared at the vet's office or being charged by a frightening dog isn't likely to cause lifelong problems in a healthy, stable dog, any more than one bad experience at the doctor's is going to leave you with a phobia about getting a physical. Of course, how you or your dog responds depends on the intensity of the experience and on whether you've been scared before in a similar situation or have a genetic predisposition toward an active amygdala.[10]

The other piece of good news about our reactions to frightening events is that as we start to understand more about the biology of fear, no matter what its source, we're also starting to develop better ways to treat fear. Some of these methods are dependent upon speech and are of no use to those of us with traumatized dogs. But other methods work without words, and can do wonders for dogs whose fears are compromising their lives. That's the subject of the next chapter, in which we'll talk about tried-and-true methods that can help you help your dog overcome his fears.

10. PTSD is more common in individuals who experienced two terrifying events, the first one seeming to "prime" the brain, and it also appears to be more common in people with genetic codings for atypical levels of neurotransmitters.

PAVLOV IN YOUR POCKET

How to help your dog overcome his fears

I remember the storm that almost killed Blue as if it had just happened. The thunder was so loud I gave up trying to sleep, and alternated between reading and attending to my dogs, who were clustered around me, panting and pacing. A huge branch, itself the size of a tree, blew off the weeping willow in the front yard. I was sure the power would go out, and it did, right on schedule, about an hour into the fury of a typical Wisconsin thunderstorm. The Midwest may seem like a quiet backwater to some, but not to those of us who live here. In part, that's because of the weather. Thanks to tornadoes, thunderstorms, and blizzards, we don't need to watch television to bring drama into our lives. I thought about that as I hunkered down on the second story of my old farmhouse, hoping that the maple tree didn't fall on the garage, and that the roof stayed on the barn for one more year.

Blue lived a mile and a half down the road. He was a working dog who lived outside, the better to protect an organic vegetable farm. It wasn't people who were the concern, it was deer. You may not think of deer as dangerous predators, but that's because you're not a cabbage. Deer can eat up a season's worth of vegetables in just one night, and they are hard to keep out once they learn that there's a buffet open in the neighborhood. Blue had proved himself invaluable to Vermont Valley Farm, living in the middle of the most vulnerable crops, barking at the first sign of deer. The smorgasbord in the fields may have tempted the local Bambis, but the presence of Blue was enough to convince them to eat elsewhere.

Surely that night the deer were hunkered down, finding what protection they could from the pouring rain and flashes of lightning. Blue had done the same in past storms, but not this time. We'll never know why this storm was the one that sent him over the edge, but it did him in. No longer content to seek shelter in his doghouse, Blue ran in terror through the tomato vines, across the cornfield, trying somehow to outrun the thunder. Tearing wild-eyed down the centerline of a county highway, Blue came within inches of being hit by a passing motorist. The driver saw him at the last instant and managed to avoid a collision. Blue's luck continued: his savior was a local, and knew where Blue belonged. Blue was happy to jump into his truck, and was escorted home to safety while the thunder still rolled and the sky flashed from light to dark.

Fear may be essential to survival, but sometimes it can work against us. That's as true for dogs as for people. Thousands of dogs die every year because, terrified of thunderstorms, they run headlong onto highways or launch themselves out of second-story windows trying to outrun the noise. Thunder phobia is only one type of fear that can do dogs more harm than good, but it's a good reminder that both people and dogs can suffer terribly from chronic and acute fear. Some individuals are so afraid of strangers that they can barely manage normal social interactions, and live their lives in a state of chronic anxiety. Others have been frightened so intensely that they develop post-traumatic stress disorder, and live in a constant state of hyperarousal. The good news is that many of these conditions, in both people and dogs, can be cured or at least substantially improved. That's what this chapter is about—how to help dogs whose fears are compromising their lives, and the lives of the people who love them. However, before we talk about what *to do*, I want to talk about what *not to do*. I wish I didn't have to bother, but the fact of the matter is, instinct often isn't enough when it comes to dealing with frightened dogs.

SPARE THE ROD—PLEASE!

There's one universal truth that relates to all fear-related behavior in both people and dogs: punishment is not a good way to fix it. You'd think it would be obvious that hitting or yelling at a frightened dog would be counterproductive, but, sad to say, people do it all the time. I suspect that the reason has more to do with our own emotions than those of our dogs. Frightened dogs can also be "aggressive" dogs, at least in the sense that some dogs growl and flash their teeth when they feel threatened. These dogs don't want to hurt anyone, although they might if trapped or pushed too far. Usually, they're just trying to defend themselves, and they're using the only means they have. We respond, understandably, with our own set of fears. As primates, we have a visceral reaction to something coming at us with teeth bared, as well we should. Nothing like a set of white, shiny teeth to get a rise out of your limbic system, even if part of you has noticed that the dog's facial expression includes signs of fear. Take it from me, never does your skin feel quite so thin and useless as when a dog is about to sink her teeth into it. If a dog is flashing her teeth, at you or someone else, it takes a special kind of training (or a high level of empathy) to focus on her fears rather than your own.

You'd be wise to try to see the world through her eyes, at least to the extent of acknowledging that fear is one component of the dog's behavior.[1] Aggression often breeds aggression, and never is that more true than if it's motivated by fear. It's a sad irony that one of the things we share with dogs is the tendency to become aggressive when we're frightened. Defensive aggression is common in both species, and it can feed on itself like a forest fire.

Surely the most common fear in all mammals is the fear of being hurt. This isn't surprising, when you think about it—being injured isn't going to help an animal pass on its genes. It's a shame dogs can't more easily tell us when they're hurt, or afraid of being hurt, because I think it's a common motivation for what we think of as aggression. If only people would be *more* anthropomorphic when their dogs are behaving badly: I'm surprised at how few of us think of pain as a motivation for the growls and snaps that some dogs are so quick to deliver. Pain is a common factor in aggression in our own species (ask any hospital nurse), and you'd think we'd be quicker to consider it when our dogs get snappy.

---

1. This doesn't mean you should ignore your own fear. I have a lot of respect for my limbic system, and I don't hesitate to acknowledge that some dogs scare the heck out of me. I've just learned to use that information to my advantage, while respecting the emotions of the dog at the same time.

I remember one dog, a lovely little Springer, who had bitten her owner repeatedly—and badly—whenever she reached toward her collar. The dog seemed sweet and submissive at all other times, perfectly happy to let me handle her paws, take away a special chew bone, and ask her to lie down and stay. The owner had been told the dog had "dominance-related aggression," but the context of the bites didn't look as if she was trying to control the household; she just couldn't tolerate anyone reaching toward her collar. In the office I noticed that her movements seemed a bit stiff, and asked whether the dog had been given a thorough medical exam. She had, but her vet had found nothing on the X-rays to suggest a problem. Because the aggression was elicited only by a reach toward her neck, and because her movements seemed just the slightest bit "wrong," I suggested a second opinion. Bless the client's heart, she took her dog for a second opinion, got referred to a certified canine chiropractor, who located a misaligned vertebra, and in just one treatment the dog was restored to her sweet, docile self. This kind of "miracle cure" is rare—it's probably one of the reasons I remember the case so well—but it serves as a good reminder that dogs can be aggressive because they are afraid of being hurt. Punishing her for growling and snapping (which the owners had tried) only exacerbated her fear and made things worse.

If you're in the middle of a vicious circle of fear-related aggression between you and your dog, don't expect your dog to figure a way out (although I've seen a number of dogs do their best to try). You're the human with the big, brilliant cortex, so if you see signs of fear in your dog, as described in Chapter 2, take a deep breath, tell your limbic system to calm down, and think yourself out of the problem. If fear could be a component in your dog's behavior, you need to take the threat away and work on teaching him what you *do* want him to do, not punishing him for what he did wrong.[2] Try to avoid getting caught up in a spiral of fear, because it can be a downhill ride to trouble.

Here's another example—a regrettably common one—of how punishment only exacerbates problems that are based on fear: someone's shy dog snaps at an unfamiliar visitor who overwhelms her by trying to kiss her on the face. Alarmed and embarrassed, the owner yells at the

2. Actually, that pretty well sums up all of dog training. If people stopped yelling "No!" at their dogs, and instead taught them what they want them *to do*, rather than *not do*, the world would be a better place.

dog and smacks her on the rump. Ask yourself, What did the dog learn? Most likely she had her fears confirmed: "Yes, unfamiliar people are just as dangerous as I thought they were, and worse, my own owner, whom I was counting on to protect me, becomes dangerous in their presence as well. I hope no one unfamiliar ever comes into our house again."

Being punished for acting out of fear is a staggeringly common problem. I've worked with countless dogs who were punished for growling when they were afraid of a person or another dog.[3] Many did indeed stop growling, but these dogs are often more dangerous than the ones that keep it up. Afraid to growl, they sit stiff and silent, but ready to blow at the slightest provocation. If people aren't aware of the meaning of a closed mouth and a stiff body, they push the dog until he can't control himself any longer, and he lashes out "without warning." "Out of the blue!" the owners tell me. "His bites come out of the blue, with no warning whatsoever." And yet, when I reach toward the dog in a consultation, his mouth closes tight, his body freezes, and his eyes round like dinner plates. All along the poor dog had been trying to tell them he was about to blow, but they took away the only warning system they understood—growling—and couldn't interpret the signals that were left.

Some dogs don't stop growling if they're punished for it. They escalate the barking and growling, in a desperate attempt to keep the approaching person as far away as possible. "You stay away from me! You're dangerous! If you get closer my owner is going to hurt me. *STAY AWAY FROM ME!* BARR RARR RARR RARR!" This, too, is a common reaction to being punished for fear-related behavior, and I've seen hundreds of dogs in my office whose quiet growls evolved into deep, hateful barks because their owners had inadvertently confirmed their worst fears.

"I SAID, 'GET OVER HERE!' "

There's another reason that people use punishment in response to fearful dogs, and it, too, relates more to our own emotions than to those of

3. I'm talking about what's called, a bit confusingly, "positive punishment," in which something aversive is done to the dog to try to eliminate an unwanted behavior. Examples are harsh yelling, grabbing the head and glaring into the dog's eyes, and striking the dog or shaking him by the scruff—all common responses to "disobedience."

our dogs. Fearful dogs are sometimes afraid to respond as asked, and dogs who don't "listen" can result in frustrated, angry owners. We'll talk about that in depth in the chapter on anger, but for now suffice it to say that getting angry at a frightened dog rarely solves the problem. This is yet another time when being anthropomorphic can help both you and your dog. Would your performance improve if someone slapped you because you were nervous before giving a speech? I'll admit that in rare cases that kind of shock might be helpful ("Thanks, I needed that"), but that's the exception, not the rule. I was so nervous when I gave my first academic speech at a scientific meeting that my goal was to make it through without fainting or throwing up. I did, but the graduate student who spoke after me dropped like a rock in a dead faint after his first few sentences. I suppose if someone had slapped him beforehand it might have improved things—he could've fainted in private instead of in front of five hundred people.

Although it's important to avoid doing things that make your dog worse, there are lots of things you can do to help your dog conquer her fears. The methods described below work as well on people as they do on dogs, a handy fact to remember next time you have to give a speech. I've used them myself to get over my own fear of public speaking and to keep myself from bolting out of the chair at the dentist's office.[4] I've written all the examples with dogs as subjects, but don't hesitate to think about how you can get these methods to work for you, too.

CLASSICAL CONDITIONING

Unless your dog was both born profoundly shy and grew up all alone in a shed, chances are you can do a lot to soothe her fears. The best way to do that is to use classical conditioning, the type of learning discovered by the Russian scientist Ivan Pavlov and his drooling dogs. Unlike most of us, who don't appreciate long, slimy strings of drool, Pavlov wanted his dogs to salivate so that he could study the extra-large chromosomes that saliva contains. However, he was frustrated when they began producing drool before he was ready to collect it. He had

4. I should state for the record here that I have never bitten a dentist—a fact of which, given my level of terror when someone jams a huge needle into my mouth, I am very proud.

expected them to start salivating when they got their food, but the dogs would start dancing and drooling long before—when they heard their dinner bowls being handled, or the sound of the keeper's footsteps approaching the door.

This is not a stunning revelation to most of us who are used to our dogs anticipating something they love with excitement, doing jumping jacks when we pick up the leash or open a can of food. No doubt dogs have been doing similar things for ages, spinning joyful circles when some humanlike primates picked up their clubs and put on animal skins on the way out of the cave.

But it was Pavlov who first realized the implications of the fact that dogs would drool in response to a sound, rather than to food. He recognized that by linking two previously unrelated things, you could get the same response to one as you did to the other. Not only that, but the response wasn't voluntary or under conscious control—you can't make yourself salivate, at least not without conjuring up an image of food, which is just another example of classical conditioning. Many of us can't stop ourselves from blinking before a camera flashes, because the "anti–red eye" feature includes a small flash that is always followed by the "real," brighter flash. Unconsciously, we've learned that the first, weaker flash, which is normally not enough to make you close your eyes, means a larger flash is coming. The sequence starts out *little flash—big flash—blink,* and turns into *little flash—blink—big flash.*[5] You can illustrate this yourself, without a camera, by pairing a clicking sound with a puff of air blown into your eye. After as few as ten trials you'll find yourself blinking just to the click, in anticipation of the puff of air. You don't decide to do it, it just happens.

Pavlov was so impressed by what he had found that he changed his scientific focus and spent the rest of his life studying the process of classical conditioning. He published 513 papers on classical conditioning, and found that it occurred in every species he studied. His work suggested that, ideally, the "neutral stimulus" (the bowl, the leash, the bell) should be presented about half a second before the stimulus that naturally evokes a response (dinner, a walk, visitors at the door), and that

---

5. Now you know why, if you are easily conditioned, you have dozens of photos of yourself with your eyes shut.

the neutral stimulus needed to come first for the association to be made. In other words, your dog associates the doorbell with visitors because it rings *before* they enter the house, not afterward. But even Pavlov would be astounded by the implications of his discovery and by what we've recently learned about the power of classical conditioning to affect emotions and behavior.

The effects of this type of learning on the lives of people and animals are extraordinarily far-reaching. In one notable example, a researcher paired a red light with the introduction of a receptive female into a male quail's cage. Sure enough, after a few repetitions, the males became excited by red lights alone, and if a female did come to visit, the males produced more sperm and more semen, and copulated faster, if there was a red light on. (You have to love the researcher's choice of color.)

Lest you start to feel smug about the foolishness of a male quail, keep in mind that people are as susceptible to conditioning as birds. Malcolm Gladwell, in the book *Blink,* recounts a study in which people's behavior could be affected by the task of creating four-word sentences from seemingly random sets of words. But the words weren't random: each set contained one word associated with old age, either directly or indirectly. Examples are "shoes give replace old the" and "sunlight makes temperature wrinkle raisins." Believe it or not, simply reading words such as "old" and "wrinkle" embedded within four neutral words was enough to cause people to walk more slowly when they left the room than they did when they entered it. At no time were the subjects aware that their brains had unconsciously focused upon the words associated with old age, and had cued their bodies to behave appropriately. Apparently, "You are what you eat" needs to be broadened to "You are what you read."

I just about fell off my chair as I finished that paragraph, realizing for the first time that there just might be a *tiny* little connection between the fact that I have become more and more fearful about my ability to do justice to the subject matter of this chapter, which would be, uh . . . fear. Good grief. I've read tall stacks of articles on fear, and the word FEAR seems to be burned into my brain. And even though I've been reading and writing about fear for several months, it *just* occurred to me that there might be a connection between that and my own emotions. This stuff is scary. Heaven help my friends: the next chapter is on anger.

Unconscious associations like these are happening all the time to every human on the planet. That's why advertisers spend so much money linking cuddly-cute puppies to their products, so you'll feel the same good feelings about toilet paper and laundry soap as you do about dewy-eyed baby dogs. It's no accident that beer commercials usually contain stunningly beautiful and scantily clad women. Long, lustrous hair and hourglass figures may have nothing to do with beer, but they evoke the kind of interest and desire that beer producers want viewers to feel for their product.

However, as we've seen, classical conditioning isn't always a good thing for either species. Remember the little boy Albert who was traumatized in the laboratory? His terror of anything furry is a perfect, though tragic, example of classical conditioning, in which the soft white rat elicited the same response as a fear-inducing noise. Examples of this phenomenon abound in daily life. You may feel a bit sad every time you hear the song that played when you broke up with your first love. Chemotherapy patients become so conditioned to feeling nauseated in a medical facility that many of them begin to feel sick any time they enter a clinic.[6] Here in my own hometown, one former cancer patient illustrated the phenomenon when she ran into her chemotherapy nurse in the supermarket. "Susan!" she said to the woman who, *two years before*, had administered the nausea-inducing medicine, "it's good to see you again," and promptly threw up on the organic broccoli.

Obviously, the same process can work against our dogs as well—and explains why some of our dogs begin to drool and whine long before a storm occurs, or start to shake uncontrollably in the vet's waiting room. However, once you know how to use it, classical conditioning can do as much to prevent fear in your dog as it does to cause it. It's also the most effective way to treat a fear that has already developed. In a satisfying irony, Blue's thunder phobia was exacerbated because of classical conditioning, but it was classical conditioning that cured him. Speaking of phobias, this is a good place to talk about them in a bit

6. This can become a serious problem for some patients, so much so that there is actually medical literature on it.

more depth, because they provide important insights into how to use classical conditioning so that it's on your side.

PHOBIAS

What's most confusing about dogs' phobias, whether thunder phobias or separation anxieties, is that they seem to come out of nowhere. Blue lived through several thunderstorm seasons at the farm without reacting fearfully. That's typical: thunder phobia usually arises between the ages of three and seven years, and isn't related to any specific event or trauma. The origins of phobias are also mysterious in people—as a matter of fact, this is one of the identifying features that distinguishes a phobia from a simple fear.

What does make sense about phobias is the object of the fear. Phobias are usually defined as persistent, extreme, and irrational fears, but they're not quite as irrational as they might seem. Phobias are most commonly directed toward things that *could* actually be dangerous. People are most often phobic about snakes or spiders or being high up in space, not about flowers or birthday cakes.[7] A person's fear may be excessive—starting to sweat when looking at a photograph of a spider doesn't make a lot of sense—but it's not unreasonable to be afraid of spiders. Spiders bite, and the bites of some, such as the black widow spider, can be serious, in some cases even fatal. Dogs suffer from phobias, too, and, just like us, they usually develop their phobias around something with real potential to cause harm, like storms with lots of thunder and lightning, or being left alone with no ability to care for themselves if their humans don't return.[8]

Sadly, many of our dogs' phobias are explained away by placing the blame squarely on the shoulders of the owners, a practice that reminds

7. Cynophobia, or a human's excessive fear of dogs, is less common than a fear of snakes or spiders, but nevertheless represents a significant percentage of phobias directed toward animals (36 percent of animal-related phobias are directed toward dogs and/or cats. Regrettably, this is not an unreasonable fear, given that there are an estimated 4.2 million dog bites a year in the United States alone).

8. Because phobias are so often associated with things that have the potential to cause harm, it's reasonable to speculate that genetics create predispositions to be more afraid of some things rather than others. Monkeys can learn to be afraid of snakes just by watching a videotape of other monkeys acting fearfully around them, but they don't make the same association if you edit the tape and replace the snakes with flowers.

me of the days when many in the health care professions blamed Down syndrome and autism on the behavior of the mother, as if she didn't have enough to cope with. In dogs, thunder phobias are often explained as a simple fear that is reinforced by owners comforting their dogs when they start to shake or pace at the sound of thunder. "Aha!" said the early American behaviorists, "You're just reinforcing the bad behavior. You must ignore your dog when he's frightened of thunder." But most animals find fear so aversive that our behavior probably plays a much smaller role in our dog's fear of thunder than some have suggested.

I bring up phobias now because it's classical conditioning that explains another confusing aspect of these extreme fears. It's classical conditioning that explains why a noise-phobic dog starts to shake long before she hears thunder, or why dogs with separation anxiety start to pace and whine long before you leave the house. Just like Pavlov's dogs learning that footsteps meant food was coming, our dogs learn that a seemingly harmless event tends to happen before something frightening occurs. A drop in atmospheric pressure predicts a storm, just as the doorbell predicts a visitor. The owner putting on his coat predicts that the dog will be left alone. Because of classical conditioning, all of these things, like Pavlov's bell, can come to elicit a powerful response.

Remember the most important part of Pavlov's discovery: when a neutral event predicts something that causes an emotional response, it develops the ability to evoke the same emotion. That means your dog may be just as scared when the clouds roll in as she is when it thunders. That's also why a dog with separation anxiety is just as nervous when she sees you pick up your keys as she is once she's been left alone. Dogs with separation anxiety learn your patterns, and become conditioned to your combing your hair, picking up your keys, or putting on your jacket as a precursor to your departing. Dogs with thunder phobia become nervous when the barometer drops or the sky darkens, long before the thunder begins to roll. That's why so many people are unsuccessful when they attempt to cure their dog's phobias by giving the dog some tasty treats as the storm rages or as they walk out the door on the way to work. It doesn't work because the dog was already scared *long before* the thunder started, or long before his owner left the house, and the food has come too late to do any good.

PAVLOV IN YOUR POCKET

As I said earlier, the good news about classical conditioning is that it can do as much to alleviate your dog's fears as it can to cause them. First, you can use classical conditioning to *prevent* a lot of fears in your dog by predicting what might make your dog fearful in the future and linking a mild version of it with something your dog adores. For example, most dogs don't like having their paws handled, being the opposite of humans who often express affection by holding hands. They particularly hate having their nails clipped. Not only does it require that their paws be handled, but it can be painful if we inadvertently cut into the quick.[9] You can use classical conditioning to prevent problems by starting with a young pup and giving her a tasty treat right after picking up one paw and holding it gently in your hand for half a second. In this case, you're starting with a relatively neutral stimulus, like Pavlov's bell, and linking it with something the dog loves—food. Don't hold onto that paw too long. If you make the mistake (as many people do) of turning what should be half a second into two or three, you'll be eliciting the very emotion you're trying to prevent.

Just pick up her paw for a *brief* moment, immediately put it down, and give her a tiny, scrumptious snack. Repeat that once or twice, and then go play ball or take her on a walk. After a few sessions of that, pick up her paw, clip off a microscopically small piece of nail, and then give her the treat. You can even condition a verbal cue—"You wanna manicure?"—and end up with a dog who wags her tail and comes running when you pick up the clippers. Granted, some dogs dislike the procedure so much that all you'll get is dutiful acceptance, but if you start by conditioning paw touches and clippers with something the dog loves, you can at least avoid meeting your dog's dark side when you need to trim her nails. Of course, you'll want to proceed more slowly if your dog has ever threatened you when you picked up her paws—if that's the case, you'll want to work with a behaviorist.

You can use the same technique to prevent separation anxiety in a young pup. If you teach your dog to associate the things you do before

9. Just like us, dogs have a lot of nerve endings inside the living part of their nails. Think how painful it is to have part of a nail pulled off your finger. Owww.

you leave with something good, you can prevent a lot of soiled carpets and chewed windowsills in the future. The key is to know what the triggers are (what sights and sounds predict that you're about to leave) and what your dog loves (best in this case might be a tough, hollow chew toy stuffed with your dog's favorite food). If you teach your pup to associate the jingle of your car keys with the feelings he has while slurping up liver paste, you're probably not going to be calling a behaviorist two years later with a dog who leaps through the window when you go to the movies. The hardest part for most people is to be patient, and to start with the mildest version possible of something potentially scary.

If I had just adopted a new puppy, I'd first condition him to love being in a crate or small enclosed area by letting him run in and out of it to get treats, without even shutting the door initially. Over the course of the day I'd shut the door and leave him in the crate for gradually increasing periods of time—first two seconds, then five seconds, then thirty seconds. During this early phase, your goal is to have the dog feel good when he's in the crate, even if it's for an outrageously brief period of time. It only takes a second or two to become fearful, and that's what you're trying to prevent, so keep him happy in the crate with treats or toys, and let him out long before he wants out himself. I'd also put him in the crate when he's sleepy, puppies having on/off switches like lightbulbs. You can make tremendous strides in just one day, by playing the "crate game" every hour or so and letting your puppy sleep in it during nap time. By nightfall you'll most likely have a puppy who has already had lots of happy emotions while being inside a crate, and is much more likely to spend his first night in it asleep, rather than raising the dead with his whimpers.

As early as day two I'd start getting him used to my departure, by picking up my keys, putting on my jacket, and putting him in his crate with a nice, plump stuffed toy. Long *before* he finished it, I'd open up the door to his crate and let him out. I want him to think, "Oh, dear, don't come back yet! I'm not finished!" rather than "Oh, no! I'm left here all alone." Gradually I'd start leaving the room for a half a minute, then leave the house for five minutes to get the mail, or run down the street to pick up some milk. As the days and weeks go on, you simply increase the amount of time you leave the pup alone.

Of course, there's that pesky occupation that many of us have that demands we leave the house for eight hours or more, and we can't all take a two-month vacation when we get a new dog. If you work Monday through Friday and you're getting a new pup, your best option is to take Friday off and get the pup early in the morning. Then you'll have three long days in which to settle him in. By Monday morning, most pups will have had enough good experiences with your brief departures that you can leave him alone for at least half the day.[10]

However you manage the details, the idea is to link good feelings with your departure, being careful to start small, and gradually lengthen the time your pup will be alone. Don't worry that this will be so successful that your pup will lie around in hopes you leave the house and stay away. If you have a good relationship with your dog, he's going to love to see you coming home no matter what. We all want to be loved, but few of us want a dog who is phobic about being left alone, so put Pavlov in your pocket and condition your pup to feel good when she sees you walking out the door.

Of course, if your dog already has a serious case of separation anxiety, you'll need to work a lot harder to turn it around. See the References section at the back of the book for more information about treatment plans.

FRIEND OR FOE?

Not long ago, I heard a ruckus in my farmyard at two in the morning, and I padded downstairs to find out what was going on. As I stepped out of the house onto my porch, an agitated, scruffy-looking man appeared from the dark shade of my willow tree and began to run full tilt toward me. Immediately my amygdala began to signal some chemical version of Uh-oh! *while my hippocampus was comparing what I was seeing with my recorded memory of what is and isn't dangerous. ("There's an unfamiliar, strange-looking man running fast toward a solitary woman standing in her nightgown in the middle of nowhere at two in the morning. This is* not *good.") All I remember is being very, very scared, and opening the door to*

10. If it's a young pup, you need to either have someone let him out of the crate at lunchtime, or restrict him to an area where he can potty, because a young pup isn't going to make it all day long without relieving himself.

let Tulip out of the house in the hope that just the sight of her would slow him down.

Just as the approaching man lengthened his stride to leap up onto the porch, I said, in the lowest, calmest voice I could muster, "Stop right there." (Did I really say that? It sounds like a bad movie script, which, on reflection, is probably where I got it from.) The guy came to a screeching halt, his eyes glued on my barking hundred-pound dog, and proceeded to ask, ever so politely, whether it would be okay if he left his motorcycle under my willow tree for the night because it had broken down in front of the farm and a friend had come to give him a ride home and he'd return in the morning for the bike, that is, if I didn't mind. I tried to explain that it was fine to leave his cycle in my yard, but that he might want to rethink his policy of running like a madman toward a solitary woman in a farmhouse in the middle of the night.

The man may have been a bit dense, but he obviously had good intentions. However, neither Tulip nor I knew that as he dashed toward us at two o'clock in the morning, and you can't blame either one of us for being alarmed. This was a dog bite waiting to happen, and I bring it up now because I suspect that's what would have happened if Tulip hadn't been conditioned to associate visitors of all descriptions with treats and ball play. She was barking, and I have no doubt she'd have tried to protect me if the man had attacked, but Tulip has learned over the years to associate people coming to the house with feeling good rather than feeling fearful. That was enough to balance her concerns, and avoid a brief incident turning into a serious problem.

I thank Pavlov in situations like that, and every time I work with a client's dog who has gotten in trouble because he's afraid of visitors. You can use this same technique for both preventing and treating fear-related aggression in dogs. This is especially important if you have a dog who is genetically shy, like Tulip, or who didn't have much socialization as a young pup, like the Border Collie Blaze we talked about in the last chapter. In this case, what you're doing is called classical *counter*conditioning because you're trying to *counter* an emotion that already exists. Classical counterconditioning is a powerful tool used by animal behaviorists to turn around behavior problems that are moti-

vated by fear. As an applied animal behaviorist, I simply don't know
what I'd do without it.

The wonderful thing about this process is that once you understand
the basics, you can use it on any kind of fear. I taught myself to be less
nervous about public speaking by envisioning an audience in front of
me and popping a Hershey's Kiss in my mouth.[11] Even if you don't
have a fearful dog, you might profit by reading the next section
carefully—you never know when it might come in handy.

SAVING BLAZE

Blaze, the troubled dog of the Irish priest, came home with me on Friday, so that I'd have the weekend to settle him in. As usual, my partner
Jim arrived after work, well warned about the dog who had already bitten three times. Before I brought Blaze home I'd worked up a plan, so
we wouldn't have to make things up as we went along. We'd arranged
that as Jim drove onto the farm, I would stand a good fifty yards away
from his car with Blaze on a leash. When he got out, Jim was to stop
and turn sideways (to minimize any perceived threat) while I gave
Blaze pieces of cooked chicken. I wanted Blaze to associate this visitor
with something that made him happy. Blaze's emotions had other
plans. Long before Jim got to the end of the driveway, Blaze was barking and lunging hysterically. His pupils were fully dilated and his commissure was retracted almost to his ears. He wouldn't have taken a piece
of chicken if he'd been starving to death; he was too aroused to have
any interest in food.[12]

Asking Jim to wait outside, I brought Blaze into the house and put
him in his crate, which I'd put in a quiet room off the living room. Unlike many dogs, Blaze seemed to be calmer in a small space, perhaps
because he couldn't generate the agitated energy that fed his emotions. Some dogs become more fearful if they're trapped, but Blaze's
fears were exacerbated by a tendency to become overly aroused, so he
actually did better when he was restricted to his crate when visitors

---

11. If you want to wear size 3 clothing you may want to choose something besides chocolate.

12. One couldn't blame Jim if his own pupils were dilated at this point, although I have to admit to
paying more attention to Blaze. Jim has my eternal gratitude for participating in a project that would have
activated anyone's amygdala.

entered. Once Blaze was settled, I gave him treats as Jim entered the
house, knowing that he could hear and smell Jim even though he
couldn't see him. As the evening went on, Jim came and stood at
the entrance to the room while I slid treats into the crate to Blaze.
Eventually Jim himself was able to sidle next to the crate, avoiding any
direct eye contact, and push treats through the crate for Blaze. I continued that routine for the next week, during which I'd ask visitors to
drive up and stay outside until I came to get them. Every time I heard
a car arrive, I'd take Blaze by the leash and put him in his crate, sliding
treats into the crate until Blaze began to respond to the noise of a car as
if he liked it.[13] During the second week, I trained Blaze to run to his
crate himself every time he heard a car drive up to the farm. On the
third week, we practiced going into the crate when someone came to
the door.

If you have a dog who is frightened in any way of visitors, teaching
him to move away from the door might seem counterproductive.
However odd it seems, following that advice can eventually lead to a
dog who happily greets visitors as they enter the house. If you first
teach your dog to move *away* from the door, you are preventing surprise encounters when everyone is crammed together in the small,
emotionally loaded space of a doorway.

This is a good time to remember that every good treatment plan begins with a *management plan* to ensure the safety of your dog and your
friends, and, as important, to prevent your dog from being conditioned in the wrong direction. Don't fool yourself into thinking that
you can make everything hunky-dory by holding your dog by the collar as visitors enter. Remember, classical conditioning is about internal
states—emotions and the physiology that goes along with them—so
forcing your dog into a situation that makes him nervous isn't going to
solve the problem; it's going to make it worse. He'll be just as nervous,
but now he'll also feel trapped because you've got a vise grip on his collar. That's not going to make him love visitors; it will condition him to
be even more nervous about them.

You can prevent trouble, and prevent your dog from learning bad
habits ("I growl, they go away. Whew, got that figured out. . . .") by first

13. I was lucky that Blaze loved his crate and was happy to go in it when asked.

People and dogs share expressions of happiness. In these pictures, notice that everyone's mouths are open and have a similar shape, and everyone has a relaxed full face and a relaxed lower jaw.

A curved line under two dots is enough to signify happiness to us; even infants respond to this simple set of stimuli. Compare this happy face with the face of the dog on the left.

Left to Right: Lassie, Tulip, Luke (lying down), and Pip. Tulip was the only dog who was nervous about being in an unfamiliar place, and she's the only one whose mouth is closed.

Look at how open and relaxed these faces are. Not only are the subjects' mouths open, but the muscles around their eyes are relaxed, and their faces have a fullness not seen when one is tense or angry.

Look at all the open mouths in these relaxed and playful individuals. In the top two photos, Tulip play bows to me and then frolics. In the bottom left photo, Marc Bekoff and his dog Jethro exchange "play faces," and on the right, little Molly opens her mouth wide in joyful exuberance. Which of the five individuals on this page would you say is the least relaxed? Why?

Lassie's mouth is closed up tight and the inside corners of the eyebrows are pulled down and together. (Lassie was in the backseat of the car, which she seems to dislike intensely.)

I asked Chelse Wieland to make an angry face—ask yourself what it is about her face that is similar to the face of the dog in the photo below.

This dog is standing over a "prized" object. Notice that his mouth is closed (although his lips are raised as he growls), his eyebrows are furrowed, and his body looks stiff and tense. This is not a dog willing to let you take the object away.

Photo courtesy of Athena Farrell

Photo © Paul Ekman

Notice in these photographs that the corners of the dogs' mouths (the commissures) are all moved forward. The dogs in the top photos are on offense, barking at intruders. You can see the same forward commissure on the face of the angry woman on the left. Notice, however, that her eyebrows are pulled down and together, just as they are on the dog on the bottom of the previous page, indicating "on offense and angry" versus simply "on offense," like the dogs above.

The "worried" faces of both Lassie and Chelse include closed mouths, and upwardly raised inner eyebrows.

Both Chelse and Lassie are concentrating on something. Both of them have closed mouths, and the commissure (the corners of the mouth) is neither pulled back as it is in a smile or fear grimace, or pushed forward as it is in anger.

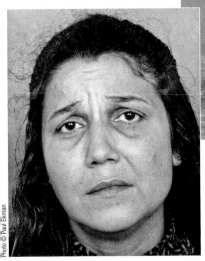

These dogs look sad to us because their eyes are large and soft, and they've raised the inner corners of their eyebrows, just as people do when they are sad.

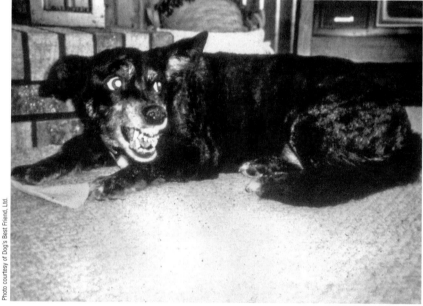

All of these photos illustrate fearful expressions, signified by the retracted corner of the mouth and the rounded eyes.

Compare the face of the dog Gus in each of these photos. In the top photo, Gus's mouth is open and his face looks relaxed and full. In the second photo, when Gus was tired after playing, Gus's mouth is closed and his face is losing its fullness. In the bottom photo, in which Gus is tired and cranky after a long day's outing, his face is drawn and tense, just like the face of a tired and cranky person.

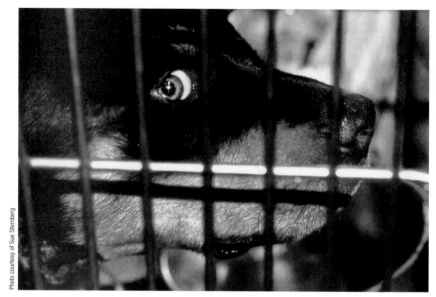

In a perfect illustration of "whale eye," this dog has turned his nose away from the visitor, but he can't take his eyes off her. The combination of a rounded eye, "whale eye," and a closed mouth is like a blinking neon sign that says, "Don't pet me!"

This dog is staring straight into your eyes, with eyes that are fixed and rounded. (The pupils are constricted because of bright light.) This dog could be fine, but because the mouth is closed, she's looking straight into your eyes, and is restrained by a short chain, you shouldn't risk petting her.

To heck with Botox, wrinkles are good. Look at how both the dog and her human have crinkly, squinty eyes as they express their mutual affection.

Who looks happier in this picture, the girl or the dog? The girl has an open mouth and squinty eyes, while the dog's mouth is closed and his eyes are showing "whale eye."

Here's another sad-looking (or worried?) dog, because the eyes are soft and the eyebrows are lifted at the corners. Notice how dogs often have different-color fur on the "eyebrows," the better to show their facial expressions. (Sometimes this pattern of fur may lead us to think that a dog is sad when he's not, especially when he's lying at our feet, looking up at us.)

All of these photos show dogs who are "tongue flicking," expressing either low-level anxiety or an appeasement gesture to an individual with more social status. You can tell when your dog is a bit anxious by how often he or she tongue flicks.

Some of these dogs appear to be expressing ambivalent emotions or motivations. The dog on the left has the rounded eyes and crouched posture of a frightened dog, but his direct stare is a clear offensive threat. One of the dogs on the right shows a fear grimace and a tongue flick, but he's standing squarely in front of the other dog and looking directly into her eyes.

The dogs in the photos above may be showing teeth, but the close-mouthed dog below might be the one most likely to bite you. His body is extremely tense and his head is being held in a stiff, unnatural position. His tail is tucked far under his belly, his mouth is closed, and he is looking directly into the eyes of the person holding the leash.

Ask yourself: What's the key feature on the white dog's face? He may look "aggressive," but the retracted commissure tells you that he is nervous. (His fur is also pilo-erected over his shoulders, indicating arousal.) Notice that the dog on the right doesn't appear to be nervous: Indeed, right after this photo was taken the dogs played well together.

Both individuals have their mouths open in this photo and are in a relaxed, comfortable state. Romy the Pit Bull is also hot, which is why her commissure is stretched back so far. ("Open mouth" doesn't always equal "relaxed"— sometimes it means the dog is hot or emotionally aroused.)

Tulip, with her head down on her paws, lay beside Harriet's body for several hours, until I finally led her away.

My first Great Pyrenees, Bo Peep. You can see she's tucked the stump of her left leg under her hip.

If there is such a thing as an "amused" look on the face of a dog, this must be it. Although you see the whites of the dog's eyes as in "whale eye," the dog's mouth is open and his body and face are relaxed. Personally, I think Luke is laughing at my hair.

Cool Hand Luke

teaching him to go into another room when there's someone at the door. Of course, your goal is to have a dog who happily greets visitors beside you at the door, but while you're working toward that it's handy to have an alternative that allows you to manage the situation and avoid trouble. Use this alternative when a busy delivery person bangs on your door, when your uncle George—the one who hates dogs—drops by to borrow a book, or when you're in a hurry yourself and can't follow the program described below. My dogs adore visitors, yet I find it handy to be able to send them into a closed room when certain kinds of company come. Even if your dog isn't aggressive, this is a great trick to teach her. Some of my clients have learned to dread visitors not because their dogs are aggressive, but because their pack goes so crazy when the doorbell rings that just opening the door qualifies as an adventure. How lovely to be able to ask your dogs to go into another room, and open the door in peace and quiet.

It's surprisingly easy to teach your dog to go away from the door after someone has knocked, although I say that with an awareness that many of you will be snorting with derisive laughter as you read this. If your dog seems to go stark raving crazy when the doorbell rings, you're not alone. If you'd like things to be a bit calmer, first understand that your chance of getting your dog's attention once he's barking hysterically at the door *after* a visitor has rung the bell is microscopic. The trick is to start *before* your dog launches himself into clinical hysteria, by first practicing when the house is quiet and calm. Knock once or twice on the door yourself, and then say, "Go to your place," in a happy tone and lure your dog with a fistful of yummy treats into the designated area (an easily accessible room with a door, or a crate in a quiet area of the house). Toss the treats onto the floor and shut the door. Wait just a few seconds, open the door, and let the dog out. Repeat that four or five times, all the while acting like it's a silly, fun game you're playing. After just a few sessions, most dogs eagerly run into the room, and don't mind the door being shut for a brief period of time. Work your way up to real life by having family members go outside and knock on the door, and eventually to friends who are happy to put up with waiting a minute or two while you lure your dog into the other room. You might want to give your dog a hollow toy (like a Kong or a Goodie Ball) stuffed with food to keep him happy there while you chat with your visitors.

"COULD WE HAVE SOME MORE COMPANY TONIGHT?"

Teaching dogs to go into another room when visitors come not only manages the situation so that it's safe, it also begins the process of classical counterconditioning. Rather than being scared, aroused, and in the thick of things at the front door, your dog has been taken out of a situation that is over his head, and has learned to associate the first signs of company with feeling calm, safe, and happy. "Ooooh, I love it when I hear the bell ring or a knock on the door, because that predicts I'm going to get chicken and I LOVE CHICKEN!!!!"

The next step is to create a safe way to have your dog out of the crate and in the same room as a visitor. The key here is to be extremely aware of every little sight and sound that could act as a "trigger" for your dog's fears. Just as a drop in atmospheric pressure can scare a dog as much as thunder can, there are a variety of stimuli that act as classical conditioners to dogs who are afraid of strangers. Common initial triggers are the sound of a car in the driveway, the sound of the doorbell, and a knock on the door.

The next set of triggers includes the sight of anyone standing at the "front" door rather than the one the family uses, the approach of an unfamiliar person, especially someone with a "weird" silhouette (produced by a backpack, a hat, or a huge beard), people with low, gruff voices, and the sight of a hand reaching out to pet them on top of the head, or a visitor standing up from a couch or a chair.[14] Keep in mind that having someone move *toward your dog* is very different (to your dog) from having *your dog move toward them*. Dogs are much more frightened of someone who approaches them than they are if the person (or other dog) stays still and lets the shy dog do the approaching. This is true of most animals. Temple Grandin relates in *Animals in Translation* that if you stand still inside a cow pen with a small white object, the cows will come over to investigate it. If you choose, on the other hand, to walk toward them with the same object in your hand, they'll spook and run away.

The better you get at identifying these triggers, the better you'll be

---

14. You can help a lot of shy dogs by having the family enter through the same door that company uses. Having a "family" door and a "door for unfamiliar people" is a setup for shy dogs. Seems obvious once you think of it, but we don't usually try to see our houses as our dogs do.

able to help your dog. Play the game now, and ask yourself what would be common triggers for dogs who have separation anxiety. There are lots of them, from taking just a few steps toward the door, to picking up your car keys, putting on your jacket, or combing your hair in the bathroom. You can play the same game with dogs who are thunder phobic—they usually begin to pace and drool when the barometric pressure drops, when the wind comes up, or when the sky darkens. Dogs with mild cases don't react until the lightning starts or the first thunder rolls are heard.

Whatever your dog's fears, it's critical to identify his triggers if you want to alleviate them. If you do have a fearful dog, sit down right now and figure out exactly what his triggers are. It doesn't matter if they make any sense to *you;* they have taken on the power to elicit fear in your dog, and that's all you need to know.

Blaze's fears of strangers were typical in that he reacted to all the usual triggers: he could be set off first by a car's approach, then by a doorbell or knock on the door, then by the sight of a stranger, by that stranger approaching him or coming into the house, by a stranger looking directly into his eyes, or by a stranger reaching, horror of horrors, to pet him. Blaze was just as aroused when people left the house as he was when they entered it (I have seen this in a small percentage of other dogs, especially the herding breeds), and at first couldn't generalize his acceptance of a person from one part of the house to another. After Blaze had accepted Jim completely (it seemed), he lunged at him in the garage, two seconds after giving him a kiss in the adjacent room. We just had to add "changing rooms" to the triggers Blaze needed to learn to handle.

Blaze's progress involved moving through each of those triggers, one step at a time. After conditioning him to enjoy people driving up and entering the house when he was in his crate, I began to work on the next trigger. I needed Blaze to become comfortable seeing people inside the house, but I wanted to avoid starting with him watching people entering through the doorway. Doorways are loaded locations to dogs, and I thought that he'd have a hard time accepting people walking in as he watched, even if he was on a leash far from the door itself. I did what behaviorists and trainers have been advising for years, which is to let the visitors enter the house without the dog seeing them. This avoided setting the dog off when someone "violated" the territorial boundary, and allowed the dog to come out on a leash when the visitor was less threatening, quiet and seated on the couch.

Blaze and I played this game for weeks, thanks to a dedicated community of friends who took the time to drive out to the farm. A carload of four or five people would drive up, and as they did Blaze and I would run to his crate, and I'd tuck him inside with a treat. Then one person at a time would come into the room and stand in the doorway, while I slipped food into Blaze's crate. Next, they'd squat down, keeping their body sideways as would any polite dog greeting another dog, and slip treats into the crate themselves. If Blaze looked relaxed and comfortable, I'd ask the visitor to go into the living room and sit down on the couch. Doors to the room safely shut, I'd let Blaze out of his crate, put on his leash, and walk him into the living room, using the door farthest from the couch. The first few times I did this he barked and lunged at the visitor. Both of us ignored this foolishness, and purposefully stayed quiet and relaxed. The visitor would begin tossing treats toward Blaze, and, because we'd worked our way up to it, Blaze was relaxed enough to eat (the treats, not the visitor).

Then Blaze would go back into his crate; the visitor would leave and send in the next person, who started the process all over again. By visitor number three in just the first session, Blaze started to associate a person sitting on the couch with chicken falling from the sky. No more barks, no more lunges. By visitor number five, Blaze was trotting out of his room looking for someone on the couch, his body loose, his mouth open, and his tail wagging. "*Yo!* Got any chicken?" he seemed to be asking, and the visitor, well equipped for that very purpose, would oblige. (If Blaze had become less relaxed as the list of visitors grew, then I would have stopped that session, and backed up several steps for the next one.)

The next step was to have Blaze out of his crate (on a leash, of course; or he could have been behind a secure gate that kept him away from the door) when a visitor entered. In this phase the visitors opened the door themselves, and stood in the doorway tossing treats like crazed flower girls refusing to walk down the aisle. Under no circumstances were they allowed to walk up to Blaze and try to hand him the treat. That would have been going way too far, way too fast. We were somewhere around step five in a twenty-step process; handing him the treats would be somewhere around step fifteen.

If you're working with dog lovers who don't have a lot of knowledge, this is the trickiest part of the treatment plan. It seems everyone wants to be the one to *hand* your dog the treat. "It's okay," they say when you ask them to throw the treat rather than hand it to the dog. "It's okay, I love dogs," they repeat, while they reach out to pet the dog cowering behind your legs. Humans seem to be hardwired with an almost uncontrollable need to touch a dog, whether you or the dog wants it or not, and it's hard to work around that. With respectful apologies to half the population, men tend to be worse about this. They often say, "Oh, it's okay, I'm not afraid of him," and so I suspect they misinterpret the instructions as concern for their well-being. Women more often say things like, "Oh, it's okay, dogs just love me." This is when a dinner party of behaviorists, contemplating the universality of this behavior, will simultaneously pick up their wineglasses and drain them in unison. In the nicest way possible, we try to explain to people that this procedure is not about them, it's about the dog, and yes, we understand that you're not afraid of the dog, or that you're so special that out of all the people in the entire world you'll be the one person whom the dog will not be afraid of, but please please please, just this once, would you do what we ask, for the dog's sake? Keep all this in mind if you're working on a treatment plan for your dog. Only ask friends to help you who will actually do what you ask, which, as we all know, turns out to be as hard for members of our own species as it often is for our dogs.

It would take a whole book to describe the entire period I spent with Blaze, and the next two months that he spent with a wonderful couple, Carol and Jim, who continued the process on their farm in northern Wisconsin. What I've written here is sufficient as a starter kit for dogs who are uncomfortable around strangers, but haven't gotten themselves (or you) into trouble yet. You can use these methods to prevent defensive aggression in shy dogs, and to manage and treat low-level problems in dogs who are nervous around strangers, but *please* don't take what I've written so far and start trying to treat a case of serious aggression without consulting a professional. You wouldn't try to neuter your own dog from information you got from a book, and treating aggression deserves to be taken as seriously as surgery. In both cases, a botched job can be fatal. This said, here is a summary of the process for those of you interested and able to pursue it:

- First, manage the situation so that, no matter what happens, everyone is safe. Saying "I *think* it will be okay" does you and your dog no favors. Be sure that no one can get hurt or scared before you go any further. For example, when Blaze lived with me, I kept my door locked at all times so that no one could walk into my house unannounced.

- Second, write out a detailed list of everything that might be a trigger to your dog's fears. Get really good at observing your dog and at noticing subtle signs of tension. Do all that you can to avoid eliciting the "wrong" emotion, and all that you can to elicit the one you want.

- Third, figure out what your dog adores most and only let him have it right *after* the appearance of a trigger. Food works best for most dogs, but ball play can be a great tool in conditioning. I played ball with my noise-sensitive dogs every time the sky darkened before a thunderstorm. It didn't make them love thunder, but it stopped Pip from clawing my face into hamburger meat when it did.

- Fourth, link up the trigger with the treat (in that order), starting with the lowest possible intensity of whatever it is that scares your dog. Gradually increase the intensity—for example, in Blaze's case, linking treats with first a car driving up, then a person on the couch, then one walking through the doorway.

- Don't go too far too fast (which, sigh, is what most people do and why the paragraph above is so important). I didn't let Blaze anywhere near anyone, except Jim, for the first six weeks that I had him, and even then it was only with dog-training professionals whom I knew and trusted.

- Don't ever stop conditioning, whether for prevention or treatment. My dogs still get treats when workmen come to the house, even though they are elderly and they've always loved workmen.

Be sure you understand that if you have a serious problem, you will have to manage it to some extent the rest of your dog's life.

- Again, don't do this by yourself if you have a dog who has injured someone or might do so. You wouldn't open up the back of your television and just start messing around with the stuff inside unless you knew what you were doing, so don't do the equivalent with your dog. Televisions can electrocute you; dogs can hurt people, and/or get their owners sued, so do everyone a favor and take this to heart.

There are lots of other things you can do for fearful dogs, from nutritional programs to exercise routines to trick training, but they are beyond the scope of this book. If you want to learn more, see the References section for a list of some sources of complete treatment plans.

YOU CAN'T FIX EVERYTHING, AND THAT'S OKAY

Blaze, I am gratified to say, is fine now. He's living on a farm with a woman who understands Border Collies and has lots of other dogs, and he gets plenty of visitors to keep him used to company. I went to see him about a year after he'd stayed with me, and drove unannounced into the farmyard. Blaze was loose in the yard, and he ran toward my car with his tail wagging in a huge, loose circle. Long before I think he recognized me, he was running up to me with his face open and relaxed, his eyes squinted, and his ears dipped in a friendly greeting. Lefty, the dog traumatized by the twelve-year-old boy, is fine, too. His family followed the steps described above, gradually exposing him to friendly men who came bearing treats and tennis balls, and eventually, with great care for safety, reintroducing the neighborhood children. The stories of Blaze and Lefty have the happiest of endings, but it's important to understand that not all stories turn out so well. No matter how good you are, you can't fix everything, any more than a great doctor can save everyone from a life-threatening disease. Blaze and Lefty had solid genetics behind them, and the resources and commitment of a large number of people for a treatment plan. That's just not true for all dogs, no matter how much you love them.

If you have a dog who is fearful, it's important to do what you can to alleviate those fears. No dog should have to live in fear all her life, and as the stories of Blaze and Lefty remind us, fearful dogs can sometimes be dangerous dogs. However, it's equally important to respect the essence of who your dog is. I work with and talk to professional dog trainers all over the country, and my impression is that many of us put too much pressure on ourselves to turn shy, inhibited dogs into bold, fearless ones. I don't know how many trainers I've talked to who broke down in tears of relief when they finally realized they didn't have to keep trying to "fix" a dog they got who simply wasn't suited for performing, or even for being comfortable at the dog park. Often the trainers have been told that they are just not skilled enough, or just not trying hard enough, when all along they have a dog who could no more do what they ask of her than most of us could win the Tour de France.

Perhaps the saddest cases are families who have a beloved dog who simply can't tolerate the addition of a toddler to the house, no matter how much training and conditioning the owners are willing to do. I meet dogs who appear to be flat-out miserable about a new child in the family, not so much because they are jealous but because they can't tolerate the noise and unpredictability of a little human scrambling around the house. Although many cases can be resolved, sometimes the only thing to do is to find the dog a quieter home, hard as that is on the family who loves him. Greater love hath no human.

And greater love had no humans than Blue's owners, who dedicated themselves to curing his thunder phobia. I had been worried, terribly worried, about his prognosis. It would have helped greatly if we could have brought him inside, but Blue couldn't do his job from the living room. Neither could he be medicated and still perform his job ("Hey, deer, how's it going?"), or be safe outside by himself. In addition, thunder phobias are especially tricky, because you can't ask the storms to represent themselves in a gradually increasing series of intensities throughout the summer. We did the best we could. Barb and Dave built him the finest "safe house" a working dog has ever had. They constructed a huge igloolike doghouse, insulated with over two feet of straw to dampen the transmission of sound. It had a double entrance so that Blue could crawl inside and turn 90 degrees to the right into a cozy, dark den, well protected from the storm. For six weeks,

Barb practiced a counterconditioning program. She ran to the doghouse at the first sign of an approaching storm, crawled into the house with Blue, and gave him lamb and chicken every time she heard the faintest crack of thunder. Every night that summer I lay in bed thinking of poor Barb, hiking across the fields to Blue whenever a storm came up. A few times I hauled myself out of bed and drove to their farm, ran across the mud in the pouring rain, and sat with Barb in a communal mix of misery and shared excitement, while Blue licked our faces and snarfed down chicken.

There were a lot of storms that summer—good for curing Blue's phobia in some ways, hard on Barb and Blue in others. One night yet another storm rolled in, but this time Barb was out of town. Husband Dave thought it was time to see if we'd made any progress, so he got out the binoculars and looked to see what Blue would do when the first thunderbolt sounded. Bless his heart, Blue ran to his safe house and stayed there until the storm passed, the emotion of fear countered by the cozy goodness of cuddling up in his house while the storm raged outside. Blue was fine all the rest of the summer, guarding the growing vegetables from the hungry mouths of deer, staying off the highway in storms, preferring his safe house to the dangers of the open road. I wish I could tell you he's still there, but one morning the next spring Barb and Dave found him lying dead in the field. He'd been healthy as a horse the day before, and he didn't have a mark on him. The vet thinks perhaps his heart gave out.

Although Blue's death was a great sadness to Barb and Dave, they are buoyed by the knowledge that his last year was full of comfort, rather than fear. Thanks to their dedication, the storms that had been a terror to Blue became a mere inconvenience. I think of him still, snoozing on a patch of rich black soil, soaking up the summer sun during the day, on guard all the night, watching over the farm like the good dog he was, taking care of the special people who took such good care of him.

6

ANGER

The good, the bad, and the ugly

Carley sat demurely in my office, soaking up attention and petting as only kids and dogs can. She was a lovely dog, a Springer Spaniel cross with limpid brown eyes and fetchingly long ears. She came when called, sat when asked, didn't jump up on company, and had been housetrained easily and permanently at a relatively young age. You couldn't get much more obedient—or cute, for that matter—than Carley. There was only one problem: the deep, nasty bite in Martha's hand. It had happened a few weeks before our appointment, when Martha tried to comb some burrs out of the fur on Carley's back legs. Carley hated having this area brushed (as many dogs do), and let Martha know it by turning her head, closing her mouth, and staring at the hand that held the hateful brush. As Carley matured, her stares moved from Martha's hand to her eyes, and Carley began to back up her threats with growls. By the time Carley was two years old, she'd begun snapping. A few weeks before our appointment, Carley had growled, lunged, and sunk her teeth into Martha's hand.

It was a bad bite, but Martha's feelings were more hurt than her hand. It's shocking when your best friend attacks you, and that's exactly how Martha felt—shocked. Carley may have been a dog, but except for their disagreement over grooming her hindquarters, she and Martha were bosom buddies. They went everywhere together and seemed to love each other equally. Carley moped when Martha left town; Martha passed up travel opportunities because she preferred being home with Carley.

Carley would let Martha take away her chew toys—although, when she thought about it, Martha admitted that sometimes Carley growled when she did so. She also confessed that she'd stopped trimming Carley's nails herself; Carley's growls seemed a bit too serious for her to handle. That was an important piece of information, because at that point in our conversation I was wondering whether there was anything about Carley's hips or back legs that might cause her pain. As we discussed that possibility, it began to seem highly unlikely. Carley's growls weren't only a matter of her back legs; she'd growl when Martha picked up her front ones, too. In addition, several veterinarians and chiropractors had done extensive evaluations, finding nothing that might have caused Carley pain.

After we talked, I sat down beside Carley and let her sniff my hand. She wiggled from the shoulders back and play-bowed. We had a great time together for a few minutes, playing and laughing (at least, I was), but once we'd established a relationship, I quieted Carley down and touched the back surface of her rear leg. Her face became serious. She turned her face toward my hand and stared at it. I gently pulled a bit on some of the hair on the back of her leg. She switched to looking directly into my eyes, and began to growl. Her face was full of emotion, but there wasn't a hint of fear in it. Carley didn't look fearful, surprised, or inquisitive. Pure and simple, Carley looked angry.

Anger and aggression can go hand in hand, and are so closely connected that many writers, including scientists, use the words interchangeably. This makes sense, given that anger probably evolved as a mechanism for recruiting the brain and body to prepare for battle. It's the "fight" part of "fight or flight." In its absence, most animals wouldn't survive, so it's no wonder it comes hardwired in so many species.

THE BIOLOGY OF ANGER

Although we have far to go, we're starting to understand a lot about the biology of anger. We know that, as part of the body's security system, the amygdala plays as important a role in anger as it does in fear. If you remove certain sections of the amygdala you can't elicit anger, no matter how hard you try. Conversely, you can stimulate those same areas with mild electrical currents and elicit a full-blown rage. That's how you get little tiny mice attacking cats in a laboratory version of David and Goliath.

Most biologists don't hesitate to attribute the emotion of anger to nonhuman animals. The neurobiologist John Ratey calls anger "the second universal emotion," as primal an experience as fear. Antonio Damasio even talks about "angry house flies," although he isn't implying that flies experience anger with the same kind of feelings that we have. Darwin has an entire chapter on anger in *The Expression of the Emotions in Man and Animals*.

That acceptance isn't universal, though, especially outside the fields of zoology and neurology. I had a client, a clinical psychologist, who said: "I know I shouldn't say this, but sometimes my dog looks so angry." Given that her dog had just shot Lassie a look that could only be described as murderous, I saw no reason not to use the term myself. I suggested that it seemed appropriate in this context. My client explained that her training had been explicit: anger was something experienced by humans; attributing it to nonhuman animals was unscientific and hopelessly anthropomorphic. Similar concerns about attributing anger to animals are not uncommon, perhaps because of the influence of the early behaviorists we talked about earlier. While surfing the web for articles on "anger management," I found a psychologist's statement that "all anger is learned." I sympathize with the author's thesis that people can learn to control their anger. I think sometimes dogs can, too, and we'll talk about how to help them do that later in the chapter. But that doesn't negate the biological basis of anger, and the fact that animals and people come hardwired to experience it.

In *The Other End of the Leash* I wrote that my noble dog Luke had a look best translated into two words, the second being "you." The first word was not "love." I'll leave it to you to figure the rest out. His sweet, docile daughter, Lassie, who has the most expressive face of any dog I've ever known, nailed her veterinary chiropractor with one of those looks after an atypically painful needle insertion. Lassie flinched, moved away, and then turned her head and looked back at Dr. Julie James—one of the kindest, gentlest veterinarians imaginable—with a look so hateful we both burst out laughing. There was no "I'm going to bite you" in it, but her eyes had such fury in them we could almost feel her anger moving through the air.

EVEN GOOD DOGS GET MAD

It's true that anger isn't the emotion most of us associate with dogs. I've had several conversations with professionals in medicine or behavior who suggested that dogs were the epitome of "pure love." Implied is that while dogs are like humans in their ability to experience love and joy (and/or are better at it), they don't share our more "negative" emotions, such as anger and hatred. A famous passage by John Cam Hobhouse about Lord Byron's loyal dog Boatswain includes the words "and all the Virtues of Man without his Vices." Jeffrey Moussaieff Masson's deeply felt book about the emotional lives of dogs speaks compellingly about their loving nature—he tells us that "the dog *is* love, that dogs are all about love." He has extensive chapters on the ability of a dog to suffer from fear and sadness, but only briefly mentions anger in the chapter on aggression. You can't blame him: most of us don't want to come home from a hard, frustrating day at work to an animal who reminds us about an emotion as aversive as anger.

In a general sense, our image of dogs as docile, loving individuals is valid. Dogs continually amaze me—they put up with treatment that would infuriate humans, remain seemingly cheerful in appalling circumstances, and, amazingly often, avoid using the weapons they carry, cocked and loaded, in their mouths. We've all known dogs who never seemed to experience even a flicker of irritation. Perhaps they felt it, but never expressed it, going through an entire life with the carefree demeanor of a happy three-year-old child at play. I suspect many dogs really are the joyful creatures that they seem. This is no accident: dogs' closest relatives are wolves, and those who know wolves are impressed by how purely they seem to express pleasure and playfulness. Additionally, domestic dogs carry a set of genes that emphasizes innocent docility, which comes as part and parcel of the joyful abandon we associate with childhood.

The evidence is growing that domestication itself, whether it resulted from natural or artificial selection (most probably both took place), includes a process of developmental inhibition in which adult individuals retain the docile characteristics of the young. Nowhere is that better exemplified than by dogs and wolves. In one sense, dogs *are* wolves—their genetics are so similar that they freely interbreed. Much of their behavior, too, is strikingly similar: a threatening or appeasing posture in a dog, for instance, is the exact replica of that posture in a wolf. And yet, dogs aren't wolves at all. Those who work with wolves unanimously agree that one never, ever commands a wolf to do anything. No matter how skilled or experienced you are, you work with wolves on their terms or not at all. It makes no difference whether the wolf was taken away from its mother at a few weeks of age and raised by humans, or captured in the wild; trying to force a wolf to do something is a poor tactic indeed. Apparently the people who have tried it have been selected out of the gene pool, because you never hear from them.

I thought about wolves once when I had to grab the collar of a frenzied and unfamiliar Husky. My friend Marilyn Fowler was doing a herding dog demonstration at a summer camp for dogs, while a group of people and dogs watched. Overwhelmed with the excitement of it all, a young Husky yanked the leash out of his owner's hands and began to chase the panicked sheep through the forest. I have a blurry video game–like memory of sheep, people, and dogs streaking around trees (and occasionally into them) while we tried to stop the dog before he did serious damage. We didn't succeed.

I was the first to find him and the sheep he had managed to catch.[1] The poor ewe was down on her side, with the Husky shaking her shoulder, his teeth sunk up to the gums in the muscles of her foreleg. Panting and shaking with adrenaline myself, I grabbed his collar, said a prayer, and began to pull him away. I knew perfectly well that even the nicest dog might bite my arm in that context. He was highly aroused, lost in a predatory haze, and he'd never even met me. Bless his heart, the dog instantly dropped the ewe and, without a flicker of anger, allowed me to pull him off. The owner was devastated at the sight of her beloved pet ravaging a sheep, but even though I felt bad for the injured ewe, I thought the dog's response to me was marvelous. This was not a

---

1. Be clear that this was a result of being in the right place at the right time, and had virtually nothing to do with any athletic ability of mine.

vicious dog. He was a dog doing what eons of evolution had primed him to do—run after moving prey and pull it down—nothing more. Of course, I'd rather he hadn't injured the ewe, but what he did wasn't about anger or aggression, it was about discovering his predatory past. He could have been angry and aggressive when I pulled him off, and he gets all the credit in the world for allowing me to do so. If he had been a wolf, I wouldn't be writing this, unless perhaps I had learned to type with my toes.

Some people object to describing dogs as "juvenilized" wolves, as if to do so demeans dogs in some way, but I don't think of it as demeaning at all.[2] I had more respect and admiration for Cool Hand Luke than I do for many of the people I know, and that's not because I don't like people. I love people, I think we're an amazing species, but the fact is that Luke was kinder and nobler than just about anyone I've ever known. I knew twenty-four hours after I got him that I was living with a very special individual. However, Luke was an intelligent, complex adult male, perfectly capable of having his own expectations and desires. As a result, there were times when he and I disagreed about what should happen next, and I have no illusions that I never made him angry. There were times when, having chosen another dog to go to the barn with, I told Luke to stay at the house, and he shot me a look I can't imagine describing as anything but angry.

Neither did he do everything I asked. When he was young, there were times when he'd lie down in front of the sheep, focused like a laser, and ignore my signals to return to me. "That'll do," I'd call, my words dissipating in the air like a trail of smoke. Nothing. Not even an ear flick. Luke stayed flattened to the ground, face riveted on the flock, his drive to work overpowering his interest in doing what I asked. This is a high-quality problem for a herding dog trainer—we love it when a young dog doesn't want to stop working—so I would gently take him by the collar and direct him away from the sheep for a moment. Luke quickly learned that coming off the sheep when called led to getting to work them again, so it didn't take long to teach him to respond to my voice. But in the beginning, I didn't hesitate to take him by the collar

2. The phenomenon is called paedomorphism, and involves a change in the development of an animal such that it retains many of its juvenile characteristics, even as a reproductively viable adult.

and coax him away. Try that with a wolf sometime. No, please, don't. The results wouldn't be pretty, although they might make great footage on *The World's Most Amazing Animal Videos.*

That dogs are juvenilized doesn't mean they are somehow lesser beings than their wild ancestors. I consider the domestic dog to be one of the world's most admirable creatures, and wouldn't want to live in a world that didn't include them. I couldn't live on my farm without my dogs, relying as I do on their ability to read sheep, their stamina, and their athletic ability on a daily basis. Dogs are better than our most advanced technologies at detecting land mines and rounding up flocks of sheep in rough terrain. They can detect lung cancer in the smell of a person's breath. That they cooperate with us in so many endeavors is nothing less than a biological miracle. I love wolves, too—I confess to getting tears in my eyes while watching two wolves rejoin the Slough Creek pack in Yellowstone National Park—but I won't be bringing one onto the farm to help me load up the market lambs.

EVEN LASSIE CAN HAVE A BAD DAY

However, just because dogs are more docile than wolves doesn't mean that every dog on the planet goes through life overcome with the joyful abandon of a floppy-eared puppy in a Kodak commercial. Although many of us do expect our dogs to radiate love and joy every minute of every day, surely it's a rare dog who never gets irritated, much less angry. After seventeen years of working with problem dogs, I can't imagine how to make sense of what I've seen without attributing the emotion of anger to dogs.

Of course, there's a danger in attributing any emotion to a dog's behavior, because we are so often wrong about it. That doesn't mean they don't have emotions, it just means that we need to get better at reading their expressions and must avoid projecting our own feelings onto them. Out of all the emotions we may or may not share with dogs, I suspect that anger is the one we're most confused about. On the one hand, we have a collective expectation that dogs should exemplify our positive emotions, such as love and joy. On the other hand, we are quick to project anger onto them inappropriately. For example, the most common assumption of novice dog owners—the same ones who will tell you that dogs are better than people because they are so loving—is that dogs urinate on the carpet because they're angry they were left home all day. However, dogs go to the bathroom in the house because they haven't been housetrained, or because they're scent marking, or because they're anxious when left alone. They don't expect us to have a trust fund that enables us to stay home all day, but it seems to be oh-so-human to imagine that those sweet, loving dogs we see in the evenings are so angry during the day that they poop on purpose just to get back at us. We also tend to imagine the worst possible motivations for any example of what we call (usually inappropriately) disobedience. People imagine their dogs are "angry" or "getting back" at them when they don't come when called or when they refuse to return the ball their owner threw. In truth, the poor dogs usually don't know what we want or, or worse, have been inadvertently trained not to do it.

However, it makes no sense to avoid inaccurate projections by pretending that our dogs can't ever be angry. Anger is too primal and too universal an emotion to be ignored, and it's absurd to imagine that we're the only species to experience it. Of course, having our big, impressive brains means that many of our inner experiences are very different from those of animals, and it may well be that humans and dogs experience anger in different ways. But the similarities are impressive, and we ignore them at our peril.

THE FACE OF ANGER

One of the many similarities between anger in humans and anger in dogs is in its expression. As you can see in the photos, the face of an angry dog resembles the face of an angry human. Imagine being five years old again, and make an angry face right now, letting your face do whatever it wants. You'll find that your mouth is closed, your lips are pushed forward, and your eyebrows move together and downward. You can see a similar expression on the face of a confident dog warning that she's about to bite. As in a human's expression of anger, the mouth moves in the opposite direction from a fear grimace. As we saw in Chapter 2, the corners of the mouth retract when we're frightened, but when we're angry, the corners of the mouth are pushed forward. In dogs this is called an offensive pucker; it can tell you a lot about the internal state of a dog, as well as what he's likely to do next. This expression is never seen on a defensive dog, but is seen on the faces of confident dogs who are on offense and are sending a clear threat that unless you change your behavior, you're at risk of being bitten.

We talked about offensive puckers relating to dogs who are on offense in Chapter 2, but I'm not sure that always means the dogs are angry. Surely both people and dogs can be threatening aggression without feeling angry. There are dogs out there that I call hit men, because their aggression seems devoid of emotional arousal and yet is chillingly serious. However, luckily for all of us, professional killers are relatively rare in both species, and when I see an offensive pucker, especially one combined with a wrinkled forehead and hard eyes, I'm inclined to believe that the dog is experiencing something akin to anger in humans.

As mentioned in Chapter 2, hard eyes are more difficult to describe than changes in the mouth or eyebrows. They're a bit like great art—you'll know it when you see it, but you can't quite articulate what it is. (I suspect this is a great example of the kind of unconscious knowledge described by Malcolm Gladwell in *Blink*.) Hard or angry eyes have a focused and rigid quality, but the best most of us can do is to describe them as "hard" or "cold." If you see a dog with hard eyes, an offensive pucker, and a stiffened body, stop doing whatever you were doing and reevaluate your options. Getting the heck out of there might be a good choice.

As you get better at reading expressions of anger, you'll see flickers of it that are so fleeting they may have escaped your attention in the past. These "micro-expressions" can occur so quickly they actually precede the feeling of anger in the person making them. The nationally known handler and trainer Sue Sternberg has a great series of videotapes of dogs looking "friendly." The dogs' mouths are open, their tails are wagging, and they leap up onto the handlers as if excited to see them. But if you look closely, the dogs' bodies aren't wagging, they're stiff. The dogs' mouths may be open, but it's because they're aroused and overheated, not because they're relaxed. If someone touches them, they turn and glare, ever so briefly, at the person's face right before they leap up toward it. These dogs are excited, all right, but not in a good way. Their eyes are rounded, cold, and hard, with none of the crinkles on the faces of friendly dogs. Sometimes the warnings they give are the briefest of looks, usually accompanied by the mouth closing and the commissure moving forward for just an instant. The message here is best read as "Stop touching me, or I'll take matters into my own teeth." Such micro-expressions occur in both people and dogs—indeed, everyone I know who has worked with aggressive dogs says they are better at reading anger on the faces of people now that they've gotten so good at seeing it on dogs.

ANGRY ON THE INSIDE?

In all animals, the external signs of anger are accompanied by a suite of internal changes. When we and our dogs get angry, our amygdalas begin a series of biochemical changes that ready us for battle. Our heart rate accelerates, our blood pressure rises, our muscles tense, and our breathing speeds up. Neurotransmitters called catecholamines flush through our bodies, producing a burst of energy. That rush of energy is one of the reasons we feel compelled to *do something* when we're angry, and why it takes maturity and experience to pause and think before acting. No wonder we blurt out hurtful words that were best left unsaid: part of our brain is compelling our body to act, even when caution is the wisest choice. Bathed in the stimulating hormones adrenaline and noradrenaline, an angry body is, by definition, aroused and looking for a fight.

As we saw in the chapter on fear, adrenaline and its relatives can take a long time to leave the body. This is one of the reasons it can be so hard to let go of anger. All of us have, at some point, been angry at a perceived injustice, only to discover that we were misinformed. But rather than immediately relaxing, it is common for us to still feel angry, even though the anger no longer makes any sense. That's because our bodies are primed for battle, and no matter how hard our rational brain tries to calm us down, it takes time for our internal chemistry to get back to normal. We can go on alert in an instant—the need for an immediate response being obvious—but we can't calm our bodies down as quickly as we can ramp them up. That's why it can be hard to calm down after someone apologizes to us. We may intellectually grant forgiveness, but our body's chemistry can't turn things around that fast.

Dogs undergo the same physiological changes as people, and they, too, can have lingering adrenaline in the system, so that their bodies remain primed for action long after the initial incident occurred. That is one of the reasons I often ask clients what happened in the hours *before* an incident occurred: residual adrenaline can make dogs more likely to react with anger, just as it can in people. This is also why it can be dangerous to use a strong physical correction on some dogs: engaging in battle with a dog who is already pumped up for a fight can make things worse. I've seen hundreds of examples of these spirals of arousal and anger in which both the person and the dog become increasingly enraged. This is a situation you want to avoid: fights don't always have winners, and too often the result is that both of you end up losing.

Anger has many similarities to fear: it's a primitive emotion that is dependent upon the amygdala, and it results in a flush of adrenaline and other substances that ready the body for action. Anger is also like fear in that its expression can be influenced by genetics, early development, and a lifetime of learning and experience. We'll talk about each of those components next, and then move on to talk about how to avoid anger-related problems between you and your dog.

GENETICS AND ANGER

Frankie, all of eight weeks old, wobbled into the offices of Dog's Best Friend, Ltd., and work pretty much came to a standstill. It's always a great day when a puppy comes to visit the office; it's a welcome change from our usual routine. Eighty percent of our cases are about aggression, and all of our staff are taught to sit on their hands when a dog enters the building. Until we've had a chance to evaluate him, who knows what his triggers are? Maybe he's fine until someone reaches out to pet him. Perhaps the dog loves women with blond hair, and only bites brunettes. You learn fast, sitting in a little room with a dog who has bitten, to be thoughtful about each and every move you make. After a while, slow, quiet movement becomes so routine it can be run out of your energy-conserving cerebellum rather than your cortex. But there's always an edge of arousal—at least, there should be, if you're going to do your job right.

But puppies are another matter. In they squirm, bodies wagging and eyes shining, and the office breathes a great, collective sigh of relief. Five-year-old children don't hold up convenience stores, and eight-week-old puppies don't tend to be aggressive. Neither do they come in with histories of growling and biting people. They waddle into the office with disproportionately large paws and foreheads, their baby-mammal "cute factor" off the charts. We do what everyone does when they see a puppy. Our voices go up and our bodies sink down, the better to pet and coo and soak up the sweetness of youth.

Frankie got all the attention that every puppy engenders, and then came into my office for an evaluation. The family was concerned about a few incidents of nipping, and wanted to get my opinion before it was too late to return the dog to the breeder. That was the last thing they wanted to do, but they had three young children and were wise enough to understand the importance of ensuring that the puppy was a good match for their family.

I was glad they'd come in, because it's impossible to evaluate this kind of case over the phone. It's hard enough to predict how a dog will behave as an adult on the basis of her behavior at eight weeks. It's downright impossible to do so over the phone. I'm also glad they understood, as many people don't, that dogs come with predispositions to behave one way or the other. That's as true of a dog's tendency to lose her temper as of the tendency to be fearful.

Frankie busily explored the office while the family and I talked about some of the incidents that concerned them. The first nipping incident had occurred when Frankie was pulled away from a chew toy, the second when she was stopped from bolting out the door. "Nipping" can mean a lot of things, from gentle mouthing of the hand to a serious bite. The family thought Frankie's version of it was troubling, and wanted a more experienced opinion. My job was to elicit the behavior in a humane way, in order to see for myself whether Frankie's behavior was typical of a puppy suited to live with a family.

I called Frankie over to me and gave her a treat for coming, and then after a few minutes of petting, I gently rolled her over on her back. I wanted to see what she'd do when she tried to get up, but couldn't. The incidents described by the family all occurred when Frankie wanted something and couldn't get it—classic frustration. By gently holding the puppy on her back long after she wanted to get up, I could see for myself how she responded when she felt frustrated. When you do this, most puppies squirm a bit; some mouth at your hand as if to make it go away. Others go stiff and silent, the corners of their mouths pulled back in a fear grimace. I tried the exercise on Tulip when she was seven weeks of age, and I can still remember her firecracker expression as she joyfully, but determinedly, tried to get up. That pretty much sums up Tulip—joyful and determined—and I've learned over the years that this particular exercise can tell me a lot about who a dog is, and how they respond to the frustrations that life always has to offer.

Rolled over on her back, with my hand resting on her chest, Frankie went still momentarily, and then began to thrash like a fish out of water. As she did, she started to growl, and began biting my hands with enough force to hurt. Her agitation increased, and the corners of her mouth moved forward in an offensive pucker. Her growls deepened into sounds too low, it seemed, to come from such a tiny chest. After just a few seconds of being held on her back, Frankie had worked herself up to a full-blown rage. Her eyes radiated fury, her mouth was forward and puckered, and her teeth were exposed. She tried desperately to sink them into my hand. She was so aroused that saliva was bubbling around her lips. I remember thinking: "This is what 'spitting mad' means."

All this was bad enough, but Frankie's response when I released her was even worse. Rather than getting up and licking my hands (a common response from sweet, docile puppies) or even moving away and glaring at me, Frankie took a split second to realize she was free, and then lunged straight at my face as if to bite it. She didn't—at eight weeks, she was easy to stop— but the look on her face chilled me to the bone. Straight out of a horror movie in which young children turn evil and violent, she had the steel-trap expression of an adult willing to kill you, on a face that should have reflected the innocence of youth.

Frankie, thank the stars, was taken back by the breeder. The family found an amiable dog from the shelter who didn't give it a thought when her tail was grabbed by the family's two-year-old.

In the right environment and with the right handler, Frankie might have turned into a fine dog, although I would never have placed her with young children. Nonetheless, sometimes you can work wonders. A veterinarian friend and colleague once brought in a Corgi puppy she had bred

who reacted very much like Frankie. Rightfully concerned, she kept the dog
and worked with him for months, rather than send Darth Vader to some
hapless family expecting Prince Charming. Working together, we developed
a doggy anger management program, and son of a gun, the pup grew into
a good dog who lives happily and politely in the home of a single woman.
He's a reminder that genetics are blueprints that can be altered by the right
architect, if you can modify them before the foundation is set in stone.

Frankie the puppy is a good example of the genetic basis of anger. People and dogs share the ability to become angry, but, in both species, the frequency and intensity of anger vary from individual to individual. We all know that some of us come out of the chute a lot grumpier than others—ask any parent with more than one child. Sporting events, with their potential for both frustration and emotional arousal, are great tests of an individual's ability to handle frustration. When he was young, John McEnroe charged onto the tennis court with a temper as powerful as his forehand. Red-faced with rage, he'd scream at the line judge and slam his racket to the ground when things didn't go his way. Older fans were appalled, accustomed as they were to the more genteel play of times past. Times may have changed, and outbursts of anger may be more acceptable now than they were before, but McEnroe's behavior wasn't just about "letting it all hang out." Look at another tennis star, Roger Federer, who's playing at the same age that McEnroe was when he was stomping around the court. Federer is so calm and polite that commentators (including the now mellow and gracious McEnroe) are surprised if he so much as raises his voice. Two different people, with two different personalities. We see it all the time, and yet we often don't focus on its importance. I've never seen anger management skills mentioned in a personal ad ("Attractive, intelligent, handles frustration with grace and aplomb . . ."), but which personality type do you want to spend the rest of your life with?

The question, of course, for both dogs and people, is how much of the difference in behavior is due to genetics, and how much to learning and early environment. As usual, the answer is clear: nature and nurture both play important roles in the likelihood that your blind date will throw his plate across the room if he doesn't like his pasta, or that your dog will go after your arm when you take away his bone. Just as with fear, genes matter when it comes to the emotional expression of anger. The delicate balance of molecules that powers our brains—a little serotonin here, a pinch of dopamine and adrenaline there—plays a big role in our temperaments, and much of that balance is inherited. Although our brains are like ongoing chemistry experiments, to which we can always make some adjustments, we're still stuck with the ingredients with which we started.

We know that babies born with uninhibited temperaments (the opposite of the cautious children we talked about in the last chapter) are likelier to have problems with anger management in adolescence. People with short tempers often have underactive frontal lobes, which normally act to inhibit impulsiveness, and it looks as though they were born that way.[3] The examples of the links between brain chemistry and anger-related aggression are endless. An imbalance of the neurotransmitter serotonin can result in aggressive behavior, which is why SSRIs like Prozac are sometimes effective in aggression-related cases. Individuals whose thyroid glands are underactive owing to inheritance or disease can have serious problems with anger and aggression until the imbalance is corrected. All these conditions are influenced by the customized set of genes that makes every individual unique. Some code for mellow, some code for prickly. You'd be wise to keep that in mind when you meet the family of your potential partner. (I would, however, avoid rolling Uncle Harry over onto his back the first time you're invited to a family dinner.)

"NATURE, RED IN TOOTH AND CLAW"

This relationship between genetics and anger is not unique to people. For example, everyone who works with common chimpanzees knows that the species is relatively aggressive, but they also know that every individual is different. In the book *Chimpanzee Politics,* Frans de Waal describes each of his research chimps as having vastly different personalities. The researchers on the study team had a range of opinions about

3. No, this is not an excuse to yell at me if something I say makes you mad. Everyone can learn to better manage anger, even if it means teaching yourself to go cool off in your crate.

who should win the "Miss Congeniality" title, but everyone agreed that one female, Puist, was the grumpiest. Described as "two-faced and mean," she terrified subordinate chimps, who never knew when she'd turn on them in a rage. The temper tantrums of common chimpanzees can be so dramatic they become funny, unless you happen to be anywhere nearby, at which point they become terrifying. One of the most important social roles of high-status female chimps is to calm and soothe agitated individuals (especially males) before they do something they're going to regret. It seems they need to do this much more often with some individuals than with others. Sound familiar?

Even pigs differ in how often and how intensely they behave in ways that we might call angry. We may think of being "piggy" as being greedy, but some pigs could have their own World Wrestling Entertainment show and get prime-time ratings. Researchers have found, after gently restraining pigs on their backs, that some pigs use aggression only when they have no other choice. Other individuals are less flexible, using aggression as a "one size fits all" solution to a variety of problems. Apparently, some are grumpier than others, in that they are quicker to respond aggressively to events that other pigs let slide.

I've seen the same personality differences in my sheep. My dear old ewe Harriet was quick to defend her lambs if she felt they were being threatened, but she'd graciously sniff noses with any of my Border Collies when they were "off duty." Not so with a younger ewe named Crystal. Long after her lamb was weaned, Crystal took any chance she could get to try to smash Lassie into the fence. Recently she barged through the flock to come after Lassie as she and I were leaving the pen. We had brought grain, water, and yummy alfalfa hay to the flock, and I had every reason to believe the sheep were chowing down with gusto as we walked back into the barn. I remember feeling the sweet glow of satisfaction that all farmers have when the chores are done and the sky is turning navy blue and the lights glow golden from the house. *Thwump.* I heard it before I saw it, a flash of white, Crystal's anvil head smashing low and fast into Lassie before my brain could make any sense of it.

It took three months of vet visits and rehabilitation for Lassie to recover, blindsided as she'd been with no chance to protect herself. There was simply no reason for the attack, except that Crystal hates dogs, even though they've never abused her in any way. Crystal is still at the farm, although I must confess her future is uncertain. I have my own anger issues to deal with now: I can't find it in myself to forgive her for her unprovoked attack on Lassie. The image of Lassie—sociable and loving to people, fair and patient to sheep—flying through the air like some furry, twisted pretzel will never leave my mind. I love Lassie with all my heart. She's willing and sweet and hardworking. She's beautiful and needy and vulnerable, and when Luke, her father, was dying, I promised him I'd take care of her. It doesn't matter if he understood what I meant, I said I would. I know that forgiveness is healthy, and I presume that, in terms of my own contentment, harboring anger toward a ewe is no better than being angry at another person. I'm working on it, but Crystal would be wise to mind her manners.

It's no surprise to dog owners that other canines, such as wolves, have their own anger management issues. Wolf researchers, rigorously trained in science, talk freely about wolves with tolerant personalities versus those with short fuses. Douglas Smith, in *Decade of the Wolf*, writes about Number 40 of Yellowstone's famous Druid pack, who became known among wolf lovers far and wide as the country's meanest wolf. She was so quick to lose her temper and take it out on others that the other members of the pack lived in constant fear of attack. In an unprecedented occurrence, she was eventually killed by a coalition of lower-status females who had had enough and weren't going to take it anymore.[4] The pack was taken over by her sister, Number 42, who was as benevolent as Number 40 was intolerant.

There's no reason why dogs would be different from wolves, pigs, and people and not vary in their tendency to beome angry. Frankie, the puppy who flew into a grown-up-like rage when I restrained her, isn't the only dog I've met who's lost her temper easily. Reactions as extreme as hers are rare, but differences in a tendency to lose one's temper occur within almost every litter. You can see them early in life, sometimes as early as three weeks of age. It's hard to imagine that experience alone accounts for such early differences. Surely much of the same brain

---

4. The exact cause of Number 40's death is unknown, but all the evidence points to a horrific battle in which her own pack turned on her and injured her so badly she died the next day.

chemistry that makes some people mellow and others quick to anger also exists in dogs.

MATCHMAKING

The influence of genetics on anger doesn't mean we're helpless victims of a dog's parentage. Far from it. In a way, it's a good thing that there's a relationship between genetics and anger. It means we can breed for docility over irritability, and select new dogs with some hope of predicting what we're going to get. Of course, the best anyone can do is play the odds—canine behavior is far more complicated than something like black or yellow coat color, and there's virtually nothing that can predict, with perfect accuracy, a dog's behavior a year down the road. We can't do that even with our own species, as should be patently obvious from a glance at the divorce rate. Predictions are particularly tricky if the dog's environment will change substantially, because, just like people, dogs behave differently in different circumstances. However, you can do a lot to get the odds on your side, and if you have the opportunity, why not take it?

If you're buying a pup from a breeder, the first step is to learn how tolerant the pup's relatives are when they're frustrated. Will Dad let you take away his bone? What does Mom do if you gently take hold of her front paw and don't let it go? Does she squint her eyes and lick your hand (good girl), or stiffen, ever so briefly, with a hard, cold stare directly at your hand or face (uh-oh)?[5] If you or the breeder is concerned about your safety if you pick up the paw of one of the pup's parents, your job is already done. Why go any further? Run, don't walk, to the car, and drive home congratulating yourself on your wisdom and maturity.

If possible, don't confine your questions to the behavior of the parents. The dam and sire of a litter can pass on genes that they don't themselves express, so their behavior isn't always enough to tell you what genes might be passed on to the pups. If you can, learn about the behavior of the pup's grandparents, aunts and uncles, and siblings from

5. Please avoid the mistake made by one of my clients, who said, "I don't know anything about the temperament of the sire. I couldn't get anywhere near him, he was barking and snarling so much." Oh, dear.

another litter. Inheritance in dogs works very much as it does in people, so if you'd like an easygoing family dog who can put up with a five-year-old, you'd be wise to choose a pup from an entire line of easygoing dogs.

PASSING THE TEST

Family histories are helpful, but we all know that every individual is unique. That, too, is as true of dogs as it is of people. That's why, along with checking up on his family, you'd be wise to test the individual puppy that you're thinking of taking home. There are myriad ways to assess a dog for frustration tolerance, and I want to be clear from the outset (again!) that these "tests" can give you a probability statement, not a guarantee. Think of them as weather predictions. They're based on good information and lots of experience, but, just as the weather is too complicated to predict with perfect accuracy, the behavior of a dog later in life can only be estimated, not guaranteed.

As noted earlier, my favorite exercise with a young pup is to *gently* roll her over onto her back and then lightly restrain her with a hand on her chest. Spend some time with the pup first, so that this isn't her introduction to you. I will usually play with a pup for a good five to ten minutes before beginning this exercise. Then I'll gently roll her, first onto her side and then over onto her back, and place one hand on her chest. I'll let my hand rest lightly on her until she begins to try to get up, and then I'll use just enough pressure to keep her from doing so.

There are a lot of different ways she can respond once she's over on her back and figures out that she can't get up when she wants to. She could replicate Frankie's response—and spiral into a primal rage so powerful it seems too big to fit inside a tiny body. The good news is that such a response is rare: I've probably seen it five or six times in seventeen years. It's also hard to miss, no matter how little experience you've had with dogs. If you see it, I suggest you move on to the next pup (or better, the next litter) as fast as you can, unless you'd like to write your own book on canine behavioral problems.

Far more common are subtle differences in behavior, and the more experienced you are at reading dogs the better you'll get at interpreting them. Some puppies will squirm a bit and mouth your hand lightly, a perfectly reasonable response that wouldn't concern me in the least.

But ask yourself: do the puppy's nips get harder, while the corners of his mouth go forward into an offensive pucker? Hmmmm—time to start paying attention if you have a house full of children. Does the pup never stop trying to get up, while his littermate gives up quickly and passively waits for you to let him up? Which pup you pick depends on what you want. If you want a search-and-rescue dog or a nationally competitive performance dog, you want one who never gives up, so you might choose the former. However, the latter might be a better choice for a family who wants a buddy to hang around with the kids in the backyard.

Pay attention to what the pup does when you let him go. I've seen puppies who have rolled over, nailed me with one of those "looks could kill" expressions, and refused to come near me again. That's not the dog I want, because I love dogs (and people) who don't take life too seriously. Neither do I want a dog who is so stressed by the procedure that his eyes round in terror and his body goes stiff, while his commissure retracts in fear. My favorite dog is the one who takes the whole thing as a silly game, and comes back for more when he gets up.

This is just one method for assessing frustration tolerance. Although these kinds of behavioral evaluations are somewhat controversial, there is an increasing amount of evidence suggesting that they can be helpful at predicting certain types of behavior. Trainer Sue Sternberg was the first to develop a test to evaluate the potential for aggression in shelter dogs. Others, like veterinarian/behaviorist Amy Marder and animal behaviorists Emily Weiss and Rebecca Ledger have developed their own tests and followed up with research that suggests some aspects of these evaluations can indeed be predictive. For example, Marder's research found that dogs who are aggressive around objects in a shelter environment ("resource guarders") are likely to behave the same way in someone's home up to six months later. She also found that dogs who are rated as being not particularly friendly in the shelter are equally aloof in their new homes. This is just the tip of the iceberg—see the References section for more sources on evaluating adolescent or adult dogs, and for ways to evaluate puppies.[6]

---

6. Perhaps we should develop a "temperament test" for dating services. It would probably not include rolling your date over on his or her back.

As I've mentioned before, I've found these assessments to be valuable if you understand that they are just probability statements, like a weather forecast. They are often called *temperament* tests, although that is not the best designation, because what is being tested is how a dog will react at any given moment to a particular event, not a long-term tendency to behave in certain ways over long periods of time (which is the definition of "temperament"). Nonetheless, it is one of many ways to gather information that can help you make predictions about a dog's behavior. Keep in mind that the further away a dog is (in both age and environment) from what you're trying to predict, the less accurate you'll be. It's useful to go back to our analogy with weather forecasts. Meteorologists are pretty darn good at predicting the weather a few hours from now, not bad with predictions for the next day, and much less accurate if asked to predict what's going to happen a month from now.

If you can, take along an experienced dog trainer; or at least read up on the topic. I can't stress enough the importance of relying on an expert evaluator if you can round one up. Although, ideally, all of these assessments would be completely objective, there's a subjective quality to them that can be valuable, *if* it's generated by someone with years of experience. Just as an art expert can take one look at a forgery and somehow know it's not "right," people who are great at reading dogs can get a sense about a dog that they find hard to describe, but that feels overwhelmingly important. I've seen dogs who made me nervous for no reason that I could discern, and dogs who growled and snarled at me who I was sure were bluffing. Often those intuitions have turned out to be good predictors of a dog's subsequent behavior. It's true that hunches aren't always right, no matter how skilled or experienced a person might be. However, given how much we're learning about the importance of intuitive knowledge, I don't think they should be ignored.

EARLY DEVELOPMENT

It's hard to imagine an emotion as important as anger not being affected by a dog's environment during early development. We know that early development affects how an animal experiences fear, and we know that anger and fear are both driven by that ever-so-important structure the amygdala. It seems impossible to imagine that an individual's experience of anger would be unaffected by his early experiences in life. I know of no research on early development and anger in dogs, but my experience with a particular type of puppy suggests that early development can have a profound effect on the emotion of anger.

The first puppy was born early in the morning, after Pip and I had napped intermittently throughout the night. Pip was an experienced brood bitch who had easy deliveries, so I wasn't terribly worried about the birthing process. Pip was also a wonderful mother who loved her puppies devotedly. She loved puppies so much she'd whine and cry when Lassie had her own litter, impatiently waiting for the day when she'd be allowed to play auntie to them. That morning, her own first puppy came slowly, the black, shiny dome of his head appearing and disappearing as she alternated between straining and resting. When he finally came, he was huge—huge and beautiful, a large tricolored male who looked healthy and hearty once he slid out of Pip and into the morning sunlight. Pip and I cleaned him off together, and I nestled him in warm towels while we waited for the next puppy. And waited. And waited some more. Usually puppies come every thirty to sixty minutes, but baby dogs don't read the books any more than baby humans do, and sometimes there'll be a gap of several hours between puppies. I went back to my mystery novel. Pip napped. I paced. Pip slept.

After several hours passed, it began to dawn on me that this might be the only puppy. You mightn't think that would be a crisis, but it felt like one to me. Over the years, I have seen what appeared to be a disproportionately large number of singleton puppies with serious behavior problems. Many of them seemed to have no frustration tolerance, and would spiral into a fury whenever they were pulled away from something they wanted. They often seemed grumpy when touched, and would growl and snap when petted, especially if disturbed when they were asleep. Many of these dogs became seriously aggressive, and their families came to me in despair, desperate to know whether their dogs could be saved. Some could, some couldn't, and I was appalled that I might be responsible for creating a dog who caused the kind of emotional suffering I see in my office every week.

I'm supposed to help people, not cause the very problems I'm trained to alleviate, so when the vet confirmed that the litter contained a total of one puppy I was beside myself. I thought about keeping him, so no one else would have to deal with him. Not a good idea at the time—I had too many dogs already, and getting another wouldn't have been fair to them. I thought about putting him down. Fat chance of that. Holding him, all warm and snuggly, against my chest, flooded with the hormones of nurturance, I would have fought off a pride of lions to protect the pup. I decided then and there to do everything I could to prevent the problems I'd seen in my office. I justified it as research, telling myself I could learn something important in the process. I did learn something, and I hope it has been of value to others, but the truth is I kept him because he was a tiny mewling baby mammal and I could no more have him put down that sunny winter morning than I could have stopped eating and drinking. I called him Solo.

I spent days asking myself why singleton pups might have less frustration tolerance than pups in litters, and whether there was anything I could do to prevent it. It seemed reasonable that the problem might relate to a lack of frustration during early development. Feeding time is great fun to watch, but it's not always peaches and cream for the puppies. They don't exactly wait in line at the cafeteria. Tiny paws and razor-sharp nails flailing, they push and claw and barge their way to the milk bar, wreaking havoc among others who were just about to settle down to a square meal. Talk about frustration—puppies spend much of their day trying to get what they want, only to lose it to another. It seemed reasonable that a single puppy would never experience this kind of irritation, and so never develop a mechanism for handling it. I tried to find someone with a litter he could join, but wasn't successful. Instead, I tried to replicate the actions of his littermates, in hopes the pup would somehow be better prepared for frustration at an older age.

And so began my daily routine of frustrating little Solo.[7] Three times a day I'd come into the nursery with his mom, and just as he connected with the milk bar, I'd use a puppy-sized stuffed animal to push him off. "Waaaaaw," he'd squeal; I'd silently apologize, and then do it again. I kept the stuffed toy (an owl, actually) in the puppy pen so it would smell like him and his mom, and I carefully kept these sessions separate from the handling and stroking from people. The last thing I wanted him to learn was

---

7. I say "little" because Solo was so small compared with everyone else in the house, but he was a huge puppy, growing by leaps and bounds, with an endless supply of creamy milk all to himself. I had to restrict his feeding times at one point, because I was concerned about him growing too big too fast.

"Oh no! Here comes a human!" That was hardly the emotional response that would lead to a friendly, sociable pup, so I spent lots of time touching and stroking him in pleasurable ways, and let the owl do the dirty work as much as I could.

He growled at me when he was five weeks old. All I had done was touch him. I remember staying calm, keeping my hand on him until he settled, stroking him in the way he most seemed to enjoy, and then walking into another room and bursting into tears. A five-week-old puppy growling at a person is like a five-year-old child stabbing his mother with the scissors. On purpose. Even though I had done all I could to touch him pleasurably, here he was growling at me. My guess, and I want to be clear that it is only a guess, is no amount of handling on my part could make up for the constant physical contact that is part of a litter's normal development.

I turned to the conditioning we talked about in the last chapter, and linked a brief touch with a tasty treat. Touch, treat. Touch, treat. Touch, treat. Over and over. Solo learned that a touch from me, anywhere on his body, led to something yummy in his tummy. In a few weeks he began to anticipate my touch and seek it out. I kept him longer than usual, until I was confident he was behaving like a sociable, normal puppy—happy to interact with people, able to handle life's little frustrations without flying into a rage. I placed him with a single woman who had no plans for children. She came to visit when Solo was an adult, and it was clear the minute they jumped out of the car together that he was the light of her life. Whew.

Solo's story is just that, a story. Science calls stories "anecdotes," and reminds us that we have no idea whether a given anecdote is representative of the big picture, or an exception to the rule. It's not clear from this story how much of an individual's ability to tolerate frustration is influenced by what happens in the first few weeks of life. It does seem reasonable that dogs need to learn to handle frustration, just as children do. Unless you're a breeder, you probably won't have much of a chance to affect a pup's early development, but you can pay attention to what your pup experienced when he was growing up at the milk bar. I don't want you to worry that every singleton puppy will grow up to be a monster; far from it. I have met scores of lovely little dogs who grew up without any siblings. Single "litters" are quite common in some of the tiny breeds—so they can't always be avoided.[8] But I do advise breeders and potential owners to be on the lookout for frustration intolerance, and, just as I did with Solo, take steps to ameliorate it while the pup is still young.

We'll talk more later in the chapter about how to handle adult dogs who have little tolerance for frustration, but first I want to talk about another common component of anger, and that's emotional arousal. Even an emotion as strong as anger can be controlled, redirected, or allowed to disperse if the angry individual stays contained. However, anger mixed with generalized arousal is a recipe for trouble, and it doesn't matter if you have two legs or four. The following story is a chilling example of how the combination of anger and arousal can have tragic results.

ANGER AND EMOTIONAL AROUSAL

I almost didn't take the case. I thought about it for days, agonizing over the decision. A ten-year-old girl had been killed by six Rottweilers, in a long and horrific attack that took place in front of the girl's best friend. From reading the newspapers, I knew that the details would be gruesome. Worse, the surviving girl, who had tried to save her friend, knew that anything she said might be held against her own mother, one of the owners of the dogs. The District Attorney was charging the surviving girl's mother and her live-in boyfriend with being parties to homicide resulting from a vicious animal and related felony and misdemeanor counts.

The DA visited my office to ask me to be an expert witness for the prosecution. Usually it's the owners who come to me, loving their dogs yet concerned about the safety of others. Sometimes they've been given a "dangerous dog" citation, and they need help designing a plan that keeps the public safe but prevents the family from having to euthanize their dog. Most come voluntarily, devastated over a bite to a neighbor, or concerned about a future bite they think is inevitable. I can't recall another case in which I've been asked to help send someone to jail, and the decision to do so didn't come easily.

8. Newborn pups are similar in size across breeds, unlike their adult counterparts; Great Dane puppies are only a few ounces larger than Miniature Poodle puppies. What is different is the size of the litter: Labrador Retrievers tend to have litters of ten to thirteen, while tiny dogs, like Chihuahuas, have only one or two.

I said yes. I said yes, because it became clear that the owners were indeed responsible for the needless and horrible death of a young girl. In my opinion, the dogs killed the child because no one had ever taught them emotional control, something every individual who lives in a social group needs to learn. Because they hadn't learned to control their own emotions, what should have been a minor incident turned into a bloody riot.

No one knows what precipitated the attack. The two girls were alone in the house, except for a total of six Rottweilers, an adult male, an adult female, and four adolescents. None of the dogs had been spayed or neutered. All were underweight and in poor condition. None of the dogs had received any training, nor had they been outside the house beyond being tied up to a chain in the yard. Neighbors reported several incidents in which the dogs had been screamed at, struck, and kicked. Social services reported that most of the surfaces in the home, including the beds, were covered in the dogs' urine and feces.

The surviving girl said her friend, Alissa, was petting one of the dogs in another room. She heard one low growl, and, in an apparent response to that, all the other dogs ran into the room toward the victim. Hearing Alissa begin to scream, she rushed into the room to find her underneath six frenzied dogs. She spent the next twenty minutes trying to save Alissa, at one point managing to drag her halfway out the door. The dogs pulled her back in. When her mother got home half an hour later, the girl was sitting beside her friend's body, the dogs lying calmly around her.[9]

None of us will ever know why the dogs killed a helpless ten-year-old girl, or what was in their minds when they did. We do know that the history and behavior of the dogs are consistent with those of dogs who have never learned to control their own emotions. We know that in the right circumstances, groups of dogs can leap from emotional excitement to emotional hysteria in a heartbeat. I think that's what happened on the horrible night when Alissa died. It is highly unlikely that the dogs consciously began an attack with the intent to kill. It's far more likely that, because of the way they'd been raised, a spark of irritation escalated into full-blown rage. Emotional arousal can be contagious, and a group of highly aroused, powerful animals, none of whom has ever learned emotional control, can

9. For those of you who are interested, the mother was sentenced to eighteen months in prison and her live-in boyfriend was sentenced to two years.

be as dangerous as a wildfire. We know this is true in our own species: it's why anger and excitement at a sporting event can morph into aggression in a few seconds. Tragically for little Alissa, the same thing can happen in dogs.

Thankfully, that's the most dramatic case I've ever had, but the link between anger, arousal, and aggression is a common one. Clients often tell me that their dogs are "out of control." Usually what they mean is that they, the owners, are unable to control their dogs, but often the dogs are so aroused they can't control themselves. You'll find the abbreviation "OOC," for "out of control," in hundreds of my office's case notes. It's written in the files of dogs who erupted in rage when another dog ran into them while they scrambled out the door, and in the files of dogs who barked themselves into hysteria as another dog walked by the window. It describes dogs who spiral into a state of emotional overload and bite whatever is nearest, whether it be a table leg, another dog, or the person standing next to them.

Emotional arousal is an important factor in aggression cases, because it can make a big difference in the level of injury caused. A veterinary student once said to me that "a bite is a bite is a bite," suggesting that it didn't matter how hard a dog bit someone. He felt that every bite, no matter how minor, should be considered an equal violation of the human-dog bond. I don't agree. Of course, no bite is acceptable, but there's a profound difference between bites; just ask a bite victim. Which would you rather receive: a carefully measured, single nip in which the dog uses just enough pressure to get his point across, or the repeated bites of a glazed-eyed dog who sinks his teeth up to his gums into your arm in a frenzy of anger and arousal? I was bitten once by a wolf-dog hybrid disciplining me for picking up his bone. He looked straight into my eyes, and, faster than seemed physically possible, sank his teeth into the fat of my hand. It was a hard bite, made by what I think was an angry individual, but one in full control over his own level of arousal. If he had become aroused and gone into an emotional frenzy, I think he might have killed me.

I show a videotape at seminars of a Border Collie named Ben, a masterful sheep and cattle dog owned by Beth Miller. I want the audience to see how he uses his mouth appropriately to get a steer out of a corner, showing complete emotional control while he nips it on the nose. One quiet, measured nip, and it's over. If I had to write a caption under the image to translate the message he conveyed, I'd write: "Just business, sir. Nothing personal; move along, please." Compare with that my dear, long-departed Misty, who, when young, was so fearful of a face-to-face confrontation with sheep she'd panic in a stare-down, exploding toward the ewe, scrunching her eyes shut and grabbing onto a wooly ear. Eyes and mouth clenched shut, she'd hang on for dear life while I ran to disentangle the hapless ewe from the small, black dog hanging from her head. After I peeled her off, Misty's emotional arousal would continue for five to ten minutes, her jaw chattering as if she was trembling from the cold. Needless to say, Misty's technique didn't get the job done, much less create the kind of peaceful management system I envisioned. I was inexperienced myself, and I cringe at the memory of our shared panic when we were in over our heads. Now, with many years of sheepherding under my belt, along with dogs whose genetics help rather than hinder, the days of herding with such unwelcome dramatics are behind us.[10]

The ability to control one's emotions is an important part of managing anger, but even we humans aren't born knowing how to do it. There's a lot to learn about controlling one's emotions; that's why a large part of being a parent includes teaching your child just that. We've all seen a two-year-old shrieking about a dropped ice cream cone, his face red and twisted with frustration. We accept that behavior in very young children, but not from adults—unless, of course, they're at a sporting event. Watching competitive sports is all about emotional arousal; that's why it's so much fun. It's no less than a biological miracle that the fate of a small ball can send thousands of people into emotional overdrive, but it can, and it does. However, the consequences of those emotions aren't always pretty. Recently I watched a tape of a near riot at a basketball game, in which players and fans began attacking one another for no discernible reason except an excess of adrenaline. There's even a familiar saying that describes emotional arousal morphing into aggression at sporting events: "I went to a fight last night and a hockey game broke out."

Usually this type of emotional arousal leads to only small problems, but sometimes it's fatal; think of sporting events in which people have

10. At least for now. Cross your paws for me when I get a new dog.

been trampled to death by rioting fans. Even police officers can become so aroused they lose control—we've all heard of cases in which discipline has collapsed, and an "attempt to restrain" a suspect has devolved into a merciless beating. These tragic cases are almost always precipitated by long, highly arousing chases. By the time the police finally catch up to the suspect, they have so much adrenaline circulating in their systems that the thinking part of their brains has been overridden by emotions so intense they were out of control. OOC: there it is again, this time in our own species.

There are a lot of reasons why emotional arousal can interfere with the more rational parts of our brains and get us and our dogs into trouble. One is the way the brain is designed: far more connections run from the amygdala to the cortex than vice versa. That means it's easier for our emotions to influence our decision-making processes than it is for our intellect to influence our emotions.[11] But once emotions become extreme, decision making is impossible, just as when I was too scared to think on the day Luke was charged by the guard dog.

We have to practice keeping our emotions in check, and the more constructive practice we get, the better we are at it. Just like people, dogs can learn to control their own impulses and deal with frustration; or, alternatively, they can learn to get what they want by losing their tempers, throwing a fit, spiraling into a rage. You can prevent a lot of those problems by helping your dog learn emotional control as he's growing up. Wolf experts tell us that the best pack leaders often use their position to influence the arousal level of the group, interfering when others begin to escalate their arousal. My attorney and I suggest you avoid the techniques of an alpha wolf (usually a bite to the muzzle that creates pressure but doesn't injure), but you can help your dog learn to control her own emotions by adding some simple exercises to her daily life that teach her to get a hold of herself.

EVERYTHING GOOD COMES TO SHE WHO WAITS

The simplest and most effective way to help a dog learn emotional control is to teach her to "stay" on cue. If you make stay training into a

11. Now you know why it's so easy for someone else to say "don't worry about it, it'll be fine" but so hard to take their advice when you're the one who's concerned.

game, she'll learn to associate controlling her impulses with feeling good. If your dog already has a rock-steady stay, then go reward yourself with a piece of chocolate. Most of us have dogs who will sit and stay if we're holding the food bowl in front of their noses in the kitchen, but who will dart off without looking back if we ask them to do the same when they're distracted. If that describes your dog, you might want to work on stay as a way of teaching your dog what psychologists call impulse control in humans.

If you're going to work on this with your dog, it helps to be realistic. Most dogs are relatively easy to teach to stay while all is calm and quiet, but that doesn't mean that you can expect a six-month-old Golden Retriever to stay in place while you welcome company into the house. Staying in place when asked, no matter what else is going on, takes a certain amount of maturity. You wouldn't expect a young child to be able to sit still for a long time in a restaurant, so don't expect the equivalent from a young dog. Most of us have enough trouble controlling our own impulses in front of a tub of mocha fudge ice cream—we can hardly expect our dogs to have it mastered when they're still just youngsters. Easily trained, mellow dogs may be able to hold a long stay at one year of age, but it's not unreasonable for a rambunctious dog to need three solid years under her belt before she can control herself when she's excited. Just like kids, dogs need practice and maturity to be able to control their emotions. Your job is to help them learn how to do it in a positive, patient manner.

Because this isn't a dog training book per se, I have put detailed instructions on teaching a solid stay in an appendix in the back of the book.[12] What's most important is to remember to go step by step. People tend to practice their stays when nothing is happening to distract the dog, and then expect the dog to stay still while three other dogs leap over her back while chasing a live rabbit. Okay, I exaggerate, but keep in mind that since the exercise is about emotional control, you need to *help* your dog work up to that skill. It helps to remember that your dog's arousal level isn't always under her voluntary control, just as your own isn't. (Do *not* be nervous when the dentist looms over your open mouth with a hypodermic. . . . Do *not* be excited if you win the lottery. . . .) Help your dog out by gradually increasing the difficulty of

12. See the References for a list of some great dog training books.

the exercise, teaching her to be successful at controlling her impulses, rather than being set up to fail.

Remember that the idea is to teach your dog that it's fun to stay when asked, and that you're on her side while she's learning. I've seen a heartbreaking number of dogs who were corrected with rough physical punishment for breaking their stays. All the poor things wanted to do was crawl away, because they'd learned to associate the stay "command" with fear and pain. Don't let that happen to your dog. Think of staying on cue as a cute trick your dog is learning, rather than a test of your authority over your dog. Your dog will thank you for it, and reward you over and over again in the years to come.

WAIT, PLEASE

Another helpful way to incorporate exercises in emotional control into your dog's daily life is to ask her to wait before you let her run out the door. I use a mini-version of stay, in which I ask my dogs to "wait" before I release them. In that case, I don't care what posture they're in, or even if they move sideways or backward; they just can't move forward through the door until I say okay. This prevents those mindless, headlong charges through doors that are sometimes amusing, often rude, and sometimes tragic. A dear friend lost a remarkable dog once because he'd learned to leap out of the back of her pickup truck when the door flap at the back opened. One horrible day it flew open while she was driving on the highway to feed sheep at another farm. Her wonderful, hardworking Border Collie leaped out as he always had—into the trailer attached to the truck going sixty-five miles an hour. A client of mine told a heart-stopping story of her little lap dog who jumped out of the car at a tollbooth when the driver opened the door to retrieve a fallen quarter. The dog survived unscathed, but the owner swears she lost five years off her life during the time she spent dodging semitrucks trying to get the dog back in the car.

You can teach your dog that everything comes to he who waits by saying "Wait," when you go to the door of your house or car. If your dog pushes ahead of you and throws himself against the door, don't open it. Your job is to encourage him to be polite—you can gently herd him backward with your body, you can toss a treat behind him, but whatever you do, don't open the door until he pauses, even just for a microsecond. The instant he pauses the tiniest bit, open the door and let him out. He'll learn that controlling his excitement gets him what he wants, and he'll get better and better at it as he matures. (Again, see the References for some good sources on how to teach this to your dog in detail.)

"WHY DON'T YOU EVER LISTEN TO ME?"

Dogs aren't the only animals who can profit by learning frustration control. Our own species causes no end of trouble when we lose our tempers, and compared to dogs, we do it a lot. Years ago, I saw a sad example of that at a herding dog trial. Peter, as we'll call him, was competing with a pregnant bitch just days before her delivery date. Swollen with puppies, Kit had no business being in a competition that pushes dogs to the limit of their abilities. She tried her best, but she was slow to respond to her owner's commands, and even stopped to urinate at one point. Her owner was well known in the trial world as someone with a hair-trigger temper; most of us were careful to avoid him late in the evening, after his second or third beer. Rumor had it that he'd take his dogs behind the trailer and beat them if they didn't perform as expected. We all talked about it on occasion, shaking our heads about how this "punishment after the fact" couldn't possibly teach his dogs anything but to be afraid of him. I hadn't seen an example of it myself— at least, not until then.

As soon as poor Kit dragged herself off the field, legs wobbly from exertion, Peter grabbed her collar and began to beat her with his crook, smack dab in front of a grandstand of onlookers. Some of my description of this incident is dependent upon the reports of others—I was otherwise engaged in the portable potty at the side of the field. Alarmed by all the commotion, I peeked out the tiny ventilation slit to see what was going on. Just as I did, I saw a woman less than half Peter's size place herself between him and the dog, and let fly with her own invective. The woman was Mary Gessert, a veterinarian and dog lover as mellow and amiable as Peter was easy to anger. At least, Mary is usually mellow, but not this time. Enraged at Peter's behavior, Mary chewed him up one side and down the other, while the rest of us silently cheered her on. Mary's bravery saved Kit that afternoon, but who knows what went on later that night or, for that matter, the rest of Kit's life.

Humans get angry for the same reasons that dogs do—they get offended or frustrated—and if you combine that with emotional arousal, the results can be ugly. Anger is such a pervasive emotion in humans, it's no wonder we think of dogs as saints. Surely the percentage of people who have been angered by their dogs is overwhelmingly larger than the percentage of dogs who are angry at their humans. We seem to be masters at anger, screaming red-faced on the interstate, furious when the referee makes what we think is a bad call. I suppose we shouldn't be surprised—just look at one of our closest relatives, the common chimpanzee. Chimps, as I mentioned earlier, can throw operatic tantrums—becoming almost hysterical with frustration and fury. Regrettably, so can we, and our dogs suffer for it terribly.[13]

One of my clients, George, came to me after dropping out of a training class run by another business. It seems the instructor had insisted that if his dog didn't sit when asked, he should violently grab the dog by the scruff and yank his front legs off the ground while screaming into his face. George was to shake the dog as hard as he could for several seconds, shrieking "I SAID SIT." Mind you, this was not military training for wartime, this was a simple family dog training class, in which people were being taught how to get their dog to sit, lie down, and come when called. When George refused to adopt this procedure, the instructor began to scream in anger at him. Wisely, in an excellent example of emotional control, George simply turned and walked out of the door with his dog.

Violent methods such as those described above were advocated at the first dog training class I attended, held in 1970 in Southern California. Even a flicker of hesitation on the part of the dog was to be taken as willful disrespect, and was to be handled immediately with a show of anger and intimidation. "Shock and awe" was the name of the game, and this "one size fits all" methodology was presented as the only way to get a dog to do what you wanted. I was there with Cosby, a floppy

13. How much anger is expressed in humans is also influenced by culture—with Asian cultures being far less likely to accept visible signs of anger than Western cultures. In the United States I suspect that our technology is making us even less tolerant of frustration, accustomed as we are to instant messaging and fast food.

seven-month-old Saint Bernard who was no more suited for Marine boot camp than I was. I hated class, but I had a dog who could eventually weigh as much as two hundred pounds, and it seemed irresponsible not to train him. On the third week of class the instructor borrowed someone's Basenji (the Basenji is the African "barkless" dog) to illustrate how we should respond to disobedience. You need to know here that Basenjis do not behave like fully domesticated animals.[14] Don't get me wrong, they are amazing dogs. I adore them, but they're much more like wild canids (such as wolves and coyotes) than like domestic dogs, in that they are independent animals who are happy to share their life with you, as long as it's on their terms.

I didn't know much about Basenjis back then, but it was clear from the outset that the instructor had his hands full. *"Sit!"* he bellowed, as if the force of his voice alone could push the dog down toward the ground. The Basenji stood still, attending to a comely little Lhasa Apso across the room. *"I said sit!"* the instructor screamed, and after giving the dog less than a second to respond, jerked on the leash hard enough to whip him backward a couple of feet. Many of us gasped, the action seemed so aggressive, but the Basenji went still, and darted his head around to look the instructor full in the face.

If I'd known then what I know now, I would've seen it coming. Ignorant of the meaning of a stiffened body and a direct stare to the face, I was surprised by the growls that began deep inside the chest of the Basenji. The entire class heard the growls, and waited, breathless and still, to see what would happen next. We didn't have to wait long. Now furious (and, I suspect, scared), the trainer jerked on the leash so hard he picked the dog up off the ground, all four feet dangling in the air. This was bad enough, but the dog had on the standard "training collar" used at the time, a slip collar that tightened continually as you pulled on it. The dog flailed in the air, strangling now as the collar got tighter and tighter, while the man continued to scream *"I said sit!"* I remember two things clearly: being appalled at what was happening in front of me while not knowing what to do about it, and being amazed at the athletic ability of the Basenji, who was somehow managing to

14. Not only is their physiology more like wild-type canids (most of them only come into estrus once a year, instead of twice a year like domestic dogs), but their behavior is also more similar to their wild cousins' than to the behavior of the Collie down the block.

launch himself upward into the air, in an attempt to bite the instructor. This seemed to go on forever, as terrible things often do, until my own dog's movements drew my attention off the center stage and onto him. Cosby had been sitting shoulder to shoulder with me, watching the drama unfold. He got up, turned his body away 180 degrees, lay down, and (I am not making this up), put his paws over his face. I took one look at him, the spell broken, and walked him to the car and drove home.

I called the instructor the next day, informing him I was dropping out of his class, even requesting my money back. I got the same response as did the Basenji, at least a verbal version of it. He explained to me, voice shaking, that I'd "better wise up, because the only way to get a dog to listen to you is to make them afraid of you." What came across most clearly was his anger. He seemed to take any response other than the one he wanted as an intentional challenge to his authority, and it infuriated him.

Although few of us are that abusive, it is nonetheless very human to assume that a disobedient dog is willfully disrespecting us, when sometimes a dog is simply too afraid or confused to comply. This is an example of that "fundamental attribution error" we talked about in Chapter 1, in which we assume that the behavior of others is based more on their disposition ("He's so stubborn!") than on other factors ("He hasn't learned to focus and he's distracted by other things").

It's frustration that seems to be the cause of most of the anger directed toward dogs by their owners. The examples above may be extreme (although not as rare as one would wish), but who among us hasn't been irritated by a dog who wouldn't come when called, or by a pup who had yet another yucky messy accident in her crate? It's human to be occasionally irritated with *anyone* we share our homes with, no matter how many legs they have. The question is, How do we handle that irritation and occasional anger? With patience, deep breaths, and a sense of humor, or with impatience and sparks of anger?

My concern about frequent expressions of anger is more than a politically correct fad. There is solid, scientific evidence that it elicits stress responses in animals who receive it, and stressed dogs are rarely well behaved. In a simple but elegant study, Amanda Jones showed that dogs who had been yelled at or pushed after running in an agility trial had significantly higher cortisol levels than dogs who had been petted or played with. Cortisol is called the universal stress hormone, and its production is one of the results of an activated amygdala. High levels of cortisol not only ready the body for danger, they can overwhelm the body and brain and thus interfere with rational thinking. We've all had times we were so shook up we couldn't think, when too much emotion simply shut down rational thought. A deeply scared dog, just like a scared person, is in no condition to be able to think clearly.

The handlers who pushed or yelled at their dogs after their agility run were only teaching their dogs to be stressed about what will happen the next time they leave the ring. The memories from the first run will increase the dogs' cortisol production during the next one, causing overstimulation of the fear-driven amygdala, and making the dogs more likely to blunder the next time they compete. Don't fool yourself: if you yell at your dog for something he did twenty seconds ago, you're not training him; you're merely expressing your own anger.

MEA CULPA

But we are all human, and few of us always react to our dogs as we wish we would every minute of every day. Just recently I yelled in frustration at wobbly, fifteen-year-old Pip. I wish I hadn't. I had been bottle-feeding a lamb whose ancient momma didn't have enough milk for him, and when the lamb finished the bottle, he looked up to discover that all the other sheep had disappeared. Panicked at having lost his flock, he began running haphazardly around the high pasture in an ovine version of hysteria. I sent Lassie to herd him down a narrow path through the woods toward his mother, but Pip stood dead center in the lamb's way. I wasn't worried about the lamb, I was worried about Pip. The lamb weighed far more than Pip and was on a path that guaranteed he'd slam into her full tilt in his dash down the hill to his momma. Worried about my old dog's safety, I called Pip to come toward me so she'd be out of the lamb's way. Pip was immobile, already nervous about the commotion in the pasture and wanting more than anything to walk away and go down the path toward home. I asked her again, confident that her aging ears still worked well enough to hear me. No response. Pip continued to stand stock-still while the lamb bounded toward her like a huge, wooly soccer ball headed for the net. Frightened for her safety, and frustrated by my lack of influence, I finally screamed, in a nasty voice full of fear and anger, *"Pip [insert words better left unwritten], get over here!"*

Pip is the most sound-sensitive dog I've ever had, and as soon as I yelled at her, she began to trot away from me, still on the path, still directly in the lamb's line of fire. Lassie saved the day by stopping the lamb before he barreled into Pip, and I eventually managed to catch up with Pip and escort her down the hill. She cheered up after we played her favorite ball game, and I assuaged my conscience by giving her an extra-long belly rub that night, but I still felt bad about yelling at her in anger. I'd done it because my own fear and frustration had resulted in a lost temper, and as soon as I did it, I knew it would only make her more scared than she already was.

It would have been easy to interpret Pip's behavior as "disobedience." I called her to come, and she didn't. Some trainers would have told me to go to Pip and smack her for being so disobedient. "Do it or I'll hurt you" is still a common philosophy in many areas of the world, including here in the United States. What's seen as a dog's blatant disregard of an owner's wishes is considered a serious offense that deserves swift and decisive punishment. Some trainers will emphasize that punishment should never be done in anger, but the reality is that it usually is. In that sense, we're not so different from dogs—combine emotional arousal with anger born of frustration, and the result isn't pretty.

Certainly, Pip has had her moments of being stubborn over the years, but in this case she was truly and deeply scared. She's fifteen, for heaven's sake, and increasingly unsteady on her feet. Physically punishing her wouldn't have made her more obedient, it would have made her more afraid than she already was. Even as a young dog, Pip was terrified of getting hurt, and no amount of force would ever have made her into a bold, gutsy dog; she was never any more capable of forcing an angry ram into the truck than she was of doing my taxes.

If Pip had lived her life in a home in which people had routinely responded to her "disobedience" with anger, I'd bet big money on what would have happened. She'd have turned into one of those pathetic dogs who hides under the porch whenever they can, or who ended up "euthanized" for defensive aggression. As it is, she's known far and wide as a sweet, loving dog who adores people and dogs, and whose gentle nature has rehabilitated scores of formerly aggressive dogs whose own fears got the better of them. Pip calmly and patiently brought these dogs out of their shells, becoming an invaluable worker in my consultation business. I bought her to be a herding dog, and I was sorely disappointed when she turned out to be worthless at the task. Little did I know then that Pip was designed for more valuable work, and that the time would come when I couldn't imagine living without her.

I tell you this story because I think we need to be honest about our emotions around dogs, and acknowledge that they aren't always what we aspire to. I'm as dewy-eyed as anyone about the relationship between people and dogs, but we must acknowledge that dogs can bring out the worst in us. Again, we are all human, so don't lose sleep over an occasional outburst of anger when you were tired, scared, or just plain sick of cleaning up diarrhea on the oriental rug. An expression of anger is just that—an expression of a primal emotion ultimately necessary for survival. However, unless you happen to be fighting for your life, it's rarely useful or effective when you're training your dog.

I think what's most important about anger and our relationship with dogs is to remember two things. First, remember the effect of emotional arousal on both you and your dog. You can train yourself, as experts in anger management will tell you, to stop and take a few breaths to lower your body's overall arousal level. Keep in mind that the word "emotion" is just "motion" with another letter added on. Remember those cases in which police officers lost control only after long, highly arousing chases? If you start to feel yourself spiraling up into real anger, you can help calm yourself by slowing your body down. Stop moving, take some breaths, and, if you can, sit down for a second or two. There's a reason that cops tell everyone to sit down when they enter the scene of a skirmish; sitting acts to deescalate emotions, and decreases the chance that arousal is going to turn into aggression.

The last thing you want to do if you think your dog is angry is to feed the fire with your own emotional arousal. If you're faced with a dog who looks angry, or who is threatening you with a stiff body and an offensive pucker, it's critical to stay calm yourself. I won't say that yelling at your dog never works in a case like this; just about anything works some of the time. I expect people could chant medieval incantations in hopes of putting a spell on their dog and, in some cases, somewhere, they would get the desired effect. However, most dogs are going to respond to yelling by increasing their own level of emotional arousal, and that's not going to be to your advantage. Your best bet is to stay calm, move slowly and deliberately, and finesse your way out of the situation. If, for example, your dog has stolen your daughter's favorite sweater and is now snarling and growling at you while he hovers over it, the last thing you want to do is start yelling "Bad dog!" while you get increasingly frantic about recovering it. You're much better off staying calm, walking to the kitchen, getting an irresistible piece of food, and tossing treats across the room to get the dog away from the sweater. This won't solve the problem, but it might prevent a bite. Then I'd review the family's policy of preventing such problems, and learn how to teach my dog to drop an object when asked. Don't try to solve the problem during the crisis; find a way to finesse yourself out of it. Child psychologists tell parents to work on their children's problem behaviors when they're not in the thick of things, and it's invaluable advice for dog owners as well. Once dog and sweater are separated, sit down and figure out how to prevent that kind of problem in the future.

The second important lesson about anger and our relationship with dogs is that it is often born of frustration, and the less you know about dog training, the more likely you are to be frustrated by your dog. It's amazing how we expect ourselves to be able to train dogs with virtually no training ourselves, but people do it all the time. No one blinks at sending their child to practice a sport three times a week, or is surprised when adults hire a coach to help them perfect their golf swing. And yet we expect that, without any prior knowledge or training, we can get individuals of another species to do whatever we want, whenever we ask. Given that we can't come close to accomplishing that even within our species, it's a mind-boggling assumption.

Perhaps we make that assumption because most of us expect our dogs to do what we ask, whether they've had any training or not. Many people seem to believe that dogs come to us able to read our minds and to translate whatever language we happen to be speaking in. Even worse is the cherished belief that dogs inherently want to "please" us. If that's what you think, then you're guaranteed to be frustrated if you expect your dog to come when called, or to not jump up on visitors, without any training or practice. The good news is that dog training has evolved, and is full of humane and effective techniques that are as enjoyable for your dog as they are for you. In the References, I've listed a number of good resources that base their training on positive methods and that focus on teaching dogs what we want them to do, rather than punishing them for what we don't. Many trainers now use food, play, and petting to condition dogs to do what we ask, and the difference between that and punishment-based training is like night and day. I can't encourage you enough to learn how to use positive reinforcement to teach your dog to listen. It creates a relationship based on mutual enjoyment and trust, rather than one based on fear and intimidation. This isn't touchy-feely New Age babble, as one trainer described it to me. It's good psychology. All animals tend to act in ways that make them feel good. Once you learn to tap into that, you've learned to take advantage of animal behavior's most basic and universal principle.

POSITIVE, NOT PERMISSIVE

Some people imagine "positive" training to mean that we treat dogs with kid gloves and let them do whatever they want. Far from it. Just because I use positive things like treats, play, and petting doesn't mean I let my dogs act like coyotes in the living room. "Positive" doesn't mean "permissive"; it just means that dogs learn to mind their manners because it makes them feel good.

As much as I love my dogs, I want and need them to be polite members of society. If dogs are going to live with us, they need to learn manners just like children do. There are lots and lots of wonderful dog trainers who avoid using punishment whenever they can, and their dogs are often more obedient than dogs who have been threatened.[15] You can be positive while still setting boundaries, being what I call a "benevolent leader" to your dog, just like a good parent or teacher.

Don't let people convince you that you have to "get dominance"

15. See the References for the names and books of some of the country's top trainers who use positive reinforcement. There are more and more of them, and their ability to create happy, well-behaved dogs can knock your socks off.

over your dog by being forceful and intimidating. "Dominance," perhaps one of the most misunderstood words in the English language, describes who gets the bone if two individuals want it. It doesn't say anything about *how* the winner gets the bone, just that she does. Certainly, one can get the bone by using aggression, but that's only one method, and a risky and expensive one at that. Social hierarchies are believed to function to avoid that kind of aggression, not encourage it. Remember that study of how piglets responded to being restrained on their backs? The ones who were most aggressive in response were *not* more likely to be the dominant members of the group when they matured. They were simply more likely to be aggressive in any kind of conflict, while the more docile pigs were able to be more flexible, and used aggression only when there was no other option available. As members of the most resourceful of species, we always have lots of options. Aggression toward our dogs should be last on the list. After all, they are our best friends.

As important, dominance has nothing to do with whether your dog comes when called or jumps on visitors. The sooner we stop invoking it to solve the problems most of us have with our dogs, the happier we'll all be. Happiness—now that's a refreshing change from fear and anger, and happily, it's the subject of the next chapter.

7

HAPPINESS

How and why dogs make us happy,
and how we can return the favor

It'd been a hard day. Too many difficult cases with heartbroken owners and dangerous dogs. Too many computer glitches and pens that ran out of ink. We all have our own versions of it, but everyone knows what it feels like to have a tough day. I remember walking into the farmhouse exhausted and depressed, burdened by the day behind me, tired from thinking about the chores that lay ahead. There were dogs to feed and walk, sheep to grain and water, baby lambs who needed bottle-feeding and a fence crushed by a fallen tree that needed repair before the ram ended up on the highway and I ended up in a whole lot of trouble.

That wasn't all. Pip had a litter of puppies, five weeks old now, and big enough to have overwhelmed their mom's efforts to clean up after them. After I fed the adult dogs I turned with a weary sigh to sprucing up the puppy pen. As I tried to move the dirty towels out from underneath the pups, they began to try to grab them and play tug-of-war. Too tired to be charmed at first, I gently pushed them aside. Everyone who's raised a young puppy knows how long that lasted. One of the pups, Rosie, continued the game with particular exuberance. Shiny-eyed and sparkling with glee, she'd leap onto the towel as I tried to pull it away, like a coyote stabbing her forelegs onto a mouse in the grass. Rosie's efforts were so endearing that I couldn't help but laugh. I forgot about the chores for a while, and began to play with her intentionally.

As we played, Rosie seemed not just overcome with happiness; she seemed to be happiness itself. Her little face radiated so much joy that *within minutes I wasn't just playing with Rosie, I was playing with the same cheerful abandon as she was. All my worries about clients and chores were forgotten. I laughed so hard I almost cried, while Rosie tried out her newfound athletic abilities, leaping and spinning—sort of—on my lap. Her efforts often ended in abject failure—she'd fall over sideways or topple backward in midspin—but her face never lost its look of pure, unmitigated joy. It makes me happy just writing about it. It made me happy all the rest of that night, when carrying water and dragging trees off fences became a pleasure, rather than a chore.*

I can't count the number of times that the happiness of a dog has flowed in my direction, but it's one of the reasons I have dogs. Surely, it's one of the reasons we all have dogs. We don't spend nine billion dollars a year on dog food just to have dog hair all over our couches. Dogs may guard our houses and herd our sheep, but that's not the primary reason we have them. Dogs make us happy, because if dogs do anything well, it's being happy themselves, and happiness—bless it—is catching.

THE JOY OF DOGS

Of all the animals on earth, few seem to express happiness and joy as well as a dog. A happy dog can't seem to contain his emotions within his own body; exuberance radiates off dogs like light from a sparkler. Of course, that's not true of all dogs, or of any dog all the time, but the vast majority of dogs seem to be overwhelmingly happy for much of their lives. Certainly, if they have food and water and companionship, most dogs seem to be happier than most people. You might argue they have every reason to be happy—a life without automobile repair bills and quarreling children sounds pretty good—but there's more to it than a lack of daily problems.

Earlier, we talked about how adult dogs retain many of the characteristics of youth. The youthfulness we see in middle-aged dogs is expressed not only as playfulness and docility, but also in their expression of happiness. Pure, unrestrained happiness is an emotion we associate with youth, not with maturity. The comedian Jon Stewart was talking about that phenomenon recently on a late-night television show, describing the giddy intensity of his young child's happiness. "When do we lose that?" he asked. "What happens to that pure sense of joy we had when we were young?"

The unmitigated joy of youth may fade as we mature, but it doesn't disappear in adult dogs, who play with the exuberance and abandon of children. Of course, most people also remain playful long into their adulthood—just check out the number of middle-aged men and women on tennis courts. But dogs play more like children play, totally in the moment, barely able to contain their happiness. "A ball?! You have a *ball*?! Oh oh oh, that's wonderful, miraculous, exquisite! Will you throw it? Oh please, please, please throw it. *Oh boy!* You threw it! I get to run after it, pick it up, and bring it back!" Of course, we all know I'm just making those words up and anthropomorphically putting them into the mouth of a dog. But if a ball-loving Labrador could talk, isn't that the gist of what he'd say?

PUT ON A HAPPY FACE

The happiness of dogs may be more childlike and exuberant than that of adult humans, but surely the experience of happiness is something that we share. There's no question that one aspect of happiness—its physical expression—is similar in dogs and people. Who could miss the expression of joy on the face of a happy dog? Without reading the accompanying text, look at the photos in the middle of the book. It's as easy to pick out the happy dogs as it is the happy people, isn't it?

Happy dogs have the same relaxed, open faces as happy people. In both species, our mouths relax and our lower jaws loosen. Remember "open mouth/closed mouth" from the chapter on expressions: the "open mouth" of a relaxed dog is unmistakable, and can be a good indication that a dog is comfortable in your presence. It's an expression that's not only easy to see but also highly relevant to us as a species. We are hard-wired to recognize the loose, relaxed jaw that goes along with a smile; people of every culture find open-mouthed smiles the easiest expressions to recognize. Newborn children even respond to an upward-curved line "smiling" under two dots. It seems we are genetically programmed to associate these patterns with something safe and good. No surprise, then, that we love seeing the curve of an open mouth on a dog's face, or that we respond by feeling happy ourselves.

The face of a happy dog or a happy person has a full, smooth look, as if the muscles underneath were plumped up like pillows at a bed-and-breakfast. In contrast, tired, angry, or fearful dogs have tight, drawn looks, just like the faces of unhappy people. Look at the three photos of the dog Gus in the middle of the book, and focus on the fullness, or lack of it, in his face. Once you notice it, it's hard to miss, and it's just as clear on a dog's face as on the face of a person.

Along with the expression of the mouth and the fullness of the skin, the eyes of a dog are a wonderful source of information about whether she's happy or not. Happy dogs, like happy people, have soft, dewy-looking eyes. This is a perfect example of the "principle of antithesis" described by Darwin, in which opposite emotions are expressed with opposite body postures. The soft eyes of a happy dog are the opposite of the hard eyes of a dog who is overaroused or threatening to bite. In our species, soft eyes are associated with happiness and love; never with anger or anxiety.[1] Old-time movie producers were so aware of this, they actually put Vaseline on the lens when filming the romantic female lead, all to make her look as soft and dewy as possible. Think of the liquid eyes of Ingrid Bergman in *Casablanca*.

Dogs also tend to crinkle the muscles around their eyes when they're happy to greet someone, be it a human or a dog. Watch your dog's face when you greet her after an absence—friendly, affiliative dogs will greet you with sloppy, relaxed faces and the squinty eyes of a smiling person. As mentioned in Chapter 2, wrinkled eyes may be most common in relatively submissive dogs, but in any case they are the exact opposite of the rounded, fixed eye of a dog who's warning you to stay away. You're most likely to see this expression when you're greeting a friendly, well-socialized dog, who drops his head, lowers his ears and tail, opens his mouth and wrinkles the muscles around his eyes. When I approach a dog who's voluntarily coming up to greet me, whose mouth is open, and whose eyes are crinkled, I think "Friendly dog," and I'm happy to crinkle my eyes right back.

There's one important difference between eye expressions and emotion in people and dogs, and that's the effect of direct eye contact. As I mentioned earlier, extended eye contact between familiar people is often an expression of love and attachment. Any of us can identify a couple in love by their long, languorous looks at each other, and any-

1. They are also associated with sadness, which makes things a bit more complicated. What seems to be universal is that soft eyes are associated with either positive emotions or passivity, but not with active, negative emotions like fear or anger.

one who's been in love can remember the warm happiness they felt when they gazed deeply into the eyes of their lover. It's always been assumed that people looked into each other's eyes because of their mutual love, but the process can go in both directions. As I mentioned earlier, if you take two willing strangers off the street and ask them to gaze into each other's eyes, they'll report strong feelings of warmth and attachment after just a few minutes.

Don't look for this exercise in your next dog training class. We spend a lot of energy *preventing* dogs from staring directly at one another, and the idea of encouraging it is enough to stimulate the amygdalas of professional dog trainers everywhere. Ask two unfamiliar dogs to stare into each other's eyes for a couple of minutes, and get ready for the fur to fly. Most dogs who know and love their humans are comfortable making direct eye contact with them, but I'm not sure they seek it out the way we do, and many of them avoid eye contact with strangers. Happy dogs may wiggle, squirm, pant, kiss, and lick us all over, but most of them don't want to get lost looking into our eyes. Speaking of happy dogs, it's worth taking some time to look at the biology of the emotion, and what biology has to tell us about our shared experience of happiness.

THE BIOLOGY OF HAPPINESS

We humans may be special, but it makes no sense for happiness to be an emotion unique to our species. That doesn't mean animals feel happy in exactly the same way that people do, but "survival of the fittest" suggests that happiness is as primal an emotion as any other. All animals move toward pleasure, because pleasure is about having everything you need to flourish. Does the air feel good on your skin right now? Not too hot, not too cold? Good: that means all the internal processes going on inside your body can do their job at maximum efficiency. Feeling not hungry but not too full? Great: that means your body is getting the fuel it needs without being overloaded trying to process it. All animals, even worms, seek out what feels good and avoid what doesn't. Feeling good can be good for you, pure and simple.

Curiously, we don't know as much about happiness as about other primal emotions, such as fear and anger, but in the last decade neurobiologists have done a great job playing catch-up. It might seem strange that scientists spent decades investigating fear long before they turned their attention to happiness, but if you look at emotions from an evolutionary perspective, it's not surprising. Happiness may be a good thing in the long run, but fear relates to things that can get you killed in an instant—perhaps fear's primal immediacy accounts for why, in years past, it has gotten more attention from neuroscientists and psychologists than more positive emotions. We can all intuitively relate: studies back up our intuition that we remember bad things better than we remember good ones. That's probably because the consequence of forgetting about something bad is usually worse than that of forgetting about something good ("Oh, gosh, that's right—now I remember: last time I tried to play with a grizzly bear it didn't work out").

But happily (she says, smiling), happiness is now a hot topic in psychology and neurobiology. We now know that, just as in other primal emotions, specific structures and chemicals in the brain are key players in the emotion of happiness. For example, an area in the forebrain called the nucleus accumbens is so central to the emotion of happiness that John Ratey calls it the "principal pleasure center of the brain." This area has a high level of sensitivity to the stimulating chemical dopamine, and is also receptive to other, more familiar chemicals, like serotonin.

Dopamine, like all neurotransmitters, plays a multitude of roles in the brain and body; one of its many duties is to focus your attention on something that you've learned might lead to something good. It's dopamine that causes that shiver of excitement when your lottery ticket starts looking like a winner, and it's dopamine that drives the feelings of infatuation when you first meet someone special.[2] Remember that flush of energy and excitement you had when you first fell in love? That's thanks to dopamine, a chemical that's as important in your dog's brain as it is in your own.

Both your brain and your dog's have other "pleasure centers" besides the nucleus accumbens with its high levels of dopamine. One especially important center is in the hypothalamus. Rats will press a lever up to four thousand times an hour, if the lever is hooked up to a tiny

---

2. Dopamine levels are also increased while you're having sex and eating chocolate. No comment.

wire that stimulates a specific area within it.[3] Not unlike human drug addicts, the rats were so motivated to seek out pleasure that they would allow themselves to starve to death, rather than stop pressing the lever.

On a lighter side, rats have also been found to produce a vocalization during play that for all the world sounds like the equivalent of human laughter. Biologist Jaak Panksepp found that these chirping noises are associated with responses in the brain correlated with pleasure, that they occur only during play, and that they can be elicited, believe it or not, by tickling from human caretakers. The tickled rats even began to seek out their human playmates and became socially bonded to them.

Now that we're starting to look, laughter—or something like it—has been found in a variety of species. We've known for years that chimpanzees have a "play pant" that closely resembles laughter, and a recent study suggests that playful dogs sometimes make a breathy vocalization that may be the equivalent of laughter. The animal behaviorist Patricia Simonet recorded dogs during play and discovered a "long, loud" panting sound that she thinks is the equivalent of human laughter. She's even tried playing it over loudspeakers at a shelter and swears it quiets barking dogs within minutes.[4] Not everyone is convinced that these sounds should be categorized as "laughter," but the examples in rats and chimps support its existence. It seems more than reasonable to me that social animals like dogs might make a similar noise. I just hope we never figure out that they're laughing at us.

HARDWIRED FOR HAPPINESS?

Laughter in other animals may be controversial, but there's no question in anyone's mind that an individual's ability to experience happiness is influenced by his or her genetics. People who are born with a low density of dopamine receptors in their nucleus accumbens have a reduced ability to feel satisfied by anything (and often suffer from addictive behavior). People whose brains have naturally low levels of dopamine have trouble feeling that anything is "enough" to satisfy them, and often

3. That's 666 times a minute, or more than ten times a second. It must feel really, really good.
4. See the References for a website where you can listen to a short recording.

indulge in high-risk behavior in a desperate attempt to feel contentment. However, excessive levels of dopamine, if unregulated by other neurotransmitters, can lead to aggression and violent impulses. But at normal levels, dopamine plays a vital role in the everyday happiness of you and your dog.

It's no surprise to any of us that some individuals seem to be inherently happy, while others view the glass as always half empty. Research supports this perception—the psychologist Nathan A. Fox found that "exuberant" four-month-old human babies (babies who became especially happy and excited by novel events; about 10 percent of the ones studied) had the same level of joyfulness at seven years of age as in infancy. Studies like this suggest that there's a kind of "set point" for happiness that comes along with your biological background. A raft of studies supports that theory. For example, lottery winners don't tend to be any happier six to twelve months after their win than they were before it, and victims of permanent injuries tend to rise to their previous level of happiness after a similar period of adjustment. Our perception of happiness even seems to be affected by the biology of sleep/wake cycles. In most people, happiness is highest between four and ten hours after getting up, and lowest at the beginning and end of our day. I find myself thinking of all the dogs I've met who snapped or bit late in the evening, after being "fine" all day, and wonder if these cycles could exist in dogs as well.

If we could do the same types of studies on dogs as we do on people, I suspect we'd find that genetics influence how happy a dog can be as much as it does a person. And if we could do a survey, my guess is we'd find a higher percentage of "very happy" dogs than of "very happy" people. But dogs seem to exhibit the same range of happiness that people do; there are "exuberant" fourteen-year-old dogs, and there are quiet, mopey puppies who don't seem to derive pleasure from much of anything. This does not mean, by the way, that we are all helpless victims of our genetics. In people, and most probably in dogs, a genetic influence on one's ability to be happy is simply that: an influence. It's not written in stone, it just means one has a particular predisposition. There is lots of research that suggests people can have a great deal of influence on their own levels of happiness no matter what their genetic baggage, and there's no question that you can have a profound effect on your own dog's level of happiness. We'll talk about how to make your dog happy (or happier) later in the chapter, but first it's instructive to talk more about the biology of happiness in both people and dogs.

HAPPINESS IS CONTAGIOUS

As Rosie the puppy illustrated in the story that opened this chapter, happiness is contagious. Unless you're feeling spiteful and envious, it's hard to see the happiness of others and not feel your spirits lifted. Cool Hand Luke loved life so much that he lifted my own spirits every single day of the twelve and a half years we had together. His love of life was like food and water to me. Luke loved working sheep and eating chicken and sitting beside me on soft summer evenings on top of our hill, but more than anything, he loved to run. When he was running, his face looked so happy I couldn't help but smile. Not so when I try to run myself—I'm designed as a sturdy hiker type, and when I try to run I feel clumsy and clunky, as if someone put weights on my feet. But when I watched Luke run, it was as though I was running with him, running like him, and somehow I became free and fluid and expansive. His happiness became my happiness, and all I had to do was stand still and watch him.

Happiness isn't the only emotion that's contagious; a spouse or partner in a bad mood can tarnish a previously good day. A nervous owner can transfer his fear to his dog as easily as water flows downstream. But, luckily for us, happiness is one of the easiest emotions to pass around. A brief interaction with a lighthearted stranger can cheer us up immeasurably. Those happy people and dogs we see on television commercials are chosen because just watching someone else be happy can make us happy ourselves, and cause us to link feeling good with a product. Research in business management has even found that groups working together were strongly influenced by the cheerfulness of an embedded "colleague." The addition of just one enthusiastic team member resulted in groups that perceived themselves as more competent and more cooperative than groups with a depressed infiltrator. Interestingly, the "cheerful" group attributed their success to their skill level, not to the general mood of the group (which was, in truth, the only difference).

I know of no studies on moods being transferred between individuals of a different species, but its occurrence seems blindingly obvious to those of us who have dogs. Surely there's no better cure for sadness than watching puppies play, because their pure, uncluttered happiness is catching. We're cheered by the enthusiastic greeting of our dogs, not just because it feels good to know someone is glad to see us, but also because their happiness is contagious. You can watch a video of a dog greeting someone you've never met, and feel almost as good as if it were your own dog. There's good, solid science behind those feelings: when you watch something as heartwarming as a happy dog, your brain chemistry changes in ways that promote feelings of love and attachment. If we're lucky, our dogs radiate the warmth of happiness day after day, year after year, from the day we get them to the day they die. Because we share the external expressions of happiness, the joy that emanates from our dogs' wiggling bodies warms us like bright white sunshine on a winter day. No wonder we love them so much.

BE A ROLE MODEL FOR YOUR DOG

If happiness can be transferred from dog to human, can it go in the other direction? Dog trainers strongly believe that, just as we can be influenced by the emotions of our dogs, dogs can be influenced by ours. Surely the happiness of an owner can have an influence on her dog. However, more negative emotions like fear and anxiety can also be transferred from person to dog, and it's important to be aware of that when you're relating to your dog. I see lots of people and dogs who are locked into a pattern of anxiety together; perhaps the dog once snapped at a dog in the neighborhood, the owner gets nervous when the same dog begins to approach, the dog senses the owner's fear and becomes nervous himself, and thus is more likely to snap . . .[5] Another common example of not-so-helpful emotional contagion occurs when agitated people try to calm down an overexcited dog. A small percentage of people automatically get quieter and calmer as their dog gets

5. If something similar has happened to you, know that this is a common, and very understandable problem. You already know from the fear chapter that just saying "I shouldn't be so scared" isn't going to help much. However, you can get out of this spiral, as have thousands of people, by conditioning yourself and your dog to have a different reaction. See References for books and articles on how to do that.

more and more excited, but they are in the minority. Most of us, before we learn to consciously calm ourselves, can become as emotionally aroused as our dogs. Ironically, this usually happens while we're trying to calm them down. "No! No! No!" we say, our voices and bodies as stressed and excited as our dogs.

It's no fun trying to control the emotions of a dog (or better yet, of a group of dogs) when your own emotions are out of control. You can avoid that by learning to stay quiet and calm yourself when you want to settle your dogs down. Use as few words as you can, be thoughtful about how you're moving your body, and take a couple of deep breaths. Once you learn to stop and quiet yourself, the effects can be amazing, but it takes conscious thought and a bit of practice. I recently watched a videotape of a client trying to calm her dog down as someone approached the house. In about three minutes she said "no" more than fifty-four times. I didn't count the number of "woofs," but I wouldn't be surprised if it was equal to the number of nos from the owner. If this sounds familiar, you're not alone. It's difficult to act calm when you're feeling panicked yourself. Remember that just as your dog's emotions can influence you, you can influence those of your dog. Try to behave as you want your dog to behave, not as an expression of how you're feeling inside.

If we want to make dogs happy, I think the most useful emotion that we can convey to them is a sense of calm, peaceful benevolence, interspersed with our own version of joyful exuberance during play. I realize peacefulness isn't the easiest emotion to convey when your three sixty-pound dogs are barking out the window, but if you're the one with the key to the house, and you're the one who can get out the dog food, then you're the one your dog counts on to keep the world safe and secure. If you're overwhelmed with agitation and angst, how's your dog going to feel? We do dogs no favors when we overload them with our own emotions, often over issues they can't possibly understand. Think of being lost in the woods with a group of people and one individual who all agree is the group's leader. Wouldn't you want that person to be calm and quietly confident? That's what your dog wants, too. To some extent, all dogs are lost in the woods of an alien world, and are counting on you to lead the way.

THE SEARCH FOR HAPPINESS

Every night, as I get ready to do the farm chores, I ask Lassie if she'd like to "go to the barn." The most expressive of dogs, Lassie has a face that lights up and softens; her mouth opens and her eyes shine like Christmas tree lights. She stretches, play-bows, and runs to get her favorite toy, which she flings toward me as I lace up my boots. It doesn't seem possible that she could be happier.

When we get to the barn, it's Lassie's job to hold the sheep away from the feeders while I pour in their grain. As soon as we enter the building, Lassie's face changes. Her joyful look of anticipation is gone, replaced by a tight and focused expression appropriate for the work at hand. Holding hungry sheep off the feeders isn't easy work; sheep love their grain and don't hesitate to fight for it if they think doing so will be to their advantage. Often, when Lassie is holding off the sheep, she looks tense, sometimes even downright nervous. At that moment, I don't think you could describe her as happy. Fully engaged and highly motivated, yes, but not necessarily brimming with the joyful emotions we usually think of as "happiness."

If you could sit in my living room and ask Lassie if she liked working sheep, I think she'd say she loves it like life itself. I say that because she never turns down an opportunity to work sheep, and because on the way to the flock she is the embodiment of happiness. Another way to describe her at that moment is in a state of "eager anticipation," and anticipation turns out to be something that plays a key role in the happiness of both dogs and people.

One of the most interesting things to come out of the research on happiness is that the search for happiness is at least as compelling as getting what you thought you wanted. Jaak Panksepp, one of the world's experts on animals and emotions, describes what is now called the "seeking" circuit in the brain. Remember the rats who would press a lever until they dropped from fatigue in order to stimulate a pleasure center in the brain? Researchers have found that this area has more to do with the anticipation of something than with actually getting it. If you think about it, these findings fit intuitively with our own life experience. Aren't you often at least as happy when you're excitedly anticipating a trip as you are when actually traveling? I went to see the comedian Jerry Seinfeld not too long ago, and he was just as funny as I hoped he would be; I must have laughed nonstop for an hour and a half. But, when I think about it, I was actually happiest as I walked into the theater, when I was brimming with what Panksepp calls "intense interest, engaged curiosity, and eager anticipation."

Think of your dog's excitement when you're mixing her dinner or getting her leash for her walk. Does she seem as excited as when she's actually eating her dinner, or on the walk? This tendency to feel excited and energized when anticipating something was first discovered by a researcher named Wolfram Schultz, who trained monkeys to press a lever for a food reward. The experiment included a light that came on right before the food was released. Schultz found that the monkeys' brains had the highest levels of dopamine *right after the light came on,* but *before the food was released.* That means that the monkeys were more excited when they were anticipating the food than they were when they actually got it. That doesn't mean that the release of dopamine made the monkeys feel good. Rather, dopamine got their attention and caused them to anticipate something good. That feeling of anticipation is exciting and energizing, which is why dopamine is a key player in all kinds of addictions.

Not only are we excited when we're anticipating something, it turns out we're most stimulated if we're not sure we're going to get it. If you first establish an association between two events—say, a light coming on, and food dropping into the cage—you get higher dopamine levels if in later trials there's only a 50 percent chance of the second event occurring: that is, food drops into the cage only half the times the light goes on. This is why Las Vegas is the most popular vacation destination in the country. Gambling is all about anticipation and all about uncertainty—no wonder people become addicted to it. The importance of uncertainty also explains why some dogs turn up their noses at the same old treats they've been getting all year. Trainers know to mix it up, so that their dog never knows what wonderful thing is coming next.

Besides varying the type of reinforcement, keep in mind that how often you reinforce is important, too. Casinos in Las Vegas are careful to ensure that people get reinforced (i.e. win) often enough to keep coming back. You need to replicate that level of reinforcement, so that your dog doesn't give up on you. If you teach a dog to expect something that he really wants, and then withhold it too much of the time, you're going to create the kind of frustration we talked about in the anger chapter. There's a balance here that can take some time to sort out, and is undoubtedly dependent on the individual and the situation. I think knowing when to reinforce and when to hold back is one of the distinctions between great animal trainers and mediocre ones, but novices can do well by following this formula: don't decrease your dog's frequency of reinforcement until you're willing to bet ten dollars that your dog will do what you ask. Most novices move to intermittent reinforcement before the dog is ready, not understanding that every change of context or increase in distraction makes the exercise more difficult for the dog, and initially requires going back to 100 percent reinforcement.

CLICK AND TREAT

You can take advantage of the phenomenon of anticipation in a good way, by teaching your dog what trainers call a bridge. A bridge is the equivalent of the light in the monkey experiment, a signal to your dog that something wonderful is about to come. A simple way to do it is to use a hand-held clicker, and start by giving your dog a tiny treat each time you click. In just a few sessions, your dog will go into that happy state of "eager anticipation" every time she hears the sound of the click. This not only takes advantage of your dog's "eager anticipation" circuit, it also means that you can time the click to the exact instant your dog does what you want.

You can use this method to train a dog to do everything from simple sits to amazingly complex tricks. You don't actually need a hand-held clicker to create a bridge; you can do the same thing with a visual signal, a tongue click, or a word you've chosen and use only for this purpose. The clicker has the advantage of being a unique and easily identified sound, but it does require that, during training, you have to remember to put it in your pocket—easier said than done, for some of us.[6] I use clicker training for teaching tricks and to sharpen my timing.

6. The acoustic properties of clicks also make them especially good at getting attention.

My dogs seem to love it; if they could talk, I suspect they'd tell me to stop writing this stupid book and get the clicker out. There's a whole world of clicker trainers out there, and I encourage you to check it out if you're interested. (I've included lots of resources in the References, including information about the queen of click-and-treat, Karen Pryor, and her clicker seminars around the country.)

It's amazing how fast you can train a dog when you use a method that, like this one, makes clear exactly what it is you want your dog to do. The same method, using positive reinforcement after a precisely timed bridge, has been shown to radically improve the skills of children in gymnastics training. There's no reason why it shouldn't, given that the basic principles of learning are universal.

ALTERNATE ROUTES (BESIDES THE STOMACH) TO YOUR DOG'S HEART

Given how much happiness our dogs give us, it's not surprising that most of us want to reciprocate, by making them happy, too. Neither is it surprising that we often use food to try to do that—what could be more universal in the animal world than the joy of getting really good food when you're hungry? However, food isn't all that dogs need, and sometimes—just ask your vet—it's the last thing they need. Being overweight isn't any better for dogs than it is for people, but many of us find it surprisingly hard to restrict how much we feed our dogs.[7]

In some ways it seems absurd that people have such a hard time regulating how much food they give their pets—after all, *we're* not the ones going without tasty snacks during the day. I suspect it's because we want our dogs to be happy and to feel loved. Food is one way to make that happen. It compensates for the times when we don't know what our dog wants, or know perfectly well, but are unable (or unwilling?) to provide it. However, treats on demand aren't enough to make a dog happy, any more than a plate of doughnuts is enough to meet our own needs. If we want to make our dogs happy, we need to expand our repertoires. The following paragraphs present some thoughts and ideas

7. If you want to get an earful, go to a vet conference and watch calm, peace-loving veterinarians gnash their teeth and tear their hair out because they see so many dogs and cats who are grossly overweight.

about what dogs need to be happy. The list isn't all-inclusive—that would require a book of its own, but it includes some of the things I think are often not obvious, even to people who love their dogs.

I'm not going to spend a lot of time on the basics. Everyone reading this book knows that dogs need fresh water and good food. I hope they also know that, almost as much as food and water, dogs need social companionship. It breaks my heart to see dogs stashed, isolated and alone, in kennels at the far end of the yard. Our dogs need us, or at least the companionship of other dogs, to be truly happy. That wild, crazy dance your dog does when you get home isn't just about getting dinner, it's about having the pack back together again and all being right with the world.

Dogs also need exercise, but I think we too often think about physical exercise and ignore the importance of mental exercise. We're not the only animals whose brains need to be stimulated. Decades ago, when dogs lived outside and mostly off leash, they pretty much entertained themselves. We didn't need to go out of our way to provide them stimulation; there was plenty of activity in the woods or the farmyard to keep them busy. Of course, we can't and shouldn't go back to letting our dogs run free, but we need to acknowledge that dogs who spend all day alone sleeping on the couch can get pretty bored if that's the sum total of their activity. If you're like me, you might be bushed when you get home from work, but if you choose to have a dog, he needs you to do more than open the back door and let him out into a fenced yard when you come home. The good news is that a little bit seems to go a long way. Fifteen minutes of trick training and fifteen minutes of playing fetch can do a lot for a dog who's been hanging out all day waiting for you to come home. If you don't have thirty minutes at least a couple of times a day, you might, just perhaps, want to rethink having a dog in the first place.

There are many ways to stimulate your dog's mind—and the same old walk around the neighborhood isn't it. Remember the effect of "same old, same old" on your dog's levels of dopamine, and see what you can do to spice things up. There are interactive toys that can entertain your dog while you're chopping up vegetables for dinner. You can teach your dog to "go find" something you've hidden upstairs while you answer your phone calls, and you can teach your dog to down and stay during the commercial breaks in the evening newscast.

Ah, but what about physical exercise? We all know dogs need exercise, but how much? People ask me constantly, "How much exercise does Ginger/Chief/Pumpkin really need?" I suspect that the subtext of this question is "What is the minimum amount of exercise I can give my dog without feeling guilty about it?" That's a perfectly reasonable question to ask, given all the other things we have to do every day.

The answer is simple: it depends on your dog. My fifteen-year-old Pip can't go on a two-hour walk anymore; she's happy to go on a twenty-minute walk twice a day. Pippy still loves to play ball, but I throw the ball no more than nine or ten times, and only about twenty feet away. Lassie is twelve, but she still loves long walks and working sheep, so I vary her exercise and ensure that she rests up one day if she worked hard the day before. Tulip is eleven (which is old for a large-breed dog like a Pyrenees), but she still loves long walks in the country and runs like a puppy when the leaves turn color and the air gets as crisp as a cold apple.

You can't help but notice that all my dogs aren't so young anymore. Neither am I. It's a bit of a retirement community out here at the farm. If your dogs are as old as mine, a short exercise period twice a day is ample. However, when Lassie first came to me at a year of age, she played nonstop with her father for hours at a time, and after a brief nap still bounced off the walls with excess energy. Young dogs of working breeds, designed to be on the move all day long, need to exercise in units of hours, not minutes. Thus, think carefully about whether you want a Border Collie or a field-bred Labrador Retriever puppy. If you do, you might be better off adopting an older dog from a shelter or a rescue group. The three factors that most influence how much time you need to spend exercising your dog are age, breed, and individual personality.[8] Consider each carefully, because many of the behavioral problems we see in dogs today wouldn't happen if the dogs got more exercise. Ouch. Sorta slipped that one in there, didn't I? I don't want to make you feel guilty, but the truth of the matter is that most pet dogs *are* underexercised, and have too little to do with both their bodies and their minds.

8. Look into this issue carefully on a breed-by-breed basis, because sometimes intuition is wrong about what breeds need exercise. Large dogs don't necessarily need more exercise than small ones. Greyhounds, for example, are the original couch potato dog, just as happy to stay inside when it's raining as you are.

Exercise is particularly relevant in a book about emotions, because of the connection between *emotion* and *motion*. Even though it's right in front of our faces, we tend to forget how closely linked those two things are. We know that, for humans, physical exercise does a lot more than keep our hearts pumping into old age. Exercise elevates mood, strengthens the immune system, and decreases stress, and there's no biological reason to believe that it doesn't have similar effects on your dog. So put on your jacket and pick up the leash, or think up a new trick to teach your dog, and while you're at it, thank your dog for helping you both have a longer, sweeter life.

"I'M SORRY; WHAT DID YOU SAY?"

As much as anything on earth, dogs want to understand us. Given that we want to be understood, you'd think there wouldn't be a problem. However, misunderstandings are so common that many trainers believe they are the primary source of the problems that people have with their dogs. It shouldn't be surprising that miscommunication is so common—look at how often it happens with our own species. And here we are trying to communicate with individuals of a whole other species. No wonder we have trouble.

Effective communication is so vital to our relationship with dogs that I wrote my first full-length book about it. In *The Other End of the Leash,* I explain at length how our primate movements and behaviors mean one thing to us, but something else altogether to dogs. I won't rewrite that book here, but it is worth mentioning a few examples that can be particularly problematic. One relates to how we move our bodies when we call our dogs to come. When we call dogs to return to us, we humans tend to look straight at their faces and move slightly toward them. Why wouldn't we? That's the polite way to initiate social interaction with another human, and it is so ingrained in us that we don't even think about it. However, in dog language, that direct stare and forward movement is a stopping signal, one that means the opposite of what we intend. Your dog is much more likely to come if you turn your body sideways and move backward a bit while you call "Come!" It's not magic—it's not going to stop your dog if he's in the middle of chasing a squirrel—but it's a simple thing that can make a difference. I got more mail about this one small aspect of *The Other End of the Leash* than about anything else in the book. Several people swore to me it saved their dog's life.

Another common cause of miscommunication between people and dogs is the act of hugging. We humans are hugging fools—we hug for comfort, we hug to express love, and we hug when we're excited. Hugging is a good thing to people, and it's natural that we'd hug our dogs for the same reasons. But dogs don't hug other dogs. The only equivalent of a hug in dog society is when a dog puts his head or foreleg over the other's shoulders and presses down. That's a display of social status, not a sign of affection. Most of our dogs, bless their hearts, put up with our hugging, but that doesn't mean they enjoy it.[9] However, some dogs don't put up with it. Every trainer and behaviorist has heard too many stories of little children who were bitten on the face when they tried to hug the family dog. There's a lot we can do about this: we can selectively breed for amiable dogs who don't take our foolishness too seriously, we can condition our dogs to enjoy hugging (in which every hug leads to a treat when they're young and impressionable), and we can teach our children not to hug unfamiliar dogs. None of those things will happen, however, if we aren't aware of the difference in communication styles between the two species.

Those are just two examples of how confusing life can be to a dog who is dependent upon an individual of an entirely different species. Anyone who has ever been in a foreign country, whose language he doesn't speak, knows how it feels when others expect you to understand them, but you can't. If dogs can be happy or sad—and I've argued throughout this book that of course they can—then they can suffer when they're confused, or worse yet, punished for something they didn't understand. That's why I think the most important thing we can do to make our dogs happy is to learn to communicate with them. That means learning about how our dogs read our own body language and learning how to teach them to want to do what we ask of them. The best way to do that is to go to dog training classes, work with a

9. I got letters about this, too—it seems to hurt people's feelings that their dog might not adore being hugged. I'm sure there are dogs out there who love any attention from their humans, but take it from me (and every trainer and behaviorist I know): your dog may love you like life itself, but that doesn't mean she loves being hugged. See the photo of a dog being hugged in the middle of this book.

trainer, and read books or watch videos on how to train and communicate with a dog. I don't understand why we, as a species, are so resistant to learning how to train our dogs when we don't hesitate to get coaching for other things. (Which is more complicated—your dog, or a piano? Would you hesitate to hire someone to teach your child to play the piano?) We need to move beyond the belief that, like Lassie and Timmy on television, a nice person and a good dog just naturally get along, and are able to understand each other just because they love each other so much. Psychologists know how well that works out between husbands and wives—sometimes not so well. In hopes of inspiring readers to learn more, I've listed some great sources on general dog training in References (cited under Chapter 6).

"I'VE GOTTA BE ME"

Each dog is different from every other dog. Surely that sentence does nothing but state the obvious. And yet, I see so many people who can't accept that, unlike their first Black Labrador Retriever, their second one doesn't enjoy playing ball but would rather use his nose tracking chipmunks in the backyard. Dog breeds aren't like brand names, with every tenth widget being checked for product consistency. The whole point (at least from a biological perspective) of sexual reproduction is to create variety, and that means that every single dog in existence is unique, just as every single human being—even those who are "identical twins"—is different from every other. That makes it essential to get to know your dog as an individual, and to do what you can to help her be the best she can be. Sometimes that means accepting that she'll never be what you had hoped for; just as Pip turned out to be worthless on sheep, your dog may be an abject failure at barking to tell you visitors have arrived, or at competing in dog shows with the drive and intensity required to get her a championship. But, like Pip, your dog may have other skills and gifts that you weren't expecting, and may turn out to be a better dog than you ever imagined.

Years ago, after my first sheep-guarding dog, Bo Peep, died, I purchased a replacement Great Pyrenees named Thulie. Her breeders had kept her longer than usual, because she'd initially seemed so, well . . . goofy. But when she was around a year and a half old, she'd seemed to come into her own, so we agreed I'd bring her to the farm for a three-month trial as the farm's new guard dog. Thulie was huge and sweet and fluffy white, and in two weeks everyone on the farm hated her. In her excitement over just about anything, Thulie knocked over sheep, dogs, and me in equal proportion. She got so excited when cars drove by the barn that she'd bowl the sheep over while running to the fence. I still remember seeing my elegant ewe Harriet suspended momentarily in the air, hooves pointing to the sky, thanks to Thulie charging through the flock to bark at a milk truck. After nursing one too many bruises on my shins, and helping one too many sheep back onto their feet, I called the breeder and told her Thulie wasn't going to work out.

Thulie wasn't the right dog for Redstart Farm, but she was, in many ways, a wonderful dog. There was just too much to stimulate her here, and it was clear she needed a home away from a road, without Border Collies dashing here and there every time she looked up. Last I heard, she'd found a perfect fit at another, quieter farm, where the environment brought out the best in her, rather than the worst.

I bring Thulie up because Patrick, my husband at the time, said, "I don't understand why you're returning her. You're a dog trainer; why don't you just train her to do what you want?" It's true that you can train dogs (and all animals) to do an amazing number of things, but you can't do personality transplants on dogs any more than you can on people. Think of your own life, and your own personality. Doesn't it sometimes feel like you're swimming upstream when you're working at one task, while others feel almost effortless? We're all suited to do different things, and aren't equally adept at everything we attempt. Trying to turn Thulie into the right dog for Redstart Farm would have been the equivalent of swimming up Niagara Falls, or trying to turn Donald Trump into someone who'd be happy as a monk. You're welcome to try, but don't call me for advice about how to do it.

Keep this in mind with your own dog. She is who she is, and the key to her happiness is knowing what parts of her you can change through training and conditioning (which, don't get me wrong, is a lot), and what parts of her need to be accepted and celebrated. Just as good parents learn who their children are as individuals rather than try to fit them into a preconceived mold, be open to who your dog really is, and help her become all she can be.

THE RIGHT TOUCH

"Oh, Pumpkin just loves petting—don't you, Pumpkin?" Cynthia said, patting her Cocker Spaniel's head as he tried to investigate the office. Pumpkin's owner had come to me for some advice about behavioral issues, and she clearly loved her dog as much as we all, human and dog, would like to be loved. Only one problem: while Cynthia beamed with love, Pumpkin didn't look quite so happy. In truth, he looked downright miserable. He kept turning his head away from her hand, trying to avoid her touch, no matter how loving it might have been.

This is not an uncommon scenario, in which a responsible, caring person pets a dog who purportedly adores petting, while the dog moves heaven and earth trying to get away. Ask any dog trainer or behaviorist: every day, in our offices, in classes, and on neighborhood streets, we see people cheerfully petting their dogs, while the dogs look miserable.

Bear with me here; I'm not saying dogs don't love to be petted. Dogs do love petting. They also don't. Understanding that can make a big difference in how happy you make your dog. If we'd just put ourselves in our dogs' paws for a minute, it would all make sense. Like most humans, you probably love a good back rub. Just thinking about one can make most of us all soft and cozy. But you don't want one every minute of every day, do you? What if you're in an important meeting, about to argue against a ridiculous new policy proposed by your boss? How about when you're playing softball in the league's quarterfinals—want your honey to come up and rub your neck when you're up at bat? I don't think so. What if you *do* want a back rub, but your would-be masseuse starts pounding on the top of your head like a woodpecker? Feel good? I think not. Dogs are just like us in this—their enjoyment of touch depends on *when* it's offered, *how* it is done, and *where* on the body it is directed. I'll talk about context first, because it's the variable most often ignored.

Do you want a massage right now? I don't; I'm busy writing this book. And I don't want one when I'm training my dogs, giving a speech, or trying to figure out why my computer has just done one of the inexplicable and irritating things it always does when I'm in a hurry. But I'd love one later, when the computer's turned off and the chores are done and I'm settled in for the night. Like us, dogs enjoy petting during quiet times, when the pack is settled in, cozied up in the living room or bedroom, the outside world shut away for awhile. They enjoy petting least when they're in high-arousal play mode. Watch a dog who's been called away from an exuberant play session and is "rewarded" with a pat on the head: most dogs turn their heads and move away. I swear, I can practically hear them saying "Awww . . . Mommmmmmmm." Neither do most dogs enjoy being petted while greeting other dogs, while eating their dinners, or while otherwise engaged in something that requires concentration. Here's yet another example of how being anthropomorphic at the right times would help our relationship with dogs, rather than hinder it.

Just like people, dogs vary tremendously when it comes to *who* they want to touch them. Some dogs are veritable streetwalkers, happy to get cuddly with anything that has hands, while others are uncomfortable having strangers touch them at all, at least before the second date. We often expect dogs to tolerate touching from anyone, just as we expect children to, but that doesn't mean they like it. They're just usually not in a position to do much about it.

Dogs are also like people in terms of *where* they like to be touched. Their favorite places may vary from ours—I've yet to see a human go goofy-eyed and thump their leg when you rub them above their tail bone—but humans don't enjoy touch equally in every part of their bodies any more than dogs do. As I write this, part of me says: "Everyone knows this, why use up valuable space talking about it?" And then I think of how often I see people slap their dogs on top of the head, or hug the dog's chest until his eyes begin to bulge. In general, dogs enjoy touch most on the sides of their heads, under their ears and chins, on their chests and bellies, and at the base of their tails. Although some dogs will turn inside out for any touch at all, most don't like their paws touched and aren't fond of you messing around with their hind legs or genitals. They dislike slappy pats on the top of their head. (Wolf researchers tell me they use head pats to get pushy wolves to leave them alone.) Of course, every dog is different, just like people. Some of us are picky about where we want to be touched; others are happy to make contact with another warm body any way they can.

How you pet your dog also makes a big difference, and individual preferences are again just as important in dogs as they are in people. In general, most of us enjoy gentle but firm strokes and rubs. I wish we'd talk more about "rubbing, stroking, or massaging" dogs instead of "petting" them, "petting" being a word close enough to "patting" to cause no end of trouble. Pats, especially rapidly repeated ones on top of the head, tend to put dogs off. (Remember this when your Border Collie drops the ball in your lap for the 561st time. You might as well use this to your advantage!)

This should not be a big shock to us. How much would you like it if some stranger walked up and patted you on the top of your head? In spite of that, people do it to dogs all the time, in yet another example of our lack of ability to be anthropomorphic when it makes sense to be. When I was taping the Animal Planet show *Petline,* a veterinarian turned sales rep asked to borrow Cool Hand Luke for a demonstration on dental care. Luke and I had just finished a segment on how much dogs dislike pats on top of the head, directing the audience's attention to Luke's look of disgust when we did it to him. Sure enough, after repeatedly jerking Luke's mouth open as if cleaning clams, the woman said "Thank you, Luke," and slapped him on the top of the head with three short, bouncy pats. We had to stop taping, because the camera crew was laughing so hard they couldn't work.

When and how you pet your dog may seem trivial, but it's actually an important topic, given the suffering that people and dogs experience when the relationship between them goes sour. Dog lovers everywhere think they are using positive reinforcement when they pat their dog's head for coming when called; the actual result is to teach him or her, with stunning effectiveness, to stay away. Before you know it, the dog is at the local shelter, because "he just won't ever listen to me."

The physical consequences of touch (or the lack thereof) aren't trivial, either. As we saw in the chapter on the brain, touch is vitally important for the physical and psychological health of social animals like people and dogs. Massage therapy on humans has been found to increase levels of serotonin and decrease excesses of dopamine, which in turn decreases incidents of aggression and acts as a calming agent. One of the many benefits of dog ownership is that the feel of their fur on our hands is good for us. Petting a dog can lower your blood pressure and your heart rate. In one study, petting a dog increased the level of one of the body's first lines of immunological defense, an immunoglobulin called IgA.[10] Certain kinds of touch can even be used therapeutically on dogs (see the comments about TTouch therapy in the References). It's simply a biological fact that petting your dog can be good for you, too, so although spending every night lying on the couch petting your dog isn't exactly a well-rounded health care plan, a little bit of it can be a good thing.

A SENSE OF SECURITY

Like humans, dogs need a sense of security. The nationally recognized speaker and trainer Trish King explains it well in her book, *Parenting Your Dog*, in which she reminds us that dogs count on us to take care of them. Involuntary Peter Pans, puppies become adult dogs who are never really allowed to grow up. We control when and what they eat (well, okay, mostly), when and where they go to the bathroom, when and where they sleep and exercise, and who belongs to their social group. They live in a world in which we expect a lot of them, but in which they are completely dependent upon us. It's hardly surprising, then, that they would look to us to be a trustworthy source of confidence and security. You know those "animal people" who seem to have a magic touch with animals, the ones your dog goes to sit beside and doesn't want to leave? In my experience, the one trait they all share is an ability to broadcast a sense of peaceful confidence and contentment that suggests they could be the benevolent leader whom we all find attractive. They're the Dalai Lamas of the animal world. The type of happiness they exude is the opposite of the frantic jolliness I sometimes see owners use to try to cheer up their dogs.

You wouldn't want to rely on someone who was paralyzed with angst all the time, so don't put your dog in that position. I see so many people who desperately want their dogs to feel loved, and who in trying to create that feeling end up catering to them in such a way that their dogs never learn any boundaries, never learn emotional control,

10. Interestingly, IgA levels increased for dog lovers even when they were petting a stuffed dog, but non–dog lovers only had increased IgA levels when they were petting real dogs.

and never feel that they can count on their human to make the hard decisions that every leader needs to make. It's been said that great leaders are not defined by their skills or their knowledge, but by their ability to promote feelings of confidence and security in others. Remember, emotions are contagious—you're not going to promote a sense of security in your dog if you don't have some of your own to share. Some people are inherently better at projecting confidence than others, but all of us can work at becoming more like them. I know of no greater gift you could give to your dog.

ARE WE CRAZY?

Someone who's not a dog lover might well be asking: "Why on earth is it so important for these crazy people to make their dogs happy? They're just dogs, for heavens sake!" I get calls about once a month from writers assigned to write articles about the lengths that people go to for their pet dogs and cats. This doesn't just happen to me. Dr. Marty Becker, the go-to vet for *Good Morning America,* tells me he gets called regularly about the same topic. The subtext is always the same: the writer has been told to get a quote from us about how foolish/pathetic/overly emotional people are about their companion animals. The focus is usually on how much money dog lovers are willing to spend on their dogs, buying hundred-dollar dog beds and designer collars. I'm the first to agree that it does dogs no good to be thought of as furry people, but I don't see why spending money on your dog is any worse than spending it on a new golf club or eating out in restaurants. What's the harm in spending a hundred dollars on a dog bed that your dog loves and that looks nice in your living room?[11] During one of these interviews I asked one reporter, who seemed bound and determined to drag out of me some remark demeaning dog lovers, how much her shoes cost. I asked because I had just seen a similar pair in a San Francisco department store priced at over seven hundred dollars. I'm the first to admit that the shoes were gorgeous, if you like shoes that are impossible to actually walk in, and that doctors tell us can cause permanent damage to your feet. Even if they'd been boots de-

11. Personal disclosure: okay, yes, there's a hundred-dollar dog bed in my living room, although truth in reporting requires me to mention that it's old and a bit scrungy and that, although my dogs love it, it doesn't really look so darn good anymore.

signed to keep your feet warm in the Antarctic—seven hundred dollars? Oh, my.

I may think it's a bit crazy to spend seven hundred dollars on shoes, but it's not my business if someone does. I just object to her laughing at those of us who spend our money on dogs instead of clothes or ski vacations. Perhaps the laughter's real source reflects a cultural discomfort with our emotional connection to another species, rather than any objection to the economics of the issue.

Of course, you don't have to spend lots of money on a dog to love him. We've all read the stories about, for example, the homeless man who has nothing but the shirt on his back and a little brown dog who follows him everywhere. In the one I remember best, the man wouldn't sleep in a shelter because they wouldn't take dogs, and the dog refused to leave his friend to scavenge in the local dump even when he was starving.

This love that we have for dogs, and that they have for us, brings untold happiness to millions of people and dogs around the world. Whether we buy them plaid raincoats and booties, or share our only can of beans, the love between people and dogs represents a special kind of happiness. From the peaceful contentment that comes while cuddling in front of a warm fire, to the giddy rush of dopamine-charged infatuation, love generates more happiness than anything else you could name. "All you need is love" isn't actually true at all—all you really need is oxygen and water and food—but without love, who could ever truly be happy? The central role of love in the pursuit of happiness has spilled over into our relationships with members of another species, which is little short of a miracle. Those of us who love dogs love them deeply and can't imagine being truly happy without a dog in our lives. In an eloquent testament to the happiness we share with our dogs, here's what two of my friends said in an e-mail about the death of their Standard Poodle, Sophie.

Beloved Poodle Sophie passed away on October 13, after a battle with cancer. She was a friend and a teacher of many—displaying an unfettered love for every human being she ever met (bar none) and an unparalleled joie de vivre. . . . She brought pleasure and comfort, in untold measure, to those who knew her—giving a lot and asking little. She will be missed and always remembered with abundant love.

8

LOVE STORY

Our extraordinary love affair with dogs

In 1992, I fell in love with a dog named Luke. I brought him home from a herding dog trial one chilly October evening, not sure whether I'd keep him, not sure I wanted another dog. A gangly adolescent, Luke had been a disappointment to his first owner, who reported that he wouldn't come when called and had failed his first herding lessons. I'd had my eye on him ever since he was a pup, and had told the owner to let me know if she ever decided to sell him. When she did I had more dogs than I needed, but every time I saw Luke something clicked inside, as if I'd finally found the combination to an old padlock I carried around, unopened. I took one last look at his bright, expectant face, wrote out a check, and drove him home through the red and orange hills of a midwestern autumn.

By sundown of the next day, Luke and I had fallen in love. I don't know any other way to describe it. I say "fallen in love" with the knowledge that eyes will roll, lips will purse, and heads will shake. "That's pathetic," someone said to me once when I described my love for Luke. It seems that people either get it or not; like the yes-no simplicity of digital computers, the world sorts us into those people who've been deeply moved by an animal, and those who can take them or leave them. I learned to censor myself, to test the waters by volunteering some platitude like "Yep, he's a great dog, Luke," instead of a deeper, more complex attempt to express how much I loved him.

I am buoyed by the knowledge that I am not alone. People come up to me at seminars, eyes full and bright with the beginnings of tears, and tell me they had a dog like Luke. "Forever dogs," we call them: the canine loves of our lives, dogs who expand our hearts and fill our souls as nothing else ever has. Old Yeller *is a book about a dog like that, a plain yellow dog who settles in the heart of a young country boy, and who is a cultural icon of the depth of devotion we can have for a dog.*

No one describes the love between a person and a dog better than the late Caroline Knapp, in Pack of Two: The Intricate Bond Between People and Dogs. *Speaking of the "remarkable, mysterious, often highly complicated dances that go on between individual dogs and their owners," she wrote:*

That dance is about love. It's about attachment that's mutual and unambiguous and exceptionally private, and it's about a kind of connection that's virtually unknowable in human relationships because it's essentially wordless. It's not always a smooth and seamless dance, and it's not always easy or graceful—love can be a conflicted, uncertain experience no matter what species it involves—but it is no less valid because one of the partners happens to move on four legs.

For twelve and a half years Luke and I danced together, sometimes so clear and so close to each other it was like moving as one, sometimes stumbling over each other's toes. We were each other's soul mates, colleagues, and best friends. I described him to everyone who would listen as my "one in a million" dog; for reasons I don't understand, he seemed to love me as much as I loved him. In some ways, Luke seemed to be having a love affair with all of humanity. He was handsome and social, the one everyone wanted to sit next to at the dinner party, and he could schmooze with the best of them at banquets and cocktail parties. He was the perfect dinner guest, who never neglected to thank the hostess and could always be counted on to flirt with the single woman in the corner. Flirt? Could someone possibly describe a dog as flirting? All I can say is that Luke adored everyone, but he loved women more than he did men, and always chose to sit beside one and charm her, head lolling like Stevie Wonder's, his face open and full of happiness, one big paw in her lap.

My life was linked with Luke's in every way. Luke was the first thing I saw in the morning, when he nosed my arm under the covers after the alarm went off, and the last thing I saw at night as I stroked his head on my way to sleep. Luke and I ran the farm together, he the trusty right-hand man, me the landed gentrywoman who knew the value of a smart, willing crew boss. It was Luke I turned to when flighty lambs needed loading or when the ram jumped the fence to breed the ewes a month earlier than planned. It was Luke who leaped over a four-foot stall and saved me from a rampaging horned ewe, and it was Luke who risked his life to stop a three-hundred-pound ram from smashing me into pulp against a fencepost.

Luke worked with me on dog-dog aggression cases with an air of calm professionalism that I still find astounding. He put up with the insanity of taping sixty television shows in two months with grace and patience. He charmed audiences at seminars, speeches, and book signings everywhere, and brought his black-and-white tuxedo of fur home to charge with abandon into mud and sheep poop to hold the ram off the feeder in the pouring rain. Luke loved being with me, herding sheep, playing ball, and running—running anywhere, after anything. He ran with the grace of a finely crafted sailboat coursing over deep water—no friction, no drumbeat of hooves on the soil—but with a smooth effortless glide that lifted my heart every time I watched it.

Luke was all of the above, but he wasn't perfect. When he was young, he'd lose his temper on sheep, chasing and even biting them, ears flat and eyes narrowed. He'd flash me looks better left untranslated when he didn't like my directions. I'm not perfect, either, but as is true of soul mates everywhere, our flaws weren't enough to undermine the love we had for each other.

When Luke was middle-aged, I fell in love again, this time as if in slow motion, with my human soul mate, Jim. After Luke's death, Jim admitted there had been a certain amount of jealousy between them early on, although they eventually became good friends. I called them my guys, reveling in the feelings of warmth and fullness that come with being loved. Jim, lucky me, is still here, but Luke died a year ago. His body is buried at the top of the farm road, where the hill pasture begins, where he would stand expectantly as I walked up the road behind him, waiting for me to catch up with him so he could play ball, or work sheep and run and run and run some more.

"I'LL NEVER LEAVE YOU"

Although the love we have for our dogs is often trivialized, there's nothing trivial about it. A few weeks after my father died, one of my mother's dogs was killed by a car. A visitor had come to help sort out my father's affairs, and unbeknownst to anyone, Jenny the exuberant Irish Setter had dashed out the door, running free and wild and no doubt, full of innocent and cheerful abandon. She was killed half a mile down the road, in front of the church where my father's service was held. My mother, stalwart and noble after my father's death, sobbed so hard and for so long about her dog's death that it seemed as if her grief would physically rip her apart. I thought at the time, as did many, that Jenny's death allowed my mom to truly grieve the death of her husband. I don't think so now. My mother loved my father, but their relationship was burdened with disappointments and perceived betrayals. But Jenny? Jenny sparkled with nothing but joy and devotion. She asked for little and gave everything she had in return. These were no hard words late at night, no angry glances or saturated silences. No baggage. She loved Mom; Mom loved her: simple as that.

We're not always comfortable with the depth of emotion we can have for our dogs, but profound love isn't uncommon. I recently read an article about a teenager who risked his life to save his dog from a burning building. A tough-minded rancher once told me he'd rather die than abandon his cattle dog in a snowstorm. The evidence is overwhelming that during the days leading up to Hurricane Katrina, hundreds if not thousands of people chose to risk death rather than leave their animals behind. The state of Florida learned this lesson well during 1992's Hurricane Andrew, when thousands of people refused to evacuate because the shelters wouldn't take pets. These decisions compromised the safety of so many people that the state now provides shelters for pets as well as for people.

The lengths that normal people will go to in order to protect their dogs testifies to the love and devotion many of us have for them. I remember a Wisconsin woman who was interviewed after a tornado destroyed her home and all of her belongings. "We're okay," she kept saying, clutching her dog to her chest, "we're okay, that's what matters." "*We're* okay" meant her husband, her children, and her dog; she wasn't sorting them out by species. After the tragedy of Katrina, I heard discussions all over the country about what each of us would do if we were told to evacuate without our pets. What would you do if you had to choose between the safety of evacuation and risking your life to stay with your dog? Everyone at my office said we couldn't imagine living with the knowledge that we'd left our dogs behind, although we'd do it if we were forced to evacuate to save our children. Merely the thought of making such a choice was so upsetting we could barely talk about it. Our response wasn't unique to people whose lives and careers are devoted to dogs. My farm's pragmatic chain-sawing, brush-clearing handyman said that someone would have to shoot him before he'd leave his Rat Terrier behind to die.

What in heaven's name is going on here? Risking your life for a member of another species? Loving your dog as much as you love a human? That's flat-out amazing if you think about it. And yet, even if some people think it's crazy, those of us who love dogs love them like family, or perhaps more accurately, like the family we always wanted.

Surely love, "an intense feeling of tender affection and compassion," is the foundation of our relationship with dogs. I remember when I got my first Border Collie, Drift. Like an infatuated teenager, I was obsessed with his every move. I thought about him constantly, watched with a sense of wonder as he licked his paws, purred with comfort and completion when we cuddled together on the couch. There are millions of people who feel the same way, whose dogs bring them a unique happiness not found in other relationships.

I'm not talking about people who love animals *more* than they love people. I'm talking about people who love people, who have enriching, healthy relationships with friends and family and co-workers, and yet who love dogs so much they describe them as one of their greatest joys in life. People who skip having drinks with co-workers after work because their dogs have been alone too long; people who take their dogs on vacation, who use limited funds to buy them toys and food, who borrow money to pay the vet bill. I meet people everywhere who just want to talk about their dogs, about the silly little trick their Cairn Terrier learned all by himself, or the endearing way their Greyhound cuddles with them on the couch.

Our love for dogs is intense, pervasive, and sometimes heroic. If you think about it, it's as remarkable as the physics of electrons and the wonder of outer space. It deserves our attention, and a good place to start is with the biology of love itself.

THE BIOLOGY OF LOVE

In a 2005 op-ed piece in *The New York Times,* the biologist Bernd Heinrich said: "Functionally, I suspect love is often [a] temporary chemical imbalance of the brain induced by sensory stimuli that causes us to maintain focus on something that carries an adaptive agenda." Doesn't make you all warm and mushy, now does it? However, Heinrich's point was not to diminish love's beauty, but to argue that love has a biological basis, and that there's no reason to believe that we can claim it as uniquely human.

We know quite a bit about the chemistry of love. It's dopamine that causes that first rush of infatuation, when you're energized and elated and can't stop thinking about that special individual. Soon after, when things calm down, the hormone oxytocin is released into the bloodstream and begins to create those longer-term feelings of caring, love, and nurturance. The biologist Sarah Blaffer Hrdy calls oxytocin "the endocrinological equivalent of candlelight, soft music, and a glass of wine." Oxytocin has its origins in parental behavior, beginning with its essential role in the birth process, during which it facilitates uterine contractions and the letdown of milk. Besides these more mechanical duties, oxytocin turns out to be a key player in the attachment of a mother to her young.[1] Oxytocin is so important that if you block its uptake in a ewe right after she's given birth, she'll reject her own lamb and aggressively push it away.

Oxytocin also plays a significant role in other kinds of love—familial, romantic, and even sexual. Oxytocin levels rise when friends hug, when mothers cuddle their babies, and when lovers have sex. It's a "one size fits all" hormone, mediating love and attachment in all social relationships that involve feelings of care and connection. Women have higher levels of it than do men, which is not surprising, given oxytocin's role in childbirth and lactation. Social animals have higher levels of it than solitary ones, a fact exemplified in two species of small mouselike animals called voles. The females of one species, which is highly social, have high levels of oxytocin, while, in the other, down-

---

1. I'm simplifying here: other substances, such as prolactin and AVP, are involved, but oxytocin seems to be the lead actor in the play.

right unsocial species, the females have exceptionally low levels. In people, higher levels of oxytocin correlate with higher levels of attachment and connection. Researchers have even found that spraying oxytocin into the nasal passages of human subjects doubled their tendency to trust others in a "game" that involved giving over custody of their money. In the not-too-distant future it will be wise to steer clear of blind dates with nasal spray bottles.

The central role of oxytocin helps explain why some people, and some dogs for that matter, seem to be more loving and nurturing than others. Individuals vary in how much of the hormone they produce and how effectively they can utilize it when it's circulating. Individual experience can have a profound effect on people's ability to feel warm and loving toward others, too; one study found that children adopted from neglectful orphanages had lower levels of oxytocin after cuddling with their mothers than normal children did. However, remember that the impact of experience is constrained by the brain and the body it acts upon. Just as a painter can only work with the canvas and colors she has in front of her, so the effect of experience is influenced by the brain that absorbs it. I often wonder about oxytocin levels when I meet a dog whose aloof behavior breaks her owner's heart—does the dog have low levels of oxytocin, owing either to genetics or to early development? At present, I know of no one who is using oxytocin therapeutically (except for medical conditions relating to birth and lactation), but perhaps someday we'll be able to spray stand-offish dogs with oxytocin and turn them into social butterflies.

LOVE'S PERFECT STORM

Missy the Weimaraner had as bad a case of separation anxiety as any dog I've ever seen. She'd cut her back into shreds going through a plate-glass window trying to find her human, Cheryl. If left alone, even for a few minutes, she'd destroy pillows, couches, and kitchen cabinets with equal abandon. As soon as Cheryl began her preparations to leave the house to go to work, Missy began to pace, her paws began to sweat, and she began to drool.

After living through months of this, Cheryl came to me for help, and we devised a counterconditioning plan to ease Missy's fears. I told her the good news: this type of plan has a high success rate. The bad news was that it's a pain in the butt to pull off. During treatment, Cheryl couldn't leave Missy alone for even a few minutes. We had to break the link between being alone and feeling panicked, so Cheryl had to hire and train a raft of helpers to dog-sit Missy whenever she was gone. When she was home, she worked on counterconditioning, but because Missy's case was so serious, progress was slow. Even with adjunctive anti-anxiety drugs from her veterinarian, Missy would go into a full-scale panic at the slightest disruption in her schedule. Cheryl's life began to revolve around organizing helpers, lining up as many as three sitters when she had to be gone all day, changing her plans if a sitter had to cancel at the last minute. Her social life dropped down to nothing, because she had "used up" all her volunteers for her job and her classes at the university.

However, Cheryl did have a social life, and to her it was worth all the hassle and disruption. Cheryl's best friend and closest family member was Missy, and to Cheryl, Missy was worth whatever it took to cure her. Cheryl loved Missy, and Missy loved Cheryl: that was all that really mattered. As a beleaguered mother still loves her troubled teenager, Cheryl felt a love for her dog that carried her through all their troubles. Cheryl loved Missy as much as you can love anyone, and the fact that Missy was a dog and Cheryl was a human didn't seem relevent.

Oxytocin and dopamine may help us understand the biology behind our strong feelings of attachment, but it doesn't explain why members of one species—ours—should be so ready to lose their hearts to a member of another species. Not only that, but why dogs? Of all the animals on earth, why is it dogs who have settled into our hearts like rain on the desert? Just sitting in a room with a dog can decrease your blood pressure and heart rate. Petting your dog makes oxytocin flood your body and increases the frequency of brainwaves associated with feelings of peace and contentment. Dogs can even elicit positive responses from emotionally damaged people when the best efforts of family and doctors have failed. Every group that takes dogs to nursing homes has its own story about an unresponsive patient who opened up for the first time in years after petting a dog. But why? Why are dogs such masters at working their way into our hearts as no other animal can?

The traditional answer to the question of why we so love dogs is that they give us "unconditional love" or "nonjudgmental positive regard." To a large extent, this rings true. The cheerful, loving nature of most dogs brings us a purity of emotion hard to find anywhere else, no matter how much we want it. But I think we need to address this question in more depth. Perhaps our love for dogs, and their love for us, is too complex to be explained by any one factor. It seems most likely that, at its best, the special bond we have with dogs is the result of a number of things, combining together into a "perfect storm" of love and devotion.

First, as we've already seen, the faces of dogs are remarkably expressive, and many of their expressions are similar to ours. More than any other animal except our own children (and possibly chimpanzees), dogs wear their hearts on their sleeves.[2] The faces of dogs are like living, breathing, fur-covered emotions, with none of the masking and censoring made possible by the rational cortex of mature adult humans. The expressiveness of dogs gives them a direct line to the primitive and powerful emotional centers of our brains, and connects us in ways that nothing else ever could. When we look at dogs, we're looking into a mirror. That they express happiness so well, and that happiness is contagious, is just icing on the cake.

Second, the sociability of dogs is similar in many ways to that of humans. Dogs evolved from one of the world's most social species and naturally seek companionship. That's why sheep-guarding dogs stay with the flock, that's why some dogs form friendships with horses that last a lifetime, and that's why your dog is waiting at the window when you drive home from work. Dogs will live alone if they have to, but as long as there are enough resources to go around, dogs will always choose the company of others. This is as true of adult dogs as of puppies. In many other species, the young can form strong attachments to others, but once they've matured, their interest in forming new bonds decreases. Not so dogs—you can become best friends with an older dog in just days or weeks, so strong is their desire for companionship.

Although dogs cling to any kind of social relationship, they don't

2. Or more accurately, dogs wear their limbic systems on their faces, but that doesn't have much of a literary ring to it.

treat humans as any port in a storm. They seem to be as attracted to us as we are to them. Even dogs who've been socialized for only minutes as puppies are able to form strong attachments to people. (Usually, however, only to a small group of highly familiar people; they remain uncomfortable around strangers all their lives.) By contrast, wolves must be taken away from their mothers at three weeks and raised by humans to be comfortable around us as adults. And dogs want more than just to hang out with us; they seem to want to understand us, and to want us to understand them. They watch our faces all the time for information, just as humans do when they're unsure of what another person is trying to communicate. You can see people do the very same thing, in a game that dog trainers play to sharpen their skills. One person uses a clicker to train another to perform some action, in a kind of "warmer/colder" game. No words or visual cues are allowed; there's just the sound of the click to tell the trainee that she's on the right track. Yet even though trainees are told they'll get no other information, they turn to look at the face of the trainer when they become confused. Dogs do exactly that when they're confused about what we want: herding dogs will break their focused stare to turn and look at their handler's face with the visual equivalent of "What?!" Dogs might even be better at decoding certain types of human signals than our closest relatives, chimpanzees. In some studies, chimpanzees, even ones familiar with people, weren't able to locate hidden food if the experimenter pointed to it. Subsequent studies on dogs suggested that they were more adept than our closest relatives at the task.[3]

A dog's desire to communicate with people fits within the bounds of a dog's evolutionary baggage, in which pack members hunted together, raised their young together, and fought to the death to keep the group together. You can't coordinate your efforts as a group without some kind of communication, so it's no wonder that dogs are as obsessed with social communication as we are. But dogs' desire and ability to communicate, and their formation of attachments, transcend species boundaries. Research found that in novel en-

---

3. Some new work on chimps *did* find evidence of chimps being able to comprehend the message of a pointing arm. Add that to the experience of most dog trainers that dogs *don't* understand a pointing gesture until trained to, and you get a good sense of how fluid science really is. Right now, I'd say we have a lot to learn about this issue. But my point remains that dogs often look to humans for information.

vironments, kenneled dogs were calmer in the presence of a human caretaker than with a dog they'd been kenneled with for over two months. It's remarkable that an animal would choose an individual of an entirely different species for comfort and companionship. Imagine being lost and alone in the jungle and stumbling upon a person and a bird—and bonding with the bird and ignoring the person. In one study, dogs living in shelters formed attachments to people after only minimal contact. It took only three ten-minute sessions of petting for dogs to become attached, and for the dogs to stand at the door, waiting, if the person left the room.

Some explanations of dogs' attachment to humans are not particularly romantic. Psychologist John Archer argues that dogs are simply social parasites, who have learned to manipulate our emotions so as to obtain free food, safety, and, in some cases, appointments with certified canine massage therapists and animal communicators. Lord knows dogs are an evolutionary success story: just compare the numbers of dogs in any given country with the number of wolves.[4] However, the biological success of dogs doesn't negate the profound feelings of love and devotion that go along with it; we don't dismiss the love of parent for child simply because it's to the parent's advantage to pass on his or her genes. I think it's shortsighted—sad, really—to dismiss the love that dogs have for us in such mechanistic terms.

Still, there is an important truth to be found in an objective view of our relationship with dogs. Painful though it might be, we need to reexamine the belief that dogs give us unconditional love. There's no question but that most of our dogs love us, and there's little doubt that, sometimes, their love is often almost epic in its intensity. However, as we saw in the chapter on anger, the chance that our dogs are never irritated with us is slim at best. How convenient, then, that they can never say so.

You may wish with all your heart that you could talk to your dog, but as we're often reminded, we'd better watch out for what we wish for, because we just might get it. The power of speech is a wonderful thing, but it comes with a price. It's not true that "sticks and stones

---

4. There are over sixty-five million dogs in the United States, compared to just a few thousand wolves in Alaska, Minnesota, Yellowstone National Park, and Wisconsin.

may break my bones but words will never hurt me." We all know that bruises and cuts often heal faster than the damage done by a cruel comment. Personally, I'm glad my dogs can't nail me with the kind of hurtful remark that can come out of the mouths of even the kindest of friends. I'm quite sure that sometimes I'd rather not know what my dogs had to say. I'm reminded of the "words" of Washoe, a chimpanzee raised by Beatrice and Robert Gardner, who ordered trainers she didn't like out of the room with the American Sign Language for "You green pile of poop."[5]

In addition to providing a kind of beneficial, before-the-fact censorship, our lack of a shared language has another, more amorphous advantage. As I said in an essay in the book *Dog Is My Co-pilot,*

> Words may be wonderful things, but they carry weight with them, and there's a great lightness of being when they are discarded. . . . Some of my happiest moments are when Luke and I sit silently together, overlooking the green, rolling hills of Southern Wisconsin. Our lack of language doesn't get in the way, but creates an opening for something else, something deep and pure and good. We dog lovers share a kind of Zen-like communion with our dogs, uncluttered by nouns and adverbs and dangling participles. This connection speaks to a part of us that needs to be nurtured and listened to, but that is so often drowned out in the cacophony of speech. Dogs remind us that we are being heard, without the additional weight of words. What a gift. No wonder we love them so much.

We might yearn to tell our dogs why they can't go on a walk while their injured foot heals, or to explain that we're only leaving town for a couple of days, but I doubt that we'd have the pure, uncluttered connections we now enjoy if the relationship were burdened by language. In *The New Work of Dogs,* Jon Katz tells a story about a man who loved his dog because the dog was the only individual he *didn't* have to talk to. Katz suspects that men often love dogs because dogs never ask them

---

5. I've modified the usual translation of what Washoe "said," in hopes of sparing the tender eyes of sensitive readers.

to talk about their feelings. Women love dogs so much, he suggests, because they see them as being so supportive. A study reported in *The New York Times* found that half of the female veterinary students surveyed said they got more emotional support from their dogs than they did from their husbands. Surely our perception that dogs are supportive is bolstered by the fact that they can't tell us to shut up when we're talking too much. The fact is, some dogs probably do give us unconditional love, but not all dogs do, and most dogs don't every minute of every day. It just feels that way, given their expressiveness, their childlike cheerfulness, and bless it, their inability to communicate in words. Overall, it seems that what we can't say to dogs is a small price to pay for what we gain from our wordless style of communication.

As if emotionality, expressiveness, a high degree of sociability, and the inability to tell us to shut up weren't enough, there's another important factor that influences our devotion to dogs. We humans have evolved to be protective and nurturing to big-eyed, dependent young mammals, and dogs elicit this state of mind from us with a force stronger than any hurricane. Like young children who stimulate our feelings of nurturance, dogs are nonverbal and have limited abilities. They can't go to the store and buy food; they can't open the door and let themselves out. If we left for work one day and never came home, they'd die, trapped and alone and unable to take care of themselves. In these ways they are the exact equivalent of young humans—nonverbal and dependent, wrapped in a fluffy, fuzzy package that says *"I'm cute and cuddly and I need you."*

Our feelings of parental love and nurturance are not to be sneezed at; they've kept primates like us going for millions of years. The parents of many animals walk away without a care once the eggs are laid or the sperm is transferred, but we shower our young with attention and care over a prolonged period. Lions may raise their young with affectionate licks and cuddles, but they'll walk away and let their babies starve to death to save their own lives. Not so humans, dogs, or wolves: we're obsessed with raising, nurturing, and protecting our young, and we'll sacrifice our own lives to save theirs. Just the sight of young, helpless mammals can change our internal hormonal balance and increase the amount of oxytocin in our bloodstream. Although our complicated brains enable us to be rational and creative, underneath that complexity are ancient structures that generate primal reactions to big-eyed, fluffy mammals. As the writer and behaviorist Karen London so aptly said in *The Bark* magazine, "Dogs, the source of so much pure joy and warm comfort, are a reminder that perhaps the passion in our lives is too great to be contained within the bounds of humanity." There's great truth to that, and it's based not on some neurotic need to replace our feelings toward people with feelings toward dogs, but on a deep-seated biological drive to nurture small, dependent things.

So there you have it, a perfect package of love, an animal whose looks and behavior leave many of us weak in the knees. Dogs elicit the love and the desire to nurture that we're designed to feel toward young dependent mammals, and their expressiveness just ups the ante. The mere sight of them bathes us with the hormones associated with love and devotion. At the same time, sometimes accurately, sometimes not, we feel from them the kind of love we want from our *parents,* that no-holds-barred, "unconditional" love that psychologists tell us we've all been seeking since infancy. It's a double whammy of epic proportions— we love them like children, and at the same time feel loved by them with the kind of pure, primal love that we needed when we were babies ourselves. Wow. Dogs get us coming and going. In truth, we're the ones who are helpless.

There's a stone I had made for Luke at the top of the hill road, where the pasture opens wide and the setting sun highlights the words carved into its face. "That'll do, Luke, that'll do," it says. The words are said to working dogs all over the world when the chores are done and the flock is settled: "That'll do, dog; come home now, your work is done." Luke's work is done, too. He took my heart and ran with it, and I hope he's running still, fast and strong, a piece of my heart bound up with his, forever.

The intense love we feel for our dogs provides us joy and happiness beyond measure, but it has a flip side: the pain we experience when we lose that love. In the next chapter, we'll look at the biology of grief and initiate an inquiry into how much our dogs understand about life, death, and the workings of their own minds.

9

ARE YOU THINKING
WHAT I'M THINKING?

Thinking about emotions
like grief, jealousy, and sympathy

Luke died on a Friday night, so thin and weak that when he squatted to pee he swayed like the plants in a tall grass prairie. There was no question of him lifting his leg anymore. He hadn't eaten in almost a week and he needed help to get up on his feet. His kidneys had failed him, as had I. While the rest of his body had been glowing with health, his kidneys had simply shut down, and nothing I or anyone else did was able to save him.

Only a few months before he had seemed fine, although a bit quiet, a tad listless about his food. I took him to his vet, John Dally, who discovered he had Ehrlichia, a tick-borne bacterial illness not unlike Lyme disease. We put him on a course of antibiotics that took care of the Ehrlichia, but noticed what I hoped was a temporary glitch in the functioning of his kidneys.

I was optimistic. Three years before, Luke had won a battle with cancer, and I felt empowered by that and by the veterinary resources at his disposal. If you want to move heaven and earth to save a dog, Madison, Wisconsin, is the place to do it. When his kidneys appeared compromised, Luke and I went to specialists at the University of Wisconsin School of Veterinary Medicine, as well as to veterinarians specializing in Chinese and homeopathic medicine. He received Western medicine, acupuncture, Chinese herbs, therapeutic massage, homeopathic supplements, and home-cooked dinners.[1] I always felt that Luke and I had a deal: you take care of

---

1. I'm aware that this sounds excessive to some people, but I'd do it again in a heartbeat. I am grateful to have the resources at this point in my life to take care of my dogs as well as I can. These expenditures don't stop me from contributing to charities or saving for retirement, and, as important, they prevent me from spending money on things like fancy shoes.

me, and I'll take care of you. That's the way it had always been. He'd saved me, and I'd saved him, and this was going to be just one more challenge for us to conquer together.

Two months later, a specialist called with new lab results and said: "It's time to start reflecting on the wonderful life you and Luke have had together." He might as well have taken a baseball bat and slammed it across my chest. I cried to my friends: "I'm not ready for the 'He's had a wonderful life' talk." I rallied, did more research, added more supplements, committed myself to proving the vet wrong, to saving my dog by sheer force of will.

But slowly, inexorably, Luke got worse. Food began to nauseate him and, in a heart-crushing example of classical conditioning, his body rejected whatever he'd eaten the day before. My life revolved around finding new kinds of food for him. I bought sardines and pumpkins and pork shoulder roast and organic brown rice. Friends brought over duck and buffalo meat and free-range eggs, but eventually, there wasn't anything Luke could eat. We couldn't keep him hydrated either, even with twice-daily sessions of subcutaneous fluids.

About a week before he died, I began to feel that my efforts were harassing Luke rather than helping him. Accepting that I couldn't save him, I switched to hospice rather than hospital care. I emptied my calendar and spent my last week with him, soaking up the touch of his nose, the smell of his fur, the pink of his tongue. I sat long hours with him in the sun up in the pasture, full of the bittersweet emotions that accompany love and grief. At the end, we slept together in a makeshift bed on the living room floor. That's where the veterinarian and I helped him pass on, peacefully snuggled up against me, nothing but bones and a shockingly beautiful black-and-white coat.

After Luke died, I was dumbstruck with grief, stumbling through the next months in a haze. I felt as if I'd been hit by a train, as though I'd been physically as well as emotionally injured. None of my senses seemed to function as they had before. The colors of the earth were different, wrong somehow, although I couldn't quite say how. I coped well enough, seeing clients, running my business, tending to my farm. But a day didn't pass that I wasn't heartsick and hurt and angry, and that I didn't agonize over whether there was something I'd missed, something I could have done to save him.

Luke's daughter didn't do so well after his death, either. Lassie wor-

shipped Luke from the day she met him, when she arrived at the farm at eleven months of age. She was meant to stay only a few weeks, as a favor to her breeder, but within twenty-four hours I asked if I could keep her, so enamored was I of her sweetness, so impressed by her natural ability on sheep. And so she stayed, becoming as much a part of the farm as her father. She fell in love with him herself, watching him, following him, licking his face while they cuddled together on the rug. They spent so much time together that I felt sorry for Pip, who had been Luke's playmate up until then, but instantly became the odd dog out when Lassie arrived.

Lassie and Luke adored each other, and of all the dogs, I wondered most what would happen to her when he passed away. The answer came readily enough. Lassie's behavior changed radically the day after Luke died. She regressed to some of the anxiety-ridden behaviors she'd had when I first got her. She began sucking on toys and kneading her paws obsessively, self-medicating herself with the hormones of a suckling puppy. She began licking again relentlessly, as she had when I first got her—tongue moving mindlessly, eyes shut, licking anything in front of her—tables, rugs, your leg, it didn't matter.[2] Worst, her work on sheep became nervous, almost desperate. She'd walk two paces toward the sheep and then stop and eat sheep poop, walk another two paces, and look for more poop to eat. Not a pretty habit, but a heartbreaking one, since I knew it was driven by anxiety. She'd done it before on occasion when she'd felt pressured, but never to that extent. It was pathetic to watch her, so for a while I kept her away from what had been her greatest joy in life, and what now seemed to cause her unbearable anxiety.

It's possible that Lassie's change in behavior was entirely due to the change in mine. My grief over Luke's death was palpable, and I can't imagine anyone in the house not being influenced by it. And yet Pip and Tulip didn't seem to be, at least not visibly. Tulip seemed unaffected by Luke's illness, his death, or my grief. True to form, she was quiet and serious some of the time, and rollicking bright at other times. I can't think of anything about her behavior that changed in any way

---

2. These kinds of repetitive actions, called stereotypies, have been found to increase the amount of serotonin in the brain, and so animals who perform them are believed to be "self-medicating."

after Luke died. Pip's behavior changed a bit, but not in the direction I would have predicted. Pip and Luke always seemed to get along well, and I can't remember one incident in twelve and a half years where there was the slightest spark of tension between them. Imagine my surprise when she seemed happier after Luke died. She seemed more playful, perkier—a notable change in a dog known for her sweetness, but not her exuberance. My only explanation is that Luke's life was so big that he took attention away from Pip, and after he was gone she got more of what she wanted—her toys, and attention from me (I suspect that is the correct order). But while Pip seemed energized, and Tulip seemed oblivious, Lassie was—there is no other way to describe it—a wreck.

DOGS, GRIEF, AND THE CONCEPT OF DEATH

Lassie behaved as if she was devastated by Luke's death, and her story is not an uncommon one. A multitude of anecdotes suggest that dogs can grieve over the death of someone they loved. A friend's Boxer startled as if she'd been hit with electricity when she entered the room in which the family's beloved cat had died. She sniffed the body, left the room, and barely got up for the next three days. She lay like a puddle in one place, eyes meltingly sad, refusing all food, including steak, chicken, and cheese.

Lassie spent the night that her father died lying in the same room as his body, with her head down and her brows furrowed. Every time I checked on her she was awake, lying still, staring at Luke's body. The next day she began doing all the crazy, obsessive things she had done when I first got her: she began spinning in tiny little circles, she started compulsively licking, and she sucked on her toys as if she'd regressed to puppyhood.

Similar stories of what looks like grief in animals are common. We've all heard about elephants staying for days with the body of a deceased herd member, and then returning months and even years later to stroke the bones. Jane Goodall riveted the world with the story of the chimpanzee named Flint, who seemingly died of grief just three weeks after his mother, Flo. Stories of animals who appear to be overwhelmed with grief aren't even restricted to mammals—an avian biologist named Marcy Houle gives a heart-rending account in *The Smile of a Dolphin* of a peregrine falcon's behavior after his mate failed to return to the nest. After three days of giving the usual contact call, used by mates to stay in touch, the bird finally let loose with "a cry like a screeching moan," and then sat motionless for an entire day before he rallied to take over feeding their chicks.

It seems reasonable that animals as complex and social as dogs could feel pain because of the death of an individual they love. Yet the concept of death isn't a simple one. It's one thing to be aware of the absence of someone you care about, another thing altogether to understand the finality of death. To understand that someone has died is to understand, at a minimum, that their absence isn't temporary, and that they won't be coming back. We often speak of dogs as living in the present, but to grieve as I did over Luke, Lassie had to understand the consequences of his death on the *future*. I knew that after Luke died I'd never again get to stroke his soft fur or watch him run across the pasture. But what of Lassie? If dogs always live in the present, how could she understand that the future would no longer include Luke?

It's no insult to dogs to question what they understand of death. After someone dies, their lifeless body can't feel, can't think, and will never again be able to laugh, cry, or yell in anger. That's a complicated set of ideas to understand. Children don't understand the concept of death until they're at least five or six. Before that, they say things like "I know Daddy is dead, but when is he coming home?"

Dogs can't ask us questions like that, but we can glean something from their behavior after someone special has died. Lassie's story suggests that she did understand the finality of Luke's passing—you'd have to work hard to convince me that she didn't. However, for every story of a dog depressed after the death of a playmate, there are hundreds if not thousands of observations of animals who seem unaffected. Remember the account, at the beginning of this book, of how Tulip seemed so sad about the death of the old ewe named Harriet? I was thinking of that episode when Amy, another of the farm's special ewes, died. I thought Tulip might react as she had when Harriet died, so I took her to Amy's body and got ready with my camera to take some interesting photographs. I got some pictures, all right—of Tulip sniffing the body for a few seconds, then moving on to sniff a pile of manure, and then, with what appeared to be joyful enthusiasm, rolling and grinding on her back in the dirt. Nothing about her behavior suggested any awareness that something special had happened, much less that she was grieving.

The difference in Tulip's response to the deaths of Harriet and Amy is emblematic of the variety of reactions that animals seem to have to the death of others. Andy Beck, an equine ethologist in New Zealand, tells a moving story of a band of horses reacting to the deaths of three foals within a few days of one another: after the last death, the herd formed a circle and stood motionless together for three days. However, stories of grieving animals may capture our interest and our imagination (not to mention our own emotions) but most accounts are less dramatic and easily fade in memory. There are numerous reports of horses sniffing the dead body of another as casually as if sniffing an old boot. Of course, we can't say from their behavior what they are feeling inside; the seemingly casual sniffing could cover a cauldron of emotions. Perhaps Tulip didn't much care for Amy, but was genuinely fond of Harriet. However, we have to be careful about dismissing behavior that *doesn't* look like grieving while paying special attention to behavior that *does*. If we're going to use behavior as an indicator of emotions like sorrow and grief, then we have to take into account all the behavior we observe, not just the behavior that supports what we want to believe.

Thanks to many advances in neurobiology, we are no longer limited to observations of behavior to help us understand what's going on in the minds of our dogs. We're learning a lot about how the brain and the body react to (and create) strong emotions like grief, and it is becoming increasingly clear that to understand how other animals experience them, we need to understand their thought processes as well as their emotions. Earlier, we defined emotions as physical changes inside and outside the body, as well as the *thoughts* that went along with them. Grief is a good example of that: thoughts like "I'll never see my dog again" are part of why it's so hard to contemplate the death of a beloved dog. Thus, if we want to understand how our emotions compare to those of our dogs, we need to understand something about how their thoughts compare to ours.

Here's where the rubber hits the road, because debates about whether animals like dogs can think can get as contentious as the nastiest of political debates. There are those who claim that animals aren't able to think; their argument is based upon the differences in the size and function of human cortexes, or on our unique linguistic ability, or on a combination of the two. It is absolutely true that those big, wrinkly cortexes of ours enable us to integrate large numbers of mental abstractions, hold them in working memory, and move them around in order to plan and strategize. If you're lying in bed trying to decide whether you should get another dog, you're integrating a vast amount of information about who dogs are, what they need, and what your life is like now compared to what you'd like it to be in the future. That's what we call "thinking," or the ability to form and manipulate "abstract mental representations" of things that are not directly in front of us. You aren't necessarily thinking in abstractions when you're looking at a puppy and wanting to pet it, but you are if you're lying in bed alone, visualizing a puppy (which is an "abstract mental representation") and wondering whether you want one. Our ability to use abstractions is so ingrained we rarely think about it, but there isn't an animal born that can approach our ability to store and manipulate large amounts of abstract information.[3] Historically some have argued that nonhuman animals aren't capable of working with abstractions at all, but as we'll soon see, the animals are proving them wrong.

In this chapter, we'll look at what we know about thinking and emotions, and how that knowledge relates to our dogs. The story at the beginning of the chapter was about grief because, sad though it may be, it's an excellent entry point to a discussion of emotions and the mind. Because grieving over the loss of a loved one necessitates an understanding of abstract concepts, such as "the future," it's a perfect introduction to the interplay between emotion and thought.

THE FLIP SIDE OF LOVE

What humans call grief has its roots in the profound social attachments that many animals form with one another, and the biology of those re-

---

3. Thinking about your ability to think is itself a great example of your ability to form and use abstract concepts. Once you start analyzing it, you might find that thinking about thinking is both fascinating and as circular as the architecture in an M. C. Escher print.

lationships appears to be as innate as anger, fear, and happiness. We know a lot about what's called separation distress in animals, and we know that many of their reactions, when they lose contact with their mother, mate, or young, can be strikingly similar to those of humans. For example, in animals who have strong social attachments, the young give "distress vocalizations" when separated from their mothers. There's been lots of research on this phenomenon; we know where in the brain such calls are generated, which chemicals elicit them, and which ones soothe them.

All these studies make it clear that the calls are much more than mindless noises produced mechanically; they are generated deep within the brain, in areas related to strong emotions. Interestingly, this type of distress involves chemical and neurological pathways different from those activated by the fear of danger or injury. Think of the way you felt when you were young and you lost track of your mother at the shopping mall, or how you felt when you looked out into the yard and discovered your dog had disappeared. It won't surprise you, then, that this neural pathway is called the panic circuit, a fitting term for any of us who have had a beloved dog go missing for even a few minutes.

In mammals and birds, these primitive circuits appear to be the flip side of the pathways related to social attachment. In other words, the brain's ability to create feelings of love and attachment entails the ability to feel panic, and eventually sadness, when the object of our affection goes away. The proposition that the brain commingles love and grief is supported by the ability of oxytocin—the hormone associated with love and attachment—to soothe animals suffering from separation distress. Take a duckling away from its mother and it will call for her in a panic. Give the duckling oxytocin and the calls quiet, while the duckling settles as contentedly as if cuddled beside her mother. This phenomenon is not unique: extensive research on social mammals shows that their neurophysiology resembles ours when it comes to social attachments and separation distress. In extreme forms, this distress verges on panic, as I inadvertently implied when I wrote, long before Luke died, that "I imagine his death to be as if someone took all the oxygen out of the air and I was left to try to survive without it."

Not only are these panic circuits primitive things, it turns out they are derived from the primordial pathways that mediate pain. The same parts of the brain activate when an animal is physically injured and when it's distressed about a separation. Additionally, opiates, such as morphine and codeine, alleviate separation distress and panic attacks, even though they are classified as painkillers. The experience of pain and the loss of social contact are so closely aligned in the brain that the administration of morphine actually reduces sociality in mammals: rodents spend less time with others, dogs wag their tails less, and primates groom less often if you give them a healthy dose of it. That's one of the reasons why addictions to this class of drugs can be so dangerous—people who become seriously addicted to morphine actually go out of their way to avoid social contact. Their brains are telling them they're getting more than they need, when in reality they're completely alone. The opposite happens if you decrease the levels of opiates in the brain—individuals seek out social contact and, if the opiate levels get low enough, can't seem to get enough of it. Thus, the chemicals that reduce physical pain also seem to provide us, at least temporarily, with the same feelings of well-being that healthy social relationships provide.

No wonder we talk about the *pain* of losing someone we love. The relationship between grief and pain is not merely metaphorical; anyone who has lost someone they loved deeply, whether a human or a dog, instantly understands the connection between grief and an actual sense of physical pain. After Luke died—and after my mother died, only six months before him—I remember feeling as if I was recovering from surgery, as if I had a raw, tender incision deep in my belly. It's no accident that we care for people who've been injured the same way we care for people who've suffered a loss: we bring them flowers and cook our best comfort food, which we deliver with sympathy cards and gentle, warm hugs. Whether someone is grieving over a death or has been hurt in a car accident, we call the process of their recovery "healing."

However, it's one thing for animals to feel emotional distress because they've been separated from their mothers or their mates. It's another thing altogether for them to fully understand that the separation is permanent. Surely it's the knowledge that the dogs we've lost are never coming back that makes our grief so intense. It seems in this case that the more sophisticated our ability to think, the stronger and more painful are our emotions. This connection between thoughts and emotions is a critical part of how we experience the world, and if we want to compare our experience with that of our dogs, it's worth taking a moment to look at new discoveries about the synergy of thoughts and emotions.

EMOTIONS—DON'T LEAVE HOME WITHOUT THEM

One of the most interesting aspects of the connection between thinking and emotion is the newly discovered importance of emotions in decision making. Certain areas of the brain integrate emotion and reason; if they are damaged—usually this happens as a result of head trauma or surgery—the victim is unable to make even the simplest decision.[4] She can create a complete list of possible options in the face of any challenge, but is unable to come to a conclusion about which one to choose. She can pass any intelligence test and solve difficult mathematical problems, but she can't make a decision.

One such patient, named Elliot in Antonio Damasio's book *Descartes' Error,* was an upstanding husband, father, and professional until a brain tumor necessitated the removal of the area of the brain that integrates emotion and rational thought. Although he performed perfectly on a raft of intelligence and personality tests, he became nonfunctional at the office. Unable to decide anything, he'd spend an entire day at work devising new ways to sort documents that could've been filed in five minutes. He seemed completely unaware of his disability. His social skills fell apart, too: he'd blurt out rude and hurtful remarks, with no idea of their effect on those around him. Eventually, Elliot lost his job and his family and ended up bankrupt and alone. When his emotions were no longer able to advise the rational part of his brain, Elliot was unable to function.

Patients like Elliot have taught us how vital the emotions are to our abilities as humans to make good, *rational* decisions. Long dismissed as somewhat embarrassing remnants of our animal nature, emotions have traditionally gotten, in the words of the late comedian Rodney Danger-

---

4. It's primarily the prefrontal cortex that communicates with the amygdala. Together they create an integration of thoughts and emotions that results in the way we feel about any given thing.

field, "no respect."[5] And yet, here they are, appearing as essential ingredients in our highly vaunted powers of reasoning. Of course, an excess
of emotion can interfere with rational thought. We all know the feeling
of having our minds freeze up when we're nervous about speaking in
public, or time-pressured during a chemistry exam. However, the link
between logic and emotion is a two-way street. We're learning that
without the influence of emotions, "rational thinking" isn't so rational
after all. It's just as likely to get us into trouble as are emotions unbal-
anced by thought. The take-home message of this discovery is this: just
as we've learned that it makes no sense to consider the brain and the
body as two separate things, we're learning that our thoughts and emotions are equally bound together. They depend upon each other, and
they are equally important to what we call the human mind.

It's hard to conclude exactly what this new knowledge tells us about
the mental lives of our dogs. Although dogs undoubtedly share much
of the basic experience of fear, anger, happiness, and love, their emotional experiences must also be different from our own. Our thought
processes are complex compared with those of dogs, and if we can't
separate our thoughts from our emotions, then we have to acknowledge that our emotions must be different from theirs, at least in some
ways.

However, thanks to the tremendous strides recently made in neurobiology, we have a lot of information that we can use to look at how
thoughts and emotions might combine differently in dogs and people.[6]
For example, you may remember, from the chapter on fear, that animals and autistic people have less active prefrontal cortexes than normal people do. Decreased activation of this area is associated with an
increased ability to feel fear. That is consistent with how autistic people
experience the world—they suffer more from fear and anxiety than
typical people (although both groups are well acquainted with these
emotions).

This finding suggests that the differences between the cognitive

5. What an irony that so many have denied animals the ability to experience emotions, when simultaneously we've described emotions as primitive and animalistic.

6. Damasio has found it useful to define "emotions" as physical changes like facial expressions and
activated amygdalas, and "feelings" as the "private" thoughts and mental experiences that accompany
them.

abilities of dogs and people might make some of the emotions that dogs experience more intense than ours, not less. Certainly the behavior of frightened dogs supports that possibility. I've seen dogs so frightened they leaped out third-story windows, or emptied their bowels, bladder, and anal glands at the approach of a stranger. Everyone in animal rescue has seen dogs whose fear rendered them virtually helpless, frozen in space and unable to move even an inch. It's not that people can't be overcome with terror; we can. But it happens much less often in our species, perhaps because we have more power to reason than our dogs, and so there's a higher likelihood that our emotions can be calmed by our thoughts.

Thoughts. There's that word again. If you want to get into an argument, start a group of people talking about whether dogs can "think." Among scientists, philosophers, and the general public, opinions on this question are not only variable but also tend to be strongly held. However, if we're going to talk about whether dogs can think, it's useful to describe clearly what we're talking about. In the next section, I discuss what thinking really is, and provide the basis for the argument that yes, dogs can think (just not like we can).

THINKING ABOUT THINKING

In his youth, Charlie was a bit of a roamer. The German Shepherd–Labrador mix terrified his owners by dashing out of their expansive yard and disappearing down the road. He'd come back hours later, after Joe and Bernadette were sick with worry and exhausted from canvassing the neighborhood. Finally, they got an "electronic fence" system to keep him in the yard. Charlie wore a collar that gave him a shock if he walked over a buried wire at the boundaries of the property. The higher priced systems, like Charlie's, warn the dog with a beeping sound if he gets close to the wire.[7] If the dog ignores the beep, he receives a shock. The idea is that the dog will only have to be shocked a few times, because the beep will tell him when he's getting too close to the boundary.

That was the theory, anyway, but Charlie had other ideas. Charlie fig-

---

7. In my experience, some dogs do well with these devices, but others do not, so please be careful and thoughtful before you invest in one. I've seen several dogs who were traumatized by them, so I don't usually recommend them.

ured out that if he lay down close enough to the wire to make the collar beep continuously, it eventually stopped. Once the beeping stopped, the collar couldn't deliver a shock anymore (because the battery had run out of juice), and Charlie could saunter out of the yard.

This story about Charlie is just that—a story. It circulated around the dog world a few years ago, and I love it because it stimulates discussion about the mental abilities of a dog. If it's true, no one can deny that Charlie is one smart dog. What's in question, though, is how Charlie figured out how to beat the system. Did he learn through trial and error that a continuous beep meant he couldn't get shocked, or did he lie in the yard thinking about it, and figure it out in a moment of insight?

We all know that the mental abilities of dogs and people are profoundly different. Dogs don't read books, design automobiles, or write sonatas. Dogs may understand a lot of words we teach them, but they don't spontaneously begin to use a complex, symbolic language early in their development. They don't lie in their dog beds planning what they should do on their evening walk next Thursday. Dogs are unable to solve problems that are trivial to us—think of dogs who have wound their leashes around a tree and can't figure out how to reverse their direction to unwind the leash. Pip, the smartest dog I've ever had, appears to be surprised every evening, as she has been for fifteen years, when she has to back away from a gate that opens inward in order to go through it.

Granted, dogs can do amazing things—anyone who earns his living with working dogs can take center stage at a dinner party relating the remarkable things the dog has done—but the problem-solving ability of the human brain leaves even the most brilliant dogs in the dust. We share ancient brain centers like the cerebellum and the limbic system with other mammals, but the "thinking" part of our brains is radically different.

We've all seen countless pictures of the human brain. If you take away the skull, you find a rather undistinguished-looking gray mass, wrinkled like a big, sodden walnut with deep nooks and crannies creasing its surface. What's most visible are the cerebral hemispheres, covered by the thin membrane called the cortex. As we saw in Chapter 2, the cortex acts as the mind's decision center, in both people and dogs. It's the neurons in the cortex that help you decide when and where to throw the ball for your dog, and it's in her cortex that your dog decides whether to bring you back the ball, or whether she should dash behind the house and hide it under the bushes. The thin but essential blanket of cells that make up the cortex is only about an eighth of an inch thick, and in humans the cerebral hemispheres beneath it are crinkled, like a wadded-up piece of paper. It's those wrinkles that make us humans so special, because by increasing the surface area of the cerebral hemispheres, they radically increase the size of the cortex that covers them.

There's a reason for those wrinkles. As we evolved as strategic thinkers (needing more and more neurons in the cortex) we couldn't keep increasing the size of our brains, or babies would never make it out of the birth canal. (Most of the mothers I know think things went too far as it is.) The solution was to create more surface area for the cortex by wrinkling the surface of the hemispheres. If you smoothed out a human cortex as you would a crumpled piece of paper, it would be as large as a full-size newspaper page laid open. If you did the same to the smoother cortex of a chimpanzee, it would be a quarter of that size. A rhesus monkey's would take up only the space of a large postcard, and your dog's would be that size or smaller.[8]

This difference in structure and function creates a profound difference between us and our dogs. We know that dogs can understand a large number of words, but it's also overwhelmingly clear that they aren't capable of anything even approaching human language. The average high school student knows more than eighty thousand words; a dog who knows two hundred words makes the national news. Humans have specialized areas in the cortex of the brain that are critical to language; our dogs have no equivalent.

However, that doesn't mean dogs can't form and manipulate "mental abstractions," which is the basis of being able to think. There's no reason to believe that what we call thinking is something you either can or cannot do. The few studies that have been done on dogs strongly

8. In many ways, this is a good thing. If our dogs were as smart as we are, I doubt that things would go so smoothly.

support the hypothesis that dogs are able to conceptualize at least simple abstractions.[9] One researcher taught dogs to select the larger of two objects to get a food treat, regardless of the shape or composition of the object. "Larger" and "smaller" are perfect examples of conceptual abstractions—there's no object called a "large" that you can ask your dog to fetch. Dogs can also be taught to select the item that's "different" in size or shape in an array of three objects. That's another example of an abstraction: you can't see, smell, or taste a "different"—it's a concept, which can only exist in one's mind.

In one experiment, it looked as though dogs weren't able to use the concept of "different" to solve a problem because they failed what's called the "delayed nonmatching to sample test." In this exercise the dogs are first shown a tray with just one item on it, and under that item is some yummy food. The dog is allowed to push it over and eat the food. The tray is then taken away, and after a delay of ten seconds the dog is presented with a tray again, this time with two objects on it. One object is the same as before, the other is different. The "right" choice is the *different* object, the one that doesn't match the object that was on the first tray. After hundreds of trials, dogs were unable to learn to choose the different object, although rhesus monkeys could figure it out pretty quickly.

But in a testament to good science, the researchers varied the task, by asking the dogs to choose an object in a different *location* than it was the first time. Dogs not only figured that out, they got it right 90 percent of the time, even when they had to wait twenty seconds between the trays. Studies like this support anecdotal observations suggesting that dogs can learn abstractions. Ken Ramirez, the head animal trainer at the Shedd Aquarium in Chicago, says it's relatively easy to teach dogs the concept of larger versus smaller, same versus different, and right versus left.

Dogs also seem to have some type of concept of number, which is also an abstraction. In one study originally done on children, dogs watched items being placed behind a screen, one at a time. After the last object was placed, the screen is removed. A subject who under-

9. It never ceases to amaze me how few studies we have on the animals we live with, compared with those on other primates, birds, marine mammals, and rodents living in laboratories.

stands something about number or quantity should expect to see the same number of objects sitting together as were lowered, one by one, behind the screen in the first place. It's these tests that taught us that children about five months old have some concept of quantity—if the "wrong" number of objects is revealed behind the screen, they stare at them for much longer than they do if they see the number they expected. Dogs do the same thing, appearing to be surprised by the "wrong" number of objects once they're revealed.

The concept of number, although we take it for granted every day, is relatively complicated. It includes the understanding that number is unrelated to size or shape (five Saint Bernards are the same number as five Miniature Poodles) and what's called the property of cardinality, which states that the last number in a count is the total number of things counted. Children don't understand this concept until they're around three and a half or four years of age; before that they don't seem to realize that if they count "One, two, three," there is a total of three things in front of them. Studies asking whether at least some animals can understand the basic concept of number are on the rise, and they overwhelmingly suggest that it's a concept many nonhuman animals can grasp.

Although we need much more research, it appears that animals of many species can keep up to about seven items in their working memory, but after that their performance begins to degrade. That's another benefit of our big, linguistically oriented brains: language and our large working memory allow us to keep far more facts or concepts in our brains at the same time than the members of any other species can. However, the research suggests that the difference between us and other animals is one of degree. It's not as simple as "Humans can think, and animals can't," but rather a matter of how much and in what ways animals think in comparison to humans.

DOGS AS PROBLEM SOLVERS

Once you start looking, you can find an infinite number of stories about dogs solving problems that suggest far more than mechanical reactions to the world around them. A dog named Izzie figured out how to get around the mousetraps that his owners had placed to prevent him from sleeping on the furniture. The owners couldn't figure out how Izzie was managing to avoid the traps—until they set up a video camera, and watched in awe as Izzie picked a blanket up in his mouth, awkwardly dragged it across the traps until they all snapped, and then cozied up on the couch with the blanket as a pillow.

Stories of dogs teaching their humans to fetch are a dime a dozen. Some special clients of mine had a Border Collie, Bear, who had learned he wasn't allowed to go off the grass into the road. His owners began noticing that when they played fetch, somehow the ball kept ending up in the road, no matter which way they threw it. They finally decided that Bear was purposely moving the ball off the grass, and then laying back, tail wagging, and watching them do the fetching. The same dog, like many I've known, played fetch with himself by trotting up the stairs with the ball in his mouth, dropping it at the top of the stairs, dashing down the stairs to catch it, and then carrying it back up again.

Another story comes from an article in *Time* magazine titled "Can Animals Think?" The article includes a story about the author's experience with a Golden Retriever named Newton, who, like Bear, created his own version of fetch. After his human friend Michael tossed the ball, Newton appeared to search high and low for it, even looking up into the trees. When Michael gave up on Newton's finding the ball and came to fetch it himself, Newton would wait until he was about ten feet away and then make a beeline to the ball and pounce on it. Michael wrote that Newton's expression as he dashed away with his prize looked "suspiciously like a grin."

Of course, often the dog's behavior in stories like these could be explained by simple trial and error, not by the dog doing what is strictly defined as thinking. In some ways, the value in these stories is that you can use them as litmus tests: tell them to other people and you'll get a good idea of how they evaluate the mental capabilities of dogs. Just be ready to hear some strongly held opinions. It's an interesting and useful exercise to ask yourself what your dog would have to do to prove to you that he's thinking. Don't hesitate to be skeptical; it's no disservice to your dog to be a critical thinker, dismissing examples that could be explained by simple trial-and-error learning. One objective way to ask if your example is a good one is to put another species in your dog's place. Your dog may come running every time she hears the can opener, but you could teach any animal to do that, even a grasshopper. Does that mean grasshoppers can think?

That's why the research I've described is so important, because it helps us sort out in a more organized fashion what animals can and can't do. An article from 2004 in the journal *Science* is a good example of how research can help us learn more about the mental experiences of our dogs. This experiment tested the ability of a Border Collie named Rico to link an unfamiliar word with an unfamiliar object. After being taught the names of two hundred different objects by his owners, Rico was asked to go into another room and fetch an object he'd never heard of before. Rico heard the phrase "Fetch the spoon" for the first time, having never been taught the word "spoon" before, and never having been asked to fetch one.[10] When Rico entered the room, he'd find seven familiar objects he knew the names of, and one unfamiliar one. In seven of ten sessions Rico was able to link the unfamiliar word with the unfamiliar object and bring back what was asked. By doing this, he not only made clear that he understood the abstract concept "unfamiliar," he also demonstrated a skill called "fast mapping" by inferring that the unfamiliar word referred to the unfamiliar object. Until this study was conducted, it was believed that only human children could fast map. The authors concluded that the "building blocks" of language acquisition may exist in other species.

The experiment on Rico brings up the second and often strongly voiced argument that dogs can't think because they don't "have language." It is true that the use of language in all its complexity is one of the defining characteristics of our species. It allows us to think in multiple levels of abstraction, to use words and thoughts to consider our actions rather than responding without reflection, and to communicate with one another on a level unimaginable in other species. But what of our dogs, and other animals like them? Is it possible to think, as we understand thinking, without being as adept at language as we are? How does our ability to use language affect our emo-

10. The article doesn't say what new words were used in this experiment. I've used "spoon" merely as an example.

tions, and how might the lack of that ability affect our dogs? We'll address these questions in the next section.

CAN DOGS THINK IF THEY CAN'T TALK?

A philosopher, R. G. Frey, is on record as arguing that animals can't have desires if they have no language. While that statement is illogical and has no basis in biology, it is understandable that we find it difficult to imagine thinking without language. Thinking and language are so closely associated in our minds that a standard psychology text links them together in the same chapter.[11] But does one really have to be able to use human language to form abstractions in the brain, to understand concepts and use them to solve problems? Perhaps the question is, How much is language an expression of what goes on inside the brain, and how much of what happens inside the brain does it actually create? That's the chicken-and-egg question of the ages, and it's keeping a lot of people busy thinking, talking, and writing in pursuit of an answer.

In one famous example of research on cognition and language, researchers attempted to teach African gray parrots to use English words by rewarding the bird with a food treat for making a sound like the one played from a tape recorder. The birds failed miserably, and it was concluded that parrots were unable to learn or use the English language functionally. That is, until the biologist Irene Pepperberg came along and taught a parrot named Alex to learn words in ways more similar to the ways we teach our children. She held up an object that Alex wanted, and asked a human assistant what it was. If the person named it by saying "cork" or "nail," Pepperberg handed her the object. All the while Alex was simply observing. When Alex finally made a noise himself that sounded something like "cork" or "nail," he was handed the object. That was enough to keep his attention, since what parrots want more than anything is to play with objects using their beaks and feet. Several years and hundreds of hours later, the world's most famous bird is able to use words to identify an object's composition (cork, wood), its shape (round, triangular), its color, and its size. Alex can tell you

11. To his credit, the author, David G. Myers, does an excellent job discussing the relationship between thinking and language, and does not argue, as do some, that thinking cannot occur without language.

which yellow, round, wooden object is "bigger" on a tray of other objects that are yellow, round, and made out of wood. He can tell you what category is "different" on a tray of five blue keys and one red one. Most amazingly, without being taught to ask questions himself, Alex asked one of his own. During the process of learning his colors, he asked "What color?" while looking at his image in the mirror. "Gray," he was told, and after that he was able to point out anything gray, no matter its size, shape, or composition.

Another study, this time on chimpanzees, looked at language from an entirely different perspective. It was done by the primatologist Sally Boyson, and its result emphasizes the importance of language on one's ability to think in the abstract. In her study, chimpanzees were first taught to associate written numbers ("1," "2," "3," etc.), with actual quantities. The chimps could look at a basket with four peaches in it and point to the number "4." They could look at a basket of two peaches and then one with three peaches, add them up in their minds, and then point to the number "5."

This finding enabled Boyson to proceed to a second study, in which one chimp got to decide which of two bowls of candy he got, and which bowl was given to a second chimp. Each bowl had a different quantity of M&M's (which chimps like as much as we do). The active chimp's job was to point to the bowl that the *other* chimp would get; the remaining bowl of candy was his to eat. Time and time again, the active chimp would point to the bowl with more candy, and look disheartened when Boyson handed the larger amount of candy to the other ape. The active chimp seemed unable to point to the bowl with fewer M&M's, even after hundreds of opportunities to learn that by pointing to the largest number of candies he'd end up with fewer himself. However, when Boyson substituted numbers in the bowls, to symbolize how much candy each bowl contained, the chimp quickly learned to point to the lower number, thereby getting more candy for himself. In other words, once the chimp was able to add a layer of abstraction between himself and the candy through the use of language-like symbols, he was able to make a smarter choice.

I can't imagine a study that makes a more compelling argument for the importance of language in our ability to think in abstractions, and to use those abstractions to our advantage. The study suggests that our linguistic abilities might often act to temper our emotions, allowing us to pause and reflect before we react. However, studies like this do not support the belief that individuals are unable to think *at all* unless they have language. If thinking is the ability to form and manipulate mental abstractions, then the chimps showed that they could think: they were able to use numbers as abstract symbols of quantity. To look at it from a wholly different perspective, that of our own species, just because a person grew up without the concept of language doesn't mean she can't think. Could Helen Keller have had no thoughts in her mind before she realized that the sign for water referred to the liquid that was splashing over her hands?

I hope we see much more research on this issue in the years to come, especially on our dogs. However, we know enough already to make a reasonable argument that although language enables us to use abstractions in ways unimaginable by other animals, it is not a prerequisite for thinking. The evidence suggests that, as we've defined thought, dogs can indeed think, although their thought processes are undoubtedly much simpler than our own.[12] The scientific evidence that some nonhuman animals can understand abstract concepts keeps getting stronger and stronger. Look at what the dolphins can do at Kewalo Basin Marine Mammal Laboratory: not only have they learned that they'll be rewarded if they create a "new" behavior, one they've never performed before, but they understand a cue called "Tandem create." This cue asks two dolphins to come up with a behavior they've never done before, communicate it to each other, plan how to execute it, and then perform it simultaneously. If that's not thinking, I don't know what is.

TURNING ON THE LIGHT

Another hot debate in science right now is about the elusive phenomenon we call consciousness. Since we are unable to deny that the bodies and brains of other animals behave in ways strikingly similar to ours, the controversy about the mental life of animals has evolved into one

12. I should note here that there are many definitions of thinking, and arguments about what it is and what it isn't could easily fill other books. The definition I've chosen is accepted by many, but not by all.

about whether animals are able to "experience" their emotions. Some people assert that while animals may "have" emotions, they aren't actually conscious of them. If ever there was a claim difficult for a dog lover to swallow, this has got to be it.

I think I can speak for most dog lovers when I say that it's impossible to imagine that our dogs "have" emotions without being conscious of them. Many scientists feel the same way. Look at what the biologist Marc Bekoff says about the mental life of his dogs: "If he [Bekoff's dog] tries to solicit play and I don't play with him, he is surprised—and he looks it. It's just wrong to say dogs don't have thoughts and beliefs about their world just because these might be different from our beliefs." The late Donald Griffin wrote an entire book arguing that *of course,* complicated animals like chimpanzees and dogs are conscious. He says, eloquently, that we need to acknowledge that and get on with learning more about it.

However, others argue that imagining consciousness in animals is foolish and problematic. In 1992, R. Boakes said: "Attributing conscious thought to animals should be strenuously avoided in any serious attempt to understand their behavior, since it is untestable, empty, obstructionist and based on a false dichotomy." *Whew.* Pretty strong stuff. It is true that trying to understand something as slippery as consciousness is a great challenge, but that's not stopped us in other endeavors of science. Physicists aren't daunted by the difficulty of studying wave theory or black holes, much less the origins of the solar system, so why should we be intimidated by the mysteries inside our brains?

It is true that consciousness is such a tricky topic that we haven't begun to understand it. Scientists haven't even agreed upon a definition of consciousness, even in our own species. Consciousness is central to our lives—indeed, it defines life as we know it—but by its very nature it's as difficult to understand as a puff of smoke.

The neurobiologist John Ratey sums up the debate about consciousness as well as anyone: "Considering that we don't know what it is or how it works, the fervor with which it is debated can be embarrassingly presumptuous." I love this man. And I love the practical, feet-on-the-ground definition offered by another neurobiologist, Deric Bownds, who argues with welcome clarity: "Consciousness is a device for focusing awareness through the linking of emotions and feeling to sensing and acting." He goes on to say that it is perfectly reasonable to grant other animals varying levels of consciousness, depending upon the complexity of their brains.

Some fuel for the argument that animals aren't conscious comes from the knowledge that more of our own behavior is driven by our unconscious than we ever might imagine. For example, if you're flashed a frightening picture so quickly that you have no conscious awareness of it, your amygdala still activates and signals your body to go on alert.

Remember the study in which people who read the words "old" and "wrinkled" walked out of the room more slowly than they entered it? A similar study by the psychologist John Bargh serves to emphasize the power of unconscious processes. In this experiment, people were asked to unscramble phrases that included words like "rude" and "intrude," or "considerate" and "polite." The subjects had no idea that the real experiment came later, when they were asked to go to the experimenter's office and ask about their next task. No matter whether the subjects had been working with "rude" words or "polite" ones, they were forced to cool their heels while someone else dominated the experimenter's attention. Bargh was interested in how long the subjects would wait before they interrupted. He figured the difference between the groups might be a matter of milliseconds, if there was any difference at all. Imagine his surprise when the subjects who had read words like "polite" turned out to be exactly that—82 percent of them *never* interrupted, even after ten minutes, while the group who had read "rude" words interrupted after an average of five minutes.

Studies like these remind us that much of who we are, and much of how we behave, is driven by unconscious processes. However, it doesn't follow, if *unconscious* processes are more important than we previously believed in *human* behavior, that *consciousness* is irrelevant in *animal* behavior. We know that consciousness does not appear to be dependent upon language; patients in whose brains the left and right hemispheres can't communicate can have consciousness in either hemisphere, even when the capacity for language is restricted to the left hemisphere of the brain. A researcher at the University of Wisconsin, Giulio Tononi, suspects that consciousness is the result of many parts of the brain communicating with one another simultaneously. He's found that when we're awake, and conscious, the various parts of our brains maintain a continuous dialogue with one another. However, when we're asleep, and are not conscious, these same areas keep to themselves.

Certainly consciousness is a difficult issue, but, thanks to our current progress in neurobiology, it shouldn't be too much longer before we get a better sense of what it is and how much of it we share with other animals. Given what we know so far, it seems reasonable to take the same approach as we did with respect to thinking in abstractions. There's simply no biological argument for the belief that consciousness could occur only in humans. It makes sense that complex mammalian brains, like our dogs', share in the ability to coordinate all the parts of their brains into something similar to what we experience when we're conscious.

THE GREEN-EYED MONSTER IN BROWN-EYED DOGS?

Brenda came to the office because her Cairn Terriers were starting to fight. Neither had been seriously injured yet, but the fights were getting worse, and it looked as if one of the dogs was going to get badly hurt in the near future. Fortunately, the fights were predictable; it's always easier to solve a behavioral problem if you can find what triggers it. Romeo, the young male, was cheerful and fun-loving—as long as he got all the petting, all the attention, and all the treats. He got along swimmingly with the other dog, Juliet, unless Juliet got something he wanted. If Brenda dared to pet Juliet without petting Romeo, he'd leap toward Juliet and begin growling and snapping.

Some people would describe this as an issue related to dominance, that overused concept about social status in dogs. But Brenda's explanation was a different one. When asked what she thought was going on between the two dogs, she said, "It's simple. Romeo's jealous."

Jealousy. Now there's an interesting emotion. Many scientists consider it one of the "higher-level" or more complex emotions, and some believe that it's exclusive to humans. Others don't hesitate to use the term "jealousy" in relation to dogs. In his book *If Dogs Could Talk,* the biologist Vilmos Csányi says anyone with kids or dogs knows exactly what jealousy looks like. The primatologist Frans de Waal is clearly comfort-able talking about jealous chimpanzees in his book *Chimpanzee Poli-tics*. But the range of beliefs about jealousy in nonhuman animals is vast. You can find differences of opinion anywhere you go, in or out-side of science. I've had clients who started sentences with: "I know dogs can't be jealous . . . ," but most dog owners I've talked to don't hes-itate to describe their dogs as being capable of jealousy.[13]

We've a long way to go before we can know how much canine jeal-ousy resembles the human version, but I see no reason why it couldn't be fundamentally similar. Jealousy doesn't strike me as a particularly complicated emotion. I see tension and aggression between dogs on a weekly basis that seem little different from behavior that we wouldn't hesitate to call jealousy in young, preverbal children. It all seems to come down to "You've got it, I don't, and I'm not happy about that." Remember our discussion on the relationship between anger and frus-tration; I can't see why dogs couldn't feel frustrated, and thus either angry or sad, because they're not getting something they want. It's unimaginable to me that they don't have some sense of missing out on something good. Surely your dog knows when you're petting another dog that he's not being petted himself.

"Himself"? "Herself"? Ah, now we're getting down to the heart of another controversy about emotions in animals. Can dogs think in those terms? Do they have a concept of "self" versus "other"? Almost all biologists agree that animals share with us basic emotions like fear, anger, and some form of happiness, but they don't agree on whether animals feel "higher-level" emotions such as jealousy, guilt, or sympa-thy, which depend on a concept of "self" and "other." The biologist Marc Hauser, in an excellent book entitled *Wild Minds,* speculates that animals probably don't experience what are often called the "social emotions" (such as jealousy), because they lack something that all hu-mans have: an awareness of *self.* If you don't have a sense of *self,* com-pared with a sense of *other,* then how could you feel jealousy or, for that matter, sympathy? It might be tempting to dismiss such comments, given how hard it is for most of us dog lovers to imagine our dogs *not* being self-aware (to say nothing of being sympathetic), but although I don't agree with Hauser's conclusion, I do agree that the question is a tricky one. Let's take a look at the issue for a moment.

ME AND YOU, YOU AND ME

Any conversation about self-awareness is complicated by the fact that knowing whether another individual is self-aware is no easy task. You know *you* are, but how do you know anyone else is? For that matter, how could you prove that you are yourself? No matter what you did, someone could argue you were just "acting reflexively," or simply following the rules of learning that apply equally to primates and parakeets. Scientists have lined up on one side or the other of this debate for decades, although the voices of those who believe that at least some animals are self-aware are strengthening.

The controversy heated up a few decades ago, when a scientist named Gordon Gallup anesthetized a variety of primates and put a red dot of paint on their foreheads. When they woke up and looked in the mirror, some of the chimpanzees and orangutans touched their forefingers to the dot on their foreheads. Gallup argued that the chimps' behavior suggested that they understood the image in the mirror was of themselves, and that their response showed they had a rudimentary concept of the self. A more recent study introduced dolphins to underwater mirrors, and then recorded what the dolphins did when the researchers put ink marks on areas of their bodies not visible to the "wearer" without the use of a mirror. Sure enough, the dolphins who found ink on their mirror images in surprising places spent more time investigating themselves in the mirror than did dolphins who had been touched by markers that had no ink.

Gallup and others cited these results to argue that some animals are self-aware, but others used the same data to debunk that suggestion. Chimps and orangutans responded to the red dots in the mirror, but other highly evolved apes, gorillas, did not. More important, what does mirror recognition really have to do with a concept of self? Mirror skills are learned: people in hunter-gatherer societies look behind a mirror to find the body of the image that they see, and have to learn that the image is actually a reflection of their own face. Six-month-old children behave as though the image in the mirror is that of another; not until fifteen to eighteen months of age do they touch their own noses if they see a spot on the nose in the mirror. For these reasons, many credible scientists argue that until we have better evidence of self-awareness, we must stay with "simpler" explanations of an animal's behavior, believing that animals are not self-aware until proven otherwise.

However, many observations do suggest self-awareness in a variety of species: subordinate male chimpanzees involved in "illicit" sexual trysts use their hands to cover their erections from passing dominant individuals; polar bears have been known to cover their black noses in order to stay camouflaged on white snow. Such behaviors suggest a sense of "self" and "other," although I'll admit they are far from definitive evidence of self-awareness.[14]

It's true that we have to be careful about believing that animals are self-aware just because we can't imagine life without self-awareness. However, neither can we imagine what it's like to do what dogs do easily—like use our noses to find a smidgen of cocaine in a warehouse of coffee beans—so our lack of imagination is not reason enough to believe other animals are self-aware. The jury is still out about how animals like our dogs experience "self" versus "other"; but, given the value of any degree of self-awareness in any highly social species, it seems most reasonable to argue that our dogs are self-aware in the absence of evidence that proves they're not.

If you live in a complex social system, as many animals do, what would be "simple" about negotiating every interaction with another individual without some concept of self? How could a wolf, for example, manage the social intricacies of the pack without at least a rudimentary concept of "self" and "other"? How could our dogs not be aware that the *other* dog got a treat and they didn't? The problem with denying self-awareness to animals with complex social relationships is that it doesn't result in a "simpler" explanation of their behavior. Remember, good science always considers the simplest explanation first, and it seems far simpler to imagine dogs as having a conscious sense of self than not.

14. Researchers are currently distinguishing "self-awareness" from a less complex concept, "self-recognition." The distinctions between them are beyond the scope of this book, but if you're interested in the topic, be sure to look up both phrases in your research.

ARE YOU THINKING WHAT I'M THINKING?

Joe wasn't a big man, but he was an ex-Marine, and I had no doubt he was capable of handling just about anything. His wife, Virginia, was as big as Joe was small, and this Mutt and Jeff couple had been visiting my office for years, lighting it up with Virginia's raucous laughter and Joe's sweet smile. They'd first come with a dog so aggressive we wondered if he'd ever be safe in public. Bear was a strikingly beautiful collie, all flashing teeth and nasty growls when I first met him—eyes rounded like pennies, black and hard and threatening, pupils expanded to the borders. After years of dedicated work, Bear had softened into a lover boy; he charmed pet-store employees and veterinary technicians and came wagging and grinning into my office, happy to say hello, looking, always looking, for his ball. Over the years, our visits became as social as therapeutic. Joe and Virginia would stop by on their way to a weekend getaway; Bear would prance in and run to the toy box, drop the ball on my lap, and wait, wait, wait for me to throw it.

One day I heard that Virginia was in the hospital; weeks later she was diagnosed with cancer. She died shockingly quick, her death coming hard and fast, leaving a hole in Joe's life that must have seemed too big to ever be filled. But Joe wasn't alone. Like millions of others, Joe had his dog, and he told me later that he couldn't imagine having made it through without him. Bear licked away his tears and cuddled against him, providing the warmth and comfort that Joe so desperately needed. Joe believes in his heart that somehow Bear knew Virginia was dying, and that Joe needed him then more than ever. Joe felt a sense of sympathy and love from him that was as strong as any he could've gotten from a person.

Surely all of us who live with dogs have had a time in our lives when a special dog came to us and provided comfort. I remember curling up on the floor with my dogs when my ex-husband left me, desperate for the touch of their fur, the sound of their hearts beating. He left in late November, and I remember the winter that followed as if it were one, long, endless night, dark, cold, and devoid of comfort except for the touch of my dogs and the love of my friends. It seemed as though the dogs stayed closer to me than usual. When I cried, as I often did, they came to me with worried eyes and moved around me as if in slow motion. They were especially obedient, the way children are when they realize that something is very wrong, though they might not know what it is.

Millions of us have been comforted by our dogs, there's no doubt about it. Just petting a dog lowers your blood pressure and decreases your heart rate. No one doubts that dogs can influence our emotions just by being there. Even people who don't believe that dogs can have emotions themselves concede that the presence of dogs can alter our own. But what's going on inside the head of a dog when he licks the tears off your face, cuddles against you, and looks deep into your eyes? Beyond a vague sense of anxiety because something is wrong, do our dogs feel true sympathy for us? To many of us, it seems impossible that they don't, but some scientists and philosophers disagree. Sympathy turns out to be an emotion that requires a lot of brainpower, and some argue that dogs don't have what it takes to experience it. Because this is a deeply felt topic to dog lovers, it's worth looking at what sympathy really is, and what kind of brainpower it requires.

Sympathy may not seem like a complicated concept—you feel bad, so I feel bad for you—but it brings up a white-hot controversy in science and philosophy about the minds of animals. Sympathy requires that an individual understand that others have minds just like her own, and that she is able to imagine the world from another's perspective. This ability to put oneself in the place of others is inconveniently known as theory of mind, although it isn't a "theory" as nonscientists use the term. It refers to something that all normal people can do, which is to be aware that other individuals have a mind that works much like their own, and to plan accordingly. When you see a dog with a broken leg, you know that her leg is like your leg, and you can imagine how she felt inside when the bones snapped. When you're in a conversation, you know that the person you're talking to is not just talking to you—he's having an internal mental conversation with himself, just as you are. But does your dog have similar powers of imagination? Does she sense that you have a mind something like her own? Your dog may be aware of how your actions predict other actions ("She got the leash, so we're going on a walk!"), but is she aware that you have an internal mental life, as she does? If not, how could she consciously know that you are suffering?

It's instructive to recognize that before the age of four or five (at the earliest), children cannot imagine the world from another's point of view. Ask a two-year-old to "show Daddy your picture," and he'll hold it up facing himself, but away from Daddy. Three-year-olds play hide-and-seek by covering their own eyes, not understanding that although *they* can't see, *you* still can. Compare that with a Standard Poodle named Luath, who plays "hide-and-seek" with his owner by running to the couch and burying his head under the pillows.

Children don't become aware until at least four years of age that others have minds just like their own. I clearly remember the moment this realization came to me; it's one of my earliest memories. I was riding in a car, looking out the window at people on the sidewalk, and I remember being dumbstruck by the insight that they had mental lives similar to my own. I was stunned at this discovery: each person I saw had his or her own version of the rich experiences inside my head. That night I lay on the floor and wondered about the mind of our family's dog, Fudge. Could she be thinking the same things that I was?

What's important in this story is that, like all children, I went for years with no awareness that others had minds like my own. The fact that young children can live and learn for so long without this awareness adds fuel to the fire that one doesn't have to have theory of mind in order to function. It also makes it especially difficult to determine what animals, like our dogs, understand about the minds of others, and the questions that raises are causing no small amount of academic fur to fly.

A flurry of clever experiments has tried to address this question by asking whether an animal appears to be able to put itself in another's place, showing some comprehension that another individual has thoughts, desires, and intentions like his own. In one study, a chimpanzee named Sarah was shown videotapes of a human actor in different problematic circumstances—shivering inside a cage; jumping to reach a banana dangling overhead—and was asked to pick a photograph that "fit" the situation. Sarah clearly understood something about what the actor was experiencing: she chose a picture of a blanket for the shivering man, and a box for him to step up onto to reach the banana. However, three-and-a-half-year-old children, too young to have theory of mind, did not. They chose pictures of things that physically related to the video they saw: a yellow flower that matched the color of the banana, for example.

In other studies, even chimpanzees have not done so well. Chimps begged at equally high rates in front of people who could and couldn't see them, which they shouldn't have done if they could imagine the world from the perspective of the people. However, studies like this are always tricky, because we're only indirectly getting evidence of what's going on in their minds—perhaps the chimps were simply unable to contain themselves, and couldn't resist begging from anyone holding tasty snacks, just as we press the elevator button multiple times when we're in a hurry, even though we know it won't help.

So far, the results of such experiments are inconsistent, so we don't know whether our dogs have theory of mind. It's a hot topic right now, so we'll undoubtedly learn a lot more in the years to come. At present, the mixed results of the studies act as a litmus test on which way a person tends to lean—is it better to mistakenly give animals credit for more brain power than they deserve, or less? In general, most dog lovers tend to vote for the former, and most scientists the latter, but we are all still just guessing. I wonder if, like consciousness, theory of mind is a capacity that can exist in a continuum, especially in highly social animals like dogs. Look at all the times that our dogs come to comfort us—would they do that if they didn't understand we were suffering in *some* way? It is undoubtedly true that some of the kisses our dogs give us when we're sad are evoked by "emotional contagion," the emotions of one individual spilling over onto the emotions of others. Emotional contagion doesn't require that either animal understand what the other is experiencing; it happens because emotions are catching, as we've talked about in earlier chapters. It offers one explanation for those sloppy kisses that our dogs tend to give in response to our tears or sad faces, but I don't think it adequately accounts for all of their actions.

Look at Marley, the out-of-control Labrador in John Grogan's *Marley and Me,* who flunked out of obedience school and systematically chewed John and Jenny's house into bite-size pieces. And yet, when the young couple returned from learning they'd had a miscarriage, Marley greeted them with none of his usual hysteria. He stood still, resting his head against Jenny's belly, until she broke down and sobbed while he stood quietly beside her. This is the dog who was oblivious to their emotions in other circumstances, no matter how strongly held or expressed. Their anger, frustration, and exhaustion seemed to bounce off him like rocks skipping across the water, with no effect on his frenetic exuberance. If emotional contagion accounted fully for his empathy, then why wasn't he equally influenced by their other emotions?

There's a recent discovery in neurobiology that might help us understand empathy in our dogs. We've learned that special brain cells called "mirror neurons" play a key role in our species' tendency to imitate others and in our ability to be empathetic. These cells are not active only when we move one way or another, but the *same* cells fire up when we watch someone else move the same way. These cells aren't restricted to humans; they were first discovered by Italian researchers Vittorio Gallese and Leonardo Fogassi, during research on how the brain controls movement in monkeys. They recorded brain cell activity as the monkeys reached for objects, and to the researchers' surprise, found that the monkeys' brain cells activated when one of the researchers reached for a raisin, just as the brain cells had when the monkeys themselves reached for the same object. Amazing.

We've since learned that humans have a vast number of these "mirror neurons," not surprising given our "monkey see, monkey do" tendency to imitate the actions of others. The other primates studied have a significantly smaller number of them, but they have them nonetheless. In humans these cells appear to play an important role in understanding the intentions of others and in feeling empathy toward them. We don't know anything yet about mirror neurons in dogs, but studies on them will no doubt provide us with a lot more information in the future.

There's another behavior that sheds light on the mental processes of other animals, and that's the phenomenon of deception. We don't tend to think of deceit as a good thing, but examples of it in nonhuman animals are interesting and instructive. It's relevant here because what's called "tactical deception" could occur only if an individual has some understanding of the thought processes of another.

There are numerous reports of animals behaving as if to deceive other animals: in one well-known example, a beleaguered Arctic fox barked out a bogus alarm call after her young had repeatedly snatched up all the food for themselves. The alarm bark sent her young scurrying for the den, which allowed the fox to get a good meal for herself for the first time in weeks. Examples of tactical deception are most common, not surprisingly, in our closest relative, the chimpanzee. Chimps not only change their behavior to keep illicit affairs quiet, they pretend to search for food in places that they know have no food. This allows them to fool dominant chimps into going away from the sites that *do* have hidden food, so the subordinate chimps can have it all to themselves.

Although deception is probably not as common in dogs, there are credible stories of dogs running to the door and barking as if visitors had arrived, causing the other dogs in the house to stop what they were doing and join in the barking. While the others continue to bark at the visitor that isn't there, the first dog quietly slips back into the living room and takes over the bone that his higher-status compatriot previously had all to himself. My own Pip has groveled and whined her way up to Tulip while Tulip chewed on a tasty bone, and licked Tulip's face so vigorously that Tulip shook her head and walked away, giving Pip exactly what she wanted: free access to the best bone in the house. These examples, although not conclusive, underscore the belief that theory of mind isn't necessarily an ability that one either has or doesn't have, but, like other mental processes, could exist in a continuum.

Earlier, I mentioned the time Luke leaped over a high wooden stall and held off a rampaging ewe until I could get out to safety. How could he have known I was in danger if he hadn't been able to put himself in my place, understanding in some way that what I was experiencing was similar to what he had experienced? I'd never been imperiled by my sheep before, but he had. Like all working sheepdogs, Luke had been trapped in tight quarters, and been in danger from flying horns and battering heads. In order to understand that I was in danger, he had to be able to put himself in my place, and imagine the world from my perspective.

To be fair, it's possible that Luke didn't leap into the pen to rescue me. Perhaps he was merely trying to get in on the action—heaven knows Luke loved drama, and he loved telling the sheep what to do. Of course, I want it to be true that Luke was consciously trying to save me. It makes me feel safe and full of the warmth that comes with feeling loved and protected. The fact that the more complicated explanation makes me feel good is a reason to be skeptical, but it's not reason enough to dismiss the possibility that Luke understood I was in danger. As I said earlier, just because an explanation makes us feel good doesn't mean it's wrong.

IN SUMMARY:
A GLASS HALF EMPTY, A GLASS HALF FULL

It's true that we'll never know exactly what goes on in the minds of our dogs, whether they're rescuing us or licking the tears from our faces. It's also true that we have much to learn about their thought processes, and how they compare with ours. However, we already know a lot. We know that we share with dogs much of the biology that creates our own emotions, and we know that we express emotions in similar ways. We know that dogs have a portion of all the components we believe make up emotions—from internal and external physical changes, to some form of the mental abstractions that go along with them.

Here's what else we know: it's time to stop apologizing for the belief that animals, like our dogs, have emotions. *Of course,* our dogs can experience emotions like fear, anger, happiness, and jealousy. And yes, as far as we can tell, their experience of those emotions is comparable in many ways to ours. People who argue otherwise might as well argue that the earth is flat.

Historically, there's been a notable lack of logic in much of what has been said about animals and emotions. Perhaps that is because we are so often uncomfortable with our own—indeed, much of the time, our emotions seem to embarrass us. Look at what Jonas Salk said when confronted with evidence that early variations of his polio vaccine actually caused polio in some victims: "*I know it's purely emotional,* but I cannot escape a terrible feeling of identification with these people who got polio" (my italics). The subtext seems to be that because Salk's feelings were "purely emotional," they must be of less value than if they'd been "purely rational." Yet, what would you think of a man who didn't care that his efforts ended up killing some children, rather than saving them? Our emotional responses are often as important as our rational ones, but in one of the great ironies of all time, it is often hard for us to give them equal credit.

During Hurricane Katrina, I heard CNN news anchor Aaron Brown defend a female reporter whose voice had trembled with emotion as she floated past desperate, dying people stranded on rooftops. Here was a reporter in the middle of one of our country's most dramatic and terrible catastrophes, helplessly passing by scenes of profound suffering. Yet even so, Brown knew she would be criticized for the emotion in her voice. Reporters are supposed to be objective and dispassionate, and there she was, speaking on the edge of tears, letting her feelings creep through on national television. Personally, I thought they were both marvelous. If she hadn't expressed some feeling, I would've thought she was mentally unsound, and I appreciated Brown's awareness that the reporter might be criticized by some for being "so emotional."

It's true that at times it's important to keep your emotions to yourself. Fighters and poker players are famous for being able to control the expressions on their faces, for obvious reasons. Perhaps that's why dogs descended from fighting lines are also often difficult to read—fighters of any species aren't negotiating or communicating, they're trying to disguise their own emotions while looking for an opening to attack. Perhaps that's one reason we equate emotions with weakness. However, emotions themselves aren't indications of weakness, any more than rational thought is superior and separate from them.

Perhaps the argument we've been having about animals and emotions isn't really about animals. Perhaps it's about us, about our discomfort with how our emotions link us to other animals. In something like a nouveau riche attempt to confirm our place in the world, we've linked our sense of worth to the distinctions between ourselves and other animals. By trying to separate rational thought from our emotions, we've put the "thinking" part of our brains on a pedestal and have treated our emotions like poor second cousins. What an irony, then, that so many have denied animals the ability to experience emotions, when simultaneously we've described emotions as primitive and animalistic.

Sometimes it seems that our irrationality about emotions, animals, and our relationship to them knows no bounds. In a strange twist of logic, we call kindness "humane," when we can be the cruelest of species. We accuse violent people of acting "like animals." In an almost desperate attempt to keep ourselves separate, we've done all we can to remind ourselves that animals aren't human, while trying to forget that we humans are still animals.

We may be special, and we may represent the most remarkable of all creatures, but, whether we like it or not, we are still animals. That the mental experiences of dogs aren't as complex as ours is no reason to dismiss those experiences altogether. It's true that when there are great differences between things it is tempting to think of them as differences in *kind* rather than differences of *degree*. I wonder whether dogs believe that we are completely unable to smell, given how impoverished our ability is compared to theirs. We *can* use our noses, but it might not seem like it to dogs. Accordingly, just because dogs don't think the way we do, it doesn't follow that they can't think at all.

I say this with some trepidation, because there is danger in overestimating the minds of dogs as well as underestimating them. Almost every day, trainers and behaviorists like me see the damage caused by people who imagine dogs as four-footed humans. These well-intentioned dog lovers behave as though their dogs have moral codes like adult humans ("How could he betray me like that?"); they feel angry when their dog won't stroll quietly beside them on a walk. But left to their own devices, dogs don't walk side by side, shoulder to shoulder; we have to teach them how to do this like it's a circus trick. Additionally, dogs don't lie around during the day thinking up ways to punish you because you left the house and went to work. They don't understand why they shouldn't eat poop, when you pick it up and act like it's special ("No! Stay away from that! It's mine!"), and they don't get angry about slights that only our own convoluted brains can imagine.

Our dogs need us to understand that they are dogs, and that they don't come speaking English. They're not born reading our minds or understanding what we want just because we want it. Without question, their thought processes are profoundly different from ours. We can't, on the one hand, say that our dogs are special because, unlike us, they always live in the present, and then turn around and expect them to think like us at other times. We have to find a balance here, one that acknowledges that dogs are different from us and at the same time celebrate what we share with them.

What we share, without question, is a rich emotional life. Emotions like fear and happiness and love simmer within us, sometimes bubbling to the surface, always linking us together. The glass of our shared experience may be half empty, but that means it's half full. How lucky we are that it's a big glass, and that, most of the time, the liquid within it is sweet and good.

AFTERWORD

As I write this, it's been a year since Luke died, almost to the day. It's snowing now, the white flakes sifting onto Luke's memorial stone in the high pasture. Lassie is lying on the sheepskin at my feet. She is better now, as am I. A few months after Luke's death, Lassie began to beg me to let her work sheep again, so I opened the gate to the pen and asked her to drive the sheep to the far corner. I helped her at first, standing behind her to back her up as she faced off the flock's toughest sheep, the sheep only Luke would've taken on before. She gathered her courage step by step, leaning forward into the job, committed to holding her ground, taking over from her father. She works like a dream now, steady and brave each night as she holds the sheep off the feeders so I don't get trampled. She sparkles with joy every evening when she picks up her toys, flings them through the air, teases me to grab hold and play tug-of-war with her.

I still miss Luke; I miss him a lot. A part of me died with him, as always happens when someone we love dies. But a part of Luke will always live on in me, and my heart doesn't hurt the way it did before. There are days when I still tear up over Luke, occasional days in which I give in to a good cry. But those days are less frequent, and it feels in my heart as if Luke and I are moving on.

I live on the farm with three dogs now, Lassie and Pip and Tulip, and I love each of them deeply. My love for each dog is different—Tulip is my clown, my stand-up comedian, whom I can count on to cheer me up on the darkest day with her puppylike gamboling and radiant eyes. She's dozing in the sun now, sprawled on the couch after staying up last night to warn the coyotes away. Pip, my sweet and gentle Pippy Tay, is old now, almost deaf and often wobbly. She follows me everywhere, refusing to be left alone even for a minute. She's lying beside me now, just a few feet away. I feel a desire that is so strong to ease her remaining days that it makes my heart expand just writing about it.

And Lassie? Oh, Lassie. I named her after the famous Lassie, the imaginary dog everyone wants but rarely gets, who seems to live and breathe just to make you happy. Lassie is creamery butter, sweet and willing and more devoted than any human deserves. Like her father, Lassie adores me, pure and simple. If Jim and I move in different directions on the farm, Lassie won't follow him. She stays with me. If a veterinary technician takes her by the leash and pulls her away for medical tests, she's too polite to protest, but her head will turn to me, her eyes pleading. As I look at her face, I think of what Alex the talking parrot said to his friend Irene when she had to leave him at a veterinary clinic: "Come here. I love you. I'm sorry. Wanna go back." When I leave Lassie, I say good-bye quickly and cheerfully, and then walk to the car, put my head down on the steering wheel, and breathe a few gulping breaths before I can drive away.

I am not alone in this love for my dogs; I am not neurotic, and I am not crazy. Millions of healthy people love their dogs so profoundly they are willing to risk their lives to save them. I don't want to romanticize our relationships with dogs—having worked with canine aggression for seventeen years, I know the dark side of human-dog interactions as well as anyone. It's not all pretty; intense, emotional relationships rarely are. We can't pretend that fear and anger, felt and expressed by members of both species, don't cause terrible and sometimes long-lasting harm to both people and dogs. Yet it's the emotions of love and happiness that bind us: a shared happiness that catches us up in giddy, joyful waves, floats us through life together, grinning and amazed at the miracle of what we share.

Last night Lassie and I played her favorite game together. Again and again, I tossed her favorite toy across the rug. Each time she leaped after it, then came back to me with her face glowing, her eyes soft and luminous. Her neat little body seemed unable to contain her joy and her love of play. At some point in the middle of our game, I realized I was beaming, a huge smile plastered across my face. For that moment, I was truly and completely happy.

In some ways, it's really that simple, isn't it? At their best, that is what dogs do: they make us happy. At our best, we make them happy, too. That can only be true because we share so very much with them, and the foundation of what we share is our emotions. Dogs are emotions—living, breathing embodiments of fear and anger and joy, emotions we can read on their faces as clearly as any language.

This emotional connection between us isn't trivial. We humans may be brilliant and we may be special, but we are still connected to the rest of life. No one reminds us of that better than our dogs. Perhaps the human condition will always include attempts to remind ourselves that we are separate from the rest of the natural world. We are different from other animals; it's undeniably true. But while acknowledging that, we must acknowledge another truth, the truth that we are also the same. That is what dogs and their emotions give us—a connection. A connection to life on earth, to all that binds us and cradles us, lest we begin to feel too alone. Dogs are our bridge—our connection to who we really are, and most tellingly, who we want to be. When we call them home to us, it's as if we are calling for home itself. And that'll do, dogs. That'll do.

APPENDIX

Teaching your dog "Stay"
as an exercise in emotional control

With any dog, the key to a good stay is to start by asking for "micro-stays," in which you expect your dog to remain in place for the briefest of moments. Start by calling your dog to you and asking her to sit or lie down. Say, "Stay," in a quiet, low voice and hold your left hand out facing forward, like a traffic cop stopping cars at an intersection. As soon as she's settled, even for an instant, release her with a clear verbal signal, such as "Okay" or "Free," praise her quietly, and give her a tiny, tasty treat with your right hand. Remember that the exercise is about emotional control, so don't praise your dog so enthusiastically that she gets too excited.

If you think about it, she hasn't done much, because if you were smart you released her before she was going to get up anyway. She has learned something, though—she's learned that there's a fun game afoot, and that the noise coming out of your mouth and the movement of your hand could be very interesting, indeed. After you've repeated this successfully two or three times, ask her to stay for one to two seconds. Now you're going to give her a treat *while* she's staying, because that's the behavior you want to reinforce. Ask for the stay with your voice (low and quiet) and with the palm of your left hand facing toward her. Rock back one *small* step to give her a little room (looming over a dog can make her nervous). Then, keeping your left hand up to block any forward motion on her part, slide your body forward and with an underhanded motion, give her a treat with your right hand. Be sure to move the treat all the way to her mouth, rather than forcing her to get up to get it. For some reason, most novice trainers stop short, and I routinely have to explain the importance of moving one's hand *all the way* to the dog's mouth. It's one of the most common mistakes that people make, so watch out for it.

Some dogs will try to get up once they get the treat, especially if they've been taught that the treat is the end of the exercise. To be most useful, "Stay" should mean "Don't get up until I say so," so if your dog starts to get up after getting a treat, you should respond by rocking your body forward, both hands extended with palms forward in the universal "Stop" signal, until she settles.[1] Use your powers of observation to watch for the slightest backward lean on her part, indicating she is responding to your signal. The instant she does so, immediately rock your own body backward and drop your hands to your side to take off the pressure. Wait a moment for her to settle, and then release her before she gets up again herself. This time, say "Okay" in a bored, bland voice and turn and walk away.

After she gets up, don't pet her, fuss over her, or give her another treat. This is hard for people to do—they either want to pat their dog on the head (which most dogs hate) or praise her to the skies. But you're trying to teach your dog that the fun part is staying still, not getting up when released, so give her treats while she's staying still, not when she gets up. It doesn't take long for dogs to catch on, and if there are no distractions you can end up with a dog who doesn't get up even after you release her. That's fine; your release should mean "Do what you want," not "Get up this instant." I love it when dogs stay in place, because that's evidence they've learned that staying in place is a great thing to do. After all, that's the whole idea, right?—teaching your dog that it feels good to control her impulses and stay still even when she didn't want to at first. Once you get this habit established, it can have long-lasting effects in all kinds of situations, by helping your dog to learn to control her emotions when you want her to.

There will be times during practice sessions when your dog gets up and goes past you before you can respond. Just lure her back to where

---

1. In *The Other End of the Leash*, I talked in much more depth about using what I call body blocks as a way of influencing your dog's behavior.

she was with the treat, like someone luring a donkey with a carrot. Avoid repeating the word "Stay"—that just starts everything all over again, and doesn't teach the dog what "Stay" really means. Not repeating the cue is also hard for people to do, so pay special attention to it when you're practicing. See if you can get a friend or family member to watch you. We all get better faster if we have someone watch us and act as a coach. Once the dog is lured back to the original spot, ask the dog to sit or lie down by pantomiming a visual signal or tapping the floor in front of her. It's also important to get the dog back to the original spot in which she was told to stay. I think dogs are conscious of their location in space at all times, and if a dog learns that "Stay" means "Stay still for a moment, then get up and sneak in a couple of steps before your owner can stop you," you're going to be in trouble down the road. Personally, I love dogs who test the definition of "Stay" by crawling forward with their bellies still firmly pressed against the floor. "I'm still lying down!" they seem to say as they and their Cheshire cat grins creep forward. I always grin back while I gently move into their space and use body blocks to move them back to their original spot.

This part of stay is easy and fun for most of us, unless we have one of those rocket-propelled dogs who can't stay still even for a second. In that case, say, "Stay," then release instantly with an "Okay" in the same breath, and immediately leave the room to search out a professional dog trainer. You wouldn't think twice about asking a coach to work with your child if he or she wanted to learn a sport, so don't expect yourself to be able to train an "advanced model" dog without help!

NEXT STEPS

Lucky for us, it turns out to be trivial to teach most dogs to stay for a few seconds when you've got treats in your pocket and there's nothing else going on. You can get that accomplished in a session or two with most dogs. This, of course, is how you should start, because you want to set your dog up to win so that you can reinforce her for the right response. But most of the effort of teaching a stay involves asking a dog to remain in place for gradually increasing lengths of time, or to stay while she's distracted by something else. Staying for thirty seconds when the two of you are alone in the kitchen is one thing; staying for five seconds while two other dogs romp together in the next room is another. I wouldn't expect the best of dogs to be able to manage that much emotional control until they'd had months, or even years, of training. A stay with no distractions is a first-grade exercise, while staying in the middle of chaos is more like graduate school. Most of us tend to get dogs started in the equivalent of first or second grade, and then immediately expect Ph.D. work out of them, having skipped junior high, high school, and college.

Avoid that mistake by being thoughtful about what level of distraction your dog has mastered. Help her by asking her to stay during distractions that are gradually more and more difficult, always making her glad she stayed when asked. While you're training, be aware that there are three different things that can make staying when asked difficult. Distinguish between the *duration* of the stay (how long she stays), the level of *distraction* (what's going on around her to cause her to want to get up) and the *distance* between you (how far away you are from her). Spend the majority of your training time on distractions; that's the part that is hardest for most dogs. Come to think of it, wouldn't that be the hardest part for you, too? Most people expect dogs to stay in situations that their children couldn't handle, so don't hesitate to be constructively anthropomorphic and put yourself in your dog's place when you ask for a stay. It's worth the time and energy to write down ten situations your dog might encounter and rank their difficulty level from 1 to 5. Maintaining a five-minute stay in the family room during a quiet evening might be a "2," while staying for two seconds when company comes might be a "5." Be sure that you don't ask for a "5" if you haven't yet worked through "4."

Your dog will learn fastest if you only push the envelope on one aspect of difficulty at a time. In other words, if you're asking for a stay when there are a lot of distractions around, keep the duration short. Work on longer durations when there are few or no distractions around. Decide for yourself how important distance is—I don't need my dogs to stay when I'm far away, so I rarely practice it, but it's important in obedience competitions.

Always be aware of your dog's current level of ability and, like any good coach, push her just a little bit beyond it in some sessions, let her relax a bit in others. Give her lots of reasons to try her hardest, and don't take minor setbacks too seriously. They happen to all of us. (Can soccer players always make the perfect shot, even after years of practice?) Eventually, work your way up to a dog who can do a half-hour down/stay in the living room when things are quiet around the house. Even then, continue occasional brief down/stays scattered throughout the day as a way of helping your dog calm herself *before* she starts to spiral up in excitement when visitors come or she's ready to go on a walk. This can be especially useful during play sessions with other dogs, in which emotional arousal can turn into nasty playground fights. If you have more than one dog, or a household with one dog and young children, a well-placed down/stay can do wonders to calm everything down. (My next book will be about teaching down/stays to children. It will be very, very long.)

REFERENCES

CHAPTER 1: EMOTIONS

There is a rich and fascinating body of books and articles about emotions in both people and animals. Here are some of the scientists whose works I have relied upon: the biologist Marc Bekoff (see for example, *The Smile of a Dolphin,* a marvelous collection of stories from field researchers about animals and emotions, and *Minding Animals: Awareness, Emotions, and Heart*); the neurobiologist Antonio Damasio (see *Looking for Spinoza: Joy, Sorrow, and the Feeling Brain*); Frans de Waal (see, for example, *The Ape and the Sushi Master: Cultural Reflections of a Primatologist*), Temple Grandin (*Animals in Translation: Using the Mysteries of Autism to Decode Animal Behavior* for a riveting comparison of the minds of typical humans, autistic people, and animals), and the books of the late Donald Griffin (see *Animal Thinking* and *Animal Minds*). Griffin's books are particularly good sources for some of the more radical objections to inquiries into the minds of animals. Equally valuable is Jaak Panksepp's amazing book *Affective Neuroscience.* It will be a bit technical for some readers, but if you are seriously interested in the biology of emotion, it is a must-read. Diane Ackerman's literary inquiry into the mind is also fascinating (*An Alchemy of Mind: The Marvel and Mystery of the Brain*). I am grateful to all those listed above (and to many others) for their thought-provoking inquiries into the emotional lives of people and animals.

There is also a legion of recent books that specifically relate to the mind and emotions of our dogs, and I highly recommend the ones below. I don't necessarily agree with everything that's in them, but then I don't agree with some of what

I've written in the past either, so don't let that stop you. Jeffrey Moussaieff Masson's book *Dogs Never Lie About Love* makes the case that *of course* dogs have emotions, and that it is our shared emotional life that binds us together. Three more recent books, *How Dogs Think,* by Stanley Coren; *If Dogs Could Talk,* by Vilmos Csányi; and *The Truth About Dogs,* by Stephen Budiansky, provide excellent reading about the mind of a dog. Elizabeth Marshall Thomas's beautifully written *The Hidden Life of Dogs* did as much to motivate others to write about dogs as Jane Goodall's work motivated primatologists to study their subjects in the wild.

If you're interested in reading a riveting historical account of early behaviorists like Watson and Skinner, and the controversial researcher Harry Harlow, don't miss Deborah Blum's book *Love at Goon Park: Harry Harlow and the Science of Affection.* A book about the horse named Clever Hans is *Clever Hans: The Horse of Mr. von Osten,* written in 1911 by Robert Rosenthal and published by Henry Holt & Co. A later edition was published in 1965, by Holt, Rinehart & Winston.

Ackerman, Diane. 2004. *An Alchemy of Mind: The Marvel and Mystery of the Brain.* New York: Scribner.

———, ed. 2000. *The Smile of a Dolphin: Remarkable Accounts of Animal Emotions.* New York: Discovery Books.

Bekoff, Marc. 2003. *Minding Animals: Awareness, Emotions, and Heart.* New York: Oxford University Press.

Blum, Deborah. 2002. *Love at Goon Park: Harry Harlow and the Science of Affection.* Cambridge, Mass.: Perseus.

Boakes, R. 1992. "Subjective experience." Review of *Animal Minds. Times Higher Education Supplement,* November 22, p. 22.

Carruthers, P. 1989. "Brute experience." *Journal of Philosophy* 89, 258–69.

Coren, Stanley. 2004. *How Dogs Think: Understanding the Canine Mind.* New York: Free Press.

Csányi, Vilmos. 2000. *If Dogs Could Talk: Exploring the Canine Mind.* New York: North Point Press.

Damasio, Antonio. 2003. *Looking for Spinoza: Joy, Sorrow, and the Feeling Brain.* Orlando: Harcourt Books.

Darwin, Charles. 1998. *The Expression of the Emotions in Animals and Man.* Paul Ekman, ed. Oxford: Oxford University Press.

De Waal, Frans. 2001. *The Ape and the Sushi Master: Cultural Reflections of a Primatologist.* New York: Basic Books.

Griffin, Donald R. 1992. *Animal Minds: Beyond Cognition to Consciousness.* Chicago: University of Chicago Press.

Kilcommons, Brian. 1992. *Good Owners, Great Dogs.* New York: Warner Press.

LeDoux, Joseph. 1996. *The Emotional Brain: The Mysterious Underpinnings of Emotional Life.* New York: Simon & Schuster.

Mack, Arien. 1995. "Editor's Introduction." In *Humans and Other Animals.* Arien Mack, ed. Columbus: Ohio State University Press.

Masson, Jeffrey Moussaieff. 1997. *Dogs Never Lie About Love.* New York: Three Rivers Press.

McConnell, Patricia B. 2002. *The Other End of the Leash: Why We Do What We Do Around Dogs.* New York: Ballantine.

Myers, David G. 2004. *Psychology.* New York: Worth.

Oshinsky, David M. *Polio: An American Story.* New York: Oxford University Press.

Panksepp, Jaak. 1998. *Affective Neuroscience: The Foundations of Human and Animal Emotions.* New York: Oxford University Press.

Ratey, John J. 2001. *A User's Guide to the Brain: Perception, Attention, and the Four Theaters of the Brain.* New York: Vintage Books.

Vauclair, J. 1996. *Animal Cognition: An Introduction to Modern Comparative Psychology.* Cambridge, Mass.: Harvard University Press.

CHAPTER 2: EMOTIONAL EXPRESSIONS

For accounts by field biologists about the expression of emotion in animals, see books, listed alphabetically by author: Marc Bekoff (*The Smile of a Dolphin;* Marc has written about emotions in all animals, but he has a soft spot for dogs), Gordon Burghard (*The Genesis of Animal Play*), Frans de Waal (*Chimpanzee Politics, Reconciliation Among the Apes, The Ape and the Sushi Master, Our Inner Ape*), Roger Fouts (*Next of Kin*), Jane Goodall (*In the Shadow of Man*), Thomas McNamee (*The Return of the Wolf to Yellowstone*), David Mech (*The Wolf: The Ecology and Behavior of an Endangered Species*), Cynthia Moss (*Elephant Memories*), Shirley Strum (*Almost Human*), Dorothy Cheney and Robert M. Seyfarth (*How Monkeys See the World*), Sue Savage-Rumbaugh (*Kanzi: The Ape at the Brink of the Human Mind*), and Bill Weber and Amy Vedder (*In the Kingdom of Gorillas*). Barbara Smuts's description of the nasty baboon mentioned in Chapter 2 is in *The Smile of a Dolphin,* a great collection of stories by scientists about emotional expressions in animals.

I used two primary sources on facial expressions in humans. One was the extensive work of Paul Ekman, who for decades has studied facial expressions around the world (see below for a partial list of his books and articles). Several of his photographs are included in the photo section. If you'd like to improve your ability to read facial expressions, get his DVD "Micro and Subtle Expressions." You can order it from his website, www.paulekman.com, and I guarantee it will entertain (and educate) you. I also relied upon David G. Myers's introductory psychology text, *Psychology.* Don't let the word "text" put you off—it's full of fascinating information and very readable. John Gottman is the researcher who did the work on expressions as predictors of marital stability—you can learn more by going to www.gottman.com or finding the article listed below authored by him and Sybil Carrère. I first learned about his work in the book *Blink,* which I talk about more in Chapter 3. The information about our reactions to infantile faces came from an article by Berry and McArthur, listed below.

Animals in Translation, by Temple Grandin, is an important and fascinating book about the inner lives of animals, and a must-read for animal lovers. See John Alcock's highly readable text *Animal Behavior* for an excellent summary of visual communication in a variety of animals. For the expressions of dogs and their relatives, some good sources are: *Dog Language,* by Roger Abrantes; *Canine Body Language: A Photographic Guide,* by Brenda Aloff; Stanley Coren's book *How to Speak Dog; Successful Dog Adoption,* by Sue Sternberg; *On Talking Terms with Dogs: Calming Signals,* by Turid Rugaas; Michael Fox's *Behaviour of Wolves, Dogs, and Related Canines;* and Erik Zimen's "A Wolf Pack Sociogram," in *Wolves of the World.* Your best bet is to watch videos and DVDs of dogs, because photographs can never do more than convey a split second, while expressions are fluid and interactive. A great set of canine expressions can be found in the video *Canine Behavior Program: Body Postures and Evaluating Behavioral Health,* from Suzanne Hetts and Daniel Estep. Also see Dr. Emily Weiss's *The SAFER Test* video, and Sarah Kalnajs's *Dog Communication Skills.* I have a video on reading visual signals in dogs (the one in which a dog reacts to someone's sunglasses); it's called *Reading Between the Lines.* Two great sources for all these books and videos are Tawzer Dog Videos, at www.tawzerdogvideos.com, and Dogwise, at www.dogwise.com. Both sites list enough resources to keep you busy for years.

Abrantes, Roger. 1997. *Dog Language: An Encyclopedia of Canine Behaviour.* Naperville, Ill.: Wakan Tanka Publishers.

Alcock, John. 2001. *Animal Behavior.* 7th ed. New York: Sinauer Assoc.

Aloff, Brenda. 2005. *Canine Body Language: A Photographic Guide.* Wenatchee, WA: Dogwise.

Berry, Diane S., and Leslie Z. McArthur. 1986. "Perceiving Character in Faces: The Impact of Age-Related Craniofacial Changes on Social Perception." *Psychological Bulletin* 100, no. 1.

Burghardt, Gordon M. 2005. *The Genesis of Animal Play: Testing the Limits.* Cambridge, Mass.: MIT Press.

Carrère, Sybil, and John Gottman. 1999. "Predicting Divorce Among Newlyweds from the First Three Minutes of a Marital Conflict Discussion." *Family Process* 38, no. 3, 293–301.

Cheney, Dorothy L., and Robert M. Seyfarth. 1990. *How Monkeys See the World.* Chicago: University of Chicago Press.

Coren, Stanley. 2000. *How to Speak Dog: Mastering the Art of Dog-Human Communication.* New York: The Free Press.

Darwin, Charles. 1998. *The Expression of the Emotions in Animals and Man.* Paul Ekman, ed. Oxford: Oxford University Press.

De Waal, Frans. 1989. *Peacemaking Among Primates.* Cambridge, Mass.: Harvard University Press.

———. 1996. *Good Natured: The Origins of Right and Wrong in Humans and Other Animals.* Cambridge, Mass.: Harvard University Press.

Dutcher, Jim, and Jamie Dutcher. 2002. *Wolves at Our Door: The Extraordinary Story of the Couple Who Lived with Wolves.* New York: Pocket Books.

Ekman, Paul. 1973. "Cross-cultural Studies of Facial Expression." In *Darwin and Facial Expression: A Century of Research in Review.* Paul Ekman, ed. New York: Academic Press.

———. 1987. "Universals and Cultural Differences in the Judgment of Facial Expressions of Emotion." *Journal of Personality and Social Psychology* 53, no. 4, pp. 712–17.

———. 2004. *Emotions Revealed: Recognizing Faces and Feelings to Improve Communication and Emotional Life.* New York: Owl Books.

Fox, Michael W. 1978. *The Dog: Its Domestication and Behavior.* New York: Garland STMP Press.

———. 1984. *Behaviour of Wolves, Dogs, and Related Canines.* Melbourne, Fla.: Krieger.

Gladwell, Malcolm. 2005. *Blink: The Power of Thinking Without Thinking.* New York: Little, Brown.

Grandin, Temple. 2000. "My Mind Is a Web Browser: How People with Autism Think." *Cerebrum* (Winter), pp. 13–22.

———. 2005. *Animals in Translation: Using the Mysteries of Autism to Decode Animal Behavior.* New York: Scribner.

Hetts, Suzanne, and Daniel Estep. 2000. Video: *Canine Behavior Program: Body Postures and Evaluating Behavioral Health.* Denton, TX: Animal Care Training.

Kalnajs, Sarah. 2003. Video: *Dog Communication Skills: Understanding What Your Dog Is Telling You.* Salt Lake City: Tawzer Dog Videos.

McConnell, Patricia. 2003. Video. *Reading Between the Lines.* Salt Lake City: Tawzer Dog Videos.

Mech, David. 1970. *The Wolf: The Ecology and Behavior of an Endangered Species.* Minneapolis: University of Minnesota Press.

Moss, Cynthia. 2000. *Elephant Memories: Thirteen Years in the Life of an Elephant Family.* Chicago: University of Chicago Press.

Myers, David G. 2004. *Psychology.* New York: Worth.

Rugaas, Turid. 2006. *On Talking Terms with Dogs: Calming Signals,* 2nd ed. Wenatchee, WA: Dogwise Publishing.

Savage-Rumbaugh, Sue. 1994. *Kanzi: The Ape at the Brink of the Human Mind.* New York: John Wiley & Sons.

Smuts, Barbara. 2000. "Child of Mine." *The Smile of a Dolphin: Remarkable Accounts of Animal Emotions.* Marc Bekoff, ed. New York: Discovery Books.

Snowdon, Charles T. 2003. "Expression of Emotion in Nonhuman Animals." In *Handbook of Affective Science,* R. J. Davidson, H. H. Goldsmith, and K. Scherer, eds. New York: Oxford University Press.

Sternberg, Sue. 2003. *Successful Dog Adoption.* New York: Howell Book House.

Strum, Shirley C. 1987. *Almost Human: A Journey into the World of Baboons.* New York: Random House.

Weber, Bill, and Amy Vedder. 2001. *In the Kingdom of Gorillas.* New York: Simon & Schuster.

Weiss, Emily. Video: *The SAFER Test.* www.emilyweiss.com.

Zimen, Erik. 1982. "A Wolf Pack Sociogram." In *Wolves of the World.* Fred H. Harrington and Paul C. Paquet, eds. Park Ridge, N.J.: Noyes Publications, pp. 282–322.

CHAPTER 3: EMOTIONS AND THE BRAIN

I am infinitely grateful to the neurobiologists Deric Bownds and John Ratey, whose informative and delightfully accessible books, *The Biology of Mind* and *A User's Guide to the Brain* were invaluable to me. I can't imagine writing this book without them. Much of my discussion about the development of the brain draws on those two books; I learned about the work of Dan Stern, on critical periods in emotional development, in the latter. Jaak Panksepp's *Affective Neuroscience* is always an excellent resource; I learn something new from it every time I pick it up. Deborah Blum's *Love at Goon Park* is an excellent source for the impact of touch on the brain's development, and is the source of my stories about children in orphanages (and of the tragic experiment by Frederick II). If you'd like to read more about touch and development, start with Tiffany Field's article, listed below.

Stanley Coren's *How Dogs Think* has the best summary available on the comparative perceptual abilities of dogs and people. I also recommend Stephen Budiansky's *The Truth About Dogs,* Vilmos Csányi's *If Dogs Could Talk,* and Bruce Fogle's *The Dog's Mind.*

Ackerman, Diane. 2004. *An Alchemy of Mind: The Marvel and Mystery of the Brain.* New York: Scribner.

Battaglia, Carmen. 1995. "Developing High Achievers." *AKC Gazette* 112, no. 5. New York: American Kennel Club. (Also see: www.breedingbetterdogs.com/achiever.html.)

Blum, Deborah. 2002. *Love at Goon Park: Harry Harlow and the Science of Affection.* Cambridge, Mass.: Perseus.

Bownds, M. Deric. 1999. *The Biology of the Mind: Origins and Structures of Mind, Brain, and Consciousness.* Bethesda, Md.: Fitzgerald Science Press.

Damasio, Antonio. 1994. *Descartes' Error: Emotion, Reason, and the Human Brain.* New York: HarperCollins.

———. 2003. *Looking for Spinoza: Joy, Sorrow, and the Feeling Brain.* New York: Harcourt.

Field, Tiffany. 2002. "Infants' Need for Touch." *Human Development* 45, no. 2, pp. 100–103.

Griffin, Donald. 2001. *Animal Minds: Beyond Cognition to Consciousness.* Chicago: University of Chicago Press.

Hauser, Marc D. 2000. *Wild Minds: What Animals Really Think.* New York: Henry Holt & Co.

Myers, David G. 2004. *Psychology.* New York: Worth.

Panksepp, Jaak. 1998. *Affective Neuroscience: The Foundations of Human and Animal Emotions.* New York: Oxford University Press.

Ratey, John J. 2001. *A User's Guide to the Brain: Perception, Attention, and the Four Theaters of the Brain.* New York: Vintage Books.

Scott, John Paul, and John L. Fuller. 1965. *Genetics and the Social Behavior of the Dog: The Classic Study.* Chicago: University of Chicago Press.

CHAPTER 4: THE MANY FACES OF FEAR

General information about the biology of fear can be found in John J. Ratey's *A User's Guide to the Brain* and Jaak Panksepp's *Affective Neuroscience.* The study mentioned on serotonin regulation and genetics was done by A. R. Hariri and is listed below. *Animals in Translation* has an especially interesting discussion about fear in animals and people with autism; I highly recommend it. The study on noise phobias and handedness in dogs was done by Branson and Rogers.

There is a plethora of material about shyness; the sources named here can get you started if you'd like to learn more. See Myers's text *Psychology* for information about the nature/nurture debate with respect to shyness in people and for references to individual studies. Carl Schwartz and colleagues did the work on "inhibited" and "uninhibited" infants, while Daniels and Plomin did the study on cross-fostered babies born of shy mothers. The story about the shy but boisterous woman, as well as the percentage of people who report themselves as shy, is in Philip Zimbardo's book *Shyness: What It Is, What to Do About It.* For more information about the relationship between genetics, brain function, and shyness, see Schwartz et al., Jenck et al., and Sinn (who knew squid could be shy, too!) and Davis for a summary of early work on the amygdala and fearful behavior.

Shyness in animals has been studied by many; see Steven Suomi's work on a variety of species as a good starting place. He is the one who cross-fostered monkeys and found that mothers who provided a secure attachment base could ameliorate the effects of "shy genes."

William Campbell, who has written many excellent books on solving behavior problems in dogs, was the first to label dogs as having "active" or "passive" defense reflexes. His most recent book, *Owner's Guide to Better Behavior in Dogs,* is a great resource. The early work on the heritability of shyness in dogs was done by Scott and Fuller (see *Genetics and the Social Behavior of the Dog*). Helen Mahut wrote as early as 1958 about the inheritance of shyness in laboratory puppies—it's her article that contains information about the brood bitch who had so many shy puppies. Also see Thorne, 1944, for a truly early work on the subject. See Ray and Lorna Coppinger's book *Dogs: A Startling New Understanding of Canine Origin, Behavior and Evolution* for an interesting discussion about shyness, wolves, and the evolution of dogs. See Stephen Budiansky's *The Covenant of the Wild* for an interesting discussion of Belyaev's work selecting for docility in fur foxes. Goddard and Beilharz did the study on the predictability of shyness in young guide dogs. See E. O. Price for a thorough review of the behavioral aspects of domestication in general.

The work on "nervous pointers" was originally done by Oddist Murphree (I did not make up that name). Currently the work is being continued by Karen Overall, a prolific researcher and writer on canine behavior and behavior problems. See the reference below and her book *Clinical Behavioral Medicine for Small Animals.*

Ian Dunbar deserves our thanks for understanding the impact of Scott and Fuller's work and initiating puppy socialization classes nationwide. See his *Before and After Getting Your Puppy* and *How to Teach a New Dog Old Tricks.* I also highly recommend Pia Silvani's video, *Kindergarten Puppy Training Gone Wrong? Avoiding the Speed Bumps,* and Trish King's *Are Puppies Really Learning What We Are Teaching?* to ensure that your puppy learns the right things, rather than being traumatized.

A good source for information about post-traumatic stress disorder is Williams and Poijula's book *The PTSD Workbook: Simple, Effective Techniques for Overcoming Traumatic Stress Symptoms.* Another is *Neuropsychology of PTSD,* by J. J. Vasterling. The story about Watson traumatizing poor young Albert is described in many sources, but a good description can be found in both Blum's *Love at Goon Park* and Coren's *How Dogs Think.* The study done on Beagles who were brought back to the room where they were shocked (using a standard electronic training collar—be aware that these collars are available for sale or rent all over the country to anyone, whether they know anything about behavior and training or not) was presented by Renate Jones-Baade at the 2005 International Veterinary Behaviour Meeting. The traumatized-rat research was described by Servatius and Shors, listed below.

Blum, Deborah. 2002. *Love at Goon Park: Harry Harlow and the Science of Affection.* Cambridge, Mass.: Perseus.

Branson, N. J., and L. J. Rogers. 2006. "Relationship between paw preference strength and noise phobia in *Canis familiaris." Journal of Comparative Psychology,* in press.

Budiansky, Stephen. 1999. *The Covenant of the Wild: Why Animals Chose Domestication.* New Haven, Conn.: Yale University Press.

Buss, Kristin A., et al. 2003. "Right Frontal Brain Activity, Cortisol and Withdrawal Behavior in 6-Month-Old Infants." *Behavioral Neuroscience* 117, no. 1, pp. 11–20.

Campbell, William E. 1995. *Owner's Guide to Better Behavior in Dogs.* 2nd ed. Loveland, Colo.: Alpine Blue Ribbon Books.

Coppinger, Raymond, and Lorna Coppinger. 2001. *Dogs: A Startling New Understanding of Canine Origins, Behavior and Evolution.* New York: Scribner.

Coren, Stanley. 2000. *How to Speak Dog: Mastering the Art of Dog-Human Communication.* New York: Free Press.

———. 2004. *How Dogs Think: Understanding the Canine Mind.* New York: Free Press.

Daniels, Denise, and Robert Plomin. 1985. "Origins of Individual Differences in Infant Shyness." *Developmental Psychology* 21, no. 1, pp. 118–21.

Davis, Michael. 1992. "The Role of the Amygdala in Fear and Anxiety." *Annual Review of Neuroscience* 15, pp. 353–75.

Dunbar, Ian. 1998. *How to Teach a New Dog Old Tricks.* Berkeley: James and Kenneth Publishers.

———. 2004. *Before and After Getting Your Puppy.* Novato, Calif.: New World Library.

Goddard, Michael, and Rolf Beilharz. 1985. "A Multivariate Analysis of the Genetics of Fearfulness in Potential Guide Dogs." *Behavior Genetics* 15, no. 1, pp. 69–80.

Hariri, A. R., et al. 2002. "Serotonin Transporter Genetic Variation and the Response of the Human Amygdala." *Science* 297, pp. 400–403.

Jenck, R., et al. 1996. "Animal Models of Panic Disorder—Emphasis on Face and Predictive Validity." *European Neuropsychopharmacology* 6, supp. 4, pp. S4.

Jones-Baade, Renate. 2005. "Stress Symptoms Caused by the Use of Electric Training Collars on Dogs in Everyday Life Situations." 5th International Veterinary Behaviour Meeting. Minneapolis: AVSAB.

King, Trish. 2001. Video: *Are Puppies Really Learning What We Are Teaching?* Salt Lake City: Tawzer Dog Videos.

Mahut, Helen. 1958. "Breed Differences in the Dog's Emotional Behaviour." *Canadian Journal of Psychology* 12, vol. 1, pp. 35–44.

McConnell, Patricia B. 2005. 2nd ed. *The Cautious Canine: How to Help Dogs Conquer Their Fears.* Black Earth, Wisc.: Dog's Best Friend.

Myers, David G. 2004. *Psychology.* New York: Worth.

Overall, Karen. 1997. *Clinical Behavioral Medicine for Small Animals.* St. Louis: Mosby.

Overall, Karen, et al. 2001. "Frequency of Nonspecific Clinical Signs in Dogs with Separation Anxiety, Thunderstorm Phobia, and Noise Phobia, Alone or in Combination." *Journal of the American Veterinary Medical Association* 219, no. 4, pp. 467–73.

Panksepp, Jaak. 1998. *Affective Neuroscience: The Foundations of Human and Animal Emotions.* New York: Oxford University Press.

Price, E. O. 1984. "Behavioral Aspects of Animal Domestication." *Quarterly Review of Biology* 59, no. 1, pp. 1–32.

Ratey, John J. 2001. *A User's Guide to the Brain: Perception, Attention, and the Four Theaters of the Brain.* New York: Vintage Books.

Rentz, Timothy O., et al. 2003. "Active-Imaginal Exposure: Examination of a New Behavioral Treatment for Cynophobia (Dog Phobia)." *Behaviour Research and Therapy* 41, pp. 1337–53.

Schwartz, Carl E., et al. 2003. "Inhibited and Unihibited Infants 'Grown Up': Adult Amygdalar Response to Novelty." *Science* vol. 300, no. 5627, June 20.

Scott, John Paul, and John L. Fuller. 1965. *Genetics and the Social Behavior of the Dog.* Chicago: University of Chicago Press.

Servatius, Richard J., and Tracey J. Shors. 1994. "Exposure to Inescapable Stress Persistently Facilitates Associative and Nonassociative Learning in Rats." *Behavioral Neuroscience* 18, no. 6, 1101–1106.

Silvani, Pia. 2004. Video: *Kindergarten Puppy Training Gone Wrong? Avoiding the Speed Bumps.* Salt Lake City: Tawzer Dog Videos.

Sinn, David L., and N. A. Moltschaniwskyj. 2005. "Personality Traits in Dumpling Squid (*Euprymna tasmanica*): Context-Specific Traits and Their Correlation with Biological Characteristics." *Journal of Comparative Psychology* 119, no. 1, pp. 99–110.

Suomi, Stephen. 1998. "Genetic and Environmental Factors Influencing

Serotonergic Functioning and the Expression of Impulsive Aggression in Rhesus Monkeys." Plenary Lecture: Italian Congress of Biological Psychiatry, Naples, Italy.

———. 2001. "How Gene-Environment Interactions Can Shape the Development of Socioemotional Regulation in Rhesus Monkeys." Round Table: Socioemotional Regulation, Dimensions, Developmental Trends and Influences, Johnson and Johnson Pediatric Round Table, Palm Beach, Florida.

Thorne, Frederick C. 1944. "The Inheritance of Shyness in Dogs." *Journal of Genetic Psychology* 65, pp. 275–79.

Vasterling, J. J., and C. R. Brewin, eds. 2005. *Neuropsychology of PTSD: Biological, Cognitive and Clinical Perspectives.* New York: Guilford Press.

Williams, M. B., and S. Poijula. 2002. *The PTSD Workbook: Simple, Effective Techniques for Overcoming Traumatic Stress Symptoms.* Oakland, Calif.: New Harbinger.

Zimbardo, Philip G. 1977. *Shyness: What It Is, What to Do About It.* Cambridge, Mass.: Perseus.

CHAPTER 5: PAVLOV IN YOUR POCKET

Both *Psychology* as an accessible text, and *Blink* as a can't-stop-reading story, are great sources for information about classical conditioning in humans. I first learned about the impact of reading words like "old" and "wrinkled" in *Blink,* which recounts the work of John Bargh and his colleagues. Michael Domjan did the study on male quail and red lights, and Michael Cook and Susan Mineka are excellent sources for nature/nurture interactions and phobias in nonhuman animals. See Doogan and Thomas below for an interesting article about cynophobia (the fear of dogs). Read *Full Catastrophe Living* by Jon Kabat-Zinn for inspiration on how meditation can reverse much fear-based physiology and boost your immune system.

There are some wonderful books that explain how to use desensitization, classical conditioning, and positive reinforcement to help dogs get over their fears. Some of my favorites are Brenda Aloff's *Aggression in Dogs: Practical Management, Prevention and Behavior Modification;* Emma Parsons's *Click to Calm;* William Campbell's *Owner's Guide to Better Behavior in Dogs;* Suzanne Hetts's *Pet Behavior Protocols;* Pat Miller's *Positive Perspectives: Love Your Dog, Train Your Dog;* Karen Overall's *Clinical Behavioral Medicine for Small Animals;* Terry Ryan's

Toolbox for Remodeling Your Problem Dog. I have written about classical conditioning in working with general fears, and separation anxiety specifically, in *The Cautious Canine: How to Help Your Dog Overcome His Fears* and *I'll Be Home Soon: How to Prevent and Treat Separation Anxiety.* However, if you have even a moderately serious problem with your dog, I strongly recommend that you consult with an expert trainer, certified applied animal behaviorist, or board certified veterinarian behaviorist. You wouldn't hesitate to hire a coach to help your child learn football or soccer, so don't hesitate to avail yourself of the help that is available. The biggest problem people have with using classical conditioning is underestimating it. The process sounds easy ("Sure, yeah, I got it, give my dog a treat when a visitor comes") but it only works if you do everything at the right time, in the right order. These things turn out to be less intuitive than you might think, so don't try it by yourself if there's any risk to your dog or others if you get it wrong.

Ader, Robert, et al. 1995. "Psychoneuroimmunology: Interactions Between the Nervous System and the Immune System." *Lancet* 345, no. 8942, pp. 99–102.

Bargh, John A., Mark Chen, and Lara Burrows. 1996. "Automaticity of Social Behavior: Direct Effects of Trait Construct and Stereotype Activation on Action." *Journal of Personality and Social Psychology* 71, no. 2, pp. 230–44.

Campbell, William E. 1975. *Behavior Problems in Dogs.* Santa Barbara, Calif.: American Veterinary Publications.

———. 1995. *Owner's Guide to Better Behavior in Dogs.* 2nd ed. Loveland, Colo.: Alpine Blue Ribbon Books.

Cook, E. W., III, R. L. Hodes, and P. J. Lang. 1986. "Preparedness and Phobia: Effects of Stimulus Content on Human Visceral Conditioning." *Journal of Abnormal Psychology* 95, no. 3, pp. 195–207.

Cook, Michael, and Susan Mineka. 1991. "Selective Associations in the Origins of Phobic Fears and Their Implications for Behavior Therapy." In *Handbook of Behavior Therapy and Psychological Science: An Integrative Approach.* Peter P. Martin, ed. New York: Pergamon Press.

Dodman, Nicholas H. 1996. *The Dog Who Loved Too Much.* New York: Bantam Books.

Domjan, Michael. 1994. "Formulation of a Behavior System for Sexual Conditioning." *Psychonomic Bulletin and Review* 1, no. 4, pp. 421–28.

Doogan, Sharon, and Glyn V. Thomas. 1992. "Origins of Fear of Dogs in Adults and Children: The Role of Conditioning Processes and Prior Familiarity with Dogs." *Behaviour Research and Therapy* 30, no. 4, pp. 387–94.

Gladwell, Malcolm. 2005. *Blink: The Power of Thinking Without Thinking*. New York: Little, Brown & Co.

Hall, Geoffrey. 1997. "Context Aversion, Pavlovian Conditioning, and the Psychological Side Effects of Chemotherapy." *European Psychologist* 2, no. 2, pp. 118–24.

Hetts, Suzanne. 1999. *Pet Behavior Protocols*. Lakewood, Colo.: AAHA Press.

Kabat-Zinn, Jon. 1990. *Full Catastrophe Living: Using the Wisdom of Your Body and Mind to Face Stress, Pain and Illness*. New York: Delta.

McConnell, Patricia. 2000. *I'll Be Home Soon: How to Prevent and Treat Separation Anxiety*. Black Earth, Wisc.: Dog's Best Friend.

———. 2005. 2nd ed. *The Cautious Canine: How to Help Dogs Conquer Their Fears*. Black Earth, Wisc.: Dog's Best Friend.

Miller, Pat. 2004. *Positive Perspectives: Love Your Dog, Train Your Dog*. Wenatchee, WA: Dogwise.

Overall, Karen. 1997. *Clinical Behavioral Medicine for Small Animals*. St. Louis: Mosby.

Parsons, Emma. 2004. *Click to Calm: Healing the Aggressive Dog*. Waltham, Mass.: Sunshine Books.

Ryan, Terry. 1998. *The Toolbox for Remodeling Your Problem Dog*. New York: Howell Book House.

CHAPTER 6: ANGER

As in previous chapters, I relied on the books of John Ratey, David Myers, and Jaak Panksepp for information about the biology of anger. Antonio Damasio's books also include fascinating discussions about anger and the brain. A vast number of books by field biologists describe the expression of anger in a variety of species; the works of primatologists are easiest to find. Frans de Waal's books have excellent descriptions of temper tantrums by chimpanzees, Shirley Strum provides compelling descriptions of grumpy baboons, and Douglas Smith doesn't hesitate to write about a particularly nasty wolf in *Decade of the Wolf*.

I highly recommend checking out Paul Ekman's interactive DVD on reading micro-expressions and subtle expressions of emotion—I found the expressions related to anger particularly interesting. His website, again, is www.paulekman.com. Charles Darwin's book *The Expression of the Emotions in Animals and Man* is still an invaluable resource; It is fascinating to look at photos of people from another age, whose features seem somehow different, and yet whose expressions are so familiar. Paul Ekman edited a new version in 1998 and added some valuable updates.

The study on aggressiveness and social status in pigs was done by J. E. Bolhuis, and the study on the behavior of owners after their dog completed an agility course was done by Amanda Jones. The correlation between high-arousal chases and breakdown of discipline among police is described in *Blink,* which draws on the book *On Killing,* by Dave Grossman. The study discussing inhibited versus uninhibited temperaments in infants (and the relationship between degree of inhibition and anger management) was done by Carl Schwartz. If you'd like to read more about paedomorphism in dogs (the retention of juvenile characteristics in the adult), you might enjoy *The Covenant of the Wild* by Stephen Budiansky and *Dogs* by Lorna and Ray Coppinger, as a start.

If you'd like to learn more about "behavioral evaluations" or "behavioral assessments" (keeping in mind that they are often called "temperament tests"), here are some sources to get you started: See Sue Sternberg's *Successful Dog Adoption,* Dr. Emily Weiss's video: *The SAFER Test,* the article by Rebecca Ledger mentioned below, or contact Amy Marder at amarder@arlboston.org. Wendy and Joachim Volhard's Puppy Aptitude Test can be accessed on their website at www.volhard.com; also see the work of Sheila Booth, mentioned below. You can learn quite a bit about your own dog by going through these procedures, but be sure not to push him if you feel either you are unsafe or your dog is becoming stressed. The psychologist Pam Reid, Ph.D., has written an interesting and informative article about what "temperament" really is. You might also want to look into the "Behavioral Wellness Program" designed by applied animal behaviorists Suzanne Hetts, Ph.D., and Dan Estep, Ph.D., available at www.AnimalBehaviorAssociates.com.

I am often asked about my "research" on teaching emotional control to a singleton puppy, so I want to emphasize here that a procedure done on one puppy can't be called research. My account of Solo's upbringing is what scientists call an anecdote—or, simply, a story. That doesn't mean it has no value, but until someone does carefully controlled research on the topic, we need to be cautious about drawing conclusions. It would be a great Ph.D. topic—anyone out there want to take it and run?

The dog-related fatality described in this chapter occurred on February 14, 2002, in Elroy, Wisconsin. The dogs were destroyed the next morning, and their adult owners eventually accepted a plea bargain and were incarcerated for eighteen months to two years. I do not know what happened to the little girl who witnessed the attack, but I hope that, wherever she is, she is very, very clear that there was nothing she could have done to save her friend.

You can help your dog learn emotional control and frustration tolerance by employing the humane training techniques described in these books, listed alphabetically by author: *Purely Positive Training*, by Sheila Booth; *Dog Behavior*, by Ian Dunbar; *Katz on Dogs*, by Jon Katz; *Good Owners, Great Dogs*, by Brian Kilcommons; *Parenting Your Dog*, by Trish King; *Lucy Won't Sit*, by Claudeen McAuliffe; *Feeling Outnumbered?* and *How to Be the Leader of the Pack and Have Your Dog Love You for It*, and *Beginning Family Dog Training*, by me; *Positive Perspectives: Love Your Dog, Train Your Dog*, by Pat Miller; *Excel-erated Learning*, by Pam Reid; *The Toolbox for Remodeling Your Problem Dog*, by Terry Ryan; *How to Behave So Your Dog Behaves*, by Sophia Yin.

For specific aggression-related problems, see *Aggression in Dogs: Practical Management, Prevention and Behavior Modification*, by Brenda Aloff; *Pet Behavior Protocols*, by Suzanne Hetts; *Handbook of Behavior Problems of the Dog and Cat*, by Gary Landsberg, Wayne Hunthausen, and Lowell Ackerman; *Handbook of Applied Dog Behavior*, by Steve Lindsay; *Feisty Fido*, by me and Karen London; *Clinical Behavioral Medicine for Small Animals*, by Karen Overall; *Click to Calm*, by Emma Parsons; *The Toolbox for Remodeling Your Problem Dog*, by Terry Ryan; and *The Dog Who Would Be King*, by John Wright.

If you have a problem with an aggressive dog, I strongly suggest that you get professional help. No one expects to be able to repair a car's engine without training, and your dog is a lot more complicated than your car. Ideally, you'll find a qualified behaviorist close by, one who is updated on humane and scientifically based methods of treating aggression. (If someone "guarantees" that they can fix your dog, hang up the phone and try again. No responsible expert would guarantee they could "fix" your dog.) Three good places to look for help are www.animalbehaviour.org for a list of Certified Applied Animal Behaviorists, www.avsab.us for board certified Veterinary Behaviorists, and www.apdt.com for dog trainers.

Aloff, Brenda. 2002. *Aggression in Dogs: Practical Management, Prevention and Behaviour Modification*. Collierville, Tenn.: Fundcraft.

Bolhuis, J. E., et al. 2005. "Individual Coping Characteristics, Aggressiveness and Fighting Strategies in Pigs." *Animal Behaviour* 69, pp. 0185–0191.

Booth, Sheila. 1998. *Purely Positive Training: Companion to Competition.* Ridgefield, Conn.: Podium.

Budiansky, Stephen. 1999. *The Covenant of the Wild: Why Animals Chose Domestication.* New Haven, Conn.: Yale University Press.

Campbell, William E. 1995. *Owner's Guide to Better Behavior in Dogs.* 2nd ed. Loveland, Colo.: Alpine Blue Ribbon Books.

Coppinger, Raymond, and Lorna Coppinger. 2001. *Dogs: A Startling New Understanding of Canine Origin, Behavior and Evolution.* New York: Scribner.

Damasio, Antonio. 1994. *Descartes' Error: Emotion, Reason, and the Human Brain.* New York: HarperCollins.

———. 2003. *Looking for Spinoza: Joy, Sorrow, and the Feeling Brain.* Orlando: Harcourt Books.

Darwin, Charles. 1998. *The Expression of the Emotions in Animals and Man.* Paul Ekman, ed. Oxford: Oxford University Press.

De Waal, Frans. 1989. *Peacemaking Among Primates.* Cambridge, Mass.: Harvard University Press.

———. 1996. *Good Natured: The Origins of Right and Wrong in Humans and Other Animals.* Cambridge, Mass.: Harvard University Press.

Dodman, Nicholas H. 1996. *The Dog Who Loved Too Much.* New York: Bantam Books.

Dunbar, Ian. 1996. *Dog Behavior: An Owner's Guide to a Happy, Healthy Pet.* New York: Howell Book House.

Ekman, Paul. 1973. "Cross-cultural Studies of Facial Expression." In *Darwin and Facial Expression: A Century of Research in Review.* Paul Ekman, ed. New York: Academic Press.

———. 1987. "Universals and Cultural Differences in the Judgments of Facial Expressions of Emotion." *Journal of Personality and Social Psychology* 53, no. 4, pp. 712–17.

Gladwell, Malcolm. 2005. *Blink: The Power of Thinking Without Thinking.* New York: Little, Brown.

Hetts, Suzanne. 1999. *Pet Behavior Protocols.* Lakewood, Colo.: AAHA Press.

Jones, Amanda. 2005. "Are We Dog's Best Friend?: Affiliating and Disaffiliating Behaviours and Their Impact on Cortisol." 5th International Veterinary Behaviour Meeting. Minneapolis: AVSAB.

Kilcommons, Brian. 1992. *Good Owners, Great Dogs: A Training Manual for Humans and Their Canine Companions.* New York: Warner Books.

King, Trish. 2004. *Parenting Your Dog.* Neptune, NJ: TFH Publications.

Landsberg, G., W. Hunthausen, and L. Ackerman. 2000. *Handbook of Behavior Problems of the Dog and Cat.* Oxford: Butterworth-Heinemann.

Ledger, Rebecca, and M. R. Baxter. 1997. "The Development of a Validated Test to Assess the Temperament of Dogs in a Rescue Shelter." *Proceedings of the 1st International Conference of Veterinary Behavioral Medicine.* pp. 87–92.

Lindsay, Steven. 2000. *Handbook of Applied Dog Behavior and Training Vol. 1: Adaptation and Learning.* Ames: Iowa State University Press.

London, Karen B., and Patricia B. McConnell. 2001. *Feeling Outnumbered? How to Manage and Enjoy Your Multi-Dog Household.* Black Earth, Wisc.: Dog's Best Friend.

Masson, Jeffrey Moussaieff. 1997. *Dogs Never Lie About Love.* New York: Three Rivers Press.

McAuliffe, Claudeen E. 2001. *Lucy Won't Sit: How to Use Your Body, Mind and Voice for a Well-behaved Dog.* Neosho, Wisc.: Kindness K9 Dog Behavior and Training.

McConnell, Patricia B. 1996. *Beginning Family Dog Training.* Black Earth, Wisc.: Dog's Best Friend.

———. 1996. *How to Be Leader of the Pack and Have Your Dog Love You for It.* Black Earth, Wisc.: Dog's Best Friend.

———. 2002. *The Other End of the Leash: Why We Do What We Do Around Dogs.* New York: Ballantine.

Myers, David G. 2004. *Psychology.* New York: Worth.

Overall, Karen. 1997. *Clinical Behavioral Medicine for Small Animals.* St. Louis: Mosby.

Panksepp, Jaak. 1998. *Affective Neuroscience: The Foundations of Human and Animal Emotions.* New York: Oxford University Press.

Ratey, John J. 2001. *A User's Guide to the Brain: Perception, Attention, and the Four Theaters of the Brain.* New York: Vintage.

Reid, Pamela. 1996. *Excel-erated Learning: Explaining in Plain English How Dogs Learn and How Best to Teach Them.* Oakland, Calif.: James and Kenneth Publishers.

Ryan, Terry. 1998. *The Toolbox for Remodeling Your Problem Dog.* New York: Howell Book House.

Schnurr, R. 1972. "Localization of the Septal Rage Syndrome in Long-Evans Rats." *Journal of Comparative and Physiological Psychology* 81, no. 2, pp. 291–96.

Schwartz, Carl E., et al. 2003. "Inhibited and Unihibited Infants 'Grown Up': Adult Amygdalar Response to Novelty." *Science* 300 (June 20). pp. 1952–53.

Smith, Douglas W., and Gary Ferguson. 2005. *Decade of the Wolf: Returning the Wild to Yellowstone.* Guilford, Conn.: Lyons Press.

Sternberg, Sue. 2003. *Successful Dog Adoption.* New York: Howell Book House.

Strum, Shirley C. 1987. *Almost Human: A Journey into the World of Baboons.* New York: Random House.

Weiss, Emily. Video: *The SAFER Test.* www.emilyweiss.com.

Wright, John C., and Judi Wright Lashnits. 1999. *The Dog Who Would Be King.* Emmaus, Pa.: Rodale Press.

CHAPTER 7: HAPPINESS

For a delightful and informative discussion on joy, playfulness, and how to tickle rats, see Jaak Panksepp's book *Affective Neuroscience.* Panksepp is probably the world's expert on "seeking circuits," and you can read about them in depth in this book. Readers interested in play, and not intimidated by science, will enjoy reading *Animal Play: Evolutionary, Comparative and Ecological Perspectives,* by Marc Bekoff and John Myers. In *The Other End of the Leash,* I talk about the rarity of play in adult mammals, and about how dogs and people share a sense of joyful playfulness seen in few other animals. (If you're interested in the topic, Google "river otters" and "Kea parrots" for descriptions of other animals appearing to have a grand time while playing.)

I learned about our innate reactions to the essence of smiles (a curved line under two dots) in Myers's *Psychology* (also the source for remembering more bad memories than good ones); also see Paul Ekman's work about the universality of responses to open-mouth smiles. See Roger Abrantes's *Dog Language* and Sue Sternberg's *Successful Dog Adoption* for descriptions of crinkled versus rounded eyes. Patricia Simonet did the research on canine vocalizations that she equates with human laughter; you can listen to a short recording by going to www.petalk.org/DogLaughSpect.html. David Watson has done lots of work on emotion and mood; the study on mood and time of day is discussed in his book, cited below. Sigal Barsade is the researcher who embedded a cheerful colleague in groups working on business-related projects.

There are many excellent resources for readers interested in learning more about "clicker training." This type of training was originally brought from the laboratory to marine mammal training by Karen Pryor, and then to dog training by Karen Pryor and Gary Wilkes. See www.clickertraining.com and *Clicker Training for Dogs* (Pryor) and www.clickandtreat.com and *On Target!* (Wilkes). For those interested in the research behind our understanding of the biology of the "seeking circuit," see below for Christopher D. Fiorillo's work on reinforcement schedules and dopamine production, and Wolfram Schultz for some of the early studies highlighting dopamine production being highest when animals expect a reward, not when they've gotten it.

If you'd like to learn more about the benefits of petting and therapeutic touch, see Charnetski et al. for the research on an increase in IgA while petting both live and stuffed dogs. See Tiffany Field's article for more information about how massage can increase the amount of serotonin in the brain, and then go out and get yourself a massage. For even more information about the health effects of petting your dog, see the early work of Beck and Katcher, and, more recently, "Proof of Power Petting" by Brad Kollus and "Dogs Are Good for People, and Vice Versa" by Marcella Durand. Linda Tellington Jones is the originator of Tellington Touch, a process of therapeutic touch that has a solid biological basis and that can be very helpful for both healthy animals and those with physical or emotional difficulties.

Abrantes, Roger. 1997. *Dog Language: An Encyclopedia of Canine Behaviour.* Naperville, Ill.: Wakan Tanka.

Barsade, Sigal. 2002. "The Ripple Effect: Emotional Contagion and Its Influence on Group Behavior." *Administration Science Quarterly,* December 2002.

Beck, Alan, and Aaron Katcher. 1983. *Between Pets and People: The Importance of Animal Companionship.* New York: G. P. Putnam's Sons.

Bekoff, Marc, and John A. Byers. 1998. *Animal Play: Evolutionary, Comparative and Ecological Perspectives.* New York: Cambridge University Press.

Charnetski, Carl, et al. 2004. "Effect of Petting a Dog on Immune System Function." *Psychological Reports* 95, pp. 1087–91.

Darwin, Charles. 1998. *The Expression of the Emotions in Animals and Man.* Paul Ekman, ed. Oxford: Oxford University Press.

Durand, Marcella. 2004. "Dogs Are Good for People, and Vice Versa." Nov. 2004.

Ekman, Paul. 1973. "Cross-cultural Studies of Facial Expression." In *Darwin and Facial Expression: A Century of Research in Review.* Paul Ekman, ed. New York: Academic Press.

———. 1987. "Universals and Cultural Differences in the Judgement of Facial Expressions of Emotion." *Journal of Personality and Social Psychology* 53, no. 4, pp. 712–17.

Field, Tiffany. 2002. "Preterm Infant Massage Therapy Studies: an American Approach." *Seminars in Neonatology,*" 7, no. 6, pp. 487–94.

Fiorillo, Christopher D., et al. 2003. "Discrete Coding of Reward Probability and Uncertainty by Dopamine Neurons." *Science* 299, no. 5614, pp. 1898–1902.

Kollus, Brad. 2005. "Proof of Power Petting." *Cat Fancy,* March 2005.

London, Karen. 2005. "Coping with Loss." *The Bark* no. 32 (Fall 2005), pp. 46–48.

McConnell, Patricia B. 2002. *The Other End of the Leash: Why We Do What We Do Around Dogs.* New York: Ballantine.

Myers, David G. 2004. *Psychology.* New York: Worth.

Panksepp, Jaak. 1998. *Affective Neuroscience: The Foundations of Human and Animal Emotions.* New York: Oxford University Press.

Pryor, Karen. 2005. *Clicker Training for Dogs.* Waltham, Mass.: Sunshine Books.

Schultz, Wolfram. 1992. "Activity of Dopamine Neurons in the Behaving Primate." *Seminars in Neuroscience* 4, pp. 129–38.

Sternberg, Sue. 2003. *Successful Dog Adoption.* New York: Howell Book House.

Watson, David. 2000. *Mood and Temperament.* New York: Guilford.

Wilkes, Gary. *On Target!* Tucson: Click! And Treat Products.

Wilson, E. O. 1978. *On Human Nature.* Cambridge, Mass.: Harvard University Press.

CHAPTER 8: LOVE STORY

Given our profound emotional connection to dogs, it is no surprise that there are a vast number of books written about our relationship with them. I can only list a few here, but these are some of my current favorites: *Dog Is My Co-Pilot,* edited by *The Bark* magazine; *Adam's Task,* by Vicki Hearne; *A Dog Year* and *The New Work of Dogs,* by Jon Katz; the exquisitely written *Pack of Two,* by Caroline Knapp; *Dogs Never Lie About Love,* by Jeffrey Moussaieff Masson; *The Rosetta Bone,* by Cheryl Smith; *What the Dog Did,* by Emily Yoffe; and the classic *My Dog Tulip,* by J. R. Ackerley. Karen London's beautiful remark about how our love for dogs spills outside of species boundaries appeared in *The Bark* magazine, noted below. For more about pending legislation that requires disaster shelters to accommodate pets, go to the website of the ASPCA at www.aspca.org.

Hardworking biologists Bernd Heinrich and Sarah Blaffer Hrdy have written highly enjoyable accounts of animal behavior; see *Mind of the Raven,* by Heinrich, and *Mother Nature,* by Hrdy (no, that's not a typo; it really is how she spells her name). No list would be complete without Goodall's *Jane Goodall: 40 Years at Gombe.* Michael Kosfeld and colleagues were the scientists who introduced oxytocin into people's noses and found that they became more trusting. If you're interested in reading about social systems and voles, there is a surprising amount of literature on the behavior of these mouselike creatures; a good place to start is the work by Steve Gaulin. See the study by Fries et al., if you're interested in oxytocin production and children raised in neglectful orphanages. David Tuber did the study on the attachment of kennel dogs to people they had met only a few times. E. O. Wilson's book *On Human Nature* recounts the story of the chimpanzee Washoe being potty mouthed to her keepers.

I read about the emotional connection between female vet students and their dogs in Jon Katz's book *The New Work of Dogs.* Brian Hare is the scientist who looked at dogs' responses to human pointing gestures. There is a rich and growing literature of studies on communication between people and dogs. Look at the work of Csányi, Miklosi, Pongracz, Povinelli, and Hare if you'd like to learn more.

Csányi, Vilmos. 2000. *If Dogs Could Talk: Exploring the Canine Mind.* New York: North Point Press.

Editors of *The Bark. Dog Is My Co-pilot: Great Writers on the World's Oldest Friendship.* New York: Crown.

Fries, A., et al. 2005. "Early Experience in Humans Associated with Changes in Neuropeptides Critical for Regulating Social Behavior." *Proceedings of the National Academy of Sciences* 102, no. 47, pp. 17237–40.

Gaulin, Steven J. C., and R. W. Fitzgerald. 1986. "Sex Differences and Spatial Ability: An Evolutionary Hypothesis and Test." *American Naturalist* 127, no. 1, pp. 74–88.

Hare, B., et al. 2002. "The Domestication of Social Cognition in Dogs." *Science* 298, no. 5598, pp. 1634–36.

Hearne, Vicki. 1986. *Adam's Task: Calling Animals by Name.* New York: Knopf.

Heinrich, Bernd. 2005. "Talk to the Animals." *The New York Times,* August 26.

Hrdy, Sarah Blaffer. 2000. *Mother Nature: Maternal Instincts and How They Shape the Human Species.* New York: Ballantine.

Katz, Jon. 2004. *The New Work of Dogs: Tending to Life, Love and Family.* New York: Villard.

Knapp, Caroline. 1995. *Pack of Two: The Intricate Bond Between People and Dogs.* New York: Dial Press.

Kosfeld, Michael, et al. 2005. "Oxytocin Increases Trust in Humans." *Nature* 435, no. 2, pp. 673–76.

London, Karen B. "Coping with Loss." *The Bark* no. 32 (Fall 2005), pp. 46–48.

Masson, Jeffrey Moussaieff. 1997. *Dogs Never Lie About Love.* New York: Three Rivers Press.

Miklosi, A. R., et al. 1998. "Intentional Behavior in Dog-Human Communication: Experimental Analysis of 'Showing' Behavior in the Dog." *Animal Cognition* 3, pp. 159–66.

Pongracz, Peter, et al. 2001. "Social Learning in Dogs I: The Effect of a Human Demonstrator on the Performance of Dogs (*Canis familiaris*) in a Detour Task." *Animal Behaviour* 62, no. 6, pp. 1109–1117.

Povinelli, D. J., et al. 1990. "Inferences About Guessing and Knowing by Chimpanzees." *Journal of Comparative Psychology* 104, no. 3, pp. 203–210.

Smith, Cheryl. 2004. *The Rosetta Bone.* New York: Howell Book House.

Tuber, David S., et al. 1996. "Behavioral and Glucocorticoid Responses of Adult Domestic Dogs (*Canis familiaris*) to Companionship and Social Separation." *Journal of Comparative Psychology* 110, no. 1, pp. 103–108.

Wilson, E. O. 1978. *On Human Nature.* Cambridge, Mass.: Harvard University Press.

Yoffe, Emily. 2005. *What the Dog Did: Tales from a Formerly Reluctant Dog Owner.* New York: Bloomsbury.

CHAPTER 9: ARE YOU THINKING WHAT I'M THINKING?

As I note in the introduction, rafts of stimulating new books have been published recently about the thought processes of nonhuman animals. Many have been mentioned already, but I repeat them here because they are so integral to this chapter. I recommend *How Dogs Think,* by Stanley Coren; *If Dogs Could Talk,* by Vilmos Csányi; and *The Truth About Dogs,* by Stephen Budiansky, as good sources on canine cognition. I encourage interested readers to pick up books on animal cognition in general, including Marc Hauser's *Wild Minds,* Donald Griffin's *Animal Minds,* and the more technical *Primate Cognition,* by Tomasello and Call.

The amazing connection between love, grief, and physical pain is well described in Jaak Panksepp's book *Affective Neuroscience.* See the following books if you want to read more about pet-related grief and its management: Julie Kaufman's *Crossing the Rubicon*; Enid Samuel Traisman's *My Personal Pet Remembrance Journal*; and Lagoni, Butler, and Hetts's book *The Human-Animal Bond and Grief.*

There is a vast literature about the relationship between thinking and language; I've only scratched the surface. Myers's *Psychology* is the text that linked thinking and language in the same chapter, although I want to reiterate that the author does not argue that thinking is not possible without the equivalent of human language. His book is the source for my discussion here about language and human development. For more about the amazing parrot Alex, see the article by Irene Pepperberg listed below. It will at least get you started. Temple Grandin's book *Animals in Translation* contains information about the relationship between the perception of pain and the ability to feel fear. For a riveting read about a man who grew up with no concept of language at all, see Susan Schaller's book *A Man Without Words.* You can read descriptions of Sally Boyson's work in Marc Hauser's *Wild Minds,* or you can refer to some of her academic articles, listed below.

See *How Dogs Think* for a description of Norton Milgram's experiment asking dogs to choose larger or smaller objects, and *The Truth About Dogs* for the experiment in which dogs were tested on "non-matching to sample." Rebecca West and Robert Young did the study asking whether dogs would be surprised by the "wrong" number of objects revealed from behind a screen, and Hank Davis did the study that asked whether rats behaved as if they have a concept of number. The *Time* magazine article about the clever Golden Retriever was written by Michael Lemonick. The story about Luah, the Poodle who played hide-and-seek by burying his head, was published in *The Bark* magazine (Summer 2005). You can read more about Rico, the dog who could fast-map, in the article by Kaminski, Call, and Fischer in *Science,* listed below.

The neurologist Antonio Damasio is responsible for educating us about the truth that emotions and rational thinking go hand in hand. For more on the unfortunate people whose emotions have become disconnected from their rational cortex, see Damasio's fascinating *Descartes' Error* and *Looking for Spinoza*. Frans de Waal can always be counted upon to write scientifically rigorous and yet highly accessible books about social behavior in primates. See his books, some listed below, for descriptions of what he doesn't hesitate to call jealousy in chimps (and his enlightening discussions of our discomfort with our animal origins). His books are also a good introduction to the controversy about self-awareness in animals; also see Hauser's *Wild Minds* and Griffin's *Animal Minds*. See Gordon Gallup's article, cited below, to begin delving into the current controversy. Reiss and Marino did the study on mirror recognition in dolphins; see Clive Wynne's book *Do Animals Think?* for criticism of the conclusion that mirror studies can tell us whether animals are self-aware. See Griffin's *Animal Minds* for more about Boakes's comment that scientific discussions of animal consciousness should be avoided. The information about children and mirror recognition is in my old friend *Psychology* by David Myers.

Discussions about theory of mind can be found in an increasing number of books, from the more academic ones, such as Panksepp's *Affective Neuroscience* and Bownds's *Biology of the Mind* to books more accessible to dog lovers, such as Coren's *How Dogs Think,* Katz's *Katz on Dogs,* and Hauser's *Wild Minds*. You can read more about "mirror neurons" in David Dobb's article, cited below, in *Scientific American Mind*. For two different perspectives on deception in animals, see *Wild Minds* and *Animal Minds*.

Consciousness—now there's a topic that can keep you reading until your dog begs to go on a walk! I found the discussions in *Biology of the Mind* and *A User's Guide to the Brain* particularly useful and clear. The latter book contains Ratey's wonderful line regarding presumptuous arguments about a phenomenon we don't even know how to define. If you'd really like to dive into the subject, try *Wider Than the Sky* by Gerald Edelman, although you're forewarned that this is not a book for the beach. Malcolm Gladwell's book *Blink* was my primary source for the workings of the unconscious, and relates the experiments of John Bargh on how embedded words affect our behavior. I learned about Giulio Tononi's work on sleep and consciousness in the *Wisconsin State Journal* (January 22, 2006). The remark by Jonas Salk that I use to illustrate our embarrassment about emotions is quoted in Oshinsky's *Polio: An American Story*. My own words about losing Luke feeling like the oxygen being taken from the air were from *Dog Is My Co-pilot: Great Writers on the World's Oldest Friendship*. The delightful book *Marley and Me: Life and Love and the World's Worst Dog* is by John Grogan.

Anonymous. Winner of "Tickle My Funny Bone" contest. *The Bark* 31 (Summer 2005), p. 24.

Bargh, John A., Mark Chen, and Lara Burrows. 1996. "Automaticity of Social Behavior: Direct Effects of Trait Construct and Stereotype Activation on Action." *Journal of Personality and Social Psychology* 71, no. 2, pp. 230–44.

Boakes, R. 1992. "Subjective Experience" (review of *Animal Minds*). *Times Higher Education Supplement,* November 22, p. 22.

Boyson, S. T. 1996. "More Is Less": The Distribution of Rule-Governed Resource Distribution in Chimpanzees. In A. E. Russon et al., eds. *Reaching into Thought: The Minds of the Great Apes.* Cambridge: Cambridge University Press.

———, and E. J. Capaldi. 1993. *The Development of Numerical Competence: Animal and Human Models.* Hillsdale, N.J.: Lawrence Erlbaum.

Budiansky, Stephen. 1999. *The Covenant of the Wild: Why Animals Chose Domestication.* New Haven, Conn.: Yale University Press.

Csányi, Vilmos. 2000. *If Dogs Could Talk: Exploring the Canine Mind.* New York: North Point Press.

Damasio, Antonio. 1994. *Descartes' Error: Emotion, Reason, and the Human Brain.* New York: HarperCollins.

———. 2003. *Looking for Spinoza: Joy, Sorrow, and the Feeling Brain.* New York; Harcourt.

Davis, H., K. A. Mackenzie, and S. Morrison. 1989. "Numerical Discrimination by Rats (*Rattus norvegicus*) Using Body and Vibrissal Touch." *Journal of Comparative Psychology* 103, no. 1, pp. 45–53.

De Waal, Frans. 1989. *Peacemaking Among Primates.* Cambridge, Mass.: Harvard University Press.

———. 1996. *Good Natured: The Origins of Right and Wrong in Humans and Other Animals.* Cambridge, Mass.: Harvard University Press.

———. 2005. *Our Inner Ape: A Leading Primatologist Explains Why We Are Who We Are.* New York: Riverhead Books.

Dobbs, David. 2006. "A Revealing Reflection." *Scientific American Mind* 17, no. 2, pp. 22–7.

Edelman, Gerald. 2004. *Wider Than the Sky: The Phenomenal Gift of Consciousness.* New Haven, Conn.: Yale University Press.

Frey, R. G. 1989. "Why Animals Lack Beliefs and Desires." In T. Regan and P. Singer, eds. *Animal Rights and Human Obligations.* Englewood Cliffs, N.J.: Prentice Hall.

Gallup, G. G. 1991. "Toward a Comparative Psychology of Self-awareness: Species Limitations and Cognitive Consequences." In *The Self: An Interdisciplinary Approach*. G. R. Goethals and J. Strauss, eds. New York: Springer-Verlag.

Goodall, Jane. 1971. *In the Shadow of Man*. Boston: Houghton Mifflin.

Grandin, Temple. 2005. *Animals in Translation: Using the Mysteries of Autism to Decode Animal Behavior*. New York: Scribner.

Griffin, Donald R. 1992. *Animal Minds: Beyond Cognition to Consciousness*. Chicago: University of Chicago Press.

Grogan, John. 2005. *Marley and Me: Life and Love and the World's Worst Dog*. New York: HarperCollins.

Hauser, Marc D. 2000. *Wild Minds: What Animals Really Think*. New York: Henry Holt & Co.

Kaminski, Juliane, Josep Call, and Julia Fischer. 2004. "Word Learning in a Domestic Dog: Evidence for 'Fast Mapping.' " *Science* 304, no. 5677, pp. 1682–83.

Kaufman, Julie. 1999. *Crossing the Rubicon: Celebrating the Human-Animal Bond in Life and Death*. Cottage Grove, Wisc.: Xenophon Publishing.

Lagoni, Laurel, Carolyn Butler, and Suzanne Hetts. 1994. *The Human-Animal Bond and Grief*. New York: W. B. Saunders.

Lemonick, Michael. 1993. "Can Animals Think?" *Time*, March 22.

McConnell, Patricia. 2003. "Love Is Never Having to Say Anything at All." In *Dog Is My Co-pilot: Great Writers on the World's Oldest Friendship*. The editors of *The Bark*, eds. New York: Crown.

Myers, David G. 2004. *Psychology*. New York: Worth.

Oshinsky, David. M. 2005. *Polio: An American Story*. New York: Oxford University Press.

Panksepp, Jaak. 1998. *Affective Neuroscience: The Foundations of Human and Animal Emotions*. New York: Oxford University Press.

Pepperberg, Irene. 1994. "Numerical Competence in an African Grey Parrot. (*Psittacus erithacus*)." *Journal of Comparative Psychology* 108, no. 1, pp. 36–44.

Povinelli, D. J., et al. 1990. "Inferences about Guessing and Knowing by Chimpanzees." *Journal of Comparative Psychology* 104, no. 3, pp. 203–210.

Ratey, John J. 2001. *A User's Guide to the Brain: Perception, Attention, and the Four Theaters of the Brain*. New York: Vintage Books.

Reiss, D., and L. Marino. 2001. "Mirror Self-Recognition in the Bottlenose Dolphin: A Case of Cognitive Convergence." *Proceedings of the National Academy of Sciences* 98, pp. 5937–42.

Schaller, Susan. 1991. *A Man Without Words.* Berkeley: University of California Press.

Tomasello, Michael, and Josep Call. 1997. *Primate Cognition.* New York: Oxford University Press.

Traisman, Enid Samuel. 1997. *My Personal Pet Remembrance Journal.* Portland, Ore.: Dove Lewis Emergency Animal Hospital.

West, Rebecca, and Robert Young. 2002. "Do Domestic Dogs Show Any Evidence of Being Able to Count? *Animal Cognition* 5, pp. 183–86.

Wynne, Clive D. 2004. *Can Animals Think?* Princeton, N.J.: Princeton University Press.

INDEX

Katz, Jon, 247–248
Keller, Helen, 270
Kilcommons, Brian, 32
King, Trish, 233
Knapp, Caroline, 237

language, 265, 267–270. *See also* body
language
laughter, 215
learning abilities of animals, 27
Ledger, Rebecca, 187
life, awareness of, xxi–xxii
limbic system, 12, 100–101, 105, 136
litters, size of, 190–192
"Little Albert," 139, 150
London, Karen, 249
love
biology of, 241–242
flip side of, 256–259
intensity of, 240
male/female differences in
(human), 247–248
unconditional, 244, 246–247, 249
Love at Goon Park (Blum), 77

Mack, Arien, 28
Marder, Amy, 187
Marley and Me (Grogan), 280–281
Masson, Jeffrey Moussaieff, xxiii, 171
McConnell, Patricia B., 14–16, 50,
65, 69, 97, 170, 226–227
medication for aggression, 182
mental states of animals, 23–29
micro-expressions, 41, 176
micro-freezes, 46
Miller, Beth, 194
mirror neurons, 281
mirror recognition, 275–276
misunderstandings, 226–228
monkeys, food experiment on, 221
morphine, 258
Morton, Eugene, 19, 68
motion of emotion, 40–41
motivations for behavior, 174–175,
202

mouths. *See also* facial expressions
interpreting positions, 60
offensive pucker, 51–52, 60,
175–176
open/closed, 43–45
position of, 50–52
Myers, David G., 268

nail trimming, 153
nature/nurture debate, 122, 129,
181–182
nervousness, 124
neurobiology/neurochemistry
anger, 169–171, 182
brain, 91–93
consciousness, 273
dopamine, 91–92, 215–216, 243
emotions in general, 7–10
empathy, 281
fear, 113
happiness, 213–215
hormones, 78
love, 241–242
pain, 113
readiness for battle, 177
thoughts/emotions, 260–261
neutral stimulus, presenting, 148–149.
See also classical conditioning
The New Work of Dogs (Katz),
247–248
nurture/nature debate, 122, 129, 181
nystagmus, 59

observation of behavior, 28–32
offense behavior, 127–128
offensive pucker (mouth), 51–52, 60,
175–176
Old Yeller (Gipson), 237
On Talking Terms with Dogs (Rugaas),
56
open mouths, 43–45
other, concept of, 274–275
The Other End of the Leash
(McConnell), 14–16, 50, 65, 69,
97, 170, 226–227

PATRICIA B. MCCONNELL, PH.D., is an adjunct associate professor of zoology at the University of Wisconsin–Madison and a certified Applied Animal Behaviorist. Her company, Dog's Best Friend, Ltd., specializes in family dog training and treating aggression in dogs, and she is an immensely popular speaker around the country. She is the co-host of Wisconsin Public Radio's *Calling All Pets,* an animal behavior advice show syndicated to a hundred public radio stations, and was the animal behaviorist on Animal Planet's *Petline.* She works daily with three dogs (two border collies and a Great Pyrenees) on her sheep farm outside of Madison. Visit Patricia McConnell's website at www.dogsbestfriendtraining.com.